In *Birth Pangs*, my dear fri   ed
a masterpiece that truly "d⌐⌐⌐⌐⌐ .

To see how the creative / redemptive purposes of our Father
for all of His family are revealed in the stories of the Scriptures
which, as Dr. Dan so insightfully shows, parallels the birthing
process is both very intriguing and extremely instructive.

So pull up a chair and fasten your seat-belt! You are about to
embark on an exciting journey through Scripture with Dr. Dan
that I am certain will birth in you a greater appreciation for the
sometimes laborious, but always glorious, work of His Spirit
in delivering us out of darkness into the light and life He has
conceived for us.

JON COURSON
AUTHOR / FOUNDING PASTOR
APPLEGATE CHRISTIAN FELLOWSHIP

BIR✝H PANGS

BIR✝H PANGS

How Pregnancy Reveals God's Plan for the Ages

by Daniel A. Tomlinson, M.D.

TATE PUBLISHING & *Enterprises*

Published by Tate Publishing & Enterprises, LLC
127 E. Trade Center Terrace | Mustang, Oklahoma 73064 USA
1.888.361.9473 | www.tatepublishing.com

Tate Publishing is committed to excellence in the publishing industry. The company reflects the philosophy established by the founders, based on Psalm 68:11,
"The Lord gave the word and great was the company of those who published it."

Book design copyright © 2008 by Tate Publishing, LLC. All rights reserved.
Cover design by Stephanie Woloszyn
Interior design by Summer Floyd-Harvey

Published in the United States of America

ISBN: 978-1-60604-886-3
1. Religion: Christianity: Theology-Eschatology
2. Theology: Systematic: Eschatology
08.08.14

Acknowledgements

First and foremost, I would like to thank my Lord and Savior, my big brother, my bridegroom and dearest friend, Jesus of Nazareth, born in Bethlehem and also known as the Christ. He, through his Spirit and his Word has inspired me countless times. I am so thankful for his grace and mercy to me as well as for the "calling" he has given me as a physician and as a lay minister. I look forward to spending eternity with him!

To my wonderful wife Julie: I thank her for her continued support as well as to my two delightful children, Alexandra (Alex) and Zach.

To Pastor Jim Wright: Pastor Jim, the senior pastor of Mountain Christian Fellowship in Medford, Oregon, was one of the first people I told of my vision to write a book dealing with obstetrics and spirituality. We were snowboarding on a beautiful winter day in Southern Oregon in 2004. Pastor Jim encouraged me to "go for it." He had been studying in the Gospel of Mark at the time and had noted the sense of immediacy and urgency that is seen in that account. I took it as a word from GOD and started the outline for this book later that day. The first words of the narrative were begun on Easter, later that Spring.

To Pastor Jim Feeney: Pastor of the Medford Christian Center and the man who inspired me to start reading through the Bible sequentially in a day by day type of format. I can't put into words how that has changed my life!

To the late Victor Paul Wierwille: Some of his unique perspectives upon the Word and especially his emphasis upon "The *Word* of GOD being the *Will* of GOD" have made a difference in my life.

To Pastor Jon Courson: Founding pastor of the Applegate Christian Fellowship in Ruch, Oregon. Pastor Jon's distinctive gift from GOD in teaching the Word and especially in revealing the countless pictures found in the Old Testament which reveal New Testament truths have been nothing short of inspirational to me! His teaching has opened my eyes to see allegories everywhere in the Bible. I would encourage any believer to read or listen to anything that Pastor Jon releases!

†able of Contents

The Future Glory|509

Foreword

From singing songs on the ski lifts in beautiful Southern Oregon to climbing Half Dome in Yosemite National Park, Doctor Dan and I have always had a relationship revolving around worship.

What Doctor Tomlinson has expressed in his book *Birth Pangs* is a necessary and exciting read for all believers. In it we get the honor of traveling with him through the scriptures and seeing God's heart for us. To see the wonder of God's creation in the birth of man is nothing less than miraculous. Having said that, there is more than meets the eye. From conception to birth are hidden wonders of intricate detail from God's Word that point out God's plan for us and the world as a whole. The types and pictures are a refreshing and valuable tool in understanding more about our Creator.

Doctor Tomlinson is a professional physician, caring father, loving husband, and an accomplished writer. He has proven to be not only a faithful friend but a mentor that I respect and cherish. His valuable counsel has proven Godly time and time again and I would highly recommend learning from him through this masterpiece. If you can't know him personally as I have had the privilege, learn from him and grow in Christ through the pages in your hands.

JIM WRIGHT
PASTOR / SONG WRITER
MOUNTAIN CHRISTIAN FELLOWSHIP

Prologue

At the outset of this book I want to make the distinction between ideas and truth. Ideas can be plagiarized, truth cannot! The reason I make this point is because the Bible is about truth. Also, when one sits under a man's teaching ministry he or she will begin to take on the flavor of that teacher. Certainly this has happened here. I thank my mentors in advance, especially Pastor Jon, for their indulgence and understanding.

Bible Translation:
All Bible verses in this book are from the King James Version

Birth Pangs: †he Past

Introduction

There is a joke we tell women in labor to help validate to them that in some way we understand what they are going through during the time of their travail. It goes like this:

How is a birth pang like a duck bite?

Answer...

Just one doesn't hurt that much...

But a thousand will kill you!

And that's very much the way it appears to be as I observe labor after labor in my calling as an Obstetrician. Contractions seem to go on and on. There is nearly always a time during the process of labor that the parturient believes it will never end!

But birth pangs, which in modern vernacular are called labor pains or contractions, are not all the same. They can actually be quite mild, even painless at times during a woman's pregnancy. Those mild tightenings are called Braxton-Hicks contractions. Also pangs can be weak at the onset of labor or during episodes of false labor. But they are incredibly severe during active labor and are especially so near the birth of the baby. At the time which is called the transition.

Contractions are caused by several chemicals coming together in the uterine wall which initiate a uterine constriction. The tightening begins at the top of the uterus and proceeds downward in a designed effort to push the contents of the uterus out.

Uterine contractions clearly occur throughout pregnancy. It's explained that these contractions are necessary to ripen and prepare the cervix to open for the upcoming birth. In fact, 4-D ultrasound studies have documented uterine contractions in the very earliest weeks of the first trimester!

When painful contractions occur near a woman's due date without effecting delivery, those contractions are called "false labor." They must be very annoying as wave after wave of moderately strong contractions often will arrive in the late evening just as the soon-to-be mother is trying to rest!

Now the difference between false and true labor hinges upon three factors. First, in the case of false labor, the pains are not close enough and are not increasing in intensity. In other words, they are painful but not worsening. They stay the same. Secondly, in the case of true labor, contractions are close *and* they increase in intensity. Lastly, false labor often changes into true labor when the "water breaks." That is, when the sack holding the amniotic fluid ruptures, then the uterus will almost immediately begin contracting vigorously and intensely.

True labor, commonly called active labor, is divided into the latent phase and the active phase. As one might imagine, the pain of the latent phase is eclipsed by the discomfort of the active phase. Also as alluded to earlier, the very end of the active phase of labor is called transition. That's the crescendo of nearly unbearable pain immediately prior to the birth.

Of course, contractions are important in effecting the delivery of the baby, but they are also needed to evacuate the uterus if a miscarriage has occurred. If the baby has passed away in utero! This is also a type of labor pain.

Lastly, true birth pangs can begin before the last month of a pregnancy in an ill-timed effort to deliver the baby. We call this pre-term labor.

Now at this point you may be thinking, "Why is he telling me this?" Hang on. I'll show you powerful analogies to all of these facets of labor in GOD's Word.

With these comments, let's look at the first mention of the pain of labor, called "sorrow" in the Bible.

> Unto the woman he said, I will greatly multiply thy *sorrow* ["issabon"] and thy conception; in *sorrow* ["eseb"] thou shalt bring forth children...
>
> GENESIS 3:16A

Wow! Birth pangs are part of the "curse" of mankind due to Adam's rebellion and Eve's deception! Presumably, GOD had not intended the birth process to be difficult and painful. This effect was the result of sin!

The first use of sorrow is the word "issabon." Issabon speaks of toil, of difficulty. GOD told Eve that it will be in difficulty that she and her progeny will conceive. We indeed know this to be true. Even in the most fertile of couples there is only a 20% chance of conception per monthly cycle. In addition, if a conception occurs there will be a 20–33% chance that the pregnancy will be lost! That is, that a miscarriage will occur. Undeniably it is difficult for humans to conceive compared to other mammals. It is "issabon."

The second usage of sorrow in our text is "eseb." Eseb speaks of pain, of travail, of intense discomfort and of agony. GOD told Eve that in eseb, in travail, thou shall bring forth children. Certainly this is the case. The pain of labor can dominate a woman's psyche as she prepares for the childbearing time of her life much like the fear of death will enter into the heart of a young man at a time of war! To be sure, the pain of labor is part of the curse that mankind (womankind!) received at the time of Adam and Eve's fall.

As an aside, the naming of Jabez illustrates this principle well. Jabez's name means "Sorrowful."

> And Jabez was more honorable than his brethren: And his mother called his name Jabez, saying, Because I bare him in sorrow.
>
> I CHRONICLES 4:9

Jabez was given a name that reminded his mother of the terrible ordeal she underwent to birth him. This is likely why he spoke the following prayer:

> And Jabez called on the GOD of Israel, saying, Oh that thou wouldest bless me indeed, and enlarge my coast, and that thine hand might be with me, and that thou wouldest keep me from evil.
>
> I CHRONICLES 4:10A

Jabez asked GOD for his blessing. He asked to have an increased influence for GOD. He prayed that GOD's hand (we would say, GOD's Spirit) would be upon him. And lastly, he pleaded for protection from evil, including protection from the evil one!

What a great prayer! Look at the answer.

> And GOD granted him that which he requested.
>
> I CHRONICLES 4:10B

You see, GOD will *always* grant a prayer that is in harmony with his will! He wants to bless you, he wants to enlarge your coasts (to take territory for him), he wants to fill you with his Spirit and he wants to protect you!

What a great prayer indeed!

•   •   •   •

Not only are sorrows such an influence upon a woman's life that she would name her son in remembrance of them, but the Lord has used this illustration time after time to show us pictures of spiritual truths.

If you have read my first literary offering, entitled *A Woman's Silent Testimony,* you will likely remember that we discussed the pain of labor as a picture of our own death in Book I. We saw sorrows as a description of the disciple's agony during Christ's passion in Book III. In Book IV, we learned of GOD's description of Israel's passage to Babylon as a woman's first travail. Paul told us in Book V that he was experiencing labor and travail to see Christ formed in his children. Lastly, we spoke of our Lord's

Passion in Book VI, where he spilled the fluids of birth, i.e. blood and water, as a type of horrific labor!

But the analogy we are about to embark upon here in *Birth Pangs* is my favorite.

It is the analogy of birth pangs to the "end time events" before the Second Coming of Jesus Christ!

> And as he sat upon the mount of Olives, the disciples came unto him privately, saying, Tell us, when shall these things be? And what shall be the sign of thy coming, and of the end of the world? And Jesus answered and said unto them, Take heed that no man deceive you. For many shall come in my name, saying, I am Christ; and shall deceive many. And ye shall hear of wars and rumors of wars: See that ye be not troubled: For all these things must come to pass, but the end is not yet. For nation shall rise against nation, and kingdom against kingdom: And their shall be pestilences, and earthquakes, in divers places. *And these are the beginning of sorrows* (emphasis mine).

Jesus told his disciples that the signs leading up to the end of the age would be as sorrows upon a woman. Specifically, he said they would be the beginning of sorrows!

And, as we have noted, sorrows are very complicated. They start at the beginning of the pregnancy, they can lead to a miscarriage, they can come early, they can come falsely, but they will ultimately get closer and closer with increasing pain and intensity culminating in the true agony of the transition phase. Then the baby is born.

Jesus was saying: Be patient, a lot is going to happen before I return! But to those with ears to hear, he was also giving a blueprint of the times prior to his return. A blueprint that mothers can best understand!

But also here in *Birth Pangs*, I desire to point out something even *bigger* than the analogy of sorrows compared to the end-times scenario.

I want to show that the entire history of the world and more specifically, the history of mankind here on this planet can be compared to a pregnant woman's course. That God's dealing with

Israel, the church, the nations and creation itself can be typified by pregnancy and delivery. A pregnancy complete with the sorrow of conception, a miscarriage, contractions remote from term, pre-term labor, false labor, rupture of membranes, true labor with it's divisions of latent phase, active phase and transition, and finally the delivery.

It's all there and I hope you enjoy seeing it as much as I will enjoy showing it to you!

> For I reckon that the sufferings of this present time *[Pregnancy and Labor]* are not worthy to be compared with the glory which shall be revealed in us *[Birth]*. For the earnest expectation of the creature waiteth for the manifestation of the sons of GOD. *[We wait for the delivery]*. For the creature was made subject to vanity, not willingly, but by reason of him who hath subjected the same in hope. *[We were made subject to emptiness so we would hope in Him!]* Because the creature itself also shall be delivered [*birthed*] from the bondage of corruption into the glorious liberty of the children of GOD. For we know that the whole creation *groaneth and travaileth in pain* together until now (emphasis mine).
>
> ROMANS 8:18–22

We are living in a world that is pregnant! Specifically, it's a world that is in "late" pregnancy. No, the water hasn't broken yet and the true labor hasn't yet started, but as we shall see, it could begin at any time! Maranatha!

✝ he Creation as Conception

The Bible clearly states that God, in the beginning, created the heavens and the earth. He also created man in his own image. That is, God placed his Spirit in man, for the Bible states that God is Spirit (John 4:24a).

To fit the type we are discussing, a conception occurred in the first chapter of Genesis. Just as a pregnancy starts with a conception, so did all of creation, including mankind. God conceived creation in all its glory. He created it out of nothing and formed man in his image.

> And God saw everything that he had made, and, behold, it was very good.
>
> GENESIS 1:31

Furthermore, a fetus is also formed in the image of its parents. He inherits chromosomal information from each parent which will project his future image. So it was with Adam. God made that first man in his own image. Adam was perfect in his genetic makeup with the potential to live and fellowship with God on into eternity! Adam was sinless!

The Earth in the beginning was also without compare. The Bible teaches the Lord caused to grow every tree that was pleasant to the sight and good for food (Genesis 2:9a).

But then Adam sinned and everything changed. GOD had told Adam that on the very day he ate of the tree of the knowledge of good and evil he would surely die (Genesis 2:17). What died in that day was the spirit GOD had placed in him. Adam lost his connection with GOD. He was no longer in GOD's image. GOD is a perfect spirit. Adam was now an imperfect man of body and soul with a spirit that had died! The obstetrical analogy is that a miscarriage was destined to occur.

Sometimes this can also happen in your life, in my life. It may seem like GOD is birthing something inside. Something is forming in my heart but then it doesn't work out, it dies. But as we shall see, GOD is faithful. If he allows something he was working in you or me to miscarry, then he will form and birth something in us that is better! Indeed, he takes us from glory to greater glory!

✝he Flood as a Miscarriage

Adam lived nine hundred-thirty years (Genesis 5:5). A study of Genesis 5 reveals that his death was one hundred twenty-eight years prior to the birth of Noah. And we are told that in the six hundredth year of Noah's life, the windows of heaven were opened (Genesis 7:11). Thus 1,658 years after GOD created Adam, GOD's creation was miscarried. Mankind, with the exception Noah and his family, underwent the "labor" of a miscarriage.

To fit the analogy we are considering, except for those animals in the ark, all of GOD's creation suffered a painful stillbirth. All of creation upon the Earth labored greatly!

Later in this study we will conclude that the Great Tribulation, also called the Day of the Lord, is analogous to labor. That seven year period of time prior to the second coming of Jesus Christ can also be seen as a woman's time of travail.

Peter taught that the flood of Noah was a foreshadowing of the Great Tribulation. He stated that GOD wants men to see that judgment will come unto those that would afterwards live unGODly.

> And spared not the old world, but saved Noah the eighth person, a preacher of righteousness, bringing in the flood upon the

world of the unGODly...making an example unto those that after should live unGODly.

II PETER 2:5,6B

And,

For this they are willingly ignorant of, that by the word of GOD the heavens were of old, and the earth standing out of water and in the water: Whereby the world that then was, being overflowed with water, perished: But the heavens and the earth which are now, by the same word are kept in store, reserved unto fire against the day of judgment and perdition of unGODly men.

II PETER 3:5–7

So it's easy to see the similarities. The flood of Noah was a horrific miscarriage. It was a picture of the Great Tribulation just as the pain of a miscarriage typifies the pain of childbirth. Only with a miscarriage, we don't get the baby! After the Great Tribulation we do! We get Jesus!

Spiritually speaking, have you had a miscarriage in your life? Was GOD forming something in you that died? A marriage, for example, that didn't work out, or an idea that seemed so good but didn't pan out. Oh, it was terrible when it occurred...but it did, or it will come to completion. Afterwards, the Lord will do something new in your life, just as he is about to demonstrate to us with his creation.

Jesus said, "In the world ye shall have tribulation *[you will have labor]:* But be of good cheer; I have overcome the world" (John 16:33b).

"Stuff" is going to happen in this life. But be of good cheer, dear reader, he has overcome the world with all of its "stuff!"

But we all, with open face beholding as in a glass the glory of the Lord, are changed into the same image from glory to glory, even as by the Spirit of the Lord.

II CORINTHIANS 3:18

Old ✝ estament Israel as Contractions of the First and Second Trimester

Introduction

After the Flood, after the miscarriage of the first earth, GOD began a new thing. If you will, a second conception had occurred. What Peter describes as the heaven & earth (which are now) was ushered into existence. The world in which we live in today was conceived.

> And GOD blessed Noah and his sons, and said unto them, Be fruitful, and multiply, and replenish the earth.
>
> GENESIS 9:1

So to fit the parallel being considered, the history of GOD's dealing with mankind can be seen as a second pregnancy. The sons of Noah multiplied and the nations were divided.

Genesis 10 tells the story,

> These are the families of the sons of Noah, after their generations, in their nations: And by these were the nations divided in the earth after the flood.
>
> GENESIS 10:32

As noted, early in a pregnancy is a time of relative quiescence. Growth of the fetus is rapid and although contractions are constantly occurring, they are mild, sometimes painless and of no consequence as far as delivering the baby. As mentioned earlier, those tightenings are called Braxton-Hicks contractions.

As it is with a pregnancy, so it is with mankind. GOD chose to reveal himself through the nation of Israel (I Corinthians 10:11). Beginning with Abraham and following with his seed, GOD elevated Old Testament Israel as a testimony to the Gentiles.

The trials and travails of Israel are documented in the Old Testament from Genesis to Malachi and to fit the type can be seen as Braxton-Hicks contractions. The Old Testament describes the pregnancy growing in maturity while documenting many contractions along the way.

Looking at some of the many lessons of Israel as Braxton-Hicks contractions will be revealing to us as we later consider mankind's preterm labor which occurred with Jesus' first coming, our false labor that Jesus spoke of in Matthew 24 as the Church Age and the true labor to be seen during the Tribulation period.

Joseph and The Seven Year Famine

Joseph, who was the oldest son of the beloved Rachel, had a favored position in the eyes of Jacob his father:

> Now Israel loved Joseph more than all his children, because he was the son of his old age: And he made him a coat of many colors.
>
> GENESIS 37:3

The coat of many colors could also be translated, "a coat of many pieces." It had big sleeves. It wasn't a working man's coat. This descriptive verse denotes that Joseph was in a position of authority over his brothers.

Hatred fueled by envy was the result.

> And when his brethren saw that their father loved him more than all his brethren, they hated him, and could not speak peaceably unto him.
>
> GENESIS 37:4

> And Joseph dreamed a dream, and he told it his brethren: And they hated him yet the more.
>
> GENESIS 37:5

Joseph dreamed that he and his brothers were sheaves of wheat standing upright. He saw in his dream that his brother's sheaves bowed down before his.

And he dreamed yet another dream, and told it his brethren...

GENESIS 37:9A

In his second dream Joseph beheld the sun, moon, and eleven stars bowing before him. Joseph, in speaking the truth to his brothers, caused them to hate him all the more.

Later, Joseph's brothers went to feed the flock in Shechem which was approximately twenty-five miles from Hebron, where Jacob lived. Israel called for Joseph and asked him to go and see if all was well with his brethren and to bring bread unto them. When Joseph came to Shechem he learned that they had taken the flock to Dothan. Thus, he traveled another thirteen miles to find his brothers. But when they saw Joseph from afar they plotted to kill him. They threw him in a pit and instead of killing him they sold him to Ishmaelite traders who were passing by on their way to Egypt. From there Joseph was sold to Potiphar, the captain of Pharaoh's guard.

Many years passed for Joseph. During that time he found grace in the eyes of Potiphar and was made overseer of his entire house. Later Joseph was falsely accused by Potiphar's lustful wife and ended up in prison. While in prison, Joseph again excelled and the jailor made him the keeper of the prison. There, he accurately interpreted the dreams of Pharaoh's butler and baker. Those dreams revealed that the butler would be restored to his position while informing the baker that he would be sentenced to death. Joseph asked the butler to remember him. But after being released, the butler promptly forgot Joseph for a period of two years.

Then, Pharaoh had two disturbing dreams which none of the wise men of Egypt could interpret. In his dreams Pharaoh saw seven well favored kine and seven full ears of corn being devoured by seven ill favored kine and seven thin ears of corn. Joseph's

GOD-given interpretive gift came to the ears of Pharaoh, and so he called for the young prisoner. Joseph explained the dreams to Pharaoh and told of their prophetic significance to the nation. They learned that seven bountiful years were to be followed by seven years of famine. Joseph explained that the abundance of the first seven years would be totally eclipsed by the severity of the second seven years. He counseled Pharaoh to store 20% of all of the nation's productivity against the seven years of famine. For that, Joseph was elevated to second in command. Only Pharaoh was over Joseph in power and prestige.

Just as Joseph had predicted, the famine came. During the first year of famine, Jacob sent all of his sons, except for Benjamin, to buy grain in Egypt. While they were there, they unknowingly crossed paths with their younger brother. Joseph kept his identity from them and started them on a series of tests to see if they had changed from the evil brothers who had years before sold him into slavery. Joseph put Simeon into jail and instructed his other brothers to bring back Benjamin in order to have Simeon released. That way he would know that they were not spies.

The brothers said one to another in Hebrew, not knowing that Joseph understood, "We are verily guilty concerning our brother, in that we saw the anguish of his soul, when he besought us, and we would not hear; therefore is this distress come upon us" (Genesis 42:21).

The sons of Israel were repenting of their evil deed and realized that their present calamity was the result of their sin.

Unfortunately for Simeon, Jacob was extremely reluctant to send his youngest son, Benjamin, to Egypt. He feared a similar fate for Benjamin which had befallen Joseph years earlier. Thus Simeon remained incarcerated for an entire year as the famine bore on.

In the second year, Jacob again commissioned his sons to travel to Egypt. But they refused unless their father would allow Benjamin to also come. They understood clearly the requirements that had been set by Joseph for their return. And at that point they did not know that Joseph was their brother whom they had betrayed. Both Reuben and Judah stepped up in integrity and stated they would guarantee the safety of Benjamin. They said they would pay the penalty if anything happened to Benjamin. Implicitly, they told their father that they would die for Benjamin.

Obviously, they were passing this first test. Earlier they wanted to kill Joseph, now they were willing to die for his younger brother Benjamin. To use an obstetrical analogy, they were in labor ready to birth something wonderful!

When the bothers returned, they bowed once again to Joseph.

> And when Joseph saw Benjamin with them, he said to the ruler of his house, Bring these men home, and slay, and make ready; for these men shall dine with me at noon.
>
> GENESIS 43:16

Joseph communed with his brethren and brought Simeon back to them. He then sent them away with food but still had another lesson to see if they had truly repented. Joseph had his steward secretly place his very valuable silver cup into Benjamin's sack as he sent them away. Soon though, he sent his steward with a company to overtake the men of Israel. He accused the bothers of rewarding evil for good in stealing away his Lord's silver cup. To this, the brothers vehemently denied their guilt and confidently said, "With whomsoever of thy servants it be found, both let him die, and we also will be my Lord's bondmen" (Genesis 44:9).

The steward answered that only the man who had the cup would be guilty. Unfortunately the cup was found in Benjamin's sack! Thus the boys rent their clothes and returned back into the city. There, they once again bowed before Joseph and confessed their guilt to him.

> And Judah said, What shall we say unto my Lord? What shall we speak? Or how shall we clear ourselves? GOD hath found out the iniquity of thy servants: Behold, we are my Lord's servants, both we, and he also with whom the cup is found.
>
> GENESIS 44:16

Judah, speaking for the group stated that they were willing

and deserved to be slaves along with Benjamin. He confessed to Joseph that GOD had revealed their previous sin. When Joseph refused to allow Judah and his brothers to stay as slaves along with Benjamin, Judah again stepped up in a sacrificial way. He drew near to Joseph and told him of their father, Jacob. He explained how Jacob had lost Benjamin's brother years before and that the loss of Benjamin would certainly bring Jacob down to the grave with grief. Judah pleaded with Joseph and said,

> For thy servant became surety for the lad unto my father, saying, If I bring him not unto thee, then I shall bear the blame to my father forever. Now therefore, I pray thee, let thy servant abide instead of the lad a bondman to my Lord; and let the lad go up with his brethren.
>
> GENESIS 44:32–33

In essence, Judah was willing to die for his brother!

With this confession, the sons of Israel had passed the test and Joseph revealed himself to his brothers. He said,

> I am Joseph...I am Joseph your brother, whom ye sold into Egypt.
> Now therefore be not grieved, nor angry with yourselves, that ye sold me hither: For GOD did send me before you to preserve life. For these two years hath famine been in the land: And yet there are five years, in which there shall neither be earing nor harvest. And GOD sent me before you to preserve you a posterity in the earth, and to save lives by a great deliverance.
>
> GENESIS 45:3A, 4–7

With that, Joseph called for his father, Jacob. He and the entire clan of seventy souls traveled to Egypt where they were preserved during the famine and beyond under the protection of Joseph, the second of all Egypt!

• • • •

Now this is a wonderful story on multiple levels. In it we see GOD's providence in calling Joseph to Egypt to preserve the tribe. We also see that things are not always as they appear. That is, Jacob believed that his son had met with an evil end while all along he was ruler in Egypt. We see the forgiveness of Joseph towards his bother's sin while also noting the importance of repentance in receiving reconciliation. On another level we see the principle of sowing and reaping as the brothers realized that their ill fate was due to the seed they had planted years before in selling Joseph and lying to their father. But the allegory I would most like you to see is the prophetic one. That is, the characters in this historical story picture future times and events.

You see, throughout this story, Joseph is a powerful picture of Israel's deliverer. He typifies the Messiah. He is analogous to Jesus Christ.

Joseph spoke the truth no matter what his brothers, who picture the unbelieving nation of Israel, thought about him. He did not keep his dreams from his brothers but always told them the truth. In fact, in analyzing Joseph's story we do not find any fault in him throughout the entire narrative.

Jacob, who early in the story pictures GOD the Father, sent Joseph from Hebron (which means fellowship) to bring bread to his brothers. First, Joseph looked for them in Shechem which was outside of the Promised Land. He then went to Dothan which means "double darkness" to find them. They plotted to kill him there and placed him into a pit before sending him away.

This of course pictures GOD sending his son, Jesus, from heaven where they fellowshipped together down to the "double dark" Earth. There, Jesus became a Jewish man and went to his brothers with bread. Bread in this allegory pictures the Word of GOD, the Bread of Life. This they did not receive but killed him and placed him into a pit!

Just as Joseph went away for a long time and ascended to power so did Jesus. He ascended into Heaven where he sits at the right hand of GOD the Father. Pharaoh of course represents the Father in this part of the analogy.

During the seven year famine, Joseph ate with his brothers at noon as well as tested them to see if they had repented. Likewise, during the seven year time of "Jacob's trouble," the time we know as the Tribulation, Jesus will sup with his brothers, the Jews. He will also test them to see whether they will repent and align with him or try to save their own necks and align with the false Messiah known as the Antichrist. Like the original sons of Jacob, those future sons will suffer labor pains of trial during that time still to come. Also, they too will be ultimately protected by the greater than Joseph, Jesus Christ, while the seven year Tribulation bears on.

It may be that the noontime lunch date with Joseph has some prophetic significance of its own. Could it be that in the middle of the Tribulation, when Antichrist declares himself to be GOD, the Jews will see him as evil and begin to dine with their true Messiah? I think it very possible.

The Bible reports that Joseph told his brothers to not be grieved nor angry with themselves for betraying him to Egypt, as they were grieving greatly. Likewise, it also tells of Israel's grief concerning Jesus in the Book of Zechariah.

> And I will pour upon the house of David, and upon the inhabitants of Jerusalem, the spirit of grace and of supplications: And they shall look upon me whom they have pierced, and they shall mourn for him, as one mourneth for his only son, and shall be in bitterness for him, as one that is in bitterness for his firstborn. In that day shall there be a great mourning in Jerusalem...
>
> ZECHARIAH 12:10–11A

Lastly, of course, we see Joseph honored among his brethren and the entire family brought to be with him. This perfectly pictures the future reality the children of Israel will obtain. They too will see Jesus as their deliverer. They will be protected by him during the remainder of the Great Tribulation and will go into the Millennial Kingdom under his authority and rule.

As Paul states in the Book of Romans concerning that day, "And so all Israel shall be saved: As it is written, There shall come out of Zion the Deliverer, and shall turn away unGODliness from Jacob" (Romans 11:26).

Truly the story of Joseph and the seven year famine is a powerful Old Testament picture of a New Testament reality!

Israel's Birth Pang in Egypt

The story of Joseph (found in Genesis chapters 37, 39, and 50) is a wonderful example of GOD's provision and of his providence. What Joseph's brothers meant for evil (the selling of Joseph into slavery), GOD meant for good. He saved the young tribe of Jacob in Egypt for four hundred years where they were able to grow into the great nation of Israel.

Joseph told his brothers, "But as for you, ye thought evil against me; but GOD meant it unto good, to bring to pass, as it is this day, to save much people alive" (Genesis 50:20).

But after Joseph's death, the Bible states a new king arose which knew not Joseph. Scholars believe that approximately seventy years after Joseph's passing, in 1730 BC, Seti I began to afflict the children of Israel. It is taught that a minor threat by the Hittites cast fear into the heart of Pharaoh.

> And he said unto his people, Behold the people of the children of Israel are more and mightier than we: Come on, let us deal wisely with them; lest they multiply, and it come to pass, that, when there falleth out any war, they join also unto our enemies, and fight against us, and so get them up out of the land.
>
> EXODUS 1:9–10

For four centuries, the children of Israel suffered a birth pang at the hand of the Egyptians. The Bible tells us they set taskmasters over Israel and forced them to build their treasure cities. But even though the Jews were afflicted, they were safe from destruction while under the Egyptian rule.

The Bible states, "But the more they afflicted them, the more they multiplied and grew" (Exodus 1:12a).

Here is a key to spiritual growth. Times of trial and testing can be the times of growth into maturity while those times of rest and ease often is not! Think of this principle like a muscle. I have to exercise it if I want it to get stronger.

After a period of time, God raised up Moses to deliver Israel out of the bondage of Egypt. God caused a labor of ten very painful contractions, called plagues, to birth Israel out of the grip of the Egyptians.

It's heartening to me when I think of this rescue. In this analogy, Israel pictures God's children; and as children of God, they picture you and me. We also understand that the nation of Egypt is a continual picture of the world and its carnal systems in type throughout the Bible. Thus, in this analogy, we can see that when you or I get caught up in the world and its system, God will do whatever it takes to rescue us from its grip. In this case we can read that five of the ten plagues also directly affected the children of Israel during the process of God's deliverance of his children. Likewise, when God comes to rescue you and me from Egypt, we too may feel some of the pain!

The plagues themselves are also very interesting to study as there is an eerie similarity between the ten plagues of Egypt and the judgments of the Tribulation period. This should not be surprising as we understand that God was judging Egypt just as he will judge the world. We know that he was rescuing and revealing himself to his people, Israel, just as he will rescue and reveal himself to those who will believe on him during that time.

Truly, like the flood of Noah which proceeded it, the deliverance of Israel from Pharaoh pictures the Great Tribulation where God will deliver his people out of the clutches of the Pharaoh of this world, Satan.

Let's look briefly at the plagues of the past and see how they are seen again when the world's true labor occurs—the Tribulation.

The first plague turned the water of the Nile into blood. This pain lasted seven days. In the seven year Tribulation we see that the rivers and oceans also have their water turned to blood (Revelation 16:3–4).

Frogs came over all of Egypt as the result of the second plague. In the Great Tribulation, three unclean devil spirits will appear like frogs out of the mouth of the dragon (Satan) and will work miracles unto the kings of the earth to gather them to the battle of the great day of God Almighty (Revelation 16:13–14). As an aside, the Egyptians worshiped frogs and their fertility God was part human and part frog. To have a population explosion of frogs in their midst was actually quite comical!

The arrival of lice was the next judgment the Egyptians suffered. During the time of Jacob's Trouble, those who have received the mark of the beast will suffer grievous sores (Revelation 16:2).

The fourth plague of Egypt was the first unique one for God said to Pharaoh, "And I will put a division between my people and thy people: Tomorrow shall this sign be" (Exodus 8:23). God sent swarms of flies upon on the Egyptians. In Goshen, where the children of Israel dwelt, there were no flies. Likewise during the seven year time of the end, God will release of swarm of locusts out from the bottomless pit. These diabolical creatures will have power to torment for five months only those who are not sealed by God upon their foreheads. They will have no affect upon the children of God. That is, those who have the Lord in their heart and in their mind!

After the plague of flies came the death of all the Egyptian's cattle. In the Bible, cattle speak of possessions and wealth. During the Tribulation period, God will judge Babylon and destroy all her riches in one day as Revelation 18 reveals.

The sixth plague to come upon the land was a birth pang of boils upon all in Egypt, both man and beast. Like the lice before it, both the Egyptians and the Jews suffered this contraction as God was birthing his children out of Egypt. During the Tribulation, the vial of grievous sores resembles this.

Next, a terrible hailstorm was prophesied to Pharaoh to occur the subsequent day. Moses told Pharaoh to gather the people and the cattle out of the field for, if they were not covered, they would die from the plague of hail. In like manner, GOD has told the world, through his spokesmen of today, of the upcoming rain of hail and fire which will fall during the Great Tribulation. That hail will be fire and brimstone, reminiscent of what was seen in Sodom and Gomorrah. In more contemporary times we may have been given a sneak preview of that fire and brimstone in what we witnessed at the end of World War II over Hiroshima and Nagasaki.

The eighth plague to come over the land was that of locusts. Like the flies that arrived previously, this plague resembles the locusts with tails like unto scorpions which will plague the world during the Tribulation.

The ninth plague was one of darkness. But it was no ordinary darkness, but one which the Bible says was palpable! For three days the Egyptians did not arise from their dwellings (Exodus 10:21–23). In like manner, the fifth angel will pour out his vial upon the seat of the Beast and his kingdom will be full of darkness (Revelation 16:10a). It also will be a darkness that can be felt. One where a man will not even be able to see his hand in front of him. It will be as "outer darkness."

The tenth and last plague to afflict Egypt does not have a corollary in the latter days. It was the plague of the firstborn of the land of Egypt. Specifically, the angel of death executed all of the firstborn in the land unless they were covered by the blood of a lamb. It was the plague which demonstrated the power of the blood to protect. During the Tribulation, this curse does not reappear as Jesus has already undergone this plague in our place! Jesus, as GOD's firstborn, already died as the spotless lamb so that we and all who call upon his name now and in the last days will be "passed-over"!

The application for me concerning the plagues of Egypt is powerful. We are told that GOD told Moses to go to Pharaoh and tell him that the Lord GOD Almighty, the GOD of the Hebrews said to "let my people go." This he repeatedly spoke in the ears of Pharaoh.

But what did Pharaoh do?

He hardened his heart!

You see, dear believer, if Pharaoh had not hardened his heart when he saw the mighty signs that GOD Almighty demonstrated, he and his people would not have had to suffer the wrath of GOD.

In like manner, when you or I harden our hearts to GOD, when he is clearly speaking in our ears, we risk the Lord taking his case to the "next level." Think of it this way. When little Johnnie is being bad and disobeying, I, as his parent, will need to discipline him. It's not because I'm mad at him but because I love him and I want him to change his mind. To see things the way I see them. In other words, he needs to repent!

That's exactly what GOD occasionally needs to do in our lives. And it's what we will see him perform in the last days in order to get the "called" of the world to wake up and come back to their Daddy!

✝he Pangs in the Wilderness

And it came to pass, that at midnight the Lord smote all the firstborn in the land of Egypt, from the firstborn of Pharaoh that sat on his throne unto the firstborn of the captive that was in the dungeon; and all the firstborn of cattle. And Pharaoh rose up in the night, he, and all his servants, and all the Egyptians; and there was a great cry in Egypt: for there was not a house where there was not one dead. And he called for Moses and Aaron by night, and said, Rise up, and get you forth from among my people, both ye and the children of Israel; and go, serve the Lord, as ye have said... . And the Egyptians were urgent upon the people, that they might send them out of the land in haste; for they said, We be all dead men... . And the Lord gave the people favor in the sight of the Egyptians, so that they lent unto them such things as they required. And they spoiled the Egyptians.
And the children of Israel journeyed from Rameses to Succoth, about six hundred thousand on foot that were men, beside children.

Ex 12:29–31, 33, 36–37

After the angel of the Lord smote the firstborn of the Egyptians while passing over the children of Israel, the Egyptians were pressed beyond measure to release the Jews. They feared greatly that their entire nation would die if they continued to enslave Israel. The power and potency of GOD had indeed opened their eyes!

In fear for their lives they gave the children of Israel all that they required so that they would leave before any further maladies came upon them. Their possessions were of little value to them as they believed they were about to lose everything if Israel, with their GOD, did not leave in haste.

So that very night the Israelites left their lives and homes in Egypt and traveled to Succoth. Succoth was the first of eight camps that the Lord led the children through on their journey to Mount Sinai, that place where he gave them the Ten Commandments.

In type, the Exodus from Egypt pictures the release of the sinner from the bondage of sin. Again, Egypt is a picture of the world. Just as the children of Israel were freed from the bondage of Egypt by the blood of a lamb, so, too, the sinner is freed from the bondage of sin in the world by the blood of *the* Lamb.

But before we reach the "promised land," the land of the Spirit-filled life, there are some stops along the way as GOD builds us up. So it was for Israel. He took them to eight places upon the way to Sinai. And in these eight camps we will see beautiful pictures of GOD's plan for the new believer's growth as well.

SUCCOTH

The first camp as we have noted above was called Succoth. What a great name for the word Succoth means "booth!"

Now that should ring a bell!

The nation of Israel to this day celebrates the Feast of Tabernacles as one of their most wonderful, important and holiest times. It is the time they remember their provision and protection by GOD in the wilderness. Another name for the celebration is the Feast of Booths!

Yes a booth is a tabernacle, it's a tent. And the first stop for the children of Israel after their release from the bondage of Egypt was to come to "tent town."

That's the way it is for the new believer in Jesus also. After GOD frees a soul from the bondage of the world, after he delivers one from the angel of death, the Lord wants that believer to realize that this world is not his home. He wants him to understand that he is just passing through! It's as if he were saying, "Don't get to busy and focused on your houses and things on earth. Your time here is short, you're moving on, passing through, going up... soon!"

Moses understood this. Look with me in his story. After he fled from the face of Pharaoh, as noted in Exodus 2, he came to the land of Midian, the back side of the desert.

There he met Jethro, who had seven daughters. The Bible states that Jethro told his daughters to call Moses that "he may eat bread." In other words, Jethro wanted Moses to stay with them, to join up with them.

> And Moses was *content* to dwell with the man: And he gave Moses Zipporah his daughter. And she bare him a son, and he called his name Gershom: For he said, I have been a stranger in a strange land (emphasis mine).
>
> EXODUS 2:21–22

Wow! Gershom means "a stranger here"!

Moses understood that the world he had come into was strange. He understood that after leaving Egypt and coming to Midian that he still wasn't home. He knew he was just passing through.

But look at the first part of the verse. It says he was *content!* You see, a wonderful key to the new covenant life that we have in Jesus Christ, that life where he writes his will upon our hearts, is to be content where he has put you or where he is taking you. A secret of contentment, a secret of life, is to understand that we are pilgrims on this earth. That something more waits.

So GOD was saying to his kids, "After your deliverance, we are coming to tent town. Don't get to comfortable, don't build houses and put down your roots yet, there's more."

Abraham, the father of faith, understood this also.

By faith Abraham, when he was called to go out into a place which he should after receive for an inheritance, obeyed; and he went out, not knowing whither he went. By faith he sojourned in the land of promise, as in a strange country, dwelling in tabernacles [*booths, tents, succoths*] with Isaac and Jacob, the heirs with him of the same promise: For he looked for a city which hath foundations, whose builder and maker is GOD... . These all died in faith...and confessed that they were strangers and pilgrims on the earth.

HEBREWS 11:8–10,13A, C

Let's look at that city the patriarchs were looking toward. It's the same city we are looking for.

And I John saw the holy city, new Jerusalem, coming down from GOD out of heaven, prepared as a bride adorned for her husband. And I heard a great voice out of heaven saying, Behold, the tabernacle of GOD is with men, and he will dwell with them, and they shall be his people, and GOD himself shall be with them, and be their GOD... . And there came unto me one of the seven angels...And he...showed me that great city, the holy Jerusalem, descending out of heaven from GOD, having the glory of GOD: And her light was like unto a stone most precious, even like a jasper stone *[diamond]*, clear as crystal... . And the building of the wall of it was of jasper: And the city was pure gold, like clear glass. And the foundations of the wall of the city were garnished with all manner of precious stones... . And the twelve gates were twelve pearls; every several gate was of one pearl: And the street of the city was pure gold, as it were transparent glass. And I saw no temple therein: For the Lord GOD Almighty and the Lamb are the temple of it. And the city had no need of the sun, neither of the moon, to shine in it: For the glory of GOD did lighten it, and the Lamb is the light thereof... . And he showed me a pure river of water of life, clear as crystal, proceeding out of the throne of GOD and of the Lamb. In the midst of the street of it, and on either side of the river, was there the tree of life...and his servants shall serve him: And they shall see his face; and his name shall be in their foreheads. And there shall be no night there; and they need no candle, neither light of the sun; for the Lord GOD giveth them light: And they shall reign for ever and ever.

REVELATION 21:2–3, 9A, 10A, C–11, 18–19A 21–23; 22:1–2A, 3B–5

Oh happy day! What a place that will be!

Jesus told us that he has gone to prepare us a place, that where he is, we will be also.

Did Jesus lie?

No!...This is really going to happen, dear believer. You are headed to heaven and he has given us a wonderful glimpse of what it will be like. A huge city with foundations whose builder and maker is GOD.

But now is the time to believe for that. Don't shrink back into unbelief.

No, GOD, in his Word, says, "This is what's in store: a mansion that makes the most glorious castle on earth seem like a garbage dump in comparison!"

But again I say...believe it. Believing is so important!

But without faith, it is impossible to please him: For he that cometh to GOD must believe that he is, and that he is a rewarder of them that diligently seek him.

HEBREWS 11:6

Lord, help us in our unbelief!

• • • •

Now, for the application.

James tells us that faith without works is dead. So how do we work out our faith concerning this idea that we are pilgrims, that we are just passing through on our way to heaven?

A key to this is found in Matthew's gospel.

Jesus, after preaching with authority the principles and precepts of his kingdom in the Sermon on the Mount found in chapters 5–7, then demonstrated his authority with power. In chapter

8, our Lord healed a leper, a centurion's servant, and a woman (Peter's mother-in-law).

As an aside, none of these three were what one would consider a "religious" person! In fact these were the three groups a good Jew looked down upon the most! To be a leper, a Gentile, or a woman was not considered "kosher"!

So the air was electric! People were excited.

And in this context we see two men speak to the Master.

> And a certain scribe came, and said unto him, Master, I will follow thee whithersoever thou goest. And Jesus saith unto him, The foxes have holes, and the birds of the air have nests; but the Son of man hath not where to lay his head. And another of his disciples said unto him, Lord, suffer me first to go and bury my father. But Jesus said unto him, Follow me; and let the dead bury their dead.
>
> MATTHEW 8:19–22

The first man said, in a sense, "Jesus you are so cool! I want to hang out with you."

Jesus said, "Okay, but it's not going to be as comfortable as you think. We're going to be cold at times and we might get rained upon."

The second man said, "You're great, Jesus, but I've got to spend time with my dad first. Then I'll follow you."

Jesus then said that famously misunderstood line of letting the dead bury their dead which means that now is the time to follow him, not later.

And that's the key. That's the application. On our journey to heaven, decide that it's not about my present comfort all of the time. Be willing to follow him wherever he takes you. And don't let relationships take priority over your relationship with him. Not *any* relationship! Period!

ETHAM

So that was Succoth, the tent town. Now on to the next camp.

And they took their journey from Succoth, and encamped in Etham, in the edge of the wilderness. And the Lord went before them by day in a pillar of a cloud, to lead them by the way; and by night in a pillar of fire, to give them light; to go by day and night: He took not away the pillar of the cloud by day, nor the pillar of fire by night, from before the people.

Exodus 13:20–22

Etham means "fort." That's the lesson of this second camp. A fort is that place where soldiers huddle. It's a place of provision and protection. As they are preparing to take territory, battling against their enemy, they come to their fort for supplies, to rest and for protection.

God would say to his people, after teaching them that they are pilgrims in this world, that he wants them to know that *he* is their provision and their protection.

The Lord taught this to Abraham as well.

After Abraham, who was still called Abram, had rescued Lot from King Chedorlaomer and his confederacy, he was offered much spoil from the King of Sodom. In Bible typology, the King of Sodom is a clear picture of Satan. Abram declined the offer but instead offered tithes of the spoil he had obtained in the victory to the King of Salem, known as Melchizedek. Now Melchizedek is plainly a type, and possibly a pre-incarnate appearance, of Jesus Christ. Thus instead of taking in an abundance of spoil, Abram gave it away (The spiritual ties here are many!).

So Abram, being human, likely became fearful that he could fall prey to retaliation by those he had defeated in the battle to rescue his nephew Lot.

That's when God came to him in a vision and told him something wonderful. He said, "Fear not, Abram: I am thy shield, and thy exceeding great reward" (Genesis 15:1b).

God said that *he* is the protection and provision that Abram needed and desired. Not possessions, gifts or abundance. It's the Lord himself that is my shield and reward!

Also, please note that in the context of God being Abram's shield and reward is "fear not." God says not to fear when circumstances look bleak, when your defenses appear down or when your finances are lacking. For *he is* your provider and protector. It's not your health or your bank account that will ultimately see you through, it's him!

David sings it in these words, "For the Lord GOD is a sun and shield: The Lord will give grace and glory: No good thing will he withhold from them that walk uprightly. O Lord of hosts, blessed is the man that trusteth in thee" (Psalm 84:11–12).

Again, it's the Lord. He is my sun and shield, my provider and protector!

BETWEEN MIGDOL AND THE SEA

And the Lord spake unto Moses, saying, Speak unto the children of Israel, that they turn and encamp before Pihahiroth, between Migdol and the sea, over against Baalzephon: Before it shall ye encamp by the sea.

EXODUS 14:1–2

The next stop for Israel was indeed a painful contraction as we will see. And as often is the case, the names tell some of the story.

Migdol means "tower." It is a place where a huge granite outcropping arises near the edge of the Red Sea. My mind thinks of El Capitan in Yosemite when I consider Migdol. For the Israelites this tower must have seemed that big as well.

The tribe of 600,000 men and their families were to camp between the tower and the sea. They were between a rock and a hard place. GOD had shut them in, for he was about to teach them of his deliverance.

To add to the picture, we need to translate Pihahiroth and Baalzephon. The former means "the temple of Hather" (Hather was an Egyptian GODdess) and the latter is translated "Lord Baal of the north."

The children of Israel found themselves in the presence of false GODs, in a tight spot.

I wonder if that's ever happened to you? Let's see how the story unfolds.

GOD told Moses that Pharaoh will see that Israel was trapped by the sea. He proclaimed that indeed the Egyptian would follow after them.

> I will be honored upon Pharaoh, and upon all his host; that the Egyptians may know that I am the Lord.
>
> EXODUS 14:4B

GOD wanted the Egyptians, the people of the world in type, to know that he is the True and Living GOD. Indeed, this account we are about to consider has been known by all throughout the ages.

As GOD predicted to Moses, Pharaoh lamented the release of Israel and he took six hundred chariots and pursued after the tribe of Jacob.

And as can happen to me when I'm stuck between a rock and a hard place, looking upon the enemy coming, the Jews panicked.

> And when Pharaoh drew nigh, the children of Israel lifted up their eyes, *[They lifted up their eyes to see the problem, but not high enough to see their Protector]* and, behold, the Egyptians marched after them; and they were sore afraid: *[We will see in the next verses that fear makes one say what one will later regret]* And the children of Israel cried out unto the Lord. And they said unto Moses, Because there were no graves in Egypt, hast thou taken us away to die in the wilderness? Wherefore hast thou dealt with us, to carry us forth out of Egypt? Is not this the word that we did tell thee in Egypt, saying, Let us alone, that we may serve the Egyptians? For it had been better for us to serve the Egyptians, than that we should die in the wilderness.
>
> EXODUS 14:10–12

What was that! Talk about fear. But wait. We, unlike them, know how the story ends. They believed they were about to be annihilated.

And they would have been had not GOD intervened. That's what he wanted them to learn. That's also a good lesson for us!

The enemy, Satan, was coming to get us. We were trapped in

our sin and perversity. But GOD, through his son, provided a way of escape. He parted the Red Sea. In type, he died for us, freeing us from the trap we were in. All we need to do is walk through to the other side. All we need to do is repent and believe.

Listen to the words of Moses. They are truly words to live by! "And Moses said unto the people, Fear ye not, stand still, and see the salvation of the Lord...The Lord shall fight for you, and ye shall hold your peace" (Exodus 14:13a, 14).

Fear not...

Stand still...

And see the salvation of the Lord!

After Moses' proclamation, the angel of the Lord stood between Israel and Pharaoh that night. Moses stretched out his hand over the sea and the Lord divided it so that the Israelites were able to walk through on dry land with a wall of water on either side. The next day, the Egyptians were allowed to pursue, and as we know, they were overcome by the sea when the waters returned.

This contraction, which was quite painful while it was happening, turned into a great lesson. After GOD told his people in Etham that he was their protector, he now demonstrated it to them at Migdol.

That's what he did for us also. "But GOD commendeth his love toward us, in that, while we were yet sinners, Christ died for us." (Romans 5:8).

GOD tells us he loves us and he demonstrated it in a way that is simply unimaginable. GOD becoming a man and then dying for us so that we might live! Incredible!

· · · ·

Before traveling on to the next camp, there is an application here for dads to see. GOD told Moses that he was to divide the waters and the children of Israel would go forth on dry ground.

Moses, as the leader, of course, typifies you fathers just as your family is pictured by the children of Israel. In the Bible, water is used by GOD to typify either the Holy Spirit or his Word. In this application we will see it as the Word of GOD. The application is this: As you dads, the spiritual leaders, are seen by your family dividing the water of the Word, your family will also will step out in faith and cross over to the other side. In so doing, they will receive all the promises and blessings that GOD has prepared for them. So divide the Word, fathers. Teach and live truth in your home and watch and see what GOD will do!

MARAH

After the place of seeing GOD's power and glory, he will often take me to a dry and sometimes bitter place to prove me.

That's what he did in the life of his only begotten Son. After Jesus was baptized, not in the Red Sea but the Jordan River, he heard his Father proclaim, "This is my beloved Son, in whom I am well pleased" (Matthew 3:17b).

Immediately the Spirit led Jesus into the desert where he hungered and was proved by the Devil.

So it should not be surprising that this is the lesson to learn for the children of Israel at their next stop.

> So Moses brought Israel from the Red sea, and they went out into the wilderness of Shur; and they went three days in the wilderness, and found no water.
>
> EXODUS 15:22

They found themselves in a dry place after seeing GOD work in their midst.

> And when they came to Marah, they could not drink of the
>
> waters of Marah, for they were bitter: Therefore the name of it was called Marah.
>
> EXODUS 15:23

As described, Marah means bitterness. The Jews were in a dry place with only bitter undrinkable water on hand.

So what do you think they did?

> And the people murmured against Moses, saying, What shall
> we drink?
>
> EXODUS 15:24

I guess this should comfort me. For after most victories I
have I can find myself doing the same thing! They murmured!

But look what the Lord did next. He wasn't mad at them. He
didn't punish them. No, he healed them!

> And he [Moses] cried unto the Lord; and the Lord showed
> him a tree, which when he cast into the waters, the waters
> were made sweet: There he made for them a statute and an
> ordinance, and there he proved them, And said, If thou wilt
> diligently hearken to the voice of the Lord thy GOD, and wilt
> do that which is right in his sight, and wilt give ear to his com-
> mandments, and keep all his statutes, I will put none of these
> diseases upon thee, which I have brought upon the Egyptians:
> For I am the Lord that healeth thee.
>
> EXODUS 15:22–26

Moses prayed and the Lord showed him a tree. In the Bible,
when a tree is mentioned, GOD is painting a picture of the cross.
There are many examples of this. One that comes to mind is the
Tree of Life. It is spoken of in Genesis and in Revelation. In both
it represents the atoning work of the Cross. Here in this example,
the casting of the tree into the bitter water made it sweet! Likewise, the work of the Cross makes our lives sweet!

We see that GOD brought Israel to that dry and bitter place
to prove them. Then he covenanted with them that if they would
follow him, he would in turn heal them. We learn of a new name
for GOD in these verses, for GOD called himself, "Jehovah-Rapah,"
meaning "the Lord who healeth thee."

The application for us is huge.

It's all about the cross. When I find myself in a dry and bitter place, in a place that makes me want to murmur, I need to
remember the cross. I need to recall what the Lord did for me
in saving my life and giving me a hope that is glorious. That will

bring sweetness to whatever situation I am in and it will bring healing to my mind and my soul!

Elim

> And they came to Elim, where were twelve wells of water, and three score and ten palms trees: And they encamped there by the waters.
>
> Exodus 15:27

The fifth camp (Elim means "big trees") is all about God's blessing. Five is the number of grace in the Bible and God is showing his kids that he just wants to bless them. No reason is given, he just wants to. So he took them to an oasis with water and food in abundance.

This camp is about numbers also. We see that there were twelve wells and seventy palm trees. In the Bible these two numbers are associated with the nation of Israel. We think of the twelve sons of Jacob, the twelve tribes of Israel and the twelve apostles as a few examples. Also the seventy elders who assisted Moses in the wilderness, the seventy making up the Sanhedrin and the seventy disciples our Lord sent out come to mind. Yes, these two numbers are placed here in the narrative to show that God wants to bless his children. And he wants to bless you also! No reason, he just wants to!

The Wilderness of Sin

I love this sixth camp. It's the place where God sent manna from heaven to his kids. There is much food for us also in this camp.

> And they took their journey from Elim, and all the congregation of the children of Israel came unto the wilderness of Sin, which is between Elim and Sinai, on the fifteenth day of the second month after their departing out of the land of Egypt.
>
> Exodus 16:1

The first Passover was at evening on the fourteenth day of the first month. They have now been traveling for only one month. Hard to believe considering all that's already happened!

> And the whole congregation of the children of Israel murmured against Moses and Aaron in the wilderness.
>
> EXODUS 16:2

The Bible speaks of the wilderness differently than we do in our day. Here in Oregon, we have wilderness areas which are lush, green, and bountiful. They are nearly unspoiled. That's not what the wilderness is in the Bible. It's exactly the opposite! It's the desert. And, in addition, it's not like the desert we have in America. It's not a place with cactus and manzanita trees. No it's a place without any life. Just sand and more sand.

We saw that the second camp, Etham, was at the edge of the wilderness. Now by this time, they are deep into the desert and are getting uncomfortable.

So why did GOD take the children of Israel this way?

We can look at a map and see that if they would have traveled along the coast they could have made it to the Promised Land in less than two weeks. The answer was given to us as they left Egypt for Succoth.

> And it came to pass, when Pharaoh had let the people go, that GOD led them not through the way of the land of the Philistines, although that was near; for GOD said, Lest peradventure the people repent when they see war, and they return to Egypt.
>
> EXODUS 13:17

You see, GOD knew that the people were not ready to enter into the Promised Land. He had taken the people out of Egypt, now he needed to take Egypt out of the people!

It's the same for you and me also. After I came to the Lord, after I was released from Egypt so to speak, I still had much of the world, much of Egypt, in me. It's taken the Lord years of work to bring me to the place where I am today. Sadly, for me, he still has much work to do!

God had a one year sabbatical in mind to tutor the nation. These lessons we are looking at are part of that plan. God was using this "quiet time" in the wilderness as a time of preparation, as Israel did not yet know him well. He wanted them to understand that he was their sufficiency.

After giving them the Law in the eighth camp, still ahead, he planned upon taking them into the Promised Land. We know that didn't happen because of the unbelief of the people after the ill report of the Land by ten of the twelve spies, but that was God's original intent.

So here they are in the desert, once again murmuring.

> Then said the Lord unto Moses, Behold, I will rain bread from heaven for you; and the people shall go out and gather a certain rate every day, that I may prove them, whether they will walk in my law, or no.
>
> Exodus 16:4

Again, God wasn't angry with them. He wasn't mad. After all, they were just children. They were still learning. No, he once again blesses them. He promises to rain down bread upon them. This bread as we shall see is a powerful picture of the Word of God and of the Word made flesh, Jesus Christ.

But, he also wanted this gift to be used as another lesson in building their trust in him as well as helping them to learn to obey his commands. He wanted to prove them like a silversmith might prove metal.

> And Moses said, this shall be, when the Lord shall give you in the evening flesh to eat, and in the morning bread to the full... . And it came to pass, as Aaron spake unto the whole congregation of the children of Israel, that they looked toward the wilderness, and, behold, the glory of the Lord appeared in the cloud. And the Lord spake...in the morning ye shall be filled with bread; and ye shall know that I am the Lord your God...and in the morning the dew lay round about the host. And when the dew that lay was gone up, behold, upon the face of the wilderness there lay a small round thing, as small as the

hoar frost on the ground. And the children of Israel saw it, they said one to another, It is manna: For they knew not what it was. And Moses said unto them, this is the bread which the Lord hath given you to eat. This is the thing which the Lord hath commanded, Gather of it every man according to his eating...And the children of Israel did so, and gathered, some more, some less...he that gathered much had nothing over, and he that gathered little had no lack; they gathered every man according to his eating. And Moses said, Let no man leave it till the morning. Notwithstanding they harkened not unto Moses; but some of them left of it until the morning, and it bred worms, and stank: And Moses was wroth with them. And they gathered it every morning, every man according to his eating: And when the sun waxed hot, it melted. And the house of Israel called the name thereof Manna: And it was like coriander seed, white; and the taste of it was like wafers made with honey.

Ex 16:8a, 10–11a, 12b, 13a-16a, 17, 18b-21, 31

Manna, wonderful manna! Oh, how it pictures the Word of God.

The children were to gather it in the morning while it was fresh and tasty. This is such a key for spiritual life. Start your day out with God by getting some bread.

Jeremiah said of the Word, "Thy words were found, and I did eat them; and thy word was unto me the joy and rejoicing of mine heart" (Jeremiah 15:16a).

The manna was sufficient to fill and the people could gather as much or as little as they desired. Whatever amount they gathered was good. So it is with the Word of God. As we take it in we are filled but we can never get "stuffed."

But note with manna, when they people gathered it but then did not eat it, it bred worms and began to stink. In like manner, that's the way it is with God's Word. If we do not digest the Word, if we simply acknowledge it but don't really take it in, then it will taste wormy and smell odious.

Have you ever read something in the Bible and thought, *well that's not for me, that seems pretty harsh*, or *I'm not going to go that far*. That's what it means to stink to you. You judged the Word instead of letting the Word minister to you.

So what must I do in order to enjoy eating GOD's Word? First I need to be hungry. If I've been feeding on "worldly" cotton candy, GOD's bread won't seem appetizing. Secondly, as with manna, I need to stoop down to pick it up. It didn't fall into their laps and it won't fall into mine either! Lastly, I've got to give GOD's Word worth. Realize that it is GOD speaking. Take it in. Don't just gather it without eating it.

• • • •

But just as manna pictures the Word of GOD, we understand that it also typifies Jesus. What did Jesus tell the Jews as recorded in John's gospel?

He said, "I am the bread which came down from heaven.... . I am the living bread which came down from heaven: If any man eat of this bread, he shall live for ever" (John 6:41b, 51a).

Look at the words of the Savior. "And he took bread, and gave thanks, and brake it, and gave unto them, saying, This is my body which is given for you: Do this in remembrance of me" (Luke 22:19).

We, like Jeremiah, can eat the Word of GOD, and we, like the disciples, can partake of his body. He has given us communion. We can commune with GOD. Give communion worth, dear reader.

REPHIDIM

We come now to the seventh and last camp before the children of Israel arrived at Mount Sinai to receive the Ten Commandments. Seven is one of those wonderful numbers that GOD uses so rigorously. As we have discussed, it is the number for spiritual perfection. And as we will see, the Israelites will be perfected in this camp for they will learn how prayer defeats the enemy within.

We also know that on the seventh day of creation GOD rested from his work. He also instructed his people to rest on the seventh day. Fittingly, Rephidim means "resting place." In this camp we will see that the Jews will learn of the "rock" which would gush forth water. That rock, Paul reveals, was Jesus in direct analogy (I Corinthians 10:4). Paul also tells us that the seventh day, the Sabbath, is a shadow of Christ (Colossians 2:16–17). Truly the people will find their rest only in and through Jesus Christ. He is the Rock and the Sabbath!

Let's see how this picture develops at Rephidim.

> And all the congregation of the children of Israel journeyed from the wilderness of Sin, after their journeys, according to the commandment of the Lord, and pitched in Rephidim: And there was no water for the people to drink. Wherefore the people did chide with Moses, and said, Give us water that we may drink. And Moses said unto them, Why chide ye with me? Wherefore do ye tempt the Lord?
>
> EXODUS 17:1–2

This is really starting to sound familiar. GOD took the people to a dry place and the people complained. But look, this time they seemed to be developing a bit of faith for, instead of telling Moses that they wanted to go back to Egypt, they begged Moses to get them water. They recalled what happened at Marah.

Of course, Moses became angry that the people were coming to him instead of crying to the Lord for deliverance.

Unfortunately the people regressed at his chiding and instead of calling upon the Lord they murmured according to their former voice.

> And the people thirsted there for water; and the people murmured against Moses, and said, Wherefore is this that thou hast brought us up out of Egypt, to kill us and our children and our cattle with thirst? And Moses cried unto the Lord, saying, What shall I do unto this people? They be almost ready to stone me.
>
> EXODUS 17:3–4

Moses did the right thing in going to GOD instead of reasoning with the people.

It's interesting to me that the people were ready to execute Moses. Later, just before entering the Promised Land, Moses told the congregation that a Prophet like him would rise up and they were to look for and listen to him (Deuteronomy 18:15). We know that prophet was Jesus and, like Moses before, instead of listening to him, they wanted to stone him also! Only with the Prophet, they did, on the altar of the cross.

But don't we do the same thing also? After GOD makes our water sweet and gives us bread and meat do we start complaining as soon as things get a little dry. Do we forget that GOD is not going to abandon us and start to murmur?

Look at GOD's grace. It's the same grace for us also.

And the Lord said unto Moses, Go on before the people, and take with thee of the elders of Israel; and thy rod, wherewith thou smotest the river, take in thine hand, and go. Behold, I will stand before thee there upon the rock in Horeb; and thou shalt smite the rock, and there shall come water out of it, that the people may drink. And Moses did so in the sight of the elders of Israel.

EXODUS 17:5–6

This is wonderful. After going to the Lord, Moses then knew what to do (this is a key for life!). He was to take the same staff he used to turn the Nile River into blood and smite the rock that stood before them. When Moses did as he was instructed torrents of refreshing water gushed forth for the people to take their fill.

• • • •

Now it's great that the people had their thirst quenched, but what's so wonderful is the picture GOD is painting for us in this Old Testament story.

Paul told the Corinthian church that Christ was that very rock that Moses smote. "And did all drink the same spiritual drink: For they drank of that spiritual Rock that followed them: And that Rock was Christ" (I Corinthians 10:4).

Remember what Jesus said to the Samaritan woman at the well. "But whosoever drinketh of the water that I shall give him shall never thirst; but the water that I shall give him shall be in him a well of water springing up into everlasting life" (John 4:14).

And to the worshipers at the Feast of Tabernacles he said,

> In the last day, that great day of the feast, Jesus stood and cried, saying, If any man thirst, let him come unto me, and drink. He that believeth on me, as the scripture hath said, out of his belly shall flow rivers of living water. (But this spake he of the Spirit, which they that believe on him should receive: For the Holy Ghost was not yet given; because that Jesus was not yet glorified.)
>
> JOHN 7:37–39

The water that came out of the rock typifies the Spirit. Note that Jesus said that water would come forth from a believer's belly "as the scripture hath said." Jesus was speaking of this story, a story that the Jews understood, when he proclaimed to the people where they could find true water.

But not only was the rock Jesus and the water the Spirit, but look what GOD told Moses to do to the rock. He instructed him to smite the rock. This act completed the analogy perfectly. Just as Moses smote the rock and out came water for the people to drink, Jesus, the rock that followed, was smitten and out came the Spirit for man to drink.

So we see in these last two camps two different layers. We see demonstrations of GOD's love and provision in providing meat, bread and water and we also see prophetic pictures of the Messiah's incarnation, death and the gift of the Holy Spirit. As Paul so eloquently states,

> O the depth of the riches both of the wisdom and knowledge of GOD! How unsearchable are his judgments, and his ways past finding out! For who hath known the mind of the Lord? Or who hath been his counselor…For of him, and through him, and to him, are all things: To whom be glory for ever. Amen.
>
> ROMANS 11:33–34, 36

• • • •

GOD was not finished teaching the people at Rephidim. After teaching the people to have a craving for him, the Living Water, he had a second lesson for them to learn. The lesson of the power of prayer. It was yet another birth pang for the people as we continue our analogy of GOD's dealing with mankind as being like the course of a woman's pregnancy.

> Then came Amalek, and fought with Israel in Rephidim.
>
> EXODUS 17:8

Amalek, according to Genesis 36, was one of the sons of Esau. He was an Edomite. You may remember that in Esau's story with Jacob, Esau, and Edom are types of the flesh while Jacob and Israel typify the spirit. Remember when Rebekah was pregnant with the twins that the children struggled within her. GOD said to her, "Two nations are in thy womb, and two manner of people shall be separated from thy bowels; and the one people shall be stronger than the other people; and the elder shall serve the younger" (Genesis 25:23).

Not only was GOD talking about the two nations but he was illustrating the two natures of man. The flesh against the spirit. What Paul in the New Testament would call the carnal man verses the spiritual man. Paul went on to say in Romans,

> That is, They which are the children of the *flesh*, these are not the children of GOD...but when Rebecca also had conceived by one, even our father Isaac; (For the children being not yet born, neither having done any good or evil, that the purpose of GOD according to election might stand, not of works, but of him that calleth;) It was said unto her, The elder shall serve the younger. As it is written, Jacob have I loved, but Esau have I hated.
>
> ROMANS 9:8A, 10B-13

This verse is quoted from Malachi and speaks of GOD's hatred of Edom. GOD hated Esau and Edom as they typified the flesh.

Thus in our story here, Amalek will illustrate the flesh. We will see in his battle with the children of Israel how GOD wants us to deal with the flesh.

> And Moses said unto Joshua, Choose out men, and go out, fight with Amalek:
>
> EXODUS 17:9A

Moses didn't tell Joshua to take all of his men, only those that were ready. Those that could do battle. Hear what Moses told the next generation nearly forty years later in recalling this story.

> Remember what Amalek did unto thee by the way, when ye were come forth out of Egypt; How he smote the hindmost of thee, even all that were feeble behind thee, when thou wast faint and weary; and he feared not GOD.
>
> DEUTERONOMY 25:17–18

That's what the enemy will do. That's what the enemy within, the flesh, will also do. It's when I'm weak, when I'm in the back of the pack that he attacks.

Dear reader, don't drop to the back. Don't say in your mind, "I'm saved, I can cruise, I can take it easy now." No, that's when you'll be taken down and wiped out! Stay close to Jesus, pray to the Father, read his Word, spend time with other believers. Don't drop back and have Amalek pick you off.

> Tomorrow I will stand on top of the hill with the rod of GOD in mine hand.
>
> EXODUS 17:9B

Moses told Joshua that while he was fighting in the valley, he would be going to the top of the hill with the rod of GOD. That rod speaks of GOD's power, as truly it is unleashed in and through prayer as we shall see.

And it came to pass, when Moses held up his hand, that Israel prevailed: And when he let down his hand, Amalek prevailed.

EXODUS 17:11

Paul told the Thessalonican believers to pray without ceasing (I Thessalonians 5:17). GOD wants me to be in constant communication with him. We see the result graphically in this story when we stop talking with him. When Moses had his hands lifted (speaking of prayer, specifically intercessory prayer), Israel prevailed, but as he tired, Amalek obtained the upper hand.

So it is with your life. As you commune with GOD, your spirit is refreshed and victorious, but as you leave conversing with him your flesh will begin to dominate.

But this verse also has another level. It is a picture of what our Lord did as he stretched out his hands on the cross of Calvary. He held his hands up for you and me. He interceded as only he could!

But Moses' hands were heavy; and they took a stone, and put it under him, and he sat thereon;

EXODUS 17:12A

Again, Jesus is the Rock. He's our Rock. He's the stone that we rest upon as we press forward in prayer.

… and Aaron and Hur stayed his hands, the one on the one side, and the other on the other side; and his hands were steady until the going down of the sun.

EXODUS 17:12B

Not only does the Father give us the Son for support in prayer, but he demonstrates that we need the support of others as we obtain the victory over the flesh. Dear believer, include other people in prayer for you. They'll help you overcome.

And Joshua discomfited Amalek and his people with the edge of the sword.

EXODUS 17:13

The victory was secured via intercessory prayer on the mountain top while the instrument of victory was the edge of the sword.

Do you remember in biblical typology what the sword represents? It's the Word of GOD (Ephesians 6:17b). We need to have some of the Word of GOD in our hand in order for prayer to obtain the victory over our flesh. That doesn't mean you have to have total command of all the nuances of GOD's Word. Joshua's men had swords, not grenades, and were victorious!

> And the Lord said unto Moses, Write this for a memorial in a book, and rehearse it in the ears of Joshua: For I will utterly put out the remembrance of Amalek from under heaven.
>
> EXODUS 17:14

GOD told Moses to write this down, don't let those who follow after forget this lesson! Don't let the people become proud as though it was by their own effort that they were victorious.

In fact, according to this verse, this is the first story in the Bible which was written down. It was written well before Moses' other contributions to scripture as the lesson was so important that GOD wanted it penned at that time. It's through prayer that the flesh is defeated and some day the flesh will be remembered no more!

> And Moses built an altar, and called the name of it Jehovah-nissi.
>
> EXODUS 17:15

Moses and the people found a fresh way to worship the Lord. And in it we see a new name for the Lord. Yet another name which describes GOD's nature. Jehovah-nissi is "The Lord My Banner."

> For he said, Because the Lord hath sworn that the Lord will have war with Amalek from generation to generation.

EXODUS 17:16

Indeed, all generations will need to battle against the flesh! But take comfort, for GOD has given us our marching orders in Rephidim. Because the Rock was smitten we can go to the him and out will gush the water of the Spirit. And, holding up our hands in prayer as we carry the sword we will realize victory over the enemy within.

THE DESERT OF SINAI

In the third month, when the children of Israel were gone forth out of the land of Egypt, the same day came they into the wilderness of Sinai. For they were departed from Rephidim, and were come to the desert of Sinai, and had pitched in the wilderness; and there Israel camped before the mount.

EXODUS 19:1–2

This eighth camp is the camp where GOD thundered the Ten Commandments. It is where the Law was received.

Paul, in the New Testament, teaches, "Wherefore the law was our schoolmaster to bring us to Christ, that we might be justified by faith. But after faith is come, we are no longer under a schoolmaster" (Galatians 3:24–25).

Here in this last camp before GOD planned to take his children to the Promised Land, he needed them to understand that his standards where not as theirs! And we need to see that, too. Before we desire a Savior, we need to see that we *need* a Savior!

Here Israel learned just what GOD required.

• • • •

So, to summarize Israel's pangs in the wilderness, let's recap what the Father desires his children to learn. First, he wants us to live for heaven. Realize we are just passing through so we won't get too caught up in this world. It's tent town! Secondly, realize that *he* is your sufficiency. He will warm you when it's cold and cool you when it gets too hot. He's our fort, our pillar of fire, our cloud in the heat of the day.

Next, realize he may put you between a rock and a hard place to demonstrate that he is your sufficiency. But the waters will part! Fourthly, after a victory, things can get dry and even bitter. It's the cross that makes life sweet. Remember the cross.

The fifth lesson reminds us that GOD is good. He blesses us just because he wants to. Oh, the grace of GOD! Sixthly, he has given us bread. He has made known to us his Word and he has given us the bread of life, his Son, that we may continually dine. Our seventh lesson was that waters of refreshment come from the sacrifice of his Son. With those waters, we are equipped in prayer to be victorious over the flesh.

Birth Pangs on The Way to the Promised Land

The remainder of the book of Exodus, Leviticus, and the first twelve chapters of Numbers detail the GOD-given Law and the order that GOD placed upon his people. But with Numbers 13 another round of birth pangs began.

There we learn that Moses sent a ruler from every tribe of Israel to look upon the Promised Land and bring word back to them. As we know, an evil report was issued by ten of the twelve spies and Israel fell back into unbelief, forgetting all of the lessons they had just learned. Their unbelief caused them to lose GOD's protection and they were beaten soundly by the Amalekites and the Canaanites when they went out under their own steam (Numbers 13–14).

After this they wandered in the wilderness for another thirty eight years while those men over twenty years of age died. Time does not allow me to speak in detail of this time but many contractions did occur which I will briefly mention.

We remember how Korah and his confederacy became envious of Moses' GOD-ordained authority and rebelled. GOD did a new thing in causing the earth to open and swallow up those false leaders (Numbers 16:1–40). The Father demonstrated in a very genuine way how he feels about pride, envy, and false teachers.

The very next day another pang occurred as the congregation murmured about GOD's treatment of Korah.

They said, "Ye have killed the people of the Lord" (Numbers 16:41b).

But they were *not* the people of the Lord and this further rebellion brought another plague upon the people.

Moses had Aaron (the High Priest) take incense from the altar to make atonement for the people. This, of course, speaks of the greater than Aaron, Jesus Christ, interceding for us. That day the Bible states 14,700 died. The loss would have been much greater had not Aaron stayed the plague (Numbers 16:41–50).

Later a birth pang of cowardice was inflicted upon Israel.

They asked for permission to pass by the border of Edom on their journey to the Promised Land but were refused passage. The Edomites came out against the Jacob, "with much people, and with a strong hand and Israel turned away from him" (Numbers 20:20b).

King Arad of the Canaanites next fought against Israel and took prisoners. Israel called upon the Lord saying they would utterly destroy the Canaanite cities if he would deliver them. GOD hearkened to their prayer and Israel did destroy their cities, calling the place Hormah which means "utter destruction" (Numbers 21:1–3).

This story has a deeper spiritual principle imbedded. GOD doesn't want only partial victory for you and me. He wants the Enemy utterly destroyed and he will partner with you if you are willing to "go for it." He wants Hormah! Here's a little limerick for this principle: Without him, I can't. Without me, he won't.

The next contraction was most intense! As we saw, the people were forced to travel far out of their way in order to avoid the land of Edom. Once again in a dry place they spoke against GOD and against Moses. And they loathed the manna that GOD was providing.

By this time GOD was expecting more from his kids. They weren't babies any more as when they had first come out of

Egypt. By now they had seen him provide time after time and thus this pang of unbelief brought fiery serpents. Many people died causing the people to realize their sin. GOD told Moses to make a fiery (brass) serpent and set it upon a pole. He said that whoever looked upon the pole after he was bitten would not die (Numbers 21:4–9).

This story of course comes up again in the Gospel of John. Jesus said to Nicodemus, "And as Moses lifted up the serpent in the wilderness, even so must the Son of man be lifted up: That whosoever believeth in him should not perish, but have eternal life" (John 3:14–15).

This story is a type of what the Savior did for me. When I was bitten by the serpent, I looked upon his finished work upon the Cross, that place where the fire of GOD's wrath fell as Jesus was lifted up, and I too did not die!

The years continued to pass by in the wilderness. Near the conclusion of their time of wandering, the children of Israel came to the border of the Amorites. The new generation was now ready to enter into the Promised Land but first they had to pass by Sihon, the Amorite king. Israel told Sihon that they meant his people no harm. They said they would not turn into the fields or drink of the waters of the wells. Nevertheless, Sihon came out with all of his people and fought against Jacob. The Amorites were destroyed and Israel came away with much spoil (Numbers 21: 21–31).

Og, the king of Bashan, made the same mistake and came against GOD's people when they were in a place of GOD's blessing. Again Israel experienced a labor pang of victory. GOD said to Moses, "Fear him not: For I have delivered him into thy hand, and all his people, and his land; and thou shall do to him as thou didst unto Sihon king of the Amorites" (Numbers 21:34).

Victory was sweet but short lived. The nation had now come to the plains of Moab which was against Jericho. There they fell prey to what the Book of Revelation calls the doctrine of Balaam.

But I have a few things against thee, because thou hast there them that hold the doctrine of Balaam, who taught Balac to cast a stumbling block before the children of Israel, to eat things sacrificed unto idols, and to commit fornication.

REVELATION 2:14

Balak who was king of Moab, hired the prophet Balaam to curse Israel. This Balaam could not do. In fact he powerfully blessed the tribe as he looked down upon the nation from a high hill and saw their camp in the configuration of a cross. But for his hire, Balaam did tell Balak that even though he could not curse them, they could curse themselves through idolatry and fornication. By looking to other GODS and by lusting after the flesh, Balaam described how Israel could bring themselves down. Numbers 25 gives the sordid story as we learn that twenty four thousand souls perished.

Jeremiah sums it up well when he said,

Thine own wickedness shall correct thee, and thy backslidings shall reprove thee: Know therefore and see that it is an evil thing and bitter, that thou hast forsaken the Lord thy GOD, and that my fear is not in thee, saith the Lord GOD of hosts.

JEREMIAH 2:19

GOD states that it's my own sin that will take me out. He doesn't get mad at me, he doesn't come down on me, it's my own sin that will wipe me out and beat me up. You see, lusting and fornication are not sins because GOD says they are bad. No, lusting and fornication are bad and that's why GOD says they are sins! He lovingly says not to go there for they are bad. I will see my family broken, I will come down with disease, I will produce fruit that is not wanted!

Solomon poetically writes it in these words,

My son, attend to my wisdom, and bow thine ear to my under-standing:...For the lips of a strange woman drop as an honeycomb, and her mouth is smoother than oil: But her end is bitter as wormwood…Her feet go down to death…Remove thy way far from her, and come not nigh the door of her house: Lest thou give thine honor unto others, and thy years unto the cruel: Lest strangers be filled with thy wealth; and thy labors be in the house of a stranger; And thou mourn at last, when thy flesh and thy body are consumed.

PROVERBS 5:1, 3–4A, 5A, 8–11

Solomon, who should know as he had many wives, states that fornication will take your reputation and title (honor), your time and your money. It will cause you to mourn and will consume your mind and body.

Instead, he offers the alternative,

Drink waters out of thine own cistern, and running waters out of thine own well… . Let thy fountain be blessed: And rejoice with the wife of thy youth. Let her be as the loving hind and pleasant roe; let her breasts satisfy thee at all times; and be thou ravished always with her love. And why wilt thou, my son, be ravished with a strange woman, and embrace the bosom of a stranger? For the ways of man are before the eyes of the Lord, and he pondereth all his goings. *His own iniquities shall take the wicked himself, and he shall be holden with the cords of his sins* (emphasis mine).

PROVERBS 5:15,18–22

· · · ·

After this, the Lord told Moses to avenge the children of Israel over the Midianites whom Balak had conspired with to cause Israel to stumble. Another pang of battle ensued and Israel slew all of the males while letting the women and children live.

This enraged Moses as those very women were the object of the men's folly immediately prior. Moses told the warriors to kill every male among the little ones and every woman which had known a man (Numbers 31:1–20).

Of course, this seems harsh to us in our age of the Geneva

Convention, but this was the rule of engagement in Biblical days. The goal was to utterly destroy the enemy.

Spiritually speaking, GOD is telling his children to completely take out the enemy. Don't spare that part of the enemy you find attractive and pleasant. It will come back to bite you!

When this contraction subdued, the children of Israel were ready to fight for the Promised Land. It was a campaign that has many interesting parallels to the spirit-filled life as well as to future battles in Israel during the Tribulation time period.

Joshua and ✝ he Promised Land

The wonderful Book of Joshua powerfully pictures the spirit-filled life as well as prophetically picturing end-times events. Specifically, numerous parallels can be seen between Joshua and Ephesians concerning our walk in the Spirit and between Joshua and Revelation concerning the Tribulation period, that time the Bible calls Jacob's Trouble (Jeremiah 30:7).

> Now after the death of Moses the servant of the Lord it came to pass, that the Lord spake unto Joshua the son of Nun, Moses' minister, saying, Moses my servant is dead: Now therefore arise, go over this Jordan, thou and all this people, unto the land which I give to them, even to the children of Israel.
>
> JOSHUA 1:1–2

Moses had earnestly desired to take the people into the Promised Land. But as you may recall from Book II of *A Woman's Silent Testimony,* Moses sinned in smiting the rock twice at the waters of Meribah after GOD had only told him to speak to the rock. Thus GOD told Moses he would not take the children into the land (Numbers 20:1–3). GOD said to Moses, "But charge Joshua, and encourage him, and strengthen him: For he shall cause them to inherit the land which thou shalt see" (Deuteronomy 3:28).

You see, Moses is a picture of the Law. Joshua is a picture of Jesus Christ. Moses received the Law and led the people to the Promised Land, but he could not take them in. The direct analogy is that the Law, the Ten Commandments, will bring a person to the realization that he needs a Savior, but it doesn't quite bring him in. The Bible states, "For all have sinned, and come short of the glory of GOD" (Romans 3:23).

Joshua, on the other hand, is a picture of the New Covenant. He is a picture of Jesus. He is the one who brought Israel into the Promised Land just as Jesus, the greater than Joshua (Joshua and Jesus are the same name), brings you and me into the promised land of the spirit-filled life. That life in which the Bible states he will write his will upon our hearts!

So after Moses, who represents the Law, came Joshua, who typifies the Spirit. And the Spirit is greater than the Law. The Bible declares that the Law kills but the Spirit gives life.

Continuing, GOD told Joshua, "Every place that the sole of your foot shall tread upon, that have I given unto you" (Joshua 1:3). In Ephesians we read, "Blessed be the GOD and Father of our Lord Jesus Christ, who hath blessed us with all spiritual blessings in heavenly places in Christ" (Ephesians 1:3).

Just as GOD told Joshua that he had *already* given him the Land, he says to you and me that we *already* are blessed with all spiritual blessings in Christ. Just like Joshua, all we need to do is to take it. We need to cross over the Jordan River and enter the land of the spirit-filled life he has already given us.

In the Promised Land there were battles.

GOD said to Joshua, "Be strong and of a good courage...Only be thou strong and very courageous" (Joshua 1:6a, 7a).

Likewise in the New Covenant life there are also battles. But GOD has equipped us well. We too can be strong and very courageous!

> Put on the whole armor of GOD, that ye may be able to stand against the wiles of the devil.
>
> EPHESIANS 6:11

. . . .

But this book is about birth pangs. It's about how the course of Israel, the church, the nations and creation itself is like the course of a woman's pregnancy. Thus, we will leave the analogy of Joshua and the spirit-filled life and speak of battles, labor pains, and of the analogy of the Book of Joshua to the Book of Revelation.

✝he Red Thread

Then Joshua commanded the officers of the people, saying, Pass through the host, and command the people, saying, Prepare you victuals; for within three days ye shall pass over the Jordan, to go in to possess the land, which the Lord your GOD giveth you to possess it.

JOSHUA 1:10–11

General Joshua told his people that within three days they would enter into the Land. There is a picture sitting in the midst of this statement. For Peter teaches concerning GOD's timing, "But, beloved, be not ignorant of this one thing, that one day is with the Lord as a thousand years, and a thousand years as one day... But the Day of the Lord will come " (II Peter 3:8, 10a).

Within three days from Joshua's commission the nation was to move into the Promised Land. So it is with Jesus. Within three days, that is, within three thousand years, Jesus will lead the nation of Israel to the place of writing his will upon their hearts. This short time interval of less than three days pictures the short time interval, from GOD's perspective, between Jesus' first and second coming. Do the math yourself...we are in the third day!

> And Joshua, the son of Nun sent out of Shittim two men to spy secretly, saying, go view the land, even Jericho. And they went, and came into an harlot's house, named Rahab, and lodged there. And it was told the king of Jericho, saying, Behold, there came men in hither to night of the children of Israel to search out the country. And the king of Jericho sent unto Rahab, saying, Bring forth the men that are come to thee, which are entered into thine house: For they be come to search out all the country.
>
> Joshua 2:1–3

The story of the battle of Jericho has many parallels to the New Testament and one is its picture of Jesus taking back Israel.

Let me be more specific. When you read this story, see Joshua as Jesus sending the spies back into the land that he wants to take back. The spies can be seen as the two faithful witnesses of Revelation 11. They witnessed to Rahab of the God of Israel just as the two witnesses in Revelation will witness to those who will hear in Israel during the latter days. The harlot, Rahab, represents the 144,000 of Israel who are given a special anointing during the Tribulation time period as seen in Revelation 7 and 14. We see that they will be protected by God just as Rahab and her family were sheltered. Lastly the king of Jericho typifies the influence of the Antichrist. He is the one during the last days who will seek to destroy the witnesses. In fact, the Antichrist will ultimately succeed and the witnesses will lay dead for three days in the streets to Jerusalem, only to be resurrected. Likewise the two spies hid for three days in the surrounding mountains. On the third day they went back to Joshua.

> And she said unto the men, I know that the Lord hath given you the land, and that your terror is fallen upon us, and that all the inhabitants of the land faint because of you...Now therefore, I pray you, swear unto me by the Lord, since I have showed you kindness, that ye will also show kindness unto my father's house, and give me a true token: And that ye will save alive my father, and my mother, and my brethren, and my sisters, and all that they have, and deliver our lives from death. And the men answered her, Our life for yours, if ye utter not

this our business. And it shall be, when the Lord hath given us the land, that we will deal kindly and truly with thee... . Behold, when we come into the land, thou shalt bind this line of *scarlet thread* in the window which thou didst let us down by: And thou shalt bring thy father, and thy mother, and thy brethren, and thy father's household, home unto thee. And it shall be, that whosoever shall go out of the doors of thy house into the street, his blood shall be upon his head, and we will be guiltless: And whosoever shall be with thee in the house, his blood shall be on our head, if any hand shall be upon him (emphasis mine).

JOSHUA 2:9, 12–14, 18–19

The two men told Rahab that she should bind a red thread upon her window so that her household would be protected. This, of course, speaks of the blood of Jesus. We are covered by the blood and cannot be taken out by our adversary just as the scarlet thread was the protection for Rahab and her family.

Jesus told the two disciples on the road to Emmaus that the scriptures speak of him. That he can be seen everywhere in the Old Testament if we have but eyes to see. Here he is manifested as the scarlet thread.

In fact, scholars have taken this verse and used it to encapsulate this principle of Jesus being found in the Old Testament. It is said, in those circles, that Jesus is the Red Thread.

For those of you who recall the movie, *Shindler's List,* this idea may come to life. Remember the movie was in black and white but every so often a little girl dressed in a red dress would be seen against the black and white background. The imagery was beautiful and I see the idea of the scarlet thread in the same light. There against the black and white background of the Old Testament would appear the Red Thread of Jesus standing out like the girl in the red dress.

But look also at what the men told Rahab. The spies told her that they needed to stay in the house, or they would not be saved. In Book II of *A Woman's Silent Testimony* we also spoke of this principle. GOD kept Noah in the ark during the storm, Paul told his sailing mates to stay in the boat and they would be saved, and here Rahab is told to stay in the house in order to be delivered safely. This pictures the importance of our continued walk in the grace of GOD; of continuing to believe in our Lord unto salvation. It would seem that if we choose to leave the protection of GOD's atoning work, we risk being destroyed.

Thus to summarize, in comparing this story to the Revelation, we see Rahab and her family picture the 144,000 Jewish believers who will hear the message from the two witnesses and will be protected by GOD during their time of testimony, and ultimately saved to be with the Lord forever, just as Rahab and her family were protected and saved during the fall of Jericho.

So on to Jericho we go!

✝he House of the Moon God

> And it came to pass, when Joshua was by Jericho, that he lifted up his eyes and looked, and, behold, there stood a man over against him with his sword drawn in his hand: And Joshua went unto him, and said unto him. Art thou for us, or for our adversaries? And he said, Nay: But as captain of the host of the Lord am I now come. And Joshua fell on his face to the earth, and did worship, and said unto him, What saith my Lord unto his servant? And the captain of the Lord's host said unto Joshua, Loses thy shoe from off thy foot: For the place whereon thou standest is holy.
>
> JOSHUA 5:13–15

Joshua encountered the "captain of the Lord's host." One might initially imagine this man with his sword drawn as a mighty angel. Michael or Gabriel come to mind. But this captain does what no angel would do, for he accepts worship from Joshua and told him to remove his shoe as he was standing on holy ground. No, this rings of deity. Just as GOD told Moses to remove his shoe at the burning bush now Joshua is told to remove his shoe in the presence of this One. This one is none other than Jesus Christ.

He is the captain of the host and he was the one that led the children of Israel in this upcoming battle.

Zechariah tells of this event in speaking of the Lord's second coming to rescue Jerusalem.

> Behold the Day of the Lord cometh...For I will gather all nations against Jerusalem to battle...Then shall the Lord go forth, and fight against those nations, *as when he fought in the day of battle.* And his feet shall stand in that day upon the mount of Olives...(emphasis mine).
>
> ZECHARIAH 14:1A, 2A, 3–4A

Zechariah was stating that the Messiah will be present in that future battle just as he was present as the Captain of the Host in this battle we are now discussing.

> Now Jericho was straitly shut up because of the children of Israel: None went out, and none came in.
>
> JOSHUA 6:1

It's time to define the word Jericho. Jericho means "moon city." Now that may ring a bell in your mind when we look at today's Middle Eastern world. Presently, that part of the globe is dominated by the Crescent Moon, that is, it is dominated by Islam. Islam is a city with huge walls. A city that is formidable. A city that hates and fears the Jews just as Jericho had shut herself up because of the children of Israel. Yes, in the type we are developing concerning end times events, Jericho is Islam. And like Jericho, which fell early in the course of taking back the Promised Land, will it be that the religion of Islam will also come crashing down early in the seven year Tribulation period? I think it very likely!

> And the Lord said unto Joshua, See, I have given into thine hand Jericho, and the king thereof, and the mighty men of valor.
>
> JOSHUA 6:2

We said earlier that the king of Jericho typifies the influence of the Antichrist. He is an Antichrist figure. But more specifically he represents those who control the power of Islam. He pictures the leaders of Islam. Those who lead the faithful of Islam hate Jews and Christians just as Satan does and the Antichrist will. But we see that the Lord said unto Joshua that the king of Jericho was about to fall!

> And ye shall compass the city, all ye men of war, and go round about the city once. Thus shall thou do six days.
>
> JOSHUA 6:3

The Lord didn't explain. He just said to quietly march around Jericho every day for six days.

Have you ever felt like that? If so, then keep plugging away. You're marching around that walled city. Nothing seems to be happening. Maybe it's that marriage that just doesn't have a breakthrough, or that health problem that keeps looming over you. Well, keep marching as something is about to happen!

> ... and the seventh day ye shall compass the city seven times, and the priests shall blow with the trumpets... . and when ye hear the sound of the trumpet, all the people shall shout with a great shout; and the wall of the city shall fall down flat, and the people shall ascend up every man straight before him.
>
> JOSHUA 6:4B, 5B

In that problem, the Lord would say to keep walking. In fact you may need to walk around the city seven times as the problem nears an end. Then shout at that wall. That speaks of fervently praying to the Father. We are to shout, not pout. That is, pray instead of complain.

When I find myself in a season of helplessness, with walls to overcome, where I can't do it by myself, I need to quietly believe the Lord, fervently pray to him about my problem, and wait for an event to suddenly happen. Wait for the walls to come down. It will always be by his power, not mine!

On another note, our story tells us that after marching for

six days, GOD's children heard the sound of the trumpet on the seventh. Then they ascended up. Does that sound familiar?

> For the Lord himself shall descend from heaven with a shout… and with the trump of GOD… . Then we which are alive and remain shall be caught up together with them in the clouds, to meet the Lord in the air: And so shall we ever be with the Lord.
>
> I THESSALONIANS 4:16–17

Here we see a picture of the rapture of the church. We, as GOD's kids, will hear the sound of the trumpet and will ascend up. That event will likely be immediately prior to the Tribulation time period just as it is seen here in our story as occurring at the beginning of the seven year campaign to take the Promised Land.

Oh, what a day that will be!

✝he Gibeonites: Death to Life

And it came to pass, when all the kings which were on this side Jordan, in the hills, and in the valleys, and in the coasts of the great sea over against Lebanon, the Hittite, and the Amorite, the Canaanite, the Perizzite, the Hivite, and the Jebusite, heard thereof; That they gathered themselves together, to fight with Joshua and with Israel, with one accord.

JOSHUA 9:1–2

Now had come the time to chose with which side to align. These six kings apparently believed they could to take on Joshua and Israel. They didn't fear the GOD of Israel. So it will be in the last days. In that future day it will become clear to all nations that Jesus *is* coming back to take the planet. People will need to choose sides. They will need to decide who they are going to follow.

We remember that the number six in the Bible is the number of man. Indeed, these six kings represent the nations of man gathering to fight against Jesus and Israel during those last days.

But there was one group, the Gibeonites, who decided not to join up with those worldly kings. Instead, they wanted Joshua's favor. We will see that the Gibeonites prophetically picture those

Gentiles who call on the name of Jesus during the Tribulation time period instead of following after the kings of the world. Instead of following after Antichrist.

> And when the inhabitants of Gibeon heard what Joshua had done unto Jericho and to Ai, They did work wilily, and went and made as if they had been ambassadors, and took old sacks upon their asses, and took wine bottles, old, and rent, and bound up; And old shoes and clouted upon their feet, and old garments upon them; and all the bread of their provision was dry and moldy. And they went to Joshua unto the camp at Gilgal, and said unto him, and to the men of Israel, We be come from a far country: Now therefore make ye a league with us.
>
> JOSHUA 9:3–6

This is beautiful! The inhabitants of Gibeon, picturing the Tribulation saints, saw what Joshua did in Jericho and Ai. They witnessed their friends leave in what the world might call "the disappearance." The event we know as the rapture. They heard the kings of the world say that beings from outer space took them or something equally farfetched. Then they saw Islam fall like a stone and along with hearing of the spiritual reawakening of the Jews and the witness of the two holy men in Jerusalem they conclude that Joshua (Jesus) is the One they want to make a league with.

Also those future believers are clothed with rags, eating moldy bread and drinking spent wine. This, of course, pictures their pathetic state as they come to Jesus. They will realize who he is at a time when it's not comfortable to follow him, a time when buying food, drink, and clothes will be regulated by the king of the world, the Antichrist. They come to Joshua in humility and fear. They come to Jesus as a child.

Also note, they come to him eating bread and drinking wine. That is, they partake in type of our Lord's death and resurrection as they take communion with him.

Dear believer, don't neglect to give the Lord's Table worth. Throughout the Bible, we see individuals sharing in GOD's blessing as they commune with him eating bread and drinking wine. Truly, GOD wants to share a meal with his children!

> And Joshua made peace with them, and made a league with them, to let them live.
>
> JOSHUA 9:15A

✝he Fate of Adonizedek

Now it came to pass, when Adonizedek king of Jerusalem had heard how Joshua had taken Ai, and had utterly destroyed it; as he had done to Jericho and her king, so he had done to Ai and her king; and how the inhabitants of Gibeon had made peace with Israel, and were among them; That they feared greatly, because Gibeon was a great city...Wherefore Adonizedek king of Jerusalem sent unto Hoham king of Hebron, and unto Piram king of Jarmuth, and unto Japhia king of Lachish, and unto Debir king of Eglon, saying, Come up unto me, and help me, that we may smite Gibeon: For it has made peace with Joshua and with the children of Israel.

JOSHUA 10:1–2A, 3–4

Who is this character, Adonizedek, who would want to form an alliance and take on Joshua? Well, let's look at his name. "Adoni" means "Lord" and "zedek" is interpreted as "righteousness." Incredibly, his name means "Lord of righteousness." But it gets even more interesting when you think about it, for Adonizedek is the king of Jerusalem. So we have the Lord of righteousness who is the king of Jerusalem taking on Joshua who as a picture of Jesus is the true Lord of Righteousness and true King of Jerusalem. Indeed, as you have by now guessed, Adonizedek directly typifies the Antichrist.

Adonizedek called upon the other kings because Gibeon had made peace with Joshua. So it will be during the latter days. Antichrist will become enraged because the Gibeonites (many Gentiles) will follow after the greater than Joshua!

> Therefore the five kings of the Amorites...gathered themselves together, and went up, they and all their hosts, and encamped before Gibeon, and made war against it.
>
> JOSHUA 10:5A, C

The kings of the world, under the command of Antichrist will war against those who follow after Jesus. Those who do not take the mark of the beast.

> And the men of Gibeon sent unto Joshua to the camp at Gilgal, saying, Slack not thy hand from thy servants; come quickly, and save us, and help us: For all the kings of the Amorites that dwell in the mountains are gathered together against us. So Joshua ascended from Gilgal, he, and all the people of war with him...And the Lord said unto Joshua, fear them not: For I have delivered them into thine hand...And the Lord discomfited them before Israel, and slew them with a great slaughter at Gibeon, and chased them along the way that goeth up to Bethhoron...And it came to pass, as they fled from before Israel...that the Lord cast down great stones from heaven upon them...and they died... . But these five kings fled, and hid themselves in a cave at Makkedah
>
> JOSHUA 10:6–7A, 8A, 10A, 11A, 16

As in that day, Jesus will rise up to defend his people in the midst of labor and travail. He will discomfit the armies of the world and once again rain the hail of judgment upon his enemies like as was seen in Sodom and Gomorrah as well as in Egypt.

"The first angel sounded, and there followed hail and fire mingled with blood" (Revelation 8:7a).

Also, like the kings at Makkedah, the kings of the earth will similarly hide from the greater than Joshua.

> And the kings of the earth...hid themselves in the dens and in the rocks of the mountains; And said to the mountains and rocks, Fall on us, and hide us from the face of him that sitteth on the throne, and from the wrath of the Lamb.
>
> REVELATION 6:15–16

Thus we see that Joshua's campaign to take the Promised Land closely pictures the conflict which will occur in the last days. According to the Bible that campaign took seven years (Joshua 14:7–10) just as the Tribulation will last seven years. After the enemy was defeated we learn of rest for the people.

> And the Lord gave them rest round about, according to all that he sware unto their fathers: And there stood not a man of all their enemies before them; the Lord delivered all their enemies into their hand. There failed not ought of any good thing which the Lord had spoken unto the house of Israel; all came to pass.
>
> JOSHUA 21:44–45

Likewise, after that future enemy will be defeated we will hear,

> Behold, the tabernacle of GOD is with men, and he will dwell with them, and they shall be his people, and GOD himself shall be with them, and be their GOD. And GOD shall wipe away all tears from their eyes; and there shall be no more death, neither sorrow, nor crying, neither shall there be any more pain: For the former things are passed away.
>
> REVELATION 21:3–4

Oh happy day that will be!

Next, we come to the second trimester of our figurative pregnancy. We leave the heady days of Joshua and come to the difficult days of the Judges of Israel.

✝he Pangs of Judges

The book of Judges is an interesting account of three hundred thirty-five years of history which illustrates the "labor pains" we humans in our fallen state undergo. In it, we see twelve Judges (there is that number of Israel again!) who are raised up to rescue the children of Israel. A better translation for the word "judge" is "deliverer." As each judge pictures an aspect of our Great Deliverer, Jesus Christ.

In this book, we note that the Israelites fall into repeated cycles of sin followed by servitude to an evil master. After serving in bondage, they would come to their senses and call out to GOD. GOD would then send a judge, a deliverer, who would save them. Then, out of response to GOD's grace, they would serve their Maker for a time, only to fall back into the sin cycle once again.

The story of the first judge illustrates this cycle shortly and succinctly.

> And the children of Israel dwelt among the Canaanites, Hittites, and Amorites, and Perizzites, and Hivites, and Jebusites:
> JUDGES 3:5

The application for me in this verse is to stay separate from the six peoples listed. Stay separate from man's system. (Six is the number of man.) Paul taught that we are in the world but not of the world.

The children of Israel didn't appreciate this truth and disaster followed.

> And they took their daughters to be their wives, and gave their daughters to their sons, and served their GODS.
>
> JUDGES 3:6

Dads, do you think it's okay for your daughters to date boys who do not know the Lord? Do you invite the "GODS" of Hollywood into your house and serve them? Dear reader, this story is not just about Israel!

> And the children of Israel did evil in the sight of the Lord, and forgat the Lord their GOD, and served Baalim and the groves.
>
> JUDGES 3:7

Baalim was the GOD of practicality. They did what seemed expedient instead of what GOD had lined out for their ultimate protection in the Law.

> Therefore the anger of the Lord was hot against Israel, and he sold them into the hand of Chushanrishathaim king of Mesopotamia: And the children of Israel served Chushanrishathaim eight years.
>
> JUDGES 3:8

GOD was angry with his children not because he has a temper but because he knew the king of Mesopotamia, who represents Satan in this story, had purchased them! The people had paid the price with their sin. As the Bible states, "and be sure your sin will find you out" (Numbers 32:23b). In Jeremiah we are told that it's our own backslidings that will reprove us (Jeremiah 2:19).

And when the children of Israel cried unto the Lord, the Lord raised up a deliverer to the children of Israel, who delivered them, even Othniel, the son of Kenaz, Caleb's younger brother.

JUDGES 3:9

Othniel of course, pictures Jesus Christ! Our Deliverer!

And the spirit of the Lord came upon him, and he judged Israel, and went out to war: And the Lord delivered Chushanrishathaim king of Mesopotamia into his hand; and his hand prevailed against Chushanrishathaim. And the land had rest forty years. And Othniel the son of Kenaz died. And the children of Israel did evil again in the sight of the Lord...

JUDGES 3:10–12A

There we see the pattern. Sin, servitude, supplication, salvation, and service followed by sin. Unfortunately, this cycle is not isolated to the Old Testament for I see it in my own life also!

The cycles repeated and we see GOD raise up Ehud who saved Israel from Eglon, the king of Moab, followed by Deborah delivering them from Jabin, the king of Canaan. After that, the Midianites prevailed over Israel and GOD used Gideon to save his people. Unfortunately, though, another cycle of sin led to the next labor pang which I want to examine in a bit more detail.

✝he Son of a King

From the book of Judges at the end of Gideon's story we learn that Gideon had many wives and seventy sons. One of his sons was the son of a concubine from Shechem. You might remember Shechem was located just outside of the Promised Land! This son was named Abimelech. Interestingly, Abimelech means "my father is a king." The meaning of this name will soon become clear.

After Gideon died, this son of an outsider went to his own people in Shechem and asked them whether they wanted all of Gideon's sons to rule over them or one of their own. Of course, he was presenting himself to them as the choice for their ruler. They agreed to this envious plot and the Bible states that Abimelech hired vain and light persons which followed him to Gideon's house where they captured and beheaded all but one of Abimelech's brothers.

The lone remaining son of Gideon was named Jotham, whose name means "Jehovah completes."

When the men of Shechem made Abimelech king, Jotham went up to Mount Gerizim, which overlooked the people and prophesied.

He said,

The trees went forth on a time to anoint a king over them; and they said unto the olive tree, Reign over us. But the olive tree said unto them, Should I leave my fatness, wherewith by me they honor GOD and man and go to be promoted over the trees? And the trees said to the fig tree, Come thou, and reign over us. But the fig tree said unto them, Should I forsake my sweetness, and my good fruit, and go to be promoted over the trees? And then the trees said unto the vine, Come thou, and reign over us. And the vine said unto them, Should I leave my wine, which cheereth GOD and man, and go to be promoted over the trees? Then said all the trees unto the bramble, Come thou, and reign over us. And the bramble said unto the trees, If in truth ye anoint me king over you, then come and put your trust in my shadow: And if not, let fire come out of the bramble, and devour the cedars of Lebanon.

JUDGES 9:8–15

Jotham noted that when the people asked the Judges to be their kings, they deferred to GOD. Gideon said to the men of Israel when they came to him with their request, "I will not rule over you, neither shall my son rule over you: The Lord shall rule over you" (Judges 8:23).

But when this false deliverer, this bramble bush, was asked to rule, he accepted!

Jotham then said that the bramble would require their trust, which is another way of saying Abimelech would require their worship and service, or they would be devoured by fire!

This, of course, did happen to the men of Shechem. Later in the chapter, we learn that, after a murderous rampage by Abimelech, both they and Abimelech were destroyed.

The Bible says, "And a certain woman cast a piece of a millstone upon Abimelech's head, and all to break his skull" (Judges 9:53).

As so often is the case, these Old Testament stories speak of New Testament realities. So it is again in this story!

Abimelech pictures the Antichrist. Indeed, his father, Satan, is the king of the world. He usurped power and desires to rule over the trees just as Antichrist will. The trees represent the nations of the world. In the last days, the nations will desire a ruler for which Antichrist, the thorny bramble bush, will gladly accept. The olive tree, fig tree, and vine all are Biblical pictures of Israel. Throughout GOD's Word, whenever one of these plants is mentioned, there is an application concerning Israel imbedded. In this case, the three fruitful trees will not accept the other tree's request for leadership.

So has been the case with Israel over the centuries. Despite her favored position as GOD's called-out child, she has not gone out to the nations with his Word. Instead she has turned inward. We will see later, during the Tribulation period, that Israel will break free from her introverted tendency. There will be 144,000 voices from Israel during that time who will take the message of GOD to the nations, telling the world to reject the bramble bush, to reject the Antichrist, and receive their true Messiah, Jesus the Christ.

In the end we see that the bramble bush did wreak havoc upon Shechem just as the Antichrist will to the nations. But ultimately he will have his head crushed by a woman just as Satan had his head crushed by the seed of a woman (Genesis 3:16).

•   •   •   •

In order to apply this to one's life, one must be careful who they follow. Is the person fruitful or thorny? Jesus said you will know a good tree by its fruit. So too, one wants to follow and listen to a man or a woman who bears fruit. Don't follow the words of a false Messiah. You will know him by his fruit!

Saul and ✝ he Men of Jabesh-Gilead

Painful contractions continued to occur intermittently as Israel's history continued. Jephthah was the next Judge, and he was prominently used in defeating the Ammonites. Sampson's interesting story followed. Sampson was a man who had many flaws. Ultimately, though, after all of his indiscretions, Sampson would stretch out his arms in the temple of his enemies, much like the One who would later stretch out his arms on the cross of Calvary. In so doing, both men defeated their foes in their deaths.

A cramp of civil war broke out after those days. The men of Gibeah, in the tribe of Benjamin's inheritance, brutally raped and killed a Levite's wife while the two were traveling back to their home. This enraged the men of Israel and they came against Gibeah to exact punishment. The other men of Benjamin learned of Gibeah's sin yet they aligned with their near kinsmen despite that knowledge. A fierce battle with thousands dying from both sides was the result.

The application is clear and that is to be careful with whom you align yourself. Family is important, but if they are totally out of harmony with the Lord, then be careful defending them, as it may take you out also!

We see this phenomenon to the highest degree today in the Middle East. Ethnic peoples defending their own brothers in a continual battle against other cultural groups. It's now to the point that they don't even remember what started their hatred.

A birth pang of famine and hunger came upon Israel next and is documented in the wonderful Book of Ruth. Elimelech, Naomi, and their sons, who picture the nation of Israel in this story, left Bethlehem-Judah and traveled to Moab, outside of the Promised Land.

You have seen by now that every time a biblical character leaves the land of promise, bad things happen! In this case it couldn't be clearer as the name of the place they left tells the story. Bethlehem means "house of bread" and Judah means "praise." In this story we see the nation of Israel, typified by Elimelech and Naomi, leaving the house of bread and place of praise in a time of dryness to seek relief outside of God's promises.

The application for you and me should be apparent. Don't stop feeding upon God's Word and praising him when things get dry. No, that's the time to press in deeper. As the Word proclaims; "Draw nigh to God, and he will draw nigh to you" (James 4:8a).

Do you want God close to your heart? Sometimes you need to make the first move!

Well, bad things did happen to Naomi in Moab. Elimelech and her two sons died just as much heartbreak and death has occurred to Israel as they have left the place of God's blessing throughout their history. Naomi came to her senses when she learned that the Lord had visited his people with bread and she returned to Bethlehem with a new name which typifies Israel's mindset. She said not to call her Naomi, which means "pleasant," but to call her Mara, meaning "bitter."

But in the place of her bitterness, Naomi, through her daughter-in-law Ruth, had an encounter with Boaz, the great-grandfather of Israel's future king, David. Boaz was Ruth's kinsman redeemer and he is a powerful picture of our Redeemer and Israel's future Redeemer, Jesus born in Bethlehem!

Read the Book of Ruth with these analogies in mind. Naomi and her family picture Israel. Ruth typifies the Gentile bride, known as the church. She marries Boaz who clearly pictures the

Savior. Also found in chapter four of the book was a kinsman redeemer who was closer to Ruth than Boaz but he could not redeem her. The man who could not save, clearly pictures the Law. Yes, just as in Ruth's story, the Law is unable to save you and me. We need the greater than Boaz! We need the Redeemer, the Lamb of God.

• • • •

After Ruth, we come to the first book of Samuel which was also called in prior days "The First Book of the Kings." In it we see the story of the first king of Israel, known as Saul.

Early in Saul's story, the king clearly reveals a preview of Israel's true King, Jesus Christ. His name means "requested" and that fit the desire of the nation at that time. For they requested a king, against Samuel's and God's desire, in order to be like their neighbors. But Saul was humble and was wonderfully filled with the Spirit and with power in the early chapters of his life. Only after his repeated disobedience was the anointing taken away and he became a picture of fleshly Israel for the remainder of his story.

But before his downfall, Saul's greatest moment, in my opinion, came in the story of his dealing with the intense contraction of the men of Jabesh-Gilead. Let's look at this story together and see what the Lord has for us.

> Then Nahash the Ammonite came up, and encamped against Jabesh-Gilead: And all the men of Jabesh said unto Nahash, Make a covenant with us, and we will serve thee. And Nahash the Ammonite answered them, On this condition will I make a covenant with you, that I may thrust out all your right eyes, and lay it for a reproach upon all Israel. And the elders of Jabesh said unto him, Give us seven days respite, that we may send messengers unto all the coasts of Israel: And then, if there be no man to save us, we will come out to thee. Then came the messengers to Gibeah of Saul...And they told him the tidings of the men of Jabesh. And the Spirit of God came upon Saul when he heard those tidings, and his anger was kindled greatly...And the fear of the Lord fell on the people, and they

came out with one consent...And it was so on the morrow, that Saul put the people in three companies; and they came into the midst of the host in the morning watch, and slew the Ammonites until the heat of the day: And it came to pass, that they which remained were scattered, so that two of them were not left together...And Saul said...for today the Lord has wrought salvation in Israel. Then Samuel said unto the people, Come, let us go to Gilgal, and renew the kingdom there. And all the people went to Gilgal; and there they made Saul king before the Lord in Gilgal; and there they sacrificed sacrifices of peace offerings before the Lord; and there Saul and all the men of Israel rejoiced greatly.

I Samuel 11:1–4a, 5b-6, 7b, 11, 13b-15

This is a great story! Once again, the names of the participants tell some of the story. Nahash means "serpent." As you surmised, if you are tracking with me, Nahash is a picture of Satan.

Nahash the Ammonite came up against the men of Jabesh-Gilead. Jabesh means "dry" and Gilead means "monument of stones." Might it be that when I'm dry, just a statue of my former self spiritually, that the enemy will attack? I think that's one of the things the Lord wants us to see in this story.

Look what the men of Jabesh, those men in a dry place, said to Nahash: "Make a covenant with us and we will serve thee!"

Now it's not a good idea to make a deal with the devil. And an even worse idea to agree to *serve* him!

Let's see Nahash's reply.

He said, "Sure, but on one condition. Let me thrust out your right eye."

And that's what Satan will do. If he can't destroy you because you're the Lord's, he will try and take out one of your eyes so as to not see well. He wants to make you unfit for battle.

So the men of Jabesh were in a bind. If they served Nahash, it was going to be painful. Thus they did something that initially seemed silly. They requested seven days respite so they could send for help.

Now why would Nahash go for that?

Well, therein lies another story. Remember the civil war that occurred over one hundred years earlier between Benjamin and Israel after the Levite's concubine was brutally raped and murdered. Well, after Benjamin was nearly destroyed the men of Israel regretted that one of their tribes was decimated. The few remaining men of Benjamin who had escaped needed wives to restore the population of the tribe. Thus Israel in considering where to find wives for the men of Benjamin realized that the men of Jabesh-Gilead, which was on the other side of the Jordan River, did not help in the effort to punish Benjamin. So they went up against Jabesh-Gilead and killed many of its men. They took virgins for the men of Benjamin and left Jabesh as sort of an outcast.

Now we can see why Nahash wasn't too worried about letting messengers leave the city to go and find help. He didn't really think anyone from Israel would come to their aid. Nahash knew of their history!

So it can be with you and me. We can be in a dry place on the other side of God's blessings and the serpent will encamp against us. And he won't be too worried if we try to find help in the flesh or with worldly philosophies and ideas. He knows they won't save us. But what he didn't count on was Saul. He didn't count on the One who Saul pictures.

Saul did come to their rescue, even though they were far away, in a dry place, and out of options. He freed them from their oppressor.

That's what Jesus does also, doesn't he?

Rebellion and Witchcraft ☦

The Philistines were a people who were a constant thorn in the side of Israel for much of their remaining history. If you will, Israel's dealings with the Philistines were a series of birth pangs which they endured. GOD was molding the children of Jacob into a group that would ultimately see his power in delivering them time after time from the stronger Philistines.

So, on with our story.

After Saul had reigned for one year, his son, Jonathan, took a thousand men and smote the Philistines at Geba.

> And Saul blew the trumpet throughout the land, saying, Let the Hebrews hear. And all Israel heard say that Saul had smitten a garrison of the Philistines.
>
> I SAMUEL 13:3B-4A

Saul took the credit even though Jonathan had clearly gained the victory. Thus began Saul's downfall from the anointed one of Israel to a fleshly, out of touch, and sometimes demon possessed despot.

After that victory the Philistines countered by massing an army which included thirty thousand chariots, planning to crush the children of Israel. Samuel told Saul to wait for him at Gilgal before the battle, but Saul became impatient and offered up sacrifices to GOD without Samuel's presence.

When Samuel arrived, he said to Saul by the Spirit of the Lord,

> Thou hast done foolishly: Thou hast not kept the commandment of the Lord thy GOD, which he commanded thee: For now would the Lord have established thy kingdom forever. But now thy kingdom shall not continue: For the Lord hath sought a man after his own heart.
>
> I SAMUEL 13:13–14A

Saul, in the remainder of his story, becomes a picture of fleshly and unbelieving Israel. They, as a nation, were given the anointing to take GOD's message to the world, but they fell back into unbelief and disobedience and thus lost the blessing that had once been bestowed. When you read Saul's story, see him first as the king of Israel, a GODly man who pictures the final King of Israel, Jesus Christ. Later after his downfall, Saul is a type of unbelieving Israel. In contrast, Jonathan his son can be seen as a picture of believing or spiritual Israel. He typifies the called out of the nation who *do* embrace the Word of the Lord.

> And the spoilers came out of the camp of the Philistines in three companies…Now there was no smith found throughout all the land of Israel: For the Philistines said, Lest the Hebrews make them swords or spears.
>
> I SAMUEL 13:17A, 19

That's what the Spoiler wants to do. He wants to take away my sword! You remember the sword pictures the Word of GOD. The devil wants to take the Word out of my heart.

> Now it came to pass upon a day, that Jonathan the son of Saul said unto the young man that bare his armor, Come, and let us go over to the Philistines garrison, that is on the other side…
> . It may be that the Lord will work for us: For there is no restraint to the Lord to save by many or by few. And his armor

bearer said unto him, Do all that is in thine heart: Turn thee; behold, I am with thee according to thy heart.

I Samuel 14:1a, 6b-7

Jonathan's armor bearer pictures the Holy Spirit as he partners with Jonathan to gain the victory over the spoilers.

And Jonathan climbed upon his hands and upon his feet, and his armor bearer after him: And they fell before Jonathan; and his armor bearer slew after him.

I Samuel 14:13

Jonathan and his mate were on their hands and feet. They were in the posture of prayer. Look at what prayer will do!

And there was trembling in the host in the field, and among all the people: The garrison, and the spoilers, they also trembled, and the earth quaked: so it was a very great trembling.

I Samuel 14:15

The earth quaked as God made the spoilers tremble. Prayer releases God's power!

And the watchmen of Saul in Gibeah of Benjamin looked; and behold, the multitude melted away, and they went on beating down one another...So the Lord saved Israel that day.

I Samuel 14:16, 23

Jonathan and his armor bearer were demonstrating the prophecy given by Moses whereby a few would chase their enemies and hundreds and thousands would fall before them (Leviticus 26:7–8).

A contrast to this victory was also prophesized by Moses as he stated what would happen to the nation if and when God withdrew his Spirit because of their unbelief and disobedience. "How should one chase a thousand, and two put ten thousand to fight, except their Rock had sold them, and the Lord had shut them up?" (Deuteronomy 32:30).

This can happen to me as I fall back into unbelief and disobedience. Dear believer, stay in that place where GOD can release his blessings to you. Don't fall back!

After that great victory GOD gave Saul yet another chance to keep the anointing he had received.

> Samuel also said unto Saul, The Lord sent me to anoint thee to be king over his people, over Israel: Now therefore hearken thou unto the voice of the words of the Lord. Thus saith the Lord of hosts, I remember that which Amalek did to Israel, how he laid wait for him in the way, when he came up from Egypt. Now go and smite Amalek and utterly destroy all that they have, and spare them not; but slay both man and woman, infant and suckling, ox and sheep, camel and ass.
>
> I SAMUEL 15:1–3

GOD told Saul to utterly destroy Amalek. Completely take out his race and all that he possessed. This sounds brutal until we recall that these physical battles in the Old Testament picture spiritual battles for us in the New Testament. Amalek, as we have developed earlier, is an unvarying picture of the flesh. Whenever he or one of his descendants is mentioned we can see application to the flesh. GOD is telling his anointed to completely and utterly destroy the flesh. He is telling you also, as you have received the anointing of his Spirit, to utterly destroy your flesh. As Paul states concerning this principle, "But put ye on the Lord Jesus Christ, and make not provision for the flesh, to fulfill the lusts thereof" (Romans 13:14).

So Saul gathered the people together and smote the Amalekites. But the Bible states that Saul took Agag, their king, alive. And King Saul spared the best of the sheep, oxen, fatlings, lambs, and all that was good.

Therefore, did Saul perform GOD's charge?

Of course not! He did his own thing and kept the trophies of victory. He took a spoil. He pictures for us our own tendency to keep living with parts of our fleshly nature. Those things which are not of GOD yet we continue to enjoy. You know what those things are!

Unfortunately, when we fast-forward to the end of Saul's life, we see that he was killed by an Amalekite.

> As I happened by chance upon mount Gilboa, behold, Saul leaned upon his spear; and, lo, the chariots and horsemen followed hard after him. And when he looked behind him, he saw me, and called unto me. And I answered him, I am an Amalekite. He said unto me again, Stand, I pray thee upon me, and slay me: For anguish is come upon me, because my life is yet whole in me. So I stood upon him, and slew him...and I took the crown that was upon his head, and the bracelet that was on his arm.
>
> II SAMUEL 1:6–10A, C

This vignette pictures what the flesh will do to you and me. Those little sins of the flesh that we think we can control, those things we believe we have contained will come back and kill us when we are down. They will take our authority and treasure for that is what Saul's crown and bracelet portray.

Paraphrasing the Apostle Paul from several scriptures...We are to mortify the flesh as we are crucified with Christ, for in my flesh dwelleth *no* good thing! We need to learn from Saul's disobedience as we see his end.

After the victory, Samuel arrived and Saul greeted him saying, "Blessed be thou of the Lord: I have performed the commandment of the Lord" (I Samuel 15:13b).

"Blessed be thou of the Lord." Saul spiritually greeted the elder prophet with religious jargon. Have you ever had that happen? A brother or a sister who are totally out of fellowship, in the midst of sin and rebellion, can still turn on the "holy language!" Be careful of spiritual jargon. As we have discussed, Jesus said you will know a tree by its fruit. So it can be in the lives of other believers. Actions always speak louder than words! The spiritual greeting or the fish on the business card does not guarantee commitment to the Lord!

> And Samuel said, what meaneth then this bleating of the sheep in mine ears, and the lowing of the oxen which I hear? And

Saul said, They have brought them from the Amalekites: For the people spared the best of the sheep and of the oxen, to sacrifice unto the Lord thy GOD: And the rest we have utterly destroyed.

I SAMUEL 15:14–15

Look at Saul passing the buck by saying that it was the people, not he, who spared the spoil. Then he came up with the weak excuse that he and the people where going to sacrifice the spoil to the Lord. This reminds me of the sort of thing one of my teenagers might say to me after being caught red-handed. My response to them is similar to Samuel's: "An excuse is *no* excuse!"

Then Samuel said unto Saul, stay, and I will tell thee what the Lord hath said to me this night. And he said unto him, Say on. And Samuel said, When thou wast little in thine own sight, wast thou not made head of the tribes of Israel, and the Lord anointed thee king over Israel? And the Lord sent thee on a journey, and said, Go and utterly destroy the sinners the Amalekites, and fight against them until they be consumed. Wherefore then didst thou not obey the voice of the Lord, but didst fly upon the spoil, and didst evil in the sight of the Lord…Hath the Lord as great delight in burnt offerings and sacrifices, as in obeying the voice of the Lord? Behold, to obey is better than sacrifice, and to hearken than the fat of rams. For rebellion is as the sin of witchcraft, and stubbornness is as iniquity and idolatry.

I SAMUEL 15:16–19, 22–23A

The Lord wants meekness and obedience in his children, and especially in his leaders. He told Saul to remember when he was little in his own sight. Remember when he was humble, that's when he had the anointing. That's when he had the power.

Samuel asked, "Is sacrifice better that obedience?" The answer is clear. Of course not! Sacrifice can take the form of fleshly works; things done in order to be seen of men. But obedience comes from the heart!

And rebellion is the same as witchcraft! Rebellion is the same as saying, "I can divine. I don't need the Lord. I can do it better in my own power!" That's why rebellion is as witchcraft. When I reflect upon these things in this light, Saul's not the only one with a problem!

> Because thou hast rejected the word of the Lord, he hath rejected thee from being king.
>
> I SAMUEL 15:23B

Do you want to lose your position of authority? Try disobedience!

> And the Lord said to Samuel, how long wilt thou mourn for Saul, seeing I have rejected him from reigning over Israel? Fill thine horn with oil, and go, I will send thee to Jesse the Bethlehemite: For I have provided me a king among his sons...And Samuel did that which the Lord spake, and came to Bethlehem...And he sanctified Jesse and his sons, and he called them to the sacrifice. And it came to pass, when they were come, that he looked on Eliab, and said, surely the Lord's anointed is before is before him.
>
> I SAMUEL 16:1, 4A, 5B-6

Samuel looked upon the oldest and most mature son whose name was Eliab, meaning "GOD is my father" and said, "Surely this is the man. He has the correct pedigree, he has the right name...This must be who and what GOD is looking for in his king."

> But the Lord said unto Samuel, Look not on his countenance, or on the height of his stature; because I have refused him: For the Lord seeth not as man seeth; for man looketh on the outward appearance, but the Lord looketh on the heart.
>
> I SAMUEL 16:7

David, whose name means "beloved one" was that man after GOD's own heart. He was the man the Lord wanted to anoint as head over Israel. David had many flaws as his story continues. He was a liar, an adulterer, and a murderer; however, he was humble and ran hard after his GOD. He was the beloved one of GOD who we will see in our next chapter in the story of David and Goliath, is a powerful picture of the future Deliverer and Anointed One of Israel, Jesus Christ.

David and Golia✝h

> Then Samuel took the horn of oil, and anointed him [David]
> in the midst of his brethren: And spirit of the Lord came upon
> David from that day forward.
>
> I SAMUEL 16:13A

Just as Jesus did not fit the outward expectation the Jews had of the King, neither did David. David's brother's witnessed the anointing just as the Jews saw Jesus' anointing in the Jordan River. For the men of Israel heard John the Baptist declare, "Behold the Lamb of GOD who taketh away the sins of the world" (John 1:29b).

The brothers heard Samuel say that GOD looks not on the outward appearance but on the inward heart, just as the children of Jacob heard GOD thunder from heaven, "This is my beloved Son in whom I am well pleased" (Matthew 3:17b). The Jews of Jesus' day asked, "can any good thing come out of Nazareth?" They were looking upon the outward. They didn't know the "heart" of the matter. This brings me to an important application.

When evaluating the behavior and motives of any man, whether he be a believer or not, I need to love him and let GOD judge him! I only see the outward expression of his life, yet GOD sees his heart. He sees the inner motives. My tendency is to judge and let GOD do the loving. It needs to be the other way around. I need to love and let GOD be the Judge. For only GOD has all of the facts of the case!

> Now the Philistines gathered together their armies to battle, and were gathered together at Shochoh...And Saul and the men of Israel were gathered together, and pitched by the valley of Elah...
>
> I SAMUEL 17:1A, 2A

The Philistines were gathered at Shochoh, meaning "a thorny place." Indeed, the men of Philistia were thorns in the sides of the children of Israel. Meanwhile, Saul and his men were in the valley of Elah. Elah is translated "mighty trees." The Israelites were in a valley surrounded by mighty trees. They were in a low place encompassed all around with huge obstacles. Have you ever felt that way?

> And there went out a champion out of the camp of the Philistines, named Goliath, of Gath, whose height was six cubits and a span.
>
> I SAMUEL 17:4

Goliath, whose name means "stripper," was the enemy's champion. He was from Gath which is translated "winepress." And he was big. You see, a cubit was the length from a man's elbow to his fingertips, approximately eighteen inches. A span was the length of a man's hand or around six inches. So for a man to be six cubits and a span would mean he was nine feet and six inches tall!

So here we have the stripper, from the nation of spoilers, from a town where they crush grapes, who is their champion. I hope you see that this guy pictures Satan!

The story continues by telling us that the armor he wore weighed 125 lbs. and incredibly the tip of his spear weighed 15 lbs. In other words, just the head of Goliath's spear carried the weight and power of a flying shot put!

> And he stood, and cried unto the armies of Israel...Choose you a man for you, and let him come down to me. If he be able to fight with me, and to kill me, then we will be your servants: But if I prevail against him, and kill him, then shall ye be our servants, and serve us.
>
> I Samuel 17:8a, 8c–9

That's the very challenge that Satan makes. He says for mankind to take your best shot. Try to follow the Law, check out the philosophies of men, and see if your crystals can defeat me. But if your best man does not prevail, then you *will* serve me!

> And the Philistine said, I defy the armies of Israel this day; give me a man, that we may fight together. When Saul and all Israel heard those words of the Philistine, they were dismayed, and greatly afraid.
>
> I Samuel 17:10–11

The stripper repeated his challenge. He said basically, I don't think you have a "man" in your entire camp. Even your supposed king is truly just a wimp! I can see this also happening to me—to us. Like Israel, we need a champion who can go up against this monster!

> Now David was the son of...Jesse; and he had eight sons...And the three eldest sons of Jesse went and followed Saul to the battle...And the Philistine drew near morning and evening, and presented himself forty days.
>
> I Samuel 17:12a, 12c, 16

God is about to introduce our champion. He was the eighth son of Jesse. You may remember that the number eight in the Bible is associated with a new beginning and with great abundance. Indeed something new and abundant was about to occur!

The Philistine taunted the children of Israel for forty days. Once again the number given adds some insight. Forty, in God's vernacular, is the number associated with trial and testing. The nation was feeling a painful contraction in this picture we are painting.

> And Jesse said unto David his son, take now for thy brethren… these ten loaves, and run to the camp to thy brethren.
>
> I SAMUEL 17:17A, C

Just as Jesse told his son to bring bread to his brothers, GOD the Father told his Son to bring the bread of his Word down to his brothers who were being taunted by the champion of the world, Satan.

> And David…came and saluted his brethren. And as he talked with them, behold, there came up the champion…and spake according to the same words: And David heard them. And all the men of Israel, when they saw the man, fled from him, and were sore afraid. And the men of Israel said, Have ye seen this man that is come up? Surely to defy Israel is he come up: And it shall be, that the man who killeth him, the king will enrich him with great riches, and will give him his daughter, and will make his father's house free in Israel.
>
> SAMUEL 17: 22A, C, 23A, 23C-25

Look at what the victor was to receive. Great riches, the king's daughter, and his house would be free. Now think about this. That's what Jesus also was looking to obtain. The Bible says that for the glory set before him he endured the Cross. It also says that we, the church, are the bride of Christ. And we know that we as the Lord's bride have truly been set free in Israel!

Beautifully, David is revealing Jesus in this story.

> And David spake to the men that stood by…For who is this uncircumcised Philistine, that he should defy the armies of the living GOD?
>
> I SAMUEL 17:26A, C

David was looking with eyes of faith and to him this warrior standing nine feet, six inches didn't look so big!

> And Eliab his eldest brother heard when he spake unto the
> men; and Eliab's anger was kindled against David, and he said,
> Why camest down thou hither? And with whom hast thou left
> those few sheep in the wilderness? I know thy pride, and the
> naughtiness of thine heart; for thou art come down that thou
> mightest see the battle.
>
> I SAMUEL 17:28

Eliab had seen Samuel anoint his younger brother but scorned
him nonetheless. In jealousy he attacked his title saying he was
but a shepherd and not the anointed, and he attacked David's
character saying that he was full of pride.

In like manner that's what Jesus' brothers did also. The
scribes and Pharisees did not accept the anointing they saw from
John but said he was just a carpenter from the backwater town of
Nazareth. One who was born illegitimately and who was doing
miracles by Beelzebub.

So David's words ultimately came to Saul and the king called
for him. "And David said to Saul, Let no man's heart fail because
of him; thy servant will go and fight with this Philistine" (I Samuel 17:32).

Jesus, through Paul, tells us also not to fear. For greater is he
that is in us, than he that is in the world (I John 4:4). Because our
champion, Jesus Christ, took on and defeated their champion, we
don't have to fear!

> And Saul said unto David, Thou art not able to go against this
> Philistine to fight with him: For thou art but a youth, and he a
> man of war from his youth.
>
> I SAMUEL 17:33

How could David, a shepherd boy from Bethlehem, take on
this experienced killing machine and hope to prevail? Likewise,
how could a carpenter from Nazareth, born in Bethlehem, take
on the stripper, the one Paul calls the GOD of this world (II Corinthians 4:4)? Thankfully, the faith of David and Jesus did not
need the support of men to be manifested.

And David said unto Saul, thy servant kept his father's sheep, and there came a lion, and a bear, and took a lamb out of the flock: And I went out after him, and smote him, and delivered it out of his mouth.

I Samuel 17:34–35a

That's what the Lord, the Good Shepherd does also. When one of his lambs is grabbed up by the lion and the bear (two animals who picture the devil in Scripture) he leaves the ninety nine to seek out the one who is lost.

And when he arose against me, I caught him by his beard, and smote him, and slew him. Thy servant slew both the lion and the bear: And this uncircumcised Philistine shall be as one of them.

I Samuel 17:35a-36a

Today's stresses prepare us for tomorrow's successes. By taking on the lion and the bear, David was now ready to take on the giant. We saw this in Jesus also. For forty days in the wilderness he battled against his mighty adversary as it prepared him for the ultimate battle three years later upon the cross of Calvary.

... seeing he has defied the armies of the living God.

I Samuel 17:36b

Also note that earlier we heard Goliath say that he defied the armies of Israel (17:10). But David understands this statement in its spiritual light. He tells Saul that Goliath is actually defying the armies of the Living God. He is bringing God into the equation. He is inviting God to join the battle!

David said moreover, The Lord that delivered me out of the paw of the lion, and out of the paw of the bear, he will deliver me out of the hand of this Philistine.

I Samuel 17:37a

Similarly, Jesus said that though he be alone in his upcoming battle, that the Father would be with him (John 16:32).

> And Saul armed David with his armor, and he put an helmet of brass upon his head; also he armed him with a coat of mail. And David girded his sword upon his armor, and he assayed to go; for he had not proved it. And David said unto Saul, I cannot go with these; for I have not proved them.
>
> I Samuel 17:38–39a

Picture this. There was young David, dressed for battle with Saul's armor. He was not familiar wearing this stuff and now he was preparing to take on the giant warrior who was very comfortable with his 125 lb. suit of armor and 15 lb. spear. It's sort of comical when you think about it, isn't it?

But we do this sometimes also. We can be pressured to enter the spiritual battle wearing clothes that don't fit. Maybe it's that pastor who makes you feel guilty if you don't street witness, or the boss that presses you to take that position that doesn't work for you.

> And David put them off.
>
> I Samuel 17:39b

David did the right thing. He told Saul that his expectations for the challenge were not the same as his. He wanted to move freely and quickly and didn't need Saul's armor, which typifies the religious non-Scriptural stuff that people can try to lay on you, weighing him down and slowing him up. He said, "I have not proved them." Street witnessing or taking that job may work for you but not for me!

Jesus did the same thing, didn't he? As the Son of God, he existed outside of time and was over all. His armor, if you will, was ultimate. No champion could stand against him. Yet he laid aside his armor and became just a clay pot. He became an earthen vessel. He became a man! As a man, with blood pulsing in his veins, emotions and feelings, susceptible to fatigue and pain, he took on the God of this world, the one the New Testament calls the Strongman, and defeated him without wearing his armor! What a champion we have!

> And he took his staff in his hand, and chose him five smooth stones out of the brook…and his sling was in his hand: and he drew near to the Philistine.
>
> I Samuel 17:40A, c

Five is the number of grace. Amazing grace. That's what David knew about his God. David planned to use the smooth stones to accurately sling them, one at a time, at the only place Goliath was vulnerable. That being his temple, just above one of his eyes. The taunter's eyes were uncovered to allow him to see. Goliath had a suit of armor, but David had a gun and he knew how to use it!

The five smooth stones accurately picture for us the Word of God. In the New Testament the Word is called the sword of the Spirit. It is an offensive weapon, very effective for battle. When the Word of God is handled correctly it is just like the bullet that David possessed in his sling. It's direct, powerful, and incredibly effective in taking down our enemy.

Jesus used the sling of the Word in the wilderness temptations. When the devil attacked, our Lord retorted with the Word. This caused the tempter to depart.

> And when the Philistine looked about, and saw David, he disdained him: for he was but a youth, and ruddy, and of a fair countenance.
>
> I Samuel 17:42

This guy is Opie from Mayberry. He's too cute with his red hair and perfect face. What kind of joke is this! I doubt the carpenter from Nazareth was what Satan was expecting from the promised Messiah either!

> And the Philistine said unto David, Am I a dog, that thou comest to me with staves? And the Philistine cursed David by his Gods.

I SAMUEL 17:43

Not a good idea to curse the greater than David. The Bible says our GOD is a consuming fire (Hebrews 12:29)!

> And the Philistine said to David, come to me, and I will give thy flesh unto the fowls of the air, and to the beasts of the field.
>
> I SAMUEL 17:44

The fowls of the air and the beasts of the field picture devil spirits in GOD's Word. When the enemy beckons me to come to him, I also risk being fed to his minions.

We know that's not what David did. No hand to hand combat. He used the sling and the stone. He attacked with the Word of GOD!

> Then said David to the Philistine, Thou comest to me with a sword, and with a spear, and with a shield: But I come to thee in the name of the Lord of hosts, the GOD of the armies of Israel, whom thou hast defied.
>
> I SAMUEL 17:45

It was the name of the Lord of hosts, the Great I AM, that David was carrying. GOD's name describes his nature, and in this case he is a warrior. It was just as Moses sang after Pharaoh and his army drowned in the Red Sea, "The Lord is a man of war: the Lord is his name" (Exodus 15:3).

Really, Goliath didn't have a chance!

On another level, we see that David didn't listen to his critics. First Eliab, then Saul, and lastly and more directly Goliath said that he was not up to the challenge. But David believed what GOD had said about him. He remembered the anointing oil that Samuel poured upon his head. He knew he was GOD's man anointed for GOD's work.

What about you? Did not GOD also anoint you with his Spirit when you believed?

Think about it. What if you actually believed that GOD was with you wherever you go and whatever you do. What would you do differently? What risks would you take?

"And, lo, I am with you always, even unto the end of the world" (Matthew 28:20b). "I will never leave thee, nor forsake thee" (Hebrews 13:5b). So go for it, dear believer. Don't fear. GOD *is* with you!

> This day will the Lord deliver thee into mine hand; and I will smite thee, and take thine head from thee; and I will give the carcasses of the host of the Philistines this day unto the fowls of the air, and to the wild beasts of the earth; that all the earth may know that there is a GOD in Israel. And all this assembly shall know that the Lord saveth not with sword and spear: For the battle is the Lord's, and he will give you into our hands.
>
> I SAMUEL 17:46–47

David said that the assembly and the entire earth would learn that there is a GOD in Israel. That's what Jesus did also. It's fair to say that the entire world has heard of his victory! As an application, when I attempt and complete the "impossible," it reveals GOD's power to the world. Dare to do something so great that without GOD's help it will fail. For with GOD's help, it cannot fail!

> And it came to pass, when the Philistine arose, and drew near to meet David, that David hasted…And David put his hand in his bag, and took thence a stone, and slang it, and smote the Philistine in his forehead, that the stone sunk into his forehead; and he fell upon his face to the earth. So David prevailed over the Philistine with a sling and with a stone, and smote the Philistine, and slew him.
>
> I SAMUEL 17:48A, 49–50A

GOD told Adam and Eve that the One to come would crush the serpent's head (Genesis 3:16b). The stone of the Word in David's hand crushed the head of his enemy just as the fulfilled prophecy of GOD's Word, that of the coming Deliverer, the suffering Servant, crushed the head of our enemy.

> But there was no sword in the hand of David. Therefore David ran, and stood upon the Philistine, and took his sword, and drew it out of the sheath thereof, and slew him, and cut off his head therewith.
>
> I Samuel 17:50b-51a

Two beautiful portraits jump from these verses. First, David did not have a sword so he used Goliath's own weapon to utterly destroy him. That's what our Lord did also. He took the incredibly cruel instrument of crucifixion and by going to the Cross himself, actually used that weapon to defeat the devil. Satan was not aware that Jesus' death would actually lead to the life of the world. Paul states it well in First Corinthians,

> But we speak the wisdom of God in a mystery, even the hidden wisdom, which God ordained before the world unto our glory: Which none of the princes of this world knew: For had they known it, they would not have crucified the Lord of glory.
>
> I Corinthians 2:7–8

Paul is teaching that God's plan of salvation was hidden, it was a mystery, but was now revealed. And that plan was not known by the princes of the world, i.e. the spiritual princes, better known as devils. For if they had comprehended that crucifying Jesus of Nazareth would lead to salvation for mankind they would not have killed him. They would have let him live so as to keep everyone else in bondage. Without Satan's weapon being used upon him, we would still be dead in our sins!

The second point to be gleaned from our text is that once again it was the sword which cut off the enemy's head. Of course, as has been emphasized time and time again, the sword is the Word of God. It did the cutting!

> And when the Philistines saw their champion was dead, they fled. And the men of Israel and of Judah arose, and shouted, and pursued the Philistines...And the children of Israel returned from chasing after the Philistines, and they spoiled their tents.
>
> I Samuel 17:51b-52a, 53

Like David, Jesus singularly defeated our enemy and then all the people, that's us, get the spoil. And what is that spoil? It's everything we could imagine and more! It's eternal life!

. . . .

Thus ends the account of Saul and David and Goliath. That labor pain of one man's rebellion and of another man's faith. But how do these two kings and their stories apply to a person practically?

First they show me the first and second Adam. Saul, in his unbelief and rebellion, pictures Adam. That first man was given a kingdom. But he also stopped believing in God's provision and rebelled by eating the forbidden fruit. David, on the other hand, demonstrates the power and potency of faith. That God driven power that can move mountains and topple giants that occur in my life. He, of course, typifies the second Adam.

These two stories are all about whether I can believe God's Word or not. Samuel told Saul to wait for him to sacrifice before fighting the Philistines and to totally destroy the Amalekites. Unfortunately, Saul only went half-way after hearing God through his prophet. David, in contrast, believed that just as God delivered him from the bear and the lion, he would likewise deliver not just him, but the entire nation.

So, do I believe it when God says a word to me? Such as… Love my wife; don't worry; love my enemy; or, remember to tithe. You see, God *does* say to me to do those things. "Husbands, love your wives" (Ephesians 5:25a). "Be anxious for nothing" (Philippians 4:6a). "Love your enemies" (Matthew 5:44a). Or in the context of tithing, "My God shall supply all your need" (Philippians 4:19a).

Realize that if God says for me to do something, then he is going to give me the power to perform it. But it takes faith. The act doesn't happen until I step out in faith. Loving my wife happens as I purpose in my heart to love her. Anxiety departs as I stop worrying. As I love my enemy, I lose that bitterness I had. As I tithe, God actually multiplies blessing to me.

The story of the man with the withered hand in Mark chapter three illustrates this very well. Jesus told the man to stretch forth his hand (vs. 5). The man could have said, "No way, Rabbi. It's paralyzed!" But he didn't. He believed that GOD's Words were also empowered by him. As has been said, GOD's commands are GOD's enablements.

Later, in the Book of Luke, the angel Gabriel told Mary, "For with GOD nothing shall be impossible" (Luke 1:37).

The literal translation in the Greek sheds additional light. The word translated "nothing" literally means "no word." The Greek word for "impossible" is literally "without power." For GOD says to you, he says to me, "For with GOD *no word is without power.*" All I have to do is believe his word and step out in *faith* by acting upon that word.

Truly, GOD's commands *are* GOD's enablements. No Word of GOD is without power!

✝he Kings and the Prophets

David reigned one thousand years before the arrival of the Christ at the dividing point of time. Yet, time does not permit me to continue to develop the remaining millennium of Jewish history in the detail we have discussed thus far. As Paul stated in the often cited eleventh chapter of the Book of Hebrews: "And what shall I more say? For time would fail me to tell of Gideon, and of Barak, and of Sampson, and of Jephthah; and of David also, and Samuel, and of the prophets" (Hebrews 11:32).

And that's how I feel as I sense I should move forward. First, to the picture of preterm labor that we see with the arrival of the kingdom of heaven (that time when the King from heaven came near to mankind during our Lord's first appearance on this planet as a man of flesh and blood). Secondly, I long to develop the false labor of the two millennia of the Church Age culminating in the true labor of the Great Tribulation. That's a lot to cover in one book so I must apologize as I will need to speed through much interesting history in order to reach our goal of seeing mankind's history as a picture of a woman's pregnancy, labor and delivery.

• • • •

David labored and travailed in eluding Saul for a number of

years after his victory over Goliath. During these trials he penned many of the beautiful psalms for which he is famous. The hardships of this time truly were molding him into a man GOD could use. So it will be for you and me! Those hard times will bring out songs we didn't know we could sing! For pain produces passion and passion brings intimacy. Intimacy with GOD!

David ultimately consolidated his power but after many years an uprising by his handsome and charming son, Absalom, whose name means "my father is peace," nearly divided the nation in a terrible civil war. As you read Absalom's story, realize that his rebellion is an Old Testament figure of the future uprising against the Greater than David, Jesus Christ, by the greater than Absalom, the one the Bible calls the Antichrist. Yes, Absalom, in his subtlety, pictures the grab for power by Antichrist during the Tribulation time period. He too will attempt to gain the favor of the Jewish nation over their true GOD ordained King!

After David's ascent to power, the nation of Israel reached a high water mark in glory under the reign of Solomon. This king, who was called the wisest man of ancient history, was given the name of "Peace." We recognize the Hebrew word "Shalom" as a derivative of the name Solomon. Of course, Solomon, in his wisdom and glory, is yet again a powerful picture of the Great King yet to come, that of the Prince of Peace, Jesus Christ!

Solomon, unfortunately, fell into idolatry under the influence of his many wives, for his insatiable lust for women was his downfall. Consequently the nation suffered greatly as a result of his idolatry. His son Rehoboam, who stubbornly refused to listen to the elder advisors of his father, led to the division of the nation as was prophesized to Jeroboam by the prophet Ahijah (I Kings 11:29–32).

A series of wicked kings arose in the northern ten tribes now called Israel. The names of Jeroboam and of Baasha and of Ahab come to mind as the nation continued their frequent labor pains under their charge.

The face-off between Elijah and the four hundred prophets of Baal occurred during Ahab's evil reign. That wonderful day in which fire came down from heaven and received Elijah's offering is forever etched into the history of Israel and of the world! Shortly after Ahab, the northern Kingdom was judged for their idolatry and was carried away in utter destruction to Assyria.

Hosea spoke over one hundred years earlier of this judgment in terms that women can understand. "Ephraim is smitten, their root is dried up, they shall bear no fruit: Yea, though they bring forth, yet will I slay even the beloved fruit of their womb" (Hosea 9:16). The Northern Tribe was going to miscarry!

And again Hosea said,

> When Ephraim spake, trembling, he exalted himself in Israel; but when he offended in Baal, he died... . The sorrows of a travailing woman shall come upon him: He is an unwise son; for he shall not stay long in the place of the breaking forth of children.
>
> Hosea 13:1, 13

The northern nation of Israel labored only to bring forth a stillborn! Indeed, they were carried away to Nineveh of Assyria, and to this day we have not seen them revived. We know the progeny of the Judeans, the Jews. But I have never met an Asherite, a Gadite, or a Reubenite! Will it be that God in the future will identify a remnant of these other sons of Abraham, Isaac, and Jacob? I don't know, but it wouldn't surprise me!

After the Assyrians routed the Northern tribes, they set their sites upon Judah and Jerusalem. Fortunately, the Godly king, Hezekiah, with the help of Isaiah the prophet, called upon the God of Israel for help. His belief in the Almighty One led to the miraculous deliverance from this strong labor pain. In one night 185,000 Assyrians were slaughtered by the Angel of the Lord without an arrow being fired by his people!

After this high point came Hezekiah's evil son, Manasseh. His twisted fifty-five year reign cursed Judah as we developed in Book IV of *A Woman's Silent Testimony*. This of course led to the travail of the Babylonian captivity which occurred in 582 b.c.

We read in the books of Ezekiel and Daniel of the labor pains in Babylon, and then we see their prophesied return in Ezra and Nehemiah. Truly God is faithful. During those days, the people living in Judah and Samaria opposed the return of the Jews, yet GOD delivered the remnant from those pangs of opposition as the Book of Nehemiah wonderfully documents.

In the fourth century b.c., we learn of the deliverance of the Jews by the courageous and beautiful Esther. That wonderful Book has many parallels which someday I would like to develop. It shows Esther as a picture of Jesus Christ. Haman, the second in the kingdom, had a deep hatred of Esther's uncle, Mordecai. These two are types of Satan and the Jews. Haman got a death sentence placed upon Mordecai and the Jews, but Esther came to the rescue by appealing to the King Ahasuerus, who pictures GOD the Father. She risked her life by going to Ahasuerus without an invitation and secured the deliverance of her people. This is what Jesus did. He gave his life to secure the deliverance of all people from the grasp of the greater than Haman, Satan.

The last book of the Old Testament, Malachi, was written in approximately 430 b.c., but the labor pangs of the Jews continued.

The Greeks, led by Alexander and then by four of his generals, were the world power from 333 to 63 b.c. This kingdom, of course, was prophesied by Daniel as the belly and thighs of brass of Nebuchadnezzar's dream (Daniel 2:32b) and the leopard with four wings and four heads of Daniel's own prophetic vision (Daniel 7:6). Daniel also foretold of the fall of the Medo-Persian Empire and of the rapid rise of Alexander followed by his untimely demise. Chapter eight of Daniel describes how the ram with two horns was lifted up. The ram represented the Medes and the Persians, and he was brought low by the goat from the west. That goat flew in without touching the ground and had one notable horn between his eyes. He came upon the ram in fury and the ram could not stand before him. History, of course, documents that this is exactly what Alexander and the Greeks did to the Medes and Persians. In a terribly swift and brutal campaign, they conquered the world just as GOD said would happen through his prophet.

But just as the goat waxed strong, the horn was broken, and four notable horns came up toward the four winds of heaven.

This foretold of Alexander's early demise at the height of his power and the subsequent division of the Greek Empire into four kingdoms. History documents this well. These four kings were consolidated later into two lesser dynasties. The Ptolemics were sensitive of the Jews, but in 198 b.c. the Seleucids took control of Israel. They were brutal towards the Jews, with the king of the north being the most evil. Daniel spoke of him as a little horn which later arose toward the south, toward the east and toward the pleasant land. The pleasant land is another name for Israel and this king, Antiochus Epiphanes, added greatly to the travail of GOD's chosen people.

Daniel revealed to us that Antiochus would magnify himself to the prince of the host (Satan) and that he would take the daily sacrifice away. Historians tell us that this blood thirsty leader murdered over one hundred thousand Jews and forced the priests to slaughter pigs in the temple as well as drink their blood!

That first abomination of desolation was spoken of by Daniel and later by Jesus in reference to the Antichrist (Daniel 11:31, Mark 13:14). Indeed, Antiochus gave the world a taste of the brutality of his spiritual son, the one the Bible calls the prince that shall come (Daniel 9:26b). Daniel prophesied to us that in the latter days Antichrist will also enter a rebuilt temple in another abomination of desolation. We learn from other scriptures that he will proclaim himself to be GOD in the temple during the middle of the Tribulation. At that time the Jews will finally understand that he is not Messiah and will call upon GOD for the true Holy One of Israel!

Finishing out the time before our Lord's arrival in fleshly form I must mention the Maccabean revolt. These brave and faithful men under the command of Judas Maccabeus rallied against the Greeks in the second century b.c. Hanukkah is the day the Jews employ to commemorate their twenty-four year travail to gain independence from the Greeks.

· · · ·

Thus, with these words, we end the first and second trimester of the pregnancy we have been discussing.

The Jews and all of creation are now about to enter the third trimester of pregnancy. The third trimester is a time filled with preterm labor and of false labor. Ultimately, though, it will end with true labor and with the birth of the baby!

✝ he Days of Jesus as Mankind's Pre-term Labor

The year was 12 a.d. and the Jews were confused. The Romans had occupied the land for over sixty years, but in that year they took away the power of the Jewish Sanhedrin to enforce capital punishment. Until that time, even though they were dominated by the Romans, the Jews pathetically believed they were in control of their own destiny. The patriarch Jacob had prophesied about the coming One who would bring justice and peace to the nation and they believed that their ability to exact the death penalty was linked to the time of the Messiah. "The scepter shall not depart from Judah, nor a lawgiver from between his feet, until Shiloh come; and unto him shall the gathering of the people be" (Genesis 49:10).

The Jews believed Shiloh was a reference to the Messiah as the translation of Shiloh is "sent one." The priests and scribes in that day of 12 b.c. feared that, indeed, the scepter had departed without the arrival of Shiloh.

But wait! Shiloh *had* been presented to the leaders as Luke documents in his Gospel. When Jesus was twelve he went up to Jerusalem with his parents as was their custom. But that year, he was led by his heavenly Father to the temple, where for three days Jesus sat with the doctors. He sat with the teachers of the nation.

> And it came to pass, that after three days they found him in the temple, sitting in the midst of the doctors, both hearing them, and asking them questions. And all that heard him were astonished at his understanding and answers.
>
> LUKE 2:46–47

GOD cannot lie! But we, in our puny understanding, do not always comprehend his Word. At the same time the scepter was taken away from Judah, Messiah came. He was in their midst and they didn't recognize it. He was a twelve year old boy! He was the Son of GOD, the Messiah, who came disguised in a way that was subtle yet very revealing. By Luke adding that Jesus was twelve years of age, we see a truth. Twelve is the number of Israel. And Israel's deliverance was upon them.

So it is for the woman. In the third trimester, the baby has developed to the point that he or she can be recognized as a complete human being. Growth and maturation is what is occurring during this time. Meanwhile, labor pains can sometimes become organized in an attempt to birth the baby before the time of full development. This of course is called preterm labor. In like manner, it was a preterm labor that the world experienced with the appearance of Jesus of Nazareth in those days at the dividing point of time.

Jesus told the multitudes that the Kingdom of Heaven was near. That it was at the very door. It seemed that the Kingdom was about to be birthed. The King from heaven was in their midst but they recognized him not!

Oh, at first, many did see the possible birth. After Jesus fed the multitudes and healed the masses, the people wanted to whisk him away and make him king. We also remember in that fateful last week of his life that his followers presented him to the nation as their King as he rode upon a donkey fulfilling that Messianic prophesy found in the Book of Zechariah (Zechariah 9:9). But ultimately, he was not received, and later that week the leaders and the people declared that they would not have this man rule over them!

Jesus understood that this preterm labor would not lead to the birth as told by Luke.

> And when he was come nigh, even now at the descent of the mount of Olives, the whole multitude of the disciples began to rejoice and praise GOD with a loud voice for all the mighty works that they had seen; Saying, Blessed be the King that cometh in the name of the Lord: Peace in heaven, and glory in the highest. And some of the Pharisees from among the multitude said unto him, Master, rebuke thy disciples. And he answered and said unto them, I tell you that, if these should hold their peace, the stones would immediately cry out. And when he was come near, he beheld the city, and wept over it, Saying, If thou hadst known, even thou, at least in this day, the things which belong unto thy peace! But now they are hid from thine eyes. For the days shall come upon thee, that thine enemies shall cast a trench about thee, and compass thee around, and keep thee on every side, And shall lay thee even with the ground, and the children within thee; and they shall not leave in thee one stone upon another; because thou knewest not the time of thy visitation.
>
> LUKE 19:37–44

Jesus wept, for he knew of Jerusalem's fate. He foresaw the Romans surrounding the city and he revealed that it was to be completely leveled. Of course, this did happen in 70 a.d. After a three year siege, Titus and his army broke into the city and utterly destroyed it.

Afterwards, over the ensuing century, the Jews were slaughtered and scattered by the Caesars in an ongoing ethnic purging that paralleled the Holocaust of WWII in scope and brutality and which eclipsed it in its duration. Caesar Hadrian was particularly devilish. Hundreds of thousands of Jews were butchered as he sought to erase the memory of Israel from the world. He changed the name of Israel to Palestine, i.e. Philistine country, and gave Jerusalem the name Aelia Capitolina in honor of himself. By his edict and in his rage against them, no two Jews could be seen together as they were scattered once again from their land.

And why did all this happen? Jesus said it was because they knew not the time of their visitation! Jesus wept as he understood that the Judeans lack of knowledge about the times they were living in as well as their rejection of their King would ultimately lead to GOD having no choice but to withdraw his protection from over them. This let Satan have his way with the Jews as history so graphically documents.

This is still the way with the Father. He does not insist that I follow him. He does not bully any man, or group of people, into loving and obeying him. But likewise, if we choose to go our own way, then we risk going it alone! We see, though, the consequences as we look at what happened to Jerusalem and the Jews.

But the question must be asked. Should the Jews have known that it was the time of their visitation? What did they miss that our Lord was alluding to? Secular as well as biblical history clearly document that first century Israel was eagerly anticipating the arrival of the Messiah. Jesus taught much of false messiahs in a way that reveals that the people were looking for the soon appearance of their Deliverer. When John the Baptist came upon the scene the people wanted to know if he indeed was the One. The Zealots were a sect of Jews who were devoted to the overthrow of Rome and they too would have welcomed a military leader to lead in that mission.

So, why were the Jews so ready for the One the Bible calls the Holy One of Israel?

Daniel the prophet gives us the answer. In 539 b.c. Daniel understood that the time of their captivity in Babylon was about to end as foretold by the prophet Jeremiah. Chapter 9 of Daniel documents this and we learn that Daniel set his face unto the Lord in prayer for the soon realization of this prophetic word concerning their seventy year captivity.

As an aside, we who also understand the times in which *we* are living should seek the Lord in prayer for the soon deliverance from our captivity. It won't be long that the Lord will meet us in the air on that day not too far away!

So, Daniel prayed and the angel Gabriel was dispatched to give understanding from GOD. He said,

> Know therefore and understand, that from the going forth of the commandment to restore and to build Jerusalem unto Messiah the Prince shall be seven weeks, and three score and two weeks:
>
> DANIEL 9:25A

The Jews clearly understood that a week in this prophetic reckoning was the equivalent of seven years. Thus, they correctly believed that seven weeks and three score and two weeks, or sixty nine weeks of seven years, would ensue from the time of the commandment to restore and rebuild Jerusalem until the coronation of Messiah. Doing the math we see that sixty nine multiplied by seven is a four hundred eighty-three year interval.

Looking to the Book of Nehemiah gives us the rest of the story. We are told in the second chapter that Nehemiah, who stood in the presence of King Artaxerxes, asked a request of him. He said unto the king,

> If it please the king, and if thy servant have found favor in thy sight, that thou wouldest send me unto Judah, unto the city of my fathers' sepulchers, that I may build it.
>
> NEHEMIAH 2:5B

The king agreed to this request and decreed that Jerusalem was to be rebuilt! The year was 445 b.c. Ninety four years after Daniel had predicted that such a decree would occur!

So when we consider that a year in Daniel's mind was three hundred sixty days in length instead of three hundred sixty-five and then we add four hundred eighty-three years to the time of Nehemiah's request, we come to the early first century a.d. The very time we are considering. Yes, the Jews understood that they were to be visited. They just wouldn't accept that the Visitor was an itinerant preacher from Galilee!

I will go further to speculate, if not to just outright say, that GOD in his exactness had the four hundred eighty-three years conclude on the very same day that Jesus was presented to the nation riding down from the Mount of Olives as their King. I believe, although I cannot prove, that the very day Jesus was proclaimed as Messiah, the One that would cause the stones to immediately cry out if the people did not, was the culmination of the 483 year prophecy of Daniel. That's why Jesus said that this was the day they should have known. The day they should have been looking to. The day of their visitation! But the day of their peace was hid from their eyes!

Don't let that happen again, dear believer. The Lord has given prophetic words to us in our day also. Signs that once again speak of our visitation from heaven!

Paul states this warning in these terms,

> But of the times and the seasons, brethren, ye have no need that I write unto you. For yourselves know perfectly that the Day of the Lord so cometh as a thief in the night... . But ye, brethren, are not in darkness, that that day should overtake you as a thief.
>
> I Thessalonians 5:1–2, 4

Paul relates that many will be caught off guard by the return of the Lord, just as were the Jews of the first century. But we who love him and have heard his Word hopefully will not be taken by surprise!

• • • •

Thus, after the King was rejected and brutally murdered, God raised him from the dead. He ascended back into heaven where he told his followers that he would prepare a place for them and for all who follow after. He promised to return and he sent the Comforter, the Holy Spirit, to fill our hearts as we wait for him.

In addition, the world's preterm labor was arrested in the redeeming work of the cross and the third trimester has continued in type up unto this very day in which we find ourselves.

In speaking of the eventual labor, we need to return to our initial text and remind ourselves that before true labor and delivery, before the Tribulation time period and the Second Coming of Jesus Christ, comes a long period of time. A time full of birth pangs which our Lord said would first occur.

> ... what shall be the sign of thy coming, and of the end of the world? And Jesus answered...For many shall come in my name, saying, I am Christ...And ye shall hear of wars and rumors of wars...but the end is not yet. For nation shall rise against nation, and kingdom against kingdom: And there shall be famines, and pestilences, and earthquakes, in divers places. All these are the beginning of sorrows.
>
> MATT 24:3B, 4A, 5A, 6A, 6C-8

With these comments Jesus gave a blueprint, an obstetrical analogy, if you will, that has described the last two thousand years.

It is to this blueprint, to the Age of Grace, to the Church Age, that we must go.

Birth Pangs: The Present

The Church Age as Mankind's False Labor

Introduction

The book of Revelation presents the outline for the days in which we live as well as for events yet to occur. Thus, for the remainder of this book I will have the joy of following the Revelation as we discuss the allegory of God's dealings with mankind as a woman's pregnancy. Specifically, in this wonderful section of Scripture we will learn of the world's false labor, the rupture of membranes, the true labor, and the delivery of the baby! So let's dive in for a blessing!

As I've heard Pastor Jon Courson say so many times, the book of Revelation is not a hard book to understand. For it is the only book of the Bible that comes with its own divine outline! That outline is found in Chapter 1 verse 19.

> Write the things which thou hast seen, and the things which are, and the things which shall be hereafter.
>
> REVELATION 1:19

God divided this revelation which was given to John into three sections. First, he told John to write down the things that he has seen. Second, he said to write about the things which are presently occurring. And thirdly, he said to write about the things which will occur hereafter.

So let's ask ourselves, what are these three things of which GOD was speaking?

• • • •

The things which thou has seen: That's the resurrected and glorified Christ. That's chapter 1 of this wonderful book! Look with me at some of the beauty of this first section.

> The Revelation of Jesus Christ, which GOD gave unto him, to show unto his servants things which must shortly come to pass; and he sent and signified it by his angel unto his servant John...blessed is he that readeth, and they that hear the words of this prophecy, and keep [treasure] those things which are written therein: For the time is at hand. John to the seven churches...and from Jesus Christ, who is the faithful witness, and the first begotten of the dead, and the prince of the kings of the earth. Unto him that loved us, and washed us from our sins in his own blood, and hath made us kings and priests unto GOD and his Father; to him be glory and dominion for ever and ever. Amen. Behold, he cometh with clouds; and every eye shall see him, and they also which pierced him: And all kindreds of the earth shall wail because of him. Even so, Amen. I am the Alpha and Omega, the beginning and the ending, saith the Lord, which is, and which was, and which is to come, the Almighty... . What thou seest, write in a book, and send it unto the seven churches...unto Ephesus, and unto Smyrna, and unto Pergamos, and unto Thyatira, and unto Sardis, and unto Philadelphia, and unto Laodicea. And I turned to see the voice that spake with me. And being turned, I saw seven golden candlesticks; And in the midst of the seven candlesticks one like unto the Son of man, clothed with a garment down to the foot, and girt about the paps (*chest*) with a golden girdle. His head and his hairs were white like wool, as white as snow; and his eyes were a flame of fire; And his feet like unto fine brass as if they burned in a furnace; and his voice as the sound of many waters...and his countenance was as the sun shineth

in his strength. And when I saw him, I fell at his feet as dead. And he laid his right hand upon me, saying unto me, Fear not; I am the first and the last: I am he that liveth, and was dead; and, behold, I am alive for evermore, Amen…Write the things which thou hast seen, and the things which are, and the things which shall be hereafter; The mystery of the…seven golden candlesticks…the seven candlesticks which thou sawest are the seven churches.
REVELATION 1:1, 3–4A, 5–8, 11B, 11D-15, 16B-18A, 19–20A, 20C, 21B

You see, the gospels are amazing, but except for the transfiguration scene as well as the Resurrection and Ascension, we do not see Jesus as the King of Kings and Lord of LORDS! He is the Servant who came for the purpose of fulfilling his Father's will. And that was to die so that we might live. We saw him as a man of flesh and blood. He was a kind and gentle man, a man who we saw weeping. One who laughed with friends and ate with sinners. One who slept out under the stars and traveled by foot wherever he went. But now in the first chapter of the book of Revelation we really get to see Jesus the Christ in all his glory and majesty!

That's the first section in GOD's divine outline! That's what Jesus meant by using the phrase, "the things which thou hast seen."

We see Jesus standing in the midst of the seven golden candlesticks and are told that they are the seven churches. He is standing in the midst of the churches! Praise GOD!

We see Jesus wearing a golden vest, having a face and hair as white as snow! His eyes are as a flame of fire and his voice, oh his voice, it is as the sound of many waters!

His countenance was as the sun! No wonder John fell at his feet as if he were dead. That's what will happen to you, what will happen to me, when we too see him in all his glory. Look back at other times when GOD revealed himself to man. Look in Isaiah or Daniel or Ezekiel and see what they did when they saw the Lord high and lifted up. They fell down upon their faces! Read what Peter, James, and John did when they heard GOD thunder from heaven that Jesus was his beloved Son. They fell facedown also! That's what John did again here and what we will do also on that day not far away!

Yes, the things which John had seen are too beautiful for words! Jesus stamped his divine fingerprint throughout this opening chapter. Every opening verse is notable for it's groupings of "threes." Three, you remember, signifies completeness. Note, in verse one, the Lord *gave, sent,* and *signified* this revelation to John. In verse two, he notes that John bore record of the *word* of the *testimony* and of *all things that he saw.* The rhythm continues, culminating in verse nineteen in the three divisions of this revelation, i.e. *the things which thou hast seen, the things which are* and *the things which shall be hereafter.*

• • • •

The things which are: Next, we learn that the Alpha and Omega, he who is and was and is to come, is writing to the "seven" churches. You will remember that seven is GOD's number for spiritual perfection. The Lord wants his church to have this revelation. He is speaking to seven literal churches in Asia Minor but also he is speaking to the Church in its entirety. That new covenant church which was born on the day of Pentecost and will continue on unto the day that we meet him in the air! That's the second section of this divine outline! The Church Age is what Jesus is speaking of by using the phrase "the things which are!"

We will see that these seven churches outline the entire course of the times in which we live. The era we call the "Age of Grace." To John these churches were not only congregations that he oversaw but also a prophetic revelation. These things had not yet occurred to him, but to us looking back we will see the awesome wonder of GOD's Word to those who would have eyes to see. In GOD's divine outline, chapters two and three are "the things which are." Also it is this time frame that our Lord spoke of when he told his disciples of those events leading up to his return. To the "Beginning of Sorrows."

• • • •

The things which shall be hereafter: In chapters four through twenty-two we find the third division of this holy outline. It's the future, if you will! In this last section we will see the Rapture of the Church, the Tribulation time period, the Second Coming, the Millennium and the New Heaven and New Earth. In our obstetrical analogy, we will see the rupture of membranes, the hard labor, the delivery of the baby and the joy that follows!

You see, John was living in the beginning of the Church Age, in the beginning of the second section. But he would not live to see the things which shall be hereafter. With hindsight we understand that the second section of the revelation has continued for the last two thousand years! But remember, dear saint, with the Lord, a day is as a thousand years and a thousand years is as a day (II Peter 3:8). In GOD's economy "the things which are" have thus far only lasted two days!

· · · ·

Thus, in considering our analogy of GOD's dealing with mankind as the course of a woman's pregnancy, we are now in this second section of the book of Revelation. The time in which we live is recorded in chapters two and three. It's "the beginning of sorrows" that Jesus spoke of to his disciples. It's that time of false labor.

Let's examine the seven churches and learn of the false labor pains which have already occurred and then reflect upon the ones still ahead as we progress to the last section of Revelation where the true labor and delivery reside!

Unto ☩ he Church of Ephesus:

Ephesus means "darling" or "lover." This church prophetically was the new, fresh and young church of approximately a.d. 33 to 100. They were the "on-fire" church of the first century. They were in love with Jesus as a young bride would be in love with her man. They only had eyes for him! This was the church which had members who had actually seen the resurrected Christ!

The literal church of Ephesus was located in Western Asia Minor, in the country we know today as Turkey. It was and is a beautiful coastal town with a temperate climate. Paul the apostle spent two years there at the school of Tyrannus and the Word of God was given free reign in that day. In Acts we read that,

> And this continued by the space of two years; so that all they which dwelt in Asia (*Turkey*) heard the word of the Lord Jesus, both Jews and Greeks. And God wrought special miracles by the hands of Paul:...And this was known to all the Jews and Greeks also dwelling at Ephesus; and fear fell on them all, and the name of the Lord Jesus was magnified... . So mightily grew the word of God and prevailed.
>
> Acts 19:10–11, 17, 20

Indeed the Ephesians had a special relationship with the

Lord. They were lovers in the truest sense of the word and out of that love an entire country, a place bigger than the state of California and Texas combined, heard the gospel of Jesus Christ!

In Jesus' words to this church, as well as to the others, we will see affirmations and warnings. Also, we will hear words of motivation to live for heaven, to live with eternity in mind, as well as see glimpses of the glorified Jesus Christ. In addition, we will look at several applications which should be made from our Lord's words to each church which we can apply to our own personal walk with the Lord as well as apply to our corporate church's walk. Finally, we will of course discuss the birth pangs that historically have occurred during each time frame as we wait for our blessed hope of the return of Christ.

Let's look at the words to this first church.

> Unto the angel of the church of Ephesus write; These things saith he that holdeth the seven stars in his right hand, who walketh in the midst of the seven golden candlesticks;
>
> REVELATION 2:1

The word angel can also be translated messenger or leader. Jesus is speaking to the leaders, the overseers, the pastors. Those entrusted to shepherd the flock. But really when you think about it, we all have been given a charge to shepherd somebody. You fathers are pastors at home, you mothers are leading those youngsters and those others in your circle, you older kids are leading those younger and even you little ones have somebody that follows you. That person may not seem significant to you but he or she is to GOD! Thus, Jesus is speaking to us all as we all are messengers.

We also learn in this verse that the Savior is in the midst of the seven golden candlesticks. He is in the midst of the churches. And he sees us as golden! As our bridegroom, he is with us!

> I know thy works, and thy labor, and thy patience, and how thou canst not bear them which are evil: And thou hast tried them which say they are apostles, and are not, and hast found

them liars. And hast born, and hast patience, and for my name's sake hast labored, and hast not fainted.

REVELATION 2:2–3

Jesus greatly affirmed this lovely young church. He told them that he could see their works and labor, how they hated evil and how they were discerning of the truth of his Word. He appreciated how they had pressed in and had not fainted despite the persecutions which Caesar Nero, the Jews, and others had initiated during this era of church history.

Paul alluded to the truth of these words in speaking of the Berean church. He said that they received the word with all readiness of mind yet searched the Scriptures daily in order to discern that the things which were being taught to them were indeed true (Acts 17:10–11).

Our Lord spoke of their patience twice in these two verses. When we hear of patience in this section it is a reference to the patience that the church has as it waits for the return of the Lord. Jesus affirmed this church as they held on to the "hope."

The Groom loved that this church did not tolerate those who spoke lies about him. He appreciated that they did not tolerate false apostles. This, of course, begs the following questions: Does the church today practice in the same spirit? Do we tolerate false doctrine in the name of tolerance?

Continuing, after these words of comfort came words of warning:

Nevertheless I have somewhat against thee, because thou hast left thy first love. Remember therefore from whence thou art fallen, and repent, and do the first works;

REVELATION 2:4–5A

Now for the hammer! The Object of their love, their Lover, had somewhat against them. They had left their first love! The Ephesian church had works and labors. They did not tolerate false doctrine and false teachers and they were looking towards the return of the Lord, but they had lost their love. Jesus was very upset about this.

We remember what Paul taught in First Corinthians concerning the relative importance of love,

> Though I speak with the tongues of men and of angels, and have not love, I am become as sounding brass, or a tinkling cymbal. And though I have the gift of prophecy, and understand all mysteries, and have all knowledge; and though I have faith, so that I could remove mountains, and have not love, I am nothing. And though I bestow all my goods to feed the poor, and though I give my body to be burned, and have not love, it profiteth me nothing.
>
> I CORINTHIANS 13:1–3

He said I can have the manifestation and power of the Spirit, speaking in tongues to GOD and to man wonderful words, and it is absolutely nothing without love! If I can foretell the future by GOD's Spirit and can interpret the scriptures with power and clarity, it also is worthless without love! If I have such great believing so as to see mountains in my life moved away or if I give all my goods to the poor, it's still absolutely nothing if not done in love. Even if I am a martyr for Jesus but my life is not given to him out of love, it is of no profit to me! Do you see now why this beautiful church was being reprimanded? They had left their love and Jesus wanted them to go back to that first love. For without love all of their good qualities were of absolutely *no* value!

Those next words from our Hero give the solution to their problem. It's the antidote for you and me, for our local church also, when we find ourselves in this loveless place. He said to *remember* from where they had fallen, *repent* (which means to turn back) and to *do the first works*.

Remember, repent, and return.

Remember the time when you were in love with the Lord. Remember the time when you were aware of his presence moment by moment in your life. When he was so real to you that breathing and talking to him were synonymous! And then repent that you've left that place. Of course, repentance just means to do an about face. Stop heading in one direction and go back in the other.

Lastly, return to that place where you were when that love was fresh and potent. To the first works, those things that you were doing when love was hot. Were you praising GOD with psalms and hymns and spiritual songs in that day prior? Were you reading his Word daily and sharing what he has done in your life with others? That's were Jesus says to return. To the place you were at first. Return to Jesus, he's your first love! That's what the church at Ephesus needed to hear.

The result of not remembering, repenting, and returning are given next.

> Or else I will come unto thee quickly, and will remove thy candlestick out of his place, except thou repent.
>
> REVELATION 2:5B

The Lord told those wonderful believers of the 1st century that if they did not return to him, to their first love, their candlestick would be taken out of its place. Remember the golden candlesticks, we are told, are the churches and Jesus is saying that this church would close down if they did not repent. Historically, that's exactly what happened. The Ephesian church, that darling and lover, died. As we shall see, she was replaced by the second church, the church of Smyrna.

That can happen to you, to me, to our church today. If we don't love GOD first and foremost, and love others as ourselves, then we are as good as dead! And your local church too will die! Jesus doesn't care if your congregation has a missions program and a healing ministry, without love it won't last.

> But this thou hast, that thou hatest the deeds of the Nicolaitans, which I also hate.
>
> REVELATION 2:6

Who are these Nicolaitans? We need to know as they come up again soon.

We get our word laity from this word. The Nicolaitans were lay people, not GOD ordained people, who sought to rule over the church. They were those false apostles that Jesus spoke of in verse two. GOD says he hates false spiritual leaders who seek to lord themselves over the flock. We are taught by Paul numerous times in his epistles to try the spirits, to test the teachers, in order to confirm that what they say is from the Lord.

Jesus once again repeats this point to his church. He says, "Don't follow blindly." There are wolves out there dressed in sheep's clothing.

Lastly, Jesus gave a motivator to live for heaven.

> He that hath an ear, let him hear what the Spirit saith unto the churches: To him that overcometh will I give to eat of the tree of life, which is in the midst of the paradise of GOD.
>
> REVELATION 2:7

Do you remember what was in that original Paradise? In that Garden of Adam and Eve? Do you recall what stood in Eden? The tree of life was there. So was the tree of the knowledge of good and evil. Adam and Eve ate of that second tree and thus could not partake of the first. That first tree, the tree of life, is Jesus. Because Jesus went to the tree and died for you and me, we will get to eat of the tree of life which is in our future Paradise! And we get to eat of it now, too. Every time I take communion I celebrate that future day when I'll be in the midst of the paradise of GOD!

So we see that that first church originally loved the Lord with all of their heart and mind and strength but then lost it. They were instructed to remember, repent, and return but did not. Ultimately, the days of the church of Ephesus ended before the Day of the Lord, before "the things that shall be hereafter." We will see this to be the case for the second and third church as well. That is, the churches of Smyrna and Pergamos will also pass away before the End. But we will see in GOD's prophetic plan for the "things which are," that the last four churches, that of Thyatira, Sardis, Philadelphia and Laodicea, will remain until the coming of the Lord. Of course, I will identify these churches to you as we encounter them in the upcoming narrative.

But before we consider our Master's words to the church of Smyrna, let us briefly recap some of the sorrows, some of the birth pangs that this church era experienced. As we have noted, the Jews rose up against the Romans and in a.d. 69 and 70 waves of Roman retaliation resulted. Ultimately, Jerusalem was destroyed and the Jews were scattered. The Jewish believers in Christ were also scattered by their non-believing brothers and this labor pang allowed the Word of Truth to be preached abroad.

Later, when Gentiles were included into the church, persecution came from all sides. That is, from the Jews and from the Romans. Nero hated the Christians almost as much as he hated the Jews. It is said that he dipped them into wax and burnt them at night as human candles because they said that they had the light of the world in them. Thousands of Christians died at the hand of this evil man and by the hands of those emperors who followed.

As we read in the Book of Acts, in Paul's epistles and in John's writings, we get a flavor that many believers felt that, because of the persecution they were experiencing, that the Day of the Lord was at hand. Paul and John on more than one occasion had to correct the people. They taught that the Day of the Lord would come on GOD's time table and would not be known exactly. Nonetheless many believed that they would live to see that day.

Now I ask...Is it bad that they lived in anticipation of the soon return of the Lord yet had it wrong and did not live to see his coming?

My answer to you is *no!*

Because they lived like Jesus could come back at any time they kept their love for their King. It may be that when they lost that expectancy of his return, when time passed by and hardships occurred without his reappearance, that they fell back from that first love!

That's a key dear believer. Keep the hope alive in your life that Jesus could come back for us today! When we do that we can live a life of victory for we are living for heaven, storing up treasure in heaven. And then, even if he doesn't come back today, we are still blessed because today we've walked with him!

Unto ✝ he Church in Smyrna:

The church in Smyrna is the second group of wonderful believers that the Lord addressed. This church was located in a beautiful coastal town forty miles north of Ephesus and was noted for two things that are significant to the words we will hear spoken to them. In this city were many who worshipped Caesar as GOD and they had a very powerful Jewish synagogue, one that was quite aggressive in its resistance to "the Way." The pastor of this local church was a Spirit-filled man named Polycarp. History tells us that Polycarp was brutally martyred for the faith after he was given a chance to recant his allegiance to the One from Nazareth of Galilee. His refusal to publicly declare his allegiance to Caesar and deny the Savior emboldened the church and typified this church prophetically as well.

In that prophetic vein, this church represents the era of history from approximately a.d. 100 to the year 313. We will see later that an important event occurred in 313 a.d. which ended the prophetic church of Smyrna and ushered in the time of the church of Pergamos.

The years of prophetic Smyrna were extremely brutal and intense. Wave after wave of persecution hit GOD's people. Both the Jews and the Church of Christ were targeted. As we have discussed, the Romans, directed by the Caesars, sought to annihilate both of these groups of GOD's children.

Certainly, on a spiritual level it is easy to comprehend that the GOD of this world, Satan, was motivating his worldly system under his control in the form of the Roman Empire to destroy the Jews and the Christians. As we have discussed, the Jews were scattered after 70 a.d. and their country was trampled and renamed. Those Jews who stayed were not allowed to even congregate together! As for the Christians, their fate was even worse! The church grew wildly among the poor of the Empire as the Good News brought to them by Paul and the many other evangelists was indeed so wonderful. But there was a terrible backlash by the Romans. Hundreds of thousands of converts were tortured, crucified, and fed to the lions. Indeed it was very dangerous to become a Christian during this era. Yet, despite this intense persecution, the church grew more and more.

We've seen this principle before, haven't we? When the children of Israel were placed in bondage by Pharaoh, they too grew and multiplied. Yes, this strategy of Satan has always backfired. Whenever he inspires his worldly leaders to take out and destroy GOD's people it only brings the Lord's children closer to him and closer to each other. I can think of many examples of this. Of course, Pharaoh and the Caesars as we have mentioned, but how about the Popes of the Middle Ages, Hitler in our recent history, and the Chinese leaders today. As these devilishly inspired leaders have sought to suppress GOD's children they have only caused them to go underground and become stronger.

Now the name of this city is also very germane to this section for the word Smyrna is a close relative to another word that has much significance in the Bible. That word being "myrrh." We remember that myrrh was one of the gifts given to Jesus by the wise men from the East (Matthew 2:11). This spice is a fragrant gum which is produced by the crushing of a particular type of wood found in the Middle East. It was one of the compounds in the sacred anointing oil of Exodus 30:23 and was offered to Jesus as he died on the cross (Mark 15:23). Esther was prepared to meet the king by bathing in myrrh (Esther 2:12); and lastly, the women were going to use myrrh to prepare our Lord's body on that wonderful Sunday morning (John 19:39).

We can see from these references that myrrh is a fragrant perfume which was made by a crushing process. In the Old Testament it was part of the anointing oil which symbolized the Spirit of GOD. That oil was placed upon the high priest's head. Also, we see that Esther was immersed in myrrh. Importantly, the high priest and Esther are powerful types of Jesus Christ in the Old Testament so it should not be surprising that Jesus himself would be given myrrh. First, as a picture of his future sacrifice when he was a child and later during the time of his sacrifice. Yes, Jesus was crushed. He was immersed in myrrh as a sweet savor to GOD. So we see that beautiful type being carried though to this section of Scripture also. The church of Smyrna was indeed crushed for their faith in Jesus Christ. They suffered and were martyred, yet we will see that they were a beautiful fragrance to Jesus as we listen to his Words.

> And unto the angel of the church in Smyrna write: These things saith the first and the last, which was dead, and is alive.
>
> REVELATION 2:8

Remember angel can mean messenger or leader. This may be a reference to Pastor Polycarp and his powerful stand for his Lord. We see another partial revelation of the person of Jesus Christ given to this church. Remember in the last section, he was walking in the midst of the churches. In this section he is revealed as the first and the last and he who was dead and is now alive. Jesus is encouraging this persecuted group of believers by telling them that he is over the Caesars and by reminding them that he died and has now conquered death. The implication, of course, is that they too will die but will also conquer death because of his sacrifice!

> I know thy works, and tribulation, and poverty, (but thou art rich)
>
> REVELATION 2:9A

Jesus affirms this group. He immediately told them that he sees their struggles and he stated that their poverty was actually storing up much wealth. He called them rich! For we know that GOD does not look upon the outside, but he sees the heart. Jesus saw that they were storing up riches in heaven. Riches that would not be moth eaten or taken away. True riches!

The Lord saw their tribulation also. Of course, when we see this word we need to consider that future time when GOD will pour out his wrath upon the world in an effort to separate the sheep from the goats. This era pictures the Great Tribulation in many ways. The Christians and the Jews were hunted down and killed by the Romans leaders just as the future believers and Jews will be persecuted by that devil possessed leader from the revived Roman Empire when they refuse to take the mark to his allegiance. But more on that later!

> And I know the blasphemy of them which say they are Jews, and are not, but are the synagogue of Satan.
>
> REVELATION 2:9B

In the Old Testament, the Jews are called the wife of Jehovah. Unfortunately, the Jews of this era are not. For they divorced their GOD when they stumbled over the One Ephesians 2:20 calls "the Chief Cornerstone." We learn that they have become the synagogue of Satan.

Jesus confirms this terrible fate in the book of John after the Jews rejected him during his presentation at the Feast of Tabernacles. Do you remember that solemn day when he called all that would thirst to come to him and drink? He promised that out of their bellies would flow rivers of living water. The next day Jesus told the nation that he was the light of the world. This is found in John 7 and 8. Unfortunately, the Jews rejected their Savior and said that he was not of GOD but was born of fornication. They did not understand the Incarnation and accused his mother of whoredom! They said that GOD was *their* Father, not his. To this Jesus said, "Ye are of your father the devil" (John 8:44).

Yes, the Jews are GOD's chosen people yet they blasphemed

and cursed themselves as they rejected their Messiah. They gave themselves over to Satan!

The Bible states that the only unforgivable sin is the blasphemy of the Holy Spirit (Matthew 12:31). That is, as the Spirit of GOD woos a man or a woman, or in this case a nation, if they continually reject him, GOD has no choice but to give that man or woman, that nation, over to Satan. They have committed the only unforgivable sin. They have rejected Jesus!

Paul said the same thing to the people of Corinth. That church in Southern Greece had an active member who was openly living with his father's wife. Paul told the believers to separate themselves from him, to give him over to Satan. The context was that as this occurred the sinner hopefully would come to his senses and repent. Later, we see in the second letter to the Corinthians that apparently this occurred as Paul instructed the church to receive the man back into fellowship.

This little vignette found in the two letters of Paul to Corinth picture what Jesus Christ has and will do with the Jews. The Jews have given themselves over to Satan for these two thousand years yet when they repent GOD will welcome them back into fellowship.

In verse 9, Jesus is telling his church that he sees their tribulation and their poverty and that he sees the blasphemy of the Jews. Next, he will tell them why they need not fear!

> Fear none of those things which thou shalt suffer: Behold, the devil shall cast some of you into prison, that ye may be tried; and ye shall have tribulation ten days: Be thou faithful unto death, and I will give thee a crown of life.
>
> REVELATION 2:10

Don't fear the things which you will suffer said the Lord! That sounds like something I might say to a laboring woman while she is in the midst of her travail! Sounds like GOD is trivializing something pretty bad here too, doesn't it! But wait! He sees the big picture. Life, like labor, is short. Then, when we endure, we get a crown of life. After she endures, she gets the baby!

So Jesus is telling this church to hang in there and he says it to you and me, too. There's going to be attacks from the devil. Some of you are going to be in prison. You're going to have prisons at work, in your ministry, with your family. Some of you are going to die. You may not even see any fruit from your trial. But when you overcome, when you have endured, in that day, you will be treated like a king. You will receive a crown from the King of Kings!

Also, look in the middle of this verse. Jesus said they would have tribulation for ten days. What does that mean?

Modern Bible teachers, such as J. Vernon Magee, Chuck Smith, and Jon Courson have said that the ten days may represent ten Roman Emperors who were responsible for this satanic onslaught. Jesus may have been speaking cryptically here that this era was to endure ten waves of persecution from ten evil rulers.

> He that hath an ear, let him hear what the Spirit saith unto the churches: He that overcometh shall not be hurt of the second death.
>
> REVELATION 2:11

What is the second death? Revelation 20 reveals that those whose names are not found written in the Book of Life will be judged by their works and will be cast into the lake of fire which is the second death (Revelation 20:14). The second death is not something anyone would desire and the promise to the believer who overcomes is that this second death will have no effect.

So how did the church of Smyrna overcome? And how do we overcome also?

> For whatsoever is born of GOD overcometh the world: And this is the victory [*Greek word "nike"*] that overcometh the world, even our faith.
> Who is he that overcometh the world, but he that believeth that Jesus is the Son of GOD?
>
> I JOHN 5:4–5

Do you believe that Jesus is who he claimed to be? Then you to have overcome and will not be hurt by the second death!

So we understand that the church of the second and third centuries truly partook in the fellowship of suffering with the Lord. They were crushed and released a sweet savor unto God as they stayed true to his Word. In fact, we have come to the end of our Lord's comments to this church and there is no correction given to them. We will see this to be the case for only one other church as five of the seven will receive reprimands from the One who stands in their midst. Smyrna, because of their persecution, clung tight to the Lord and had no need to be corrected.

Then came the year 313 a.d. and things changed radically. Emperor Constantine became a Christian!

Unto ✝ he Church in Pergamos

The name of this church, Pergamos, is an interesting word. It has two components, "Per" and "gamos". We recognize "gamos" in relationship to words concerning marriage (e.g. "monogamous" or "polygamy"). And in this case, "Pergamos" also speaks of marriage, but not a marriage you would be fond of, for Pergamos means "objectionable marriage!" Indeed, in this section of Scripture, we will see the marriage of politics and religion. We will hear how the faith of Jesus Christ and the politics of the world's false religion do not and should not mix, how they are a "Pergamos"—an objectionable marriage in the eyes of our husband, Jesus Christ.

Pergamos itself was the northernmost city of the actual seven churches to which John was writing. It was located in Northwest Turkey approximately twenty miles from the seashore. Significantly to the narrative, it was held to be the birthplace of the chief GOD of Roman mythology, Zeus. Yes, the false religion which started thousands of years earlier in Babylon was now ruled by the GOD Zeus who, as legend had it, was born in Pergamos!

Prophetically, the church era spoken of in this section covers the years 313 to approximately 600 a.d. Initially, Constantine was the Emperor and he was embroiled in a power struggle with a rival from the western part of the Empire. So, in what many military historians have called a brilliant tactical move, overnight he declared that he had become a Christian, and more important militarily, he proclaimed that Christians were no longer to be ostracized and persecuted, but to be embraced! This infused his army with thousands of previously unwilling souls who now wanted to see the victory of Constantine over his rival. They understood that if Constantine consolidated power, they too would be victorious. They saw that they could be released from the intense trial and labor pain of the days of Smyrna.

Historically we understand that this did occur. The Christians were no longer tortured and killed but they were welcomed as viable members of the Roman Empire. Christianity was declared the state religion and all was going to be well!

Or so it seemed.

Even though the Christians were outwardly welcomed, there were many powerful and wealthy people in the Empire who had embraced the Babylon mystery religion of their culture. They were not going to sit idly by and just accept all of the teachings of true Christianity without watering it down with their own traditions. Examples of this mixed marriage are many. Resurrection Sunday which occurred in the Spring during Passover was incorporated with the Roman holiday of Ishtar. We know this day as Easter and celebrate it with the bunny and the eggs just as the Romans did two thousand years ago! The Romans also celebrated a winter holiday to mark the beginning of the Sun's return back toward the Northern Hemisphere which was called Saturnalia. The celebrants would decorate evergreen trees with silver ornaments and burn a commemorative family fire with fuel known as the Yule Log. The date of this popular holiday is, as you may have surmised, on December 25th! Of course, since the Christians weren't exactly sure when their Savior was born, it wasn't too difficult for those in power to combine the two traditions into one. Indeed as we shall see, in the literal and the prophetic city of Pergamos, Christianity was married to the Babylonian Religion. Not a marriage made in heaven, but one from hell!

> And to the angel of the church in Pergamos write: These things saith he which hath the sharp sword with two edges.

Again, we see a partial revelation of the glorified Christ. In Ephesus, he walked in the midst of the churches. In Smyrna, he was dead and is alive. Here in Pergamos, he has the sharp two edged sword. You may recall the sword in Bible typology always represents the Word of GOD. Truly Jesus cannot be separated from the Word. The Bible declares that the Word was GOD and yet the Word was made flesh (John 1:1, 14).

The people of Pergamos needed to know that the Word of GOD, that the two edged sword will separate truth from error. Fact from fiction. True faith from false religion. That's the way it is for me in our day also. Whenever I am enticed by the world's system to incorporate another world view of life, I can go to the Word of GOD for direction. Whether it be the call to embrace homosexuality that we hear so loudly in these days or the cry to accept Marijuana and other drugs with questionable medical benefits, I can go to the Bible and see what it says. When society says abortion is legal and that maybe we should consider euthanasia and assisted suicide as good ideas, I can see from the Bible that this is not the spirit we see present there. When the world tells me it's okay to believe one view yet the Bible says it's not, which one am I going to follow? I can't have it both ways. So the people living with the Pergamos mentality needed to remember that Jesus has the sharp two edged sword.

> I know thy works, and where thou dwellest, even where Satan's seat is: And thou holdest fast my name, and hast not denied my faith, even in those days wherein Antipas was my faithful martyr, who was slain among you, where Satan dwelleth.
>
> REVELATION 2:13

In this verse we read of the commendation our Lord has for this group of believers. He knew their works and appreciated that they held onto his name, not denying him while living in the midst of Satan's kingdom. Indeed, dwelling in the city of Zeus or in the era of this objectionable marriage was to be exposed to a strong yet subtle force which would pull at the Christian to move that believer away from the truth and simplicity of the Gospel. The GOD of this world realized that he was losing the battle for the souls of men by persecuting "the Way" during the historical church of Smyrna. Now he's improved his strategy by joining up with the church, so to speak. That is, Satan became a member of the congregation. The wolf put on sheep's clothing!

The historical reference to Antipas here is a contraction of Antipater who was killed for the faith in the days of John.

> But I have a few things against thee, because thou hast there them that hold the doctrine of Balaam, who taught Balac to cast a stumbling block before the children of Israel, to eat things sacrificed unto idols, and to commit fornication. So hast thou also them that hold the doctrine of the Nicolaitans, which thing I hate. Repent; or else I will come unto thee quickly, and will fight against them with the sword of my mouth.
>
> REVELATION 2:14–16

As with the Ephesian church, Jesus has strong words of correction to this backsliding church as well! They were holding onto the doctrine of Balaam. You may remember in the Book of Numbers, chapters 22–24, that the Spirit-filled, yet carnal prophet, Balaam, was hired by the king of the Moabites, named Balac, to curse the nation of Israel. GOD would not allow Balaam to carry out that contract yet Balaam did instruct Balac how Israel could curse themselves, as verse 14 suggests. He told the king to have women from his nation enter into the camp of Israel and that the men of Israel would subsequently fall prey to their lure. Sure enough, the Bible says that the people began to commit whoredom with the daughters of Moab, they sacrificed, ate and bowed down to their GODs (Numbers 25:1–2).

This is the doctrine of Balaam. It's Christians joining with pagans, it's believers in Christ joining with unbelievers to commit spiritual fornication. It's sleeping with the false GODs of this world's system.

In considering this doctrine of Balaam, the word for my church, for you and me, is to be careful of with whom we join up. Is it a good idea for my congregation to jump in totally with the Democrats or the Republicans? Should we partner with the Elks club or the Boy Scouts to improve our community? It may sound good initially but it could be to our detriment spiritually. We may end up compromising our values in the name of political expediency. We've all seen this, haven't we? I have a friend who became a politician and started out with such great intentions. Unfortunately, as he became immersed in the day to day grind of the political world, he started to compromise his beliefs. He agreed to back things he doesn't believe in, so as to bring forward the things he does. This is not the way our Lord has for us! Don't get sucked into the doctrine of Balaam, dear saint! Say yes to things that matter spiritually and no to those that don't! I want to say yes when I can make a difference eternally, and no when I won't!

Also, we see that the Nicolaitans have come up again. They were those lay leaders who were able to lord their power over the body of Christ even when they had received no authority from God. During the Pergamos time period, people started following after "infallible" leaders in a prototype to be developed more completely by the next church, that of Thyatira. In 325 a.d. the noted Council of Nicaea occurred. Early leaders, called bishops, formulated official church doctrine which unfortunately was mixed in with the Roman culture and was officially "sanctioned" as truth! Also, since Rome was in control, it was a natural extension of this council to proclaim that the bishop of Rome should be the supreme church leader!

The Good Shepherd, the Teacher himself, told these believers that he hates this unholy priesthood! Our Lord then told them to repent, to turn back to pure and undefiled religion, or else he would fight against them with the sword of his mouth. In other words, he would speak the word against them ending their time as a congregation both locally and historically.

> He that hath an ear, let him hear what the Spirit saith unto the churches: To him that overcometh will I give to eat of the hidden manna, and will give him a white stone, and in the stone a new name written, which no man knoweth saving he that receiveth it.

What a wonderful motivator to them and us to live with heaven in mind. Here we learn that over-comers, those who are born of GOD, will eat of hidden manna, will be given a white stone and will receive a new name unknown to other men.

Jesus, who is pictured as manna from heaven, will reveal himself in new and fresh ways to the over-comers. That's the hidden manna. Next, the Romans used white and dark stones as yes and no votes for elections. In receiving a white stone, Jesus is voting yes for the one who overcomes. Lastly, Jesus will give the over-comer a new name. It will be a personal name known only to the believer and his Lord.

• • • •

The application that we need to see in our day from Jesus' words to Pergamos is to watch out for politics and religion. The Pergamos mentality that I can find myself falling into, that we in our church can walk head-first into, is that it's okay to mix with the world. After all, we don't want to just hole up and be irrelevant, do we?

Paul said it well when he said we are *in* the world but not *of* the world. We need to realize that we are a peculiar people, a royal priesthood, a holy nation. As we stay separate from the world and its carnal system we will avoid the correction our Lord had to give to this group. Dear believer, don't commit spiritual fornication. You won't be happy. As a child of GOD you have too much of him in you to enjoy the world. So don't have too much of the world in you to enjoy the Lord! Stay separate spiritually. Go into the world as we all have to, but don't take it home with you!

With this we end Jesus' comments to this third church. Our next stop is to examine the first of four epic church administrations which have persisted from their inception on unto our present day. This fourth church is the powerful and pervasive church of Thyatira! And just as GOD signifies the number four with the world, this fourth church can truly be said to be the "world's church," for it has dominated the world for nearly 1,500 years.

Unto ✝ he Church in Thyatira

And unto the angel of the church in Thyatira write;
REVELATION 2:18A

Thyatira was a small town on the trade route in northwest Turkey between Europe and Asia. They were noted for their production of colorful dye and for making and selling little idols of the GODS. You may remember from the book of Acts when Paul met Lydia near Philippi. We read that Lydia was from Thyatira and she sold beautiful purple garments (Acts 16:14).

This industrial connection is important to the section we are discussing but is eclipsed by the meaning of the word itself. For Thyatira means "continual sacrifice." Prophetically, the continual sacrifice is naming the Catholic Church. This section is speaking of the Church which has subjugated the world economically and politically for over 1,500 years.

The continual sacrifice is the Mass which is celebrated in the Catholic Church every day. The broken body and the shed blood is the central point of the Mass, and every Catholic Church building has a cross with the dying Lord over the altar of sacrifice. Truly, Thyatira is the continual sacrifice. Jesus' words apply to them. But as we have seen previously, these words not only apply to a specific church, but to *all* believers in *all* churches for *all* time.

I have been taught by my mentors that the time frame of the church in Thyatira is from 600 a.d. to the present, but the prophetic time is from approximately 600 to 1500 a.d. Around the year 1500 a.d. the church in Sardis was born as we will review in the next section.

> These things saith the Son of GOD, who hath his eyes like unto a flame of fire, and his feet are like fine brass.
>
> REVELATION 2:18B

Here is yet another partial revelation of the risen Christ! His eyes are as fire and his feet as brass. He is the Judge! His eyes penetrate my heart as he sees and knows my every thought and intention. In the Old Testament, brass in the metal is associated with judgment. Jesus wants to remind this church and you and me that he will one day judge in righteousness.

> I know thy works, and charity [love], and service, and faith, and thy patience, and thy works; and the last to be more than the first.
>
> REVELATION 2:19

Being raised as a youngster in the Catholic Church, this verse warms my heart! This church is full of works! Throughout history, the corporate Catholic Church and her local churches have been noted for their abundance of work and service for their communities. Hospitals, relief organizations, schools, shelters, and on and on have been gifts to the people of the world by this hard working church. Note also that their last works are even more than the first. As this church era has progressed they have become even more generous and magnanimous in their works. Their works now are even greater than at first!

This church has great charity. Jesus sees many lovers in the Catholic Church and as we have already mentioned, GOD calls charity (love) the greatest of all (I Corinthians 13:13).

This church has faith. They hold onto their beliefs with a

death grip. We see this as a blessing and a curse. For it is a blessing if I hold tight to the commandments of God but a curse if I cling relentlessly to the doctrine of men!

Lastly, the One whose eyes are like a flame of fire notes their patience. Recall that this word biblically refers to the hope of the soon return of the Lord. The believers in the Catholic Church have looked and are looking for the blessed hope of the return of the Lord. In their beautiful profession of faith which they audibly pray during every Mass they proclaim that they believe that Jesus is coming back to judge the living and the dead. They affirm that they believe in the resurrection of the dead and the life in the world to come. This church has patience. Many true believers in the Catholic Church look and pray for the return of their Lord. Jesus commends this church for they have not lost their faith, hope and love!

What about me. Are my works greater now at the last than at the first? Do I give myself in service without regard to what I will receive in return? Do I love God and man as the greatest commandments? Is my faith unmovable? And do I have patience, looking daily for the coming back of my Lord? Those questions are for you too!

> Notwithstanding I have a few things against thee, because thou sufferest that woman Jezebel, which calleth herself a prophetess to teach and to seduce my servants to commit fornication, and to eat things sacrificed unto idols.
>
> REVELATION 2:20

Apparently the local church in Thyatira tolerated a literal woman named Jezebel to spiritually rule over them. They were led away from the simplicity of the Gospel into fleshly lusts and false teaching by this woman. But the parallels to the Roman Church in this verse are huge!

Let's look at the infamous Jezebel of the Old Testament to more fully understand what Jesus through John is alluding. Her story is found in First Kings.

The first mention of Jezebel is when we are introduced to her husband the king. We read that Ahab was more evil than all the kings which were before him. It was a light thing for him to walk in the sins of Jeroboam. You may remember Jeroboam was the first king of the Northern tribes who introduced idolatry to the people in order to keep them from traveling to Jerusalem every year for true worship as GOD had commanded.

Well, we learn that Ahab took to wife Jezebel the daughter of the Zidonian king. He subsequently worshiped the Zidonian GOD Baal and erected a house for this false GOD in Samaria (I Kings 16:30–33).

Later, through Ahab's dealings with the prophet Elijah, we learn that Queen Jezebel had many prophets of the Lord killed (I Kings 18:4, 13) and that she was intending to kill Elijah after the four hundred prophets of Baal were defeated and executed. That happened on the day when GOD rained down fire from heaven in front of the people on Mount Carmel. She sent a messenger to Elijah, saying, "So let the GODS do to me, and more also, if I make not thy life as the life of one of them by tomorrow about this time" (I Kings 19:2b).

But the most notorious evil that Jezebel is credited with was in her dealings with her neighbor Naboth. In First Kings chapter 21 we learn that Ahab wanted to purchase his neighbor's vineyard and was willing to buy or trade for it. Naboth had no intention of selling the land as it was his family inheritance and was dear to him. Thus, Ahab came back to his house heavy and displeased with his failure to purchase the land. For this, Jezebel taunted the king. She basically said, what's wrong with you, man! Are you not the king! Let me take care of it since you are so impotent!

And take care of it she did! She proclaimed a fast and elevated Naboth above the people. Then she secretly hired false witnesses to say that Naboth had blasphemed GOD and should be stoned. The people followed blindly and indeed the innocent Naboth was brutally killed. Ahab was able to grab up the vineyard and we are told at the conclusion of the story, "But there was none like unto Ahab, which did sell himself to work wickedness in the sight of the Lord, whom Jezebel his wife stirred up" (I Kings 21:25).

Ahab was indeed brought low as he joined in league with his evil wife. He was sucked into the spiritual fornication of false worship and he condoned the murder of an innocent man in order to satisfy his lust for wealth and property. This story is a preview of the wrongs throughout the centuries of the Catholic Church!

This powerful church is noted for its wealth and possessions. The practice of buying indulgences for the dead brought the Church vast amounts of wealth. Wealth that is apparent today to anyone who travels to the Vatican and gazes upon the opulence of the city. This money was stolen from the poor of Europe. They were taught that salvation for their loved ones who had died could be purchased from the Church! Hundreds of millions of dollars were given blindly by the masses in the name of this false doctrine!

Another false teaching was that of praying to the saints and to Mary. The followers in this church's heyday were taught to worship idols just as Israel did in the days of Jeroboam and Ahab and Jezebel.

The Catholic Church has had their own Queen Jezebels, otherwise known as the Queens of the Church, i.e. the Popes. Many evil church leaders have executed good and GODly men who would dare to question their authority in relation to GOD's Word. Thinkers like Huss, Wycliffe, and many others unnamed, were persecuted and murdered. History calls this time the Dark Ages for good reason as the light of GOD's Word was covered greatly by this evil Church hierarchy.

The Inquisitions first conceived by Pope Gregory IX in the 13th Century was a tool used by the Franciscans and others to root out "heretics" of all kinds in France, Italy, and Germany. After that, the infamous Spanish Inquisition of the 15th Century documents thousands of true believers being cruelly burned at the stake by the Spanish monarchs Ferdinand and Isabella in their effort to consolidate power with the Roman Catholic Church. These martyrs needed only to recant their Biblical belief and declare allegiance to the Pope and they would be spared. Of course, in those days salvation by grace was obscured and the people were confused as to what was biblical. When I read accounts of those inquisitions I see a foreshadowing of the days to come. Those days when Antichrist will execute all those who do not publicly declare allegiance to him.

During the reign of the Popes the labor pain of the Crusades and the death and misery that was associated with these unwise military adventures was conceived by the leaders of this politically connected Church. Yes, the historical Catholic Church leaders from 600 to 1500 a.d. can be seen clearly in the allusion to Jezebel! They were power hungry and greedy men. Men who worshipped idols and lusted for land and money!

Jesus is telling the true believers in this Church to stop suffering, or putting up with these Jezebels! This is what he says for us today also. Don't follow after false spiritual leaders. You know who I mean. That man with his "healing ministry" or with his "holy spirit movement;" false doctrines which lead believers away from following Christ and into following men. You can always tell them though by their fruit. Is the focus on Jesus or on someone else? Do they emphasize God and his kingdom or are they raising money for their earthly empire?

But the application doesn't stop there. What about your church? Do you have a charismatic pastor who everybody loves? Is he a man that your church cannot do without? Watch out! That's also the Jezebel mentality. Nobody's indispensable. When a church doesn't get that, there's going to be trouble.

> And I gave her space to repent of her fornication; and she repented not.
> Behold, I will cast her into a bed, and them that commit adultery with her into great tribulation, except they repent of their deeds.
>
> REVELATION 2:21–22

The words "great tribulation" will hopefully catch your attention. Indeed those in this church who do not overcome will see that time called the Great Tribulation as they refuse to repent of their idolatry.

And I will kill her children with death; and all the churches

shall know that I am he which searcheth the reins and hearts:
And I will give every one of you according to your works.

REVELATION 2:23

Those unbelieving followers in this church will die the second death spoken of in Revelation chapter twenty. Those who do not believe in Jesus as Lord will be judged according to their works and will be found wanting. Jesus teaches here that the others churches will learn from the church in Thyatira of the folly of the doctrine of salvation by works. Indeed, for centuries the Protestants and the Evangelicals have contrasted their belief in Christ with that of the Catholic Church and her emphasis upon works.

But unto you I say, and unto the rest in Thyatira, as many as have not this doctrine, and which have not known the depths of Satan, as they speak; I will put upon you none other burden. But that you hold fast till I come.

REVELATION 2:24–25

Again, this church, unlike those which have preceded it, will see the Second Coming of Christ! Jesus comforts those true believers in the Catholic Church, those who have not known the depths of Satan, that he has no other burden for them. He implies that the "depths of Satan" is burden enough. The word "depths" is the Greek word "bathos." This speaks of the secret doctrines of the church. Those in the inner circle of the Roman church spoke a language, Latin, which the followers did not understand. Until the 1960's the members of this Church suffered through the continual sacrifice in a mass that they didn't even understand as it was given in Latin! Truly the Lord tells us where this originated. From Satan himself!

And he that overcometh, and keepeth my works unto the end, to him will I give power over the nations.

REVELATION 2:26

How do I overcome? What are the works of the Lord? You

187

know! Believe in God's only begotten Son (John 3:16). Ironically this Church wanted and has gained temporary power over the nations. But Jesus says that those who overcome will be given lasting power over the nations. Once again, it's the first shall be last and the last shall be first paradox that Jesus offers to those who overcome!

> ... And I will give him the morning star.
>
> REVELATION 2:28

The morning star is the planet Venus. Biblically this brilliant star pictures Jesus Christ. This gift from Jesus to the overcomer pictures the marriage relationship they will have in the ages to come!

• • • •

Thus, I can learn much from our Lord's words to this largest of all the churches. He teaches that I should not get sucked into the Thyatira mentality of idols and hierarchy. Like the Pergamos mentality before it, where we learn not to mix faith and politics, here we see the folly of confusing faith in the Invisible God with faith in things made by the hands of men and faith in the words given by fallible leaders who say they are infallible.

The words of Jesus given to the Pharisees and scribes in the book of Mark ring true when I am tempted to fall into the Thyatira mentality of idols and hierarchy.

> He answered and said unto them, well has Isaiah prophesied of you hypocrites, as it is written, this people honoreth me with their lips, but their heart is far from me. Howbeit in vain do they worship me, teaching for doctrines the commandments of men. For laying aside the commandments of God, ye hold the tradition of men...And he said unto them, full well ye reject the commandment of God, that ye may keep your own tradition.
>
> MARK 7:6–8A, 9

My prayer is that I will not get seduced by the traditions of men and miss the commandments of GOD!

• • • •

During the prophetic era of the church in Thyatira, painful sorrows, as upon a woman in labor, occurred. The Crusades, the Dark Ages, the One Hundred Year War between France and England and the Inquisitions were felt along with the pestilence of the Black Plague of 1347 a.d.

Next, we have come to the 16th Century, specifically to October 31, 1517 when a German monk nailed his ninety-five objections to the cathedral door in Wittenberg! GOD raised up Martin Luther and the church in Sardis was born!

Unto The Church in Sardis

The historic church of Sardis was in the centrally located city of these literal seven Asian churches. Sardis was the chief city of the province of Lydia, in present-day Turkey, and was very proud of and famous for its arts and crafts. Significantly to the revelation, Sardis was a city built upon a cliff and thus its citizens felt impregnable and safe from attack. In fact, throughout their history to this point, they had only been defeated in battle twice. Both were nighttime attacks! We will see these associations as applicable to the prophetic church of Sardis as well.

The word "sardis" means "remnant," and this church prophetically pictures the mainline Protestant Church. This remnant of believing faiths began in the days of the Reformation as many seekers of the Lord broke away from the vice-grip of the Catholic Church during the 16th Century. This church obviously has persisted unto our day and will also see the Coming of the Lord, but its prophetic time frame is from 1517 to approximately 1800 a.d. We will see that the next church, that of Philadelphia, was prophetically birthed at that time.

The early history of the Protestant Church was grand and glorious. Martin Luther, Ulrich Zwingli, John Calvin, John and Charles Wesley and others where led by the Spirit of GOD, and were protected during the time of their ministries by the same.

They courageously stood up to the "antichrists" of the day and started a movement of faith that restored a huge remnant of true believers to GOD. The various denominations became strong and their progeny are with us today as the Lutherans, the Presbyterians of Calvin, the Episcopalians from the Church of England and the Methodists after the Wesleys. These tight-knit groups also greatly influenced the early history of America. Many traveled to North America to escape the persecution that came with their stand for Christ. Their beliefs have been well documented to have greatly influenced our founding fathers in the formation of our National Constitution.

Indeed, the beginning of the Protestant churches was wonderful. Unfortunately though today, many, but not all, of those same churches have become monuments to their past glory. Grand churches with nearly empty seats on Sunday are peppered across Europe and North America. Most of those same churches have their lights out for the rest of the week. In the words of our Lord to this church we will learn why this has happened as well as make application to our own personal and corporate church lives!

> And unto the angel of the church in Sardis write: These things saith he that hath the seven Spirits of GOD, and the seven stars;
>
> REVELATION 3:1A

Here we have yet another partial revelation of the risen Lord. He has the seven Spirits of GOD and the seven stars. Soon, we will see in chapter 4 of this Revelation that the seven Spirits of GOD are seven lamps burning before the throne of GOD (Revelation 4:5). Bible scholars teach that this heavenly scene is an illusion to the seven fold nature of the Spirit upon Jesus as described in Isaiah 11.

> And there shall come forth a rod out of the stem of Jesse, and a Branch shall grow out of his roots: And the spirit of the Lord shall rest upon him, the spirit of wisdom and understanding,

the spirit of counsel and might, the spirit of knowledge and of the fear of the Lord.

ISAIAH 11:1–2

In chapter 1 of Revelation we read that the seven stars are the seven angels or the seven messengers of the churches (Revelation 1:20).

Thus we see the One with the Spirit of the Lord upon him is holding and caring for the leaders of his church and thus by extension is holding on to all of us. For as we have discussed, we all are overseers to somebody!

I know thy works, that thou hast a name that thou livest,

REVELATION 3:1B

This church, like its predecessor has much good work which has been well documented historically. The Protestant churches have made a difference in the world as a result of their work.

They also have a name. This is a reference to the denominational splits which occurred early in the Reformation time period. The Protestants went back to the Scriptures but their differences in interpretation led to multiple denominations. Thus they go by a name. They are identified with a group.

And they are alive! They resembled a living organism which started out like a fragile baby, then grew up into adulthood.

But after adulthood comes the twilight years and then... death!

And art dead. Be watchful, and strengthen the things which remain, that are ready to die: For I have not found thy works perfect before GOD. Remember therefore how thou hast received and heard, and hold fast, and repent. If therefore thou shalt not watch, I will come on thee as a thief, and thou shall not know what hour I will come upon thee.

REVELATION 3:1C-3

This church is dead and dying. Why? Because their works are not perfect before GOD.

Jesus answered and said unto them, This is the work of GOD, that ye believe on him whom he hath sent.

JOHN 6:29

The Protestant churches which started out so strongly, standing upon the Scriptures, have left their roots. Some denominations today even question the basic doctrine of the Good News! We see abortion and homosexuality tolerated, if not accepted, in many of these same churches now. Often, a social gospel is favored from the pulpit over the simple Gospel of Christ and him crucified!

Jesus is telling this church, like Ephesus before it, to remember where they came from and repent. Turn back to that place where Jesus is found. Turn back to that One with the seven-fold spirit of GOD upon him.

If they don't repent, the Lord proclaims that he will return at an hour in which they are not expecting. At an hour in which they will be surprised and overcome. He will come like a thief in the night! Obviously, this section is a reference to the rapture of the church. For indeed, the gathering together of believers is a doctrine which is generally not understood in today's Protestant churches.

These verses summarize succinctly what has been the downfall of the mainline Protestant church. Again, I am not saying every Protestant church falls into this category. And I am saying this can happen to any church, whether it be Catholic, Protestant, or Evangelical (also, this can happen to any individual believer). But the ancient church in Sardis, and the Protestant churches which Sardis typifies, stopped believing first and foremost in the work of GOD. They stopped embracing the Good News of Jesus as Savior and Lord. They also have dismissed the work of the Spirit. Thus, Jesus showed himself to this church as the One who hath the seven Spirits of GOD. Lastly, the Protestants generally disregard the doctrine of the Rapture and the Second Coming of Christ. Thus Jesus warns that unless they repent, they will be surprised by this very event they have left off believing!

I want you to see this Sardis mentality which is being alluded to here. Like the people of literal Sardis, that city built on a cliff which was proud of their fine art and crafts. The Protestant churches have rested on their laurels. They were noted historically to be the church which freed the world from the tyranny of the medieval Catholic Church. Thus, they were filled with pride and have become complacent. Instead of pressing in and growing in the Lord, this church has coasted! But unfortunately, when a church, or a person, puts it on cruise control and start coasting, they eventually will stop moving forward. They wake up one day and realize that they are at a standstill and wonder how that happened. This is what Jesus is saying to Sardis and what he is speaking to you and me also. Don't rest on your laurels. Just because you've been to the mountain, so to speak, with the Lord don't think that now it's time to kick back. If you do, you may find yourself in a valley not knowing which way out. The Christian walk is not static. If you are not moving forward, then you are moving back. Keep pressing forward, dear believer. Keep your eyes upon Jesus, first and foremost. Listen to his Spirit and remember daily of the hope of his soon return.

> Thou hast a few names even in Sardis which have not defiled their garments; and they shall walk with me in white: For they are worthy.
>
> REVELATION 3:4

How do I keep my garments undefiled? How do I keep them white, being worthy and getting to walk with the Lord? Read on...

> He that overcometh, the same shall be clothed in white raiment;
>
> REVELATION 3:5A

As we have discussed, First John 5:5 tells us that he that overcomes is the one who believes that Jesus is the Son of GOD.

Just believe the Gospel and you will walk with him in white!

. . . .

Thus we come to the end of the Church in Sardis. Many labor pangs also occurred in those days. Europe's most destructive war up unto that point was fought over religious doctrine and was called the Thirty Years War. It occurred in 1618–1648. The French Revolution with its middle class rebellion in 1789 was quite brutal and of course the American Revolutionary War was a labor pain with parallels to many Old Testament stories of God's deliverance.

Next, we come to the 1800's and to the Church in Philadelphia. Like the persecuted church in Smyrna before it, the Lord has no words of correction for this group of believers, for Philadelphia is the church of brotherly love!

Unto ✝ he Church in Philadelphia

> And to the angel of the church in Philadelphia write;
> REVELATION 3:7A

Wonderful Philadelphia! The word means "brotherly love." We remember that love is the greatest virtue, and in this revelation to Philadelphia we will see the apex of the Church Age because this church is filled with love. They love GOD and they love their neighbor. They follow the two greatest commandments spoken of by our Lord.

> Master, which is the great commandment of the law? Jesus said unto him, Thou shalt love the Lord thy GOD, with all thy heart, and with all thy soul, and with all thy mind. This is the first and great commandment. And the second is like unto it, Thou shalt love thy neighbor as thyself. On these two commandments hang all the law and the prophets.
> MATTHEW 22:36–40

As an aside, I find it very intriguing that the city where our nation was birthed from is also named Philadelphia! I think there are parallels to the early days of America and to the words of this revelation to the church in Philadelphia for the reader to consider. Truly, America was formed upon the premise of brotherly love and Christian faith!

The literal township of ancient Philadelphia was located in west-central Turkey between Sardis and Laodicea. It was not a notable city outwardly by any means. We will see in a moment that Jesus will say they had but a little strength!

The prophetic church of Philadelphia represents the Evangelical church movement which sprouted in the 1800's. This prophetic church is also weak in comparison to the two other churches that are still on the scene which we have just reviewed, that of the powerful Catholic Church and the once strong Protestant denominations.

The call to eliminate denominational tags started in the early 1800's and the followers called themselves the Church of Christ. The progeny of this movement is found today in the non-denominational Evangelical mega-churches which have sprouted across America. For it is in America where we predominately find the prophetic church of Philadelphia!

The Baptists, which also are included, can be traced to the early 1600's but they too really started evangelizing in the late 18th and early 19th centuries. The Assemblies of GOD and the Pentecostal movements of the early 20th century are also included in Jesus' words concerning Philadelphia.

You see, the prophetic church of Philadelphia is the missionary church which has proceeded out from America and has taken the Word of GOD to the world. From the U.S. we have seen an uncoordinated, yet massive effort by thousands of dedicated missionaries over the past two hundred years to take the Gospel of Jesus Christ to the entire planet. In my opinion, it is largely due to this single historical event which has led to the abundant GOD-given blessings America continues to enjoy, despite our many national sins. Oh, there is one more reason GOD continues to mercifully bless our nation. I will discuss that when we come to our discussion of the newly reborn nation of Israel.

Now let's look at the words of our King.

> These things saith he that is holy, he that is true, he that hath the key
> of David,
>
> REVELATION 3:7B

Here we are getting yet another partial revelation of the risen Lord.
He is holy and true and holds the key of David.

I wish I could tell you what this key is, but I can't. In pondering this
though, I remember that David, despite his many flaws, was a man after
GOD's own heart. Could it be that the key of David is to give my heart
wholly to the Lord? I don't know. But it's not a bad idea!

> … he that openeth, and no man shutteth; and shutteth, and no man
> openeth.
>
> REVELATION 3:7C

If Jesus opens a door, then it's open. Nothing can shut it. Con-
versely, if he closes a door, then nothing I do will open it. This is a key
to life. "If GOD be for us, who can be against us?" (Romans 8:31b). "The
Lord is my light and my salvation: Whom shall I fear? The Lord is the
strength of my life; of whom shall I be afraid?" (Psalm 27:1).

Again, if the One who is holy and true says for me to walk through
an open door, then nothing man or the devil can say or do will stop me.
We understand this to be true when we consider the church in Philadelphia. A door to evangelism has been open wide for the last two hundred years. When it looks like the devil will shut it down and close it up,
the door just swings open wider. Satan's world system has tried to stop
the spread of the Gospel just about everywhere it travels, yet the Lord
is holding the door open! If you doubt this last statement, just look
at China today for verification. This devilishly inspired government is
actively suppressing the Gospel yet it is spreading like wildfire in that
country. In fact, more believers live in China, a nation which officially
denies Christianity, than in any other nation on Earth!

> I know thy works: Behold, I have set before thee an open door, and
> no man can shut it: For thou hast a little strength,
>
> REVELATION 3:8A

Because of this church's work, that of love, Jesus has opened the door which no man has been able to shut. No one would say that the Evangelical movement has power, it has but a little strength in the words of our Lord, but because the One who has the key of David is holding the door open, nothing has been able to stop it! Why has Jesus held the door open? The answer may be found in his next comments to them.

> ... and hast kept my word, and hast not denied my name.
>
> REVELATION 3:8B

This church believes the reality of the Word concerning who Jesus is. We will see that the next church, Laodicea, will stumble over this truth.

> Behold, I will make them of the synagogue of Satan, which say they are Jews, and are not, but do lie; behold, I will make them to come and worship before thy feet, and to know that I have loved thee.
>
> REVELATION 3:9

Earlier, Jesus spoke to the church in Smyrna of the synagogue of Satan. We learned that these were Jews who had rejected Messiah and had cursed themselves. Here we have some additional information about this devilishly inspired religious group. Those of the synagogue of Satan say they are Jews and are not! This one hits close to home! For this statement is directed at Christians!

The Catholic and later the Protestant Church for centuries have interpreted the many promises in the Old Testament concerning the Jews as if they were written to them. It has been propagated that since the Jews rejected Jesus, GOD rejected them and thus the Church became GOD's "chosen people." It was taught that all of the promises concerning the revival of the Jews were actually allegories which dealt with the Church. After all, the Jews no longer existed! Or so it seemed.

Martin Luther was notably one of these men who taught that the Jews were cursed and that GOD was finished with them. An unfortunate footnote to his legacy is that much of this doctrine was subconsciously at the root of Germany's feelings towards the Jews seen in the 1940's!

But Paul, in his wonderful letter to the Romans stated clearly that GOD was not finished with the Jews even though they had rejected their Messiah.

> Brethren, my hearts desire and prayer to GOD for Israel is, that they might be saved...I say then, Hath GOD cast away his people? GOD forbid...Even so then at this present time also there is a remnant according to the election of grace...I say then, Have they stumbled that they should fall? GOD forbid: But rather through their fall salvation is come unto the Gentiles, for to provoke them to jealousy...And they also, if they abide not still in unbelief, shall be grafted in: For GOD is able to graft them in again...For I would not, brethren, that ye should be ignorant of this mystery, lest ye should be wise in your own conceits; that blindness in part is happened to Israel, until the fullness of the Gentiles be come in. And so all Israel shall be saved: As it is written, There shall come out of Zion the Deliverer, and shall turn away unGODliness from Jacob: For this is my covenant unto them, when I shall take away their sins. As concerning the gospel, they are enemies for your sakes: But as touching the election, they are beloved for the father's sakes. For the gifts and calling of GOD are without repentance.
>
> ROMANS 10:1; 11:1A, 5, 11, 23, 25–29

GOD does not change his mind. If he promises something, he delivers! Paul is clear that the fall of the Jews resulted in a huge benefit for the Gentiles. But he emphatically stated that GOD was not through with Israel. The Deliverer will turn away unGODliness from Jacob and the remnant will be saved.

This section of Scripture was hidden from much of the church in days past as it didn't make any sense without the nation of Israel existing on the planet! But then Israel was reborn in 1948. We in the Church now can look back with hindsight and see that GOD has had Israel in mind all along!

The take home point to all of this is don't attend the synagogue of Satan. Let's not be ignorant of GOD's plan for the Jews.

God loves his people and has used them to tell the Gentiles of himself. The Old Testament Law, the Gospels and the New Testament Epistles all are derived from God's dealing with Israel. And after the fullness of the Gentiles come, God will once again use Israel as his primary instrument to reveal himself to the world. This we will see during mankind's labor and travail known as the Tribulation!

> Because thou hast kept the word of my patience, I also will keep thee from the hour of temptation, which shall come upon all the world, to try them that dwell upon the earth. Behold, I come quickly:
>
> REVELATION 3:10–11A

Once again we read of "the word of my patience" and understand this to be a reference to the return of the Lord. This church has faithfully looked to the return of Christ and consequently we learn that they will be kept from the hour of temptation which shall come upon the entire world!

Paul states it this way, "And to wait for his Son from heaven, whom he raised from the dead, even Jesus, which delivered us from the wrath to come" (I Thessalonians 1:10).

The members of this church, as well as those from the other churches, who are looking for the Son from heaven, will be delivered from the Tribulation time period. They will be delivered from the wrath to come!

How does this happen?

Jesus states that, "behold, I come quickly." A better translation would be, "when I come, it will be quick." It will be sudden. It will be like lightning flashing across the sky. It will be in the twinkling of the eye. It's called the rapture!

This prophetic church, as well as many individual believers and churches which are present during the end times will be saved from the hour of temptation because they have overcome. Because they (we) call Jesus, Lord!

> … hold that fast which thou hast, that no man take thy crown
>
> REVELATION 3:11B

Jesus tells this church to hang on. Don't let go. Finish strong! If they do, they will keep their crown. What is this crown of which the Lord is speaking? Paul gives us the answer, "For what is our hope, or joy, or crown of rejoicing? Are not even ye in the presence of our Lord Jesus Christ at his coming? For ye are our glory and joy" (I Thessalonians 2:19–20).

The crown is made up of people. Specifically, it is those people to whom we've shared Christ and his Word—those we've brought to the Lord. They will be in the presence of the Lord at his coming and we will rejoice because he partnered with us to bring them along with us into his Kingdom.

• • • •

So the application for you and me, and for our local church corporately, is to have the Philadelphia mentality. That is, choose to walk in brotherly love, tell people about Jesus and what he means to you, and hold fast.

To amplify, be a man or a woman who loves people. That might mean stop being selfish and self-centered and see people the way GOD sees them.

And be an evangelist. Tell your story. You may not have the ministry of an evangelist but no one can refute what the Lord has done for you! Just think where you would be without him. You were dead without him!

Lastly, hold fast. Paul wrote that we should work out our own salvation with fear and trembling (Philippians 2:12b). That means we must guard our hearts from outside attacks, for they will come. I don't want to be embarrassed when I meet the Lord because I've fallen back.

• • • •

By now in this revelation it's hard to believe that I would need more motivation to live for heaven, but GOD in his grace nonetheless gives me a wonderful promise.

Him that overcometh will I make a pillar in the temple of my

GOD, and he shall go no more out: And will write upon him the name of my GOD, and the name of the city of my GOD, which is new Jerusalem, which cometh down out of heaven from my GOD: And I will write upon him my new name.

REVELATION 3:12

Just like GOD gave Abram, Sarai, and Simon new names. He will give you and me new names also. Why not, for we too are his friends!

When we are told of the name of GOD and of the name of the city of GOD, this speaks of the glory and government of GOD. The people of this prophetic church will be given glory and responsibility in the ages to come. The irony is that this weak church that loves, evangelizes, and holds fast will rule with him while the strong church of Thyatira which has desired and held the rule for nearly 2,000 years will lose that role.

• • • •

So we come to the end of the words given to Philadelphia. During their prophetic time many birth pangs have also occurred. The Napoleonic Wars rocked Europe from 1793–1815. In America we suffered through the Gold Rush chaos, the Mexican–American War, the brutal Civil War of the 1860's and it's aftermath, and the Indian Wars of the late 19th Century. It would seem as time has progressed that more intense and frequent labor pangs have occurred.

But then we come to the 20th Century. The time of the prophetic church of Laodicea and a time where the frequency of the labor pangs would indicate that the true labor is just around the corner. For indeed this last century has brought wars, earthquakes, famines and pestilences to a degree such as the world has never before seen!

Unto ✝ The Church of the Laodiceans

Laodicea was the southern and eastern most church of the seven literal churches that Jesus spoke to. They were located on the main road through the area and were totally unable to defend themselves. Because of that, they became very adept at compromising with their neighbors. They had a well developed entertainment industry and were notably very wealthy. There also was a wonderful hot aqueduct which sprang out of nearby Colossae to the east. But before the hot spring entered Laodicea it mixed with a cold river rendering the mixture warm but not hot. Lastly, the Laodiceans were noted as a center for the production of eye medications. People with visual problems would travel to Laodicea to medicate their eyes with a balm produced in Laodicea.

The word "Laodicea" is also very germane to the story. Like the word "Nicolaitans," we see the root word "laity" once again. Laodicea means "people rule." In the church of the Laodiceans, the people rule, not the Lord! Yes, we saw in chapter one of Revelation that Jesus was in the midst of the churches, for all seven are his church, but this church has pushed him out, so to speak. We will see that this church will uniquely receive no words of affirmation from the Lord and we will get a better understanding of the famous evangelistic verse found in this section, for Jesus is asking this church to let him back in!

Behold, I stand at the door and knock: If any man hear my voice, and open the door, I will come in to him, and will sup with him, and he with me.

REVELATION 3:20

The prophetic church of Laodicea is seen primarily in the 20th century. But it has had it roots in the 19th Century The largest group of modern-day Laodiceans is the Church of Jesus Christ of Latter-day Saints. The Mormon Church teaches that their prophet Joseph Smith received revelation from the angel Moroni in New York State between 1820 and 1830. But it has not been until the last few generations that they have elevated to their present status as a rich and powerful American church.

The Unitarians and the Jehovah's Witnesses can also be traced back many years. But again, their influence has been felt more recently.

Mary Baker Eddy founded the Christian Science movement in 1875, and her group remains viable unto this time. Lastly, among other groups of lesser importance is The Way Ministry. The Way was founded by Victor Paul Wierwille in Ohio during the 1950's. These religious groups make up the prophetic church of Laodicea.

The one things that all of these groups have in common is that they have lowered the status of Jesus Christ. Yes, they do see him as Lord and Savior but they do not call him GOD. They are unified in their belief that Jesus and the Father are not part of a triune GODhead. To the church of Laodicea, Jesus is not GOD. He is a created being, one who is enlightened and elevated, but he does not receive nor deserve equality with the Father according to their thinking.

Now, I don't pretend to understand all of the nuances of the doctrine of the Trinity, but it has been a primary belief of most of Christendom for centuries. Could it be that so many lovers of the Lord who have gone before have been wrong about Jesus while these modern-day "saints" have it right? I think not!

But we Evangelicals, who call this church a cult, need to lighten up on them. Jesus, as we will see, loves this church as he loves the others. Yes, they have erred and we will see that the Lord has strong words of reprimand for them. But he still walks in their midst. We Trinitarian Christians need to love them and leave the judging to GOD!

> And unto the angel of the church of the Laodiceans write: These things saith the Amen, the faithful and true witness, the beginning of the creation of GOD;
>
> REVELATION 3:14

Jesus wastes no time getting to the heart of the problem with this church. They've got him all wrong!

He is the Amen.

Amen is one of a short list of words that every tongue speaks and every ear understands. Jesus is the Amen. He is the Alpha and the Omega. So be it. Amen!

He is the Faithful and True Witness. Jesus told Philip that he who has seen him has seen the Father (John 14:9). Jesus has explained GOD to mankind in a way that we can comprehend, for GOD became a man. He stooped down to our level so that we could begin to grasp eternity and infinity!

He is the beginning of the creation of GOD. This does not mean that Jesus was the first thing GOD created. No, it means creation began with him. The Son of GOD, created everything!

Look with me into the book of Hebrews;

> GOD...Hath in these last days spoken unto us by his Son...by whom also he made the worlds; Who being the brightness of his glory, and the express image of his person, and upholding all things by the word of his power, when he had by himself purged our sins, sat down on the right hand of the Majesty on high.
>
> HEBREWS 1:1A, 2A, C, 3

Jesus not only is the express image of GOD but we also learn from the author of Hebrews that he made the worlds and he sustains everything by the word of his power. To simplify, Jesus made and sustains *everything!* If that's not GOD, then I don't know what is!

So this is the opening word our Lord has for this church, "Wake up Laodicea, I am GOD!"

. . . .

As mentioned earlier, Laodicea means "people rule." And we see this in the modern-day church of Laodicea. The Mormons have laymen who become bishops over the people in small groups they call wards. Similarly we see ordinary men in charge of doctrinal interpretation for the followers of the Jehovah's Witnesses, the Unitarians and the other groups which make up this church.

Paul explains to us in the book to the Ephesians that the true leaders in the church are given to it from Christ. They are ordained with power from him which is evident to all who look upon them.

> Wherefore he saith, When he ascended up on high, he led captivity captive, and gave gifts unto men...And he gave some, apostles; and some, prophets; and some evangelists; and some, pastors and teachers. For the perfecting of the saints, for the work of the ministry, for the edifying of the body of Christ:
>
> EPHESIANS 4:8, 11–12

The Lord intends for the overseers, the leaders of his church, to be those whom he has gifted with ability in one of these five ministerial areas. He does not intend for the shepherd to lead the sheep without his gifting. Unfortunately, in the church of Laodicea, this has occurred.

> I know thy works, that thou art neither cold nor hot: I would thou were cold or hot.
>
> REVELATION 3:15

Jesus calls this church lukewarm. Like the water that flowed into literal Laodicea, they are not refreshing to the Lord. They are not hot, nor are they cold. They are not burning with love and passion for him nor are they without awareness of his presence at all. It's ho-hum in this church. They are going through the motions of playing church but they really are somewhere else as soon as they leave the Lord's house.

This can happen to you and me also, to my church and yours! This mentality is not just limited to Laodicea! In fact, I will go so far as to say that in our fallen state, it is unusual for this not to happen to the believer and his church from time to time. They key is to be aware of this tendency and to go back to that first love as was told to the first of the seven churches, that of the church in Ephesus. To remember, repent, and return to that place where you were when the Lord was real and hot in your life. Like the word to the church in Philadelphia. Hold fast to the things he has given to us. In Laodicea this does not happen. In fact we will soon see that they believe they are in an exalted place because of these very same lukewarm works!

The Lord would rather they were hot or cold. That's because those are the people he can work with. Those who are hot will be loving on people and talking about him to others. Those who are cold he can reach also. A cold person can realize that he is in a bad place and can come back. A cold person can wake up and return to the Lord. But the lukewarm person doesn't even realize that there's a problem. They don't get hot and thus are not useful nor do they get cold and see that they need their Savior's grace.

> So then because thou art lukewarm, and neither cold nor hot, I will spue thee out of my mouth.
>
> REVELATION 3:16

This is not something I want to hear the Lord say to me! I like my coffee hot. Also iced coffee can be tasty. But lukewarm... Yuck!

That's what our Friend is saying to this church and to those who fall into this pseudo-spiritual mentality. "You're not refreshing to me at all. I can't swallow your works, for you are doing them without my gifting and without any concept of my grace. You're works are without me. You're working on your own steam!"

The Lord goes on to amplify upon the reason for their lukewarm state in the next verse.

Because thou sayest, I am rich, and increased with goods, and have need of nothing;

REVELATION 3:17A

This church has misunderstood GOD's grace and goodness to them. They have believed that their wealth and self-sufficiency are evidences of GOD's approval. Not only that, but they say to others that GOD's material blessings correlate with his feelings toward them.

We see this in the modern-day church of Laodicea. The Mormons, Jehovah's Witnesses, The Way, and the others have separated themselves from the other churches on the scene today. There is a "we are better than you mentality" that is pervasive in these present day denominations!

We will see that nothing could be farther from the truth!

And knowest not that thou art wretched, and miserable, and poor, and blind, and naked:

REVELATION 3:17B

In their self-glorification they have become wretched. They stink!

Work done in the flesh stinks. Paul stated, speaking of the flesh; "O wretched man that I am! Who shall deliver me from the body of this death?" (Romans 7:24).

They are miserable. You know when you are miserable, you're just not happy and you're not even sure why that is! This church and all those who fall into that lukewarm place are really miserable.

They are poor. Remember the church in Smyrna, that persecuted church. They were poor but really rich. This church is rich but really poor! Again, the financial status of the believer has no correlation to his spiritual state! This rich church is really poor in the true treasures. Those treasures stored up in heaven!

They are blind. In Laodicea they made eye balm to help people see. What an irony that they were really blind. In our day, the Mormon sons travel far and wide when they are eighteen or nineteen to reach people about the Book of Mormon...the Jehovah's Witnesses go from door to door, but in thinking that they see, they are really blind! How sad!

They are naked. The Bible teaches that we have been clothed with the garments of salvation and are covered with the robe of righteousness (Isaiah 61:10). Those in this church have demoted the Son and are naked!

The antidote to this mentality...

> I counsel thee to buy of me gold tried in the fire, that thou mayest be rich;
>
> REVELATION 18A

Gold is that metal we use to symbolize wealth, yet GOD uses to symbolize his glory and presence. And the gold the Lord tells this church to buy has been heated and perfected. This, of course, speaks of adversity and trial. The One who possesses the true riches is telling his people in their lukewarm place that trials and adversity will be needed to perfect them!

> And white raiment, that thou mayest be clothed, and that the shame of thy nakedness do not appear;
>
> REVELATION 3:18B

Put on the garments of salvation as Isaiah proclaimed. In this church, as in every church, are people who are not born again. These are folks who have not embraced the grace of GOD. They have not received the free gift of GOD but continue to try and work for salvation. Jesus says that until I am clothed in white, clothed in his righteousness, I am naked and ashamed!

> And anoint thine eyes with eye-salve, that thou mayest see.
>
> REVELATION 3:18C

I think of the blind man who was anointed with Jesus' saliva and made to see. The blind in this church need their eyes intimately touched by the Savior.

As many as I love, I rebuke and chasten:

REVELATION 3:19A

Please note my dear Evangelical brothers and sisters who call this church a cult...Jesus loves this church just as he loves you!

Be zealous therefore, and repent.

REVELATION 3:19B

A zealous person is a hot person. Jesus wants this church to move up stream, where the water is hot.

And repent. Just change direction, stop working your way to heaven. You don't have to leave home to evangelize when you are still young in the faith to impress GOD. It's not mandatory to give 10% of your money to the church. Yes, it's good and you'll be blessed, but your salvation doesn't depend upon it! And certainly you don't have to have a large family in order to enjoy heaven to its fullest!

Jesus wants to come in, but he won't break the door down.

Behold I stand at the door, and knock: If any man hear my voice, and open the door, I will come in to him, and sup with him, and he with me.

REVELATION 3:20

He's standing there. He's knocking. His voice can be heard unless the outside noise is too loud. Will I open the door and invite him in? Will this church, or any church, make the Lord its head? If I do, if we do, we get to have a heavenly dinner right here and now!

To him that overcometh will I grant to sit with me in my throne, even as I also overcame, and am set down with my Father in his throne.

REVELATION 3:21

Here is a motivator for heaven. To him that overcomes, to the man or woman who calls Jesus, Lord. That person will sit with him on his throne. I'm not sure what that means exactly, but certainly it will be a profound blessing and privilege!

• • • •

We have come to the end of our Lord's words to this latter-day church. That happy, wishy-washy church of the 20th Century. And we have come to the end of his words to the churches in totality. Next, the Book of Revelation takes us to chapter 4 where we immediately behold a door in heaven opened and hear a trumpet sound with a voice saying to come up hither! (Revelation 4:1). We have arrived at the end of the Church Age, to the end of the age of Grace. We have arrived at what the Bible calls the fullness of the Gentiles (Romans 11:25). We have come to the Rapture of the church. In our obstetrical analogy, we have come to the point of the water breaking. To the rupture of the membranes. To the onset of true labor. We have come to the Day of the Lord. We have come to the Tribulation!

But before we continue forward in Revelation and examine these wonderful and yet, for others, dreadful times, let me make an application from the Master's words to Laodicea. Also in the next chapters we must consider the frequent birth pangs, the beginning of sorrows that our Lord spoke of, which we have felt in this last century and examine the budding of the fig tree which Jesus told his followers would occur before the Day of the Lord.

• • • •

I have alluded to the attitude of mind that is present in Laodicea. And have said not to have that mindset. So just what is the Laodicean mentality that the Lord wants me not to have?

Well, it's the pervasive philosophy which can creep into the church that says, "It's okay, I'm really a good person, I'm a good Christian!" The Laodicean mentality is the place that forgets that I am saved by grace through faith and not of works that no one may boast (Ephesians 2:8–9). It's the comfortable place that doesn't need to confess sin and doesn't think to repent and turn back to him when I fall. It's "I deserve to be blessed, look at all I've done for him and sacrificed to him!"

You see, dear reader, this mentality isn't just owned by the Mormons or the Jehovah's Witnesses. I get sucked down this path all too often, you probably do too. I've seen it in my Evangelical church and it exists with the Catholics and the Protestants also. This worldview is in all the churches and the Lord has *nothing* good to say about it. No words of affirmation come to this church for this mentality only makes him want to spit up!

Get rid of the Laodicean mentality. Remember his grace. Without him we can do nothing! In my flesh dwelleth no good thing (Romans 7:18). It's all by his unbelievable, unfathomable, unquenchable grace.

G.R.A.C.E: God's Riches At Christ's Expense.

✝he Beginnings of Sorrows

The 20ᵗʰ century has seen the words which our Lord spoke to Peter, James, John, and Andrew come alive in a way which is charged with anticipation to those with eyes to see.

> And as he sat upon the mount of Olives over against the temple, Peter and James and John and Andrew asked him privately, Tell us, when shall be the sign when all these things be fulfilled? And Jesus began to say, Take heed lest any man deceive you: For many shall come in my name, saying, I am Christ; and shall deceive many. And when ye shall hear of wars and rumors of wars, be ye not troubled: For such things must needs be; but the end is not yet. For nation shall rise against nation, and kingdom against kingdom: And there shall be earthquakes in divers places, and there shall be famines and troubles [pestilences, Matthew 24:7]: These are the beginnings of sorrows.
>
> MARK 13:3–8

Luke adds in his parallel account of these days that the seas and the waves will roar (Luke 21:25b).

The reader may recall that "sorrows" is a biblical term for labor pains. Also from the introduction you may remember that birth pangs do not start all at once but is a process full of false alarms before the actual day of travail arrives. In answering his disciple's question, Jesus told them that the aforementioned signs of his return would be as false labor precedes true labor.

Jesus first told his men not to be deceived. The implication, of course, is that men will try to deceive.

The Teacher proclaimed the he is the way, the truth, and the life and that no man could come to the Father but by him (John 14:6). Yet here he taught that many will come as another way to the Father, as another way to reach GOD.

We have seen this prophecy to be true. Millions worldwide have been and are being deceived by the false messiahs of Mohammed and Buddha. Others are being sucked into the New Age movement, the Age of Aquarius, where all men are GODS and there are no absolutes. Yes, false Christs have appeared and we can unfortunately expect to see even further fulfillment of these words in the days to come. Of course, during the Tribulation time period the Antichrist will ultimately complete this prophecy!

Next, Jesus said that men would hear of wars and rumors of wars. That nation would rise against nation and that kingdom would battle kingdom.

Certainly this has been true since the days of Abraham. In fact, the Bible's first mention of war was in Abram's day as noted in Genesis 14. That was the battle of the nine kings over Sodom. But war has been taken to a new level in the last century. The 20th Century has been called "the century of war" as we have seen conflicts on a scale never before witnessed.

In these days of increasing birth pangs, we have seen the introduction of chemical, biological, and nuclear warfare as well as witnessed the incredible increased efficiency of conventional weapons in their ability to kill and maim other men.

A summary of some of the wars this last one hundred years has endured is in order.

The 1900's opened with the assignation of the American President, James McKinley and was immediately followed by the Mexican Revolution of 1910. In 1912 the Balkan War began which led into World War I by 1914. Fifteen million men died in that terrible war which witnessed chemical weapons as well as airpower being used for the first time. Thousands of young men died on a front that inched back and forth without any breakthroughs for months on end. Ultimately, though, the coalition led by England and America prevailed over Germany and the Treaty of Versailles was the result. This treaty punished Germany very severely and historians are quick to point out that the backlash of this treaty made Germany ripe for her Nazi conversion under the reign of the Third Reich and the infamous Adolph Hitler.

The Marxist Revolution spearheaded by Vladimir Lenin in Russia from 1918–1922 led to the spread of Communism across the globe. Communist Russia and her satellite countries were the cause of much human suffering, bondage and death from her inception until 1985 and the fall of the Soviet Union. Unfortunately, this evil form of totalitarian control still exists in China and North Korea in our present day.

1929 saw the stock market crash and the Great Depression which followed. Global suffering on an economic scale not seen in the Western developed countries was the result. By 1933 Germany was in the throes of the Depression and desperately wanted to regain her position and status as a major world power after her defeat in WWI. Thus, the Nazis and Adolph Hitler were allowed to crawl out of their hole with a message of salvation to the people of the Arian Nations. In a rapid rise to power that may again be seen in the days of Antichrist, Hitler, who as a pre-figure of the evil world leader to come, grabbed the reins of the Nazi Party and carried Germany onto a course of utter depravity. The Third Reich closed down Germany and by 1939 began to conquer Europe. Concomitantly, the Japanese were also positioning themselves in Asia to dominate and control. The behavior of those two rogue nations led to World War II. Thirty five million people died in this largest of wars. With the rise in population of the 20th Century, this war saw more die than nearly the sum total of all wars which had come before!

The first and second atomic bombs were dropped over Japan at the end of WWII. This ended that conflict but paved the way for the Cold War between the Communist block and the West. Red scares, bomb shelters and air raid drills were common in

America during the 50's and early 60's as the Nuclear Age seemed to be developing unchecked! The Korean War, the Cuban Missile Crisis, and the terrible Vietnam War were byproducts of the labor pain of the Cold War.

The 1980's brought the Soviet–Afghanistan War of '79–'89. Death and destruction without the more powerful nation being the victor was the result. Interestingly, this seemed to be a preview of our own country's quagmire in that land in our day today!

Muslim extremists led by the Ayatollah Khomeini gained control of Iran in the 70's. The four hundred forty six day American Hostage Crisis preceded Iran's bloody war with Iraq and Saddam Hussein. This decade long war saw its cease fire only shortly before Hussein invaded the American and European ally of Kuwait. The short Gulf War of 1991, known as Desert Storm, was the result. "Smart weapons" were first introduced to the world during this conflict as a preview of coming attractions, if you will, for the end times

The words of Jeremiah seem appropriate as we consider this pang.

> For, lo, I will raise and cause to come up against Babylon [Iraq] an assembly of great nations from the north country: And they shall set themselves in array against her; from thence she shall be taken: Their arrows shall be as of a mighty expert man; none shall return in vain.
>
> JEREMIAH 50:9

Remarkably, though, America's president, George H. W. Bush, let Hussein stay in power in Iraq when he had the opportunity to remove him. In retrospect, many believe that the continued instability of the region at the hands of this man led to the younger President Bush to call America back into the region for another round of false labor pains!

The 1990's were not without its wars and rumors of wars. The Serbian war with its ethnic cleansing dominated William Clinton's presidency, along with his "domestic affairs." Simultaneously, tribal genocide in Africa reached tragic heights which has continued unabated into our present decade.

In September 2001 America was attacked and, like a sleeping dog when aroused, it bit back. An undeclared religious war which may have strong ties to the end times has been the result. More recently we have seen Spain and England suffer in this terrorist war.

Yes, this incomplete summary of the wars over last one hundred years would seem to bring the obstetrical point home concerning the beginning of sorrows and our Lord's words about the increase in war as time marches toward his return. Of course, in this review I did not even mention the nation of Israel and her many conflicts with her Middle Eastern neighbors. This I will do in the next chapters as we consider the budding of the fig tree and Israel's role as a predictor of end times events.

•　•　•　•

After speaking of kingdom warring against kingdom, the Prophet mentioned earthquakes. Significantly, he placed the phenomenon of the Earth shaking into this obstetrical formula of increasing frequency and intensity near the end.

Of course we read of the Earth quaking in the Bible from early days. At Mount Sinai, the Earth shook violently as GOD prepared to give the Ten Commandments to the people as seen in Exodus 19:18. Later, the Earth quaked after Jonathan and his armor bearer defeated the Philistine garrison near Gibeah. This routed the camp of the Philistines and gave the victory to Israel (I Samuel 14:15). And most notably, on that glorious morning of our Lord's Resurrection, the Earth quaked and the stone was rolled away, not so Jesus could get out but so that we could see in! So that we could see that the tomb was empty!

But the point of these words concerning earthquakes is not that they have occurred from days long ago, but that in these last several generations they have increased with alarming frequency and intensity. Experts who study these things say that there has been a logarithmic increase in the number of major earthquakes over the last one hundred years. It is interesting also that with the population explosion of the 20th century we have seen major metropolitan centers growing up directly on top of earthquake zones. A certain recipe for disaster has been written. Mexico City, Los Angeles, San Francisco, Anchorage, Tokyo with all of Japan, Indonesia, and Istanbul have all experienced destructive and deadly earthquakes during our lives or those of our parents and grandparents.

Indeed, the words of Paul bear repeating at this point, "For we know that the whole creation groaneth and travaileth in pain until now" (Romans 8:22).

Yes the Earth itself is laboring as it readies itself for the Day of the Lord!

. . . .

Jesus predicted that famine would also be as the beginning of sorrows. We can go back to the book of Genesis and find mention of famine, but the intensity in these days is nothing short of mind boggling!

We remember the predicted seven year famine in Egypt which Pharaoh dreamed and Joseph interpreted. Recall also that that seven year famine was a picture of the seven year Tribulation. The nation of Egypt as a type of the world is seen, along with the tribe of Jacob picturing Israel and Joseph starring as the Lord. Strong allegories to the time of Jacob's Trouble were developed earlier in this book.

Yes, famine has always been around and many times it was even used by GOD in the Bible to correct his children, but in this day it is pervasive.

It has been stated that over one-third of the world's population is in a state of starvation. That's over two billion people! I've heard it estimated that a person dies from starvation every four seconds on planet Earth!

Indeed famine, like war and earthquakes, has taken on a labor-like rhythm which seems to point to the King's soon return!

. . . .

Next, the Prophet mentioned pestilences.

The Bible clearly states that men lived long lives after the fall of Adam and Eve. Sin entered the world, yet one of its consequences, that of death by disease, really did not begin to become so evident until after the flood of Noah. It was typical for a person's life span to last many centuries. Afterwards, though, we saw a steady decline in longevity so that by the days of the Judges, a life span of forty to seventy years was all that one would expect due to the effects of aging and disease.

In biblical times, leprosy was the disease that was feared above all others. And, of course, until the last century with the introduction of antibiotics, that disease continued to be a plague. The young and old have always succumbed to pneumonia and influenza as well as the Black Plague of the Middle Ages, but in recent decades this prophecy of Jesus is coming alive with a birthing-like increase. The Spanish flu killed millions in the early 20th Century. Also, tuberculosis, cholera, and other waste-borne pathogens have ravaged the 3rd World due to its overcrowding and lack of sanitation. Polio was a virus my parents feared greatly in the '50s. Recently, we have seen new diseases come onto the scene, most notably the Human Immunodeficiency Virus. HIV is responsible for the demise of millions world-wide, with central Africa being particularly devastated with this disease and its sequelae. STD cases from Herpes Virus and Human Papilloma Virus have skyrocketed in the last thirty years. Also we have also been introduced to and have come to fear contagions such as the Ebola Virus, the West Nile Virus, the Avian flu, Methacillin Resistant Staph Aureus and the SARS virus. Indeed, pestilence is going unabated despite medical advances. Just as our Lord said it would!

• • • •

Lastly, in considering Jesus' words to his four questioners, let us look at the words Luke includes to the discussion.

> ... and upon the earth distress of nations, with perplexity; the sea and the waves roaring.
>
> LUKE 21:25B

This last decade has seen killer hurricane after killer hurricane make landfall in Central America and the U.S. as well as in the Western Pacific nations. The names of Ivan and Katrina have been imbedded in our minds as we consider the raging of the ocean against our own shores. Death and destruction from the windblown sea has been at an all-time high. That was until the "tsunami"! In 2005, the world witnessed death from the waves roaring in a very spine-chilling way. The nations surrounding the Indian Ocean were overwhelmed by the shear power of the earth quaking under the sea near Indonesia. The largest single natural disaster occurred and the words quoted in Luke's gospel cannot be emphasized enough. The signs Jesus spoke as the beginning of sorrows is happening before our eyes in the news of the day.

Look up, dear believer, our redemption draws nigh!

• • • •

But what do I make of all this death and destruction. How can a loving GOD let all of this happen?

Well, two things need to be said when I get thinking along this line of thought. First, remember GOD gave free will to mankind. He has let us have our way to some degree. The death and carnage from war certainly cannot be blamed upon GOD. But what about earthquakes, storms, famine, and disease? One cannot blame mankind for those maladies, can we? No, they are from the GOD of this world, Satan. The Bible clearly teaches that originally GOD gave mankind dominion over the Earth. But with sin, we gave the dominion of the planet over to Satan. Thus, we see that by the time Satan was tempting Jesus in the wilderness, as noted in Matthew 4, he was in a position to offer Jesus all the kingdoms of the world if only the Messiah would bow down and worship him (Matthew 4:8–9). Jesus did not refute that part of the offer as he well understood that the world *did* belong to the one formerly called Lucifer. Jesus understood that the way to purchase back dominion of the planet was through the cross. Thus we read in Revelation that it was by the cross that the Lion of the tribe of Judah has prevailed and has opened the seven sealed book (Revelation 5:5)—the title deed to planet Earth, if you will. Yes, it is important to consider who is temporarily on the throne of the Earth when I look upon all of the ills of our world!

Secondly, when I want to indict GOD, who is greater than Satan, concerning the many terrible problems of the world today, I need to remember what he did on the cross of Calvary. Jesus was pinned up on that wooden beam, although he was the only innocent man who has ever lived! He knows my sorrows and travail as he took it all upon the cross. We will never understand this side of eternity just how bad that was. He died for the sins of the world! I must always look at circumstances through the lens of the cross. I must be cross-referenced! I must be cross-eyed!

Thus, with these comments completed, let's now look at the nation of Israel to see how she points to the soon coming Day of the Lord. Let's examine the budding of the fig tree found in that very famous discourse of our Lord. That being the exciting and intense Olivet Discourse of Matthew 24 and 25!

☦he Budding of the Fig tree

In the Old Testament times GOD used the nation of Israel to demonstrate and tell the people of the world of his power and love and mercy and grace. Then at the crossroads of history he sent his only begotten Son, born into the tribe of Judah to bring rest, comfort and salvation for all. The men of Israel rejected their Messiah and seemingly the nation perished much like the fig tree which our Lord cursed when it had no fruit for him (Matthew 21:18–19).

As we know, in 70 a.d. the Romans crushed Israel and the nation appeared to have withered away. But as Paul has taught in Romans Chapters 9–11, GOD is not through with the Jews. He has revived them, as he repeatedly said in his Word that he would, and he once again is and will use them to point the way to him. First, as an indicator of the onset of the end times and secondly Israel will be a light to the rest of the people of the world during the day of wrath, during the Tribulation time period.

Now to comprehend the "budding of the fig tree" we must first understand something of the word "tree." In the Bible "tree" is one of those words dripping with significance as the Author uses trees to typify spiritual truths. When we read of a lone tree, it often is used to represent the work of the cross (Exodus 15:23–25). Trees can picture people as seen in Matthew 12 from Jesus' statement to the Pharisees that a tree is known by its fruit. Also, trees can typify the nations as seen in Gideon's son Jotham's parable against Abimelech found in Judges 9:6–15. But certain trees always speak of Israel when spoken of in Scripture. Those trees are the vine, the olive tree and the fig tree. Again Jotham's parable is helpful in our understanding of this allegory as are the following words of Jesus, Paul, Hosea, and Joel.

First, you may recall our study of the birth pangs of the book of Judges and specifically the section entitled "The Son of a King" that the trees of the field represented the nations. The trees asked the olive and fig tree, as well as the vine, to rule over them. This pictured Israel's role over the nations as God's ambassador to them. Israel was unwilling to take this responsibility as the parable indicated. Then we saw the bramble bush who we understand to be a type of Antichrist. He very much wants to dominate and control the nations as Abimelech desired in Jotham's day.

In our next example, Jesus, again in speaking to the Pharisees, told the parable of the men of the vineyard. He indicted the nation of Israel for their unbelief and rejection of the prophets and of the Son. He used the vine as the analogous picture of Israel (Matthew 21:33–46). He ended his prophecy against them by saying, "Therefore say I unto you, The kingdom of God shall be taken from you, and given to a nation bringing forth the fruits thereof" (Matthew 21:43). Paul spoke of Israel as an olive tree as noted in his explanation of the grafting in of the Gentiles into the blessings of God through Jesus Christ (Romans 11:17–26).

Lastly, Hosea and Joel give us insight towards the fig tree and its meaning in Bible typology.

> I found Israel like grapes in the wilderness: I saw your fathers as the first ripe in the fig tree at her first time:
>
> HOSEA 9:10A

We see Israel likened to both the vine and the fig tree in Hosea's imagery. In prophesying of the soon coming world dominance of Babylon followed by the revival of Israel, Joel speaks in these figurative terms.

He hath laid my vine waste, and barked my fig tree: He hath made it clean bare, and cast it away; the branches thereof are made white...The vine is dried up, and the fig tree languisheth; the pomegranate tree, the palm tree also, and the apple tree, even all trees of the field, are withered: Because joy is withered from the sons of men...Fear not, O land; be glad and rejoice: For the Lord will do great things. Be not afraid, ye beasts of the field: For the pastures of the wilderness do spring, for the tree beareth her fruit, the fig tree and the vine do yield their strength.

JOEL 1:7, 12; 2:21–22

Yes, it is a recurring theme in Scripture. The fig tree always speaks in some way of the nation of Israel just as does the number twelve which we have spoken of previously. GOD's ways are so above our ways that it should not be surprising that his writing is most exacting! As a postscript to this point we can look to modern Israel. Along with the Star of David, the Fig tree is the country's national emblem!

• • • •

Thus with these opening comments, the words of our Lord should grab our attention as we consider the times in which we are living.

In chapters 24 of Matthew, 13 of Mark and 21 of Luke, we read of the account of the apostles questioning Jesus of the signs of his coming and of the end of the world. After speaking of many of the birth pangs we have already discussed as well as some that we will cover when we speak of mankind's time of labor and delivery, the Tribulation time period, Jesus said these very telling words to help them and us get a handle on this question.

He said,

Now learn a parable of the *fig tree:* When his branch is yet tender, and putting forth leaves, ye know that summer is nigh: So likewise ye, when ye shall see all these things, know that it is near, even at the doors. Verily I say unto you, This *generation* shall not pass, till all these things be fulfilled (emphasis mine).

MATTHEW 24:32–35

Jesus told his men to look at the fig tree in parable—to look at the nation of Israel. After the long winter, when the tree appears dead, will come the springtime buds and leaves which will lead to the fruit of summer. He said when you see the nation of Israel bringing forth leaves once again, even before the fruit is present, know that his return is at the door! And the Prophet said that the generation which was alive when the fig tree budded would not pass away until all his words be fulfilled!

Well, goodness sake! In 1948 the nation of Israel was reborn. This historical fact is incredibly significant as it points to his return and the end times. For I repeat, Jesus said that the generation that witnesses the budding of the fig tree would not pass away until all his words concerning the end times be fulfilled!

First, let's look at the rebirth of Israel as prophesied in Scripture then undertake a study of how long a generation is in biblical terms.

> Come, and let us return unto the Lord: For he hath torn, and he will heal us; he hath smitten, and he will bind us up. After two days will he revive us: In the third day he will raise us up, and we shall live in his sight.
>
> HOSEA 6:1–2

Hosea, in prophesying to Israel in the 7th century b.c., revealed Israel's soon demise followed by her revival. He preached that the revival would occur "after two days."

You may remember that with GOD a day is as a thousand years.

> For a thousand years in thy sight are but yesterday...
>
> PSALM 90:4A

And,

> But, beloved, be not ignorant of this one thing, that one day

is with the Lord as a thousand years, and a thousand years as one day.

II Peter 3:8

Moses and Peter reveal time in God's economy. One day equals a thousand years. Thus, we can understand Hosea's words to mean that after two thousand years, Israel will come back to life!

We are living in the third day dear reader, and Israel has been revived!

Again Jesus taught, that when you see the fig tree budding, look up for your redemption draws nigh!

But there is much more! Look with me at the words of Jeremiah.

The fierce anger of the Lord shall not return, until he hath done it, and until he have performed the intents of his heart: In the latter days ye shall consider it.

Jeremiah 30:24

What is it that the Lord would perform in the latter days?

For, lo, the days come, saith the Lord, that I will bring again the captivity of my people Israel and Judah, saith the Lord: And I will cause them to return to the land that I gave to their fathers, and they shall possess it...Alas! For that day is great, so that none is like it: It is even the time of Jacob's trouble; but he shall be saved out of it. For it shall come to pass in that day, saith the Lord of hosts, that I will break his yoke from off thy neck, and will burst thy bonds, and strangers shall no more serve themselves of him: But they shall serve the Lord their God, and David their king, whom I will raise up unto them. Therefore fear not, O my servant Jacob, saith the Lord; neither be dismayed, O Israel: For, lo, I will save thee from afar, and thy seed from the land of their captivity; and Jacob shall return...For I will restore health unto thee, and I will heal thee of thy wounds, saith the Lord; because they called thee an Outcast, saying, This is Zion, whom no man seeketh after.

Thus saith the Lord: Behold, I will bring again the captivity of Jacob's tents, and have mercy on his dwelling places; and the city shall be builded upon her own heap, and the palace shall remain after the manner thereof.

JEREMIAH 30:3, 7–10A, 17–18

Jeremiah revealed that the time of Israel's revival and the time of Jacob's trouble, also known as the Tribulation, are related. He taught that Israel, that nation that was an outcast, will serve the Lord and David their king. We understand this to mean that the complete fulfillment of this prophecy will occur when Israel calls upon the greater than David, the son of David, Jesus Christ, during the time of Jacob's Trouble.

Jeremiah went on to say that during the end times,

Again I will build thee, and thou shalt be built, O virgin of Israel…Thou shalt yet plant vines upon the mountains of Samaria: [Today we call "the mountains of Samaria" the West Bank.]…For there shall be a day, that the watchmen upon the mount Ephraim shall cry, arise ye, and let us go up to Zion, unto the Lord our GOD…Behold, I will bring them from the north country, and gather them from the coasts of the earth… a great company shall return thither…Hear the word of the Lord, O ye nations, and declare it in the isles afar off, and say, He that scattered Israel will gather him, and keep him, as a shepherd doth his flock.

JEREMIAH 31:4A, 5A, 6, 8A, C, 10

This is so wonderful, for before our very eyes this is happening! The Good Shepherd is gathering his flock.

Also of particular note in this prophecy is the revelation that "watchmen" would say, "Arise, and let us go up to Zion." In Hebrew the word translated "watchmen" is also translated "Nazarenes." I believe that the prophet is saying that in the latter days, the Nazarenes, those followers of the One from Nazareth, will go up to Zion unto the Lord their GOD. This is what we have seen in this last century. Scores of Christians have traveled to the Holy Land to experience the glory of that special place. I was privileged to be one of those Nazarenes, for in 1999 and 2006 I toured Israel and experienced firsthand of the wonder and mystery of the Holy Land. I am blessed to understand that the Lord used me as one of the "watchmen" to fulfill his prophetic Word!

Now back to the revival of Israel, to the budding of the fig tree. With these words of Hosea and Jeremiah, we come to the incredible prophecy of Isaiah concerning this time.

> Hear the word of the Lord...Who hath heard such a thing? Who hath seen such things? Shall the earth be made to bring forth in one day? Or shall a nation be born at once? For as soon as Zion travailed, she brought forth her children. Shall I bring to birth, and not cause to bring forth? Saith the Lord: Shall I cause to bring forth, and shut the womb? Saith thy GOD.
>
> ISAIAH 66:5A, 8–9

Isaiah audaciously predicted that a nation, that Zion, would be birthed, would be brought forth in one day! He basically said that GOD would be showing off! GOD was going to do something unique to demonstrate his power to those with eyes to see! And, as an obstetrician, I like the imagery. He used my favorite people, pregnant women, to paint the picture!

On May 14, 1948 this occurred. After centuries of persecution, the children of Israel who had been scattered across the globe were given a homeland by the pen of the United Nations. After the Holocaust of Hitler's Third Reich, the sympathy of the world for a brief time allowed enough momentum for that governing body to give Israel back to the Jews. Of course, GOD all along was orchestrating the event and the times!

I will show you in the next chapter that the revival of Israel was predicted in GOD's Word over three thousand years earlier to be on that very day! It will be a study that hopefully will chill and tingle your spine as you consider in a new way that the book we hold in our hand, the Bible, contains the very words of the Maker of the universe!

GOD promised to revive Israel and indeed that has happened. How does that affect me today? Well, it should bless me immensely. If GOD will keep his promise to the Jews, he will also keep his promise to me. He said in John 3:16 that if I believe in the only begotten Son then I will have eternal life. I too will be revived. After my labor and travail on this planet, I will come back to life, so to speak, in his presence on that day not too far away!

But it's even more than that! Today, now in my life, GOD is in the business of revival. He changes beauty for ashes whenever I call upon him. Whenever I give worth to his Son and his Word.

> And thou shalt do that which is right and good in the sight of the Lord: That it may be well with thee, and that thou mayest go in and possess the good land which the Lord sware unto thy fathers.
>
> DEUTERONOMY 6:18

. . . .

Continuing, what about the exact day of his return? Can we tell when this will be? The answer is, no! That would be in direct opposition to GOD's Word, for in the very next verse after Jesus spoke of the budding of the fig tree and of the generation that would see it, he said this, "But of that day and hour knoweth no man, no, not the angels of heaven, but my Father only" (Matthew 24:36).

Jesus said we could know the times of the end, but not the exact day! Remember, he has said through the Apostle Paul that he doesn't want us to be caught off guard and be overtaken like a thief in the night (I Thessalonians 5:1–6). That presumes that we *can* know the times of the end and be ready!

So let's get back to our Lord's words to his men. He said that the generation which witnessed the budding of the fig tree would not pass away. Thus, the question is, in the Bible, how many years is a generation? For Jesus said the end would occur *before* that generation passed.

I have to smile when I consider this question as GOD has used the word "generation" as an imprecise measure of time in Scripture. He wants us to know the times of the end but not the exact day or time. He wants you and me to be ready all of our days, for as we continue to hope for heaven, we experience heaven here on Earth!

As far as I can tell in looking at the length of time of a generation in Scripture, there are four different time periods. Let's briefly look at them.

> And the Lord's anger was kindled against Israel, and he made them wander in the wilderness forty years, until all the generation, that had done evil in the sight of the Lord, was consumed.
>
> NUMBERS 32:13

This verse from the Book of Numbers speaks of a generation as forty years. Hmm, that can't be it! For if I add forty years to 1948 I get 1988. In retrospect, his return did not occur in that time frame, so that can't be the meaning as it relates to the Master's words.

The next description of "generation" is found in Moses' very reflective Psalm.

> Lord, thou hast been our dwelling place in all generations... .
> The days of our years are threescore years and ten; and by reason of strength they be fourscore years.
>
> PSALM 90:1, 10A

In this reckoning of a generation we see the length as seventy to eighty years.

Now I like this one better! Add eighty trips around the sun from 1948 and I come up with the year 2028. I'll be seventy three years old in 2028 so I'm hoping it will come by then!

But wait! GOD told Abram yet another period of time he uses for this word.

> And he said unto Abram, Know of a surety that thy seed shall be a stranger in a land that is not theirs, and shall serve them; and they shall afflict them four hundred years...But in the fourth generation they shall come out again:

Genesis 5:13,16a

Now we're up to a hundred years! The end could go out all the way to 2048! Looking bad for me to hold out in this body of mine for that long! That's okay though. Jesus didn't say that the end would be on the last day of that generation anyway. It could be anytime within that one hundred year time frame of the budding of the fig tree.

One more usage though.

And Joshua the son of Nun, the servant of the Lord, died...
And also all that generation were gathered unto their fathers:
Judges 2:8a,10a

In the case of the budding of the fig tree, this usage of the word "generation" presumes that some people who were alive in 1948 will live to see all of Jesus' words fulfilled.

And that, my friends, is the meaning! Jesus told his apostles that people alive at the time of the budding of the fig tree would not be outlived by the day of his return. He purposely kept it vague so that we couldn't lock in to an exact day and fall asleep in the time prior. He wants me to be ready *every* day!

• • • •

There is so much more to speak about concerning Israel and God's prophetic timetable. We will speak of their pure language, the dry bones imagery and the revival of the fruitful countryside. We must consider that in the end times the nation will be a cup of trembling to the world, and, of course, we will review the battles they have already fought and how Jehovah has protected them as he said he would. We will see the benefits to any nation that loves Israel and the curses to those peoples who hate them. Later in this section of the days a false labor leading up to the time of true labor, we will discuss the certain battle between Russia with her confederates against Israel. But now it is time to uncover and consider God's exacting prediction concerning the revival of the nation, for May 14, 1948 was predicted centuries earlier in a way that was hidden from men's eyes until these last days.

✝he End of the 2,520 Year Curse: May 14ᵗʰ, 1948

Let me show you how GOD predicted in a very obscure yet powerful way that Israel would once again be birthed on May 14, 1948. The story will first take us to the powerful book of Ezekiel—to that prophet who was given abundant revelation concerning future events.

The time of Ezekiel's prophecy was between 593–560 b.c. His words were given during Judah's seventy year captivity in Babylon. Much of Ezekiel's vision is a very heavenly scene, yet our text here concerning Israel is quite earthy, as you will see!

> Thou also son of man, take thee a tile, and lay it before thee, and portray upon it the city, even Jerusalem:
>
> EZEKIEL 4:1

Now stay with me here, dear reader. GOD told Ezekiel to take a tile. We might say, "build a sand castle on the beach" to show what is going to happen to Jerusalem.

> And lay siege against it, and build a fort against it, and cast a mount against it; set the camp also against it, and set battering

rams against it round about...and set thy face against it, and it shall be besieged, and thou shalt lay siege against it. This shall be a *sign* to the house of Israel (emphasis mine).

EZEKIEL 4:2.3B

The Almighty told the prophet to use the model of the city as a sign to the people of the upcoming siege against it.

Lie thou also upon thy left side, and lay the iniquity of the house of Israel upon it: According to the number of days that thou shalt lie upon it thou shalt bear their iniquity. For I have laid upon thee the years of their iniquity,

EZEKIEL 4:4–5A

Picture this, if you can. GOD instructed Ezekiel to lie on his left side day after day to bear the iniquity that was due the men of Israel. He said that every day you lay on your side represents a year that they will be punished and besieged for their sins.

Now, we've seen this principle of a day for a year before, haven't we?

In punishing the children of Israel for their unbelief in listening to the ill report of the ten spies instead of believing the words of Joshua and Caleb, GOD sentenced the nation to wander in the wilderness for forty years. One year for every day that the twelve spies searched out the land.

After the number of the days in which ye searched the land, even forty days, each day for a year, shall ye bear your iniquities, even forty years.

NUMBERS 14:34A

... three hundred and ninety days: So shalt thou bear the iniquity of the house of Israel.

EZEKIEL 4:5B

Just as Ezekiel was to lie in front of the model of the besieged city for three hundred ninety days as a sign to the people of GOD's wrath towards the nation, that wrath was going to last three hundred ninety years!

But there was more work for Ezekiel!

> And when thou hast accomplished them, lie again on thy right side, and thou shalt bear the iniquity of the house of Judah forty days: I have appointed thee each day for a year.
>
> EZEKIEL 4:6

This *really* happened! Ezekiel, the man of GOD for his generation, laid down on his side for over one year for all the people to see and know what GOD was going to do. This was sort of bad news/good news. The bad news is that they were going to be besieged for a long time as punishments for their iniquity. But the good news is that there would be an end. They were not going to be utterly destroyed! We learn here of another forty years added to the sentence. That brings us to a four hundred thirty year debt which the nation as a whole had stored up due to their continued disobedience from the days in which Moses received the Law until that time.

Okay, now is where it becomes a bit obscure. Stay with me.

So they have a four hundred thirty year debt. That means that from the time of the Babylonian takeover until the time of the nation's revival would only be four hundred thirty years. The temple was burned and the city destroyed in 586 b.c., so the revival should have been in 156 b.c. But this isn't what happened, so understanding the prophecy in this way would be wrong. In hindsight, we need to bring into the equation two other variables from GOD's Word to know the exact duration of the curse they had called upon themselves.

First, the children of Israel paid seventy years off the debt with their Babylonian captivity.

> Therefore he brought upon them the king of the Chaldees, who slew their young men in the house of their sanctuary... and they burnt the house of GOD, and brake down the wall of Jerusalem...and them that escaped from the sword carried he away to Babylon; where they were servants to him and his sons

until the reign of the kingdom of Persia: To fulfill the word of the Lord by the mouth of Jeremiah, until the land had enjoyed her sabbaths: For as long as she lay desolate she kept Sabbath, to fulfill threescore and ten years.

II CHRONICLES 36:17A, 19A, 20–21

It's an historical fact that the totality of the Babylonian captivity was seventy years, just as Jeremiah prophesied it to be. The first wave of Nebuchadnezzar's attacks came in 605 b.c. and Cyrus, the king of Persia, decreed the return of the people in 536 b.c. Taking into account that a year was only three hundred sixty days in Biblical reckoning and not the celestial three hundred sixty four and three fourths days we know it takes for the Earth to orbit the Sun, we see the prophecy to be powerfully correct.

So, subtracting seventy years from their four hundred thirty year debt brings us to a shorter time of payment due—to a shorter time of labor and travail for the people. Only three hundred sixty years left to pay.

So, was Israel revived as a sovereign, independent nation three hundred sixty years later? We know that was also not the case. That's because we need to consider the second factor from GOD's Word which reveals when the curse will end. It's found in the Law of Moses. Specifically, the third book of the Torah, the book of Leviticus.

Chapter 26 of Leviticus tells of the blessings and of the curses which would await the children of Israel based upon their ability to keep the covenant which GOD had made with them.

The Lord told his people that if they did not worship idols, if they kept the Sabbaths, and if they walked in his statutes, that they would have rain in due season, they would have peace in the land, they would chase away their enemies, they would be fruitful and multiply, and that he would set his tabernacle among them and walk with them. But, if they did not hearken to his commandments, it would be appointed for them to have terror, consumption, and sorrow of heart. He said he would set his face against them and that their enemies would slay them and reign over them (Leviticus 26:1–17).

Then GOD revealed the key point in our consideration for this study.

> And if ye will not yet for all this hearken unto me, then I will punish you *seven times more* for your sins... . And if ye walk contrary unto me, and will not hearken unto me; I will bring *seven times more* plagues upon you according to your sins... . Then will I also walk contrary unto you, and will punish you yet *seven times* for your sins (emphasis mine).
>
> LEVITICUS 26:18, 21, 24

The debt was to be multiplied seven times! GOD repeated the curse three times. We remember three is the number of completeness in the Bible and GOD completely states that the curse will be multiplied by seven!

So, now we have the variables we need to understand GOD's power and sovereignty over the affairs of men. GOD, the Righteous Judge, stated that the nation had a four hundred thirty year debt which was reduced to three hundred sixty years because of the payment they made at the hand of Nebuchadnezzar. But we must add the multiplication of seven to the account. That is the factor which gave the Children of Israel their 2,520 year debt!

Since we want to know the *exact* day of Israel's revival, as we remember Isaiah predicted that the nation would be born in a day, we need to convert 2,520 years into days. Remember, in scripture a year is three hundred sixty days. Thus we come up with 907,200 days that Israel would be besieged by their enemies before they would be revived as an independent nation once again.

Israel's seventy year captivity ended with the edict to rebuild the temple. That occurred on 536 b.c. Hopefully, if you have been able to stay with me here, you've guessed it! If you travel in time 907,200 days from July 23, 536 b.c., the day Cyrus issued his decree to rebuild Jerusalem, we come to May 14, 1948! The very day that Israel became a nation as agreed upon by the United Nations. Somehow I don't think the people at the U.N. understood this prophecy when they picked that day to be the beginning of the new nation. Truly GOD ways are far beyond our ways. He raises up kings and he sets them down. GOD is in control!

This is so beautiful to me! If GOD's Word is that precise then it tells me that what he says for you and me is also going to come to pass. Absolutely! No doubt about it! When Jesus said he was leaving to build me a mansion and that he would return one day to take me there, I can be sure that it will happen. When the Lord says to you that in this world you will have tribulation, but be of good cheer for I have overcome the world, you can relax.

When I learn of things like this prophecy concerning the revival of the Jews it enlarges my mind concerning GOD and his Word. For now I see dimly but truth like this helps me to see a bit more clearly!

One last thing, then we will move on. GOD told his people that he would use prophecy to show off to man. For GOD will not give his glory to another. In Isaiah we read of GOD's boasting!

> Produce your cause, saith the Lord; bring forth your strong reasons, saith the King of Jacob. Let them bring them forth, and show us what shall happen: Let them show the former things, what they be, that we may consider them; or declare us things for to come. Show the things that are to come hereafter, that we may know that ye are GODS: Yea, do good, or do evil, that we may be dismayed, and behold it together. Behold, ye are of nothing, and your work of naught: An abomination is he that chooseth you.
>
> ISAIAH 41:21–24

> Behold, the former things are come to pass, and new things do I declare: *Before* they spring forth I tell you of them (emphasis mine).
>
> ISAIAH 42:9

> Thus saith the Lord, the Holy One of Israel, and his Maker, *Ask* me of things to come concerning my sons, and concerning the work of my hands *command* ye me… . For thus saith the Lord that created the heavens…I have not spoken in secret (emphasis mine).
>
> ISAIAH 45:11, 18A, 19A

It's as if GOD is daring us to prove him in this arena of prophecy!

> Remember the former things of old: For I am GOD, and there is none else; I am GOD, and there is none like me. Declaring the end from the beginning, and from ancient times the things that are not yet done, saying, My counsel shall stand, and I will do all my pleasure.
>
> ISAIAH 46:9–10

> I have even from the beginning declared it to thee, before it came to pass I showed it thee: Lest thou shouldest say, Mine idol hath done them, and my graven image, and my molten image, hath commanded them.... . For mine own sake, even for mine own sake, will I do it: For how should my name be polluted? And I will not give my glory unto another.
>
> ISAIAH 48:5, 11

There it is! GOD taunts other GODS to foretell the future. He says that the fact that they can't reveals to all that those GODS are nothing! The Almighty declares that he will reveal things before they come to pass. The Holy One of Israel actually tells us to ask him of things to come. He states that he has not spoken in secret and that he has declared the end from the beginning! Why? So that mankind would know that it's him, and not another. Not an idol or the work of men's hands. For he alone is to receive all glory and honor, blessing, and power. Now, and in eternity to come!

✝he Pure Language

The Prophet Zephaniah was a man of GOD to the tribe of Judah during a fifteen year time from 635–620 b.c. Josiah was the king and revival was taking place in Jerusalem under the leadership of that wonderful sovereign. In that light, Zephaniah had much to say during the time of his prophecy concerning end-times events and the role his people would play in that scenario.

Most of his words concerning the Tribulation time period and the battle of Armageddon are covered in greater detail in other Scriptures which I will discuss later when we reach the time of mankind's labor and travail, but Zephaniah does speak of one particular item which is not really found in any of the other prophet's writings. That is a reference to a pure language that the Judeans would speak in the latter days.

> For then will I turn the people a pure language, that they may all call upon the name of the Lord, to serve him with one consent.
>
> ZEPHANIAH 3:9

Scholars believe that the pure language that GOD is alluding to through Zephaniah is the Hebrew language. It is taught that another sign of the latter days would be the revival of the Hebrew language.

It is understood that after the Jews were scattered in the first century a.d. they lost their language as they were assimilated into the Gentile nations. Even though GOD miraculously kept them together as a close knit group, their language was dead in the sense that no one spoke it. In a way, Hebrew took the same path as the Latin tongue. It was a language in written form only. No Jew could actually speak the ancestral words.

Then in the late 19th Century as Jews began migrating back to Palestine in small numbers a man by the name of Ben Yehuda who was a leader in the community began to insist that his family learn and speak Hebrew. This caught on in what many consider a GOD-ordained way and the people developed a hunger to learn and speak their historic language. Today, of course, Hebrew is the official language of Israel and this pure language is yet another indicator on the fig tree, from the nation of Israel, that GOD's words concerning the Day of the Lord are soon to be fulfilled!

Now before we discuss more of the predictors of the return of Jesus Christ which are given to us by the nation of Israel, I want to you to think about the "pure language." In our text, the pure language is Hebrew, but on another level the pure language is the language of love. Jesus taught that people of the world would know that we are his disciples by our love one for another. Yes, we who are living late in the days of false labor also have the opportunity to speak the "pure language" as we speak words that are gracious and loving at every opportunity. Don't miss a chance to bless people with your words. For in blessing others with words of love, grace, mercy, and faith you too will be built up and revived! Lastly, on that day when we stand before the Lord, we will be sorry for the times we *didn't* speak words of love, not for the times we did!

He Will Make Her Wilderness Like Eden

A common theme throughout the Old Testament is the revival of the remnant of the children of Israel. After receiving punishment for their sins, and appearing to have all but died in a national sense, they were promised to be resurrected. Along with this theme is one that the nation would once again become fruitful and the people would multiply in the land.

Let's look at a few of the many references to this and develop them in the historical context of the last four thousands years. Of course, there will be an application or two in it for you and me also!

> For the Lord shall comfort Zion: He will comfort all her waste places; and he will make her wilderness like Eden, and her desert like the garden of the Lord; joy and gladness shall be found therein, thanksgiving, and the voice of melody.
>
> ISAIAH 51:3

O Lord, thou art my GOD; I will exalt thee, I will praise thy name; for thou hast done wonderful things; thy counsels of old are faithfulness and truth.... . He will swallow up death in victory;

and the Lord GOD will wipe away tears from off all faces; and the rebuke of his people shall he take away from off all the earth: For the Lord hath spoken it... . In that day shall this song be sung in the Land of Judah; We have a strong city; salvation will GOD appoint for walls and bulwarks... . In that day the Lord... He shall cause them that come of Jacob to take root: Israel shall blossom and bud, and fill the face of the world with fruit.

ISAIAH 25:1, 8 26:1 27:1A, 6

The word that came to Jeremiah from the Lord, saying...For, lo, the days come, saith the Lord, that I will bring again the captivity of my people Israel and Judah, saith the Lord: And I will cause them to return to the land that I gave to their fathers, and they shall possess it. And these are the words that the Lord spake concerning Israel and concerning Judah... . Thus saith the Lord; Behold, I will bring again the captivity of Jacob's tents...And out of them shall proceed thanksgiving and the voice of them that make merry: And I will multiply them, and they shall not be a few; I will also glorify them, and they shall not be small...Again I will build thee, and thou shalt be built, O virgin of Israel...Thou shalt yet plant vines upon the mountains of Samaria: The planters shall plant, and eat them as common things.

JEREMIAH 30:1, 3–4, 18A, 19; 31:4A, 5

Also, thou son of man, [Ezekiel] prophesy unto the mountains of Israel, and say, Ye mountains of Israel, hear the word of the Lord...But ye, O mountains of Israel, ye shall shoot forth your branches, and yield your fruit to my people of Israel; for they are at hand to come. For, behold, I am for you, and I will turn unto you, and ye shall be tilled and sown: And I will multiply men upon you, all the house of Israel, even all of it: And the cities shall be inhabited, and the wastes shall be builded: And I will multiply upon you man and beast; and they shall increase and bring fruit: And I will settle you after your old estates, and will do better unto you than at your beginnings: And ye shall know that I am the Lord.

EZEKIEL 36:1, 8–11

I don't think it could be any clearer! The Lord time and time again stated that he would bring the people back to the land. He said it would be associated with the day that tears would be wiped away. It would be a day when the people would again multiply upon the Land and that the entire nation would once again become fruitful, from the temperate costal region to the Eastern deserts. In the Bible, those two areas are called the Mountains of Samaria and the Wilderness. Wonderfully, his comments were ended with the statement that their end would be better than their beginning! In considering this statement in light of what has happened historically in Israel, we need to look back at their beginning.

When GOD told Abraham to travel west to a new homeland it was not the dry and dusty land we may think of today. No, Israel was much like coastal California and Oregon. Located on a temperate latitude with a large body of water to the west, Israel was always blessed with rain during the Spring and late Autumn (called the early and latter rains). In between those two periods of precipitation was a warm summer with abundant sunshine. Perfect for the land to be one flowing with milk and honey. Forests were abundant in the north and on the western slopes of the mountains and the coastal plains were ideal for agriculture. Even the eastern desert was green. The Bible tells us when Abraham and Lot separated their flocks because they were too numerous together as one, that Lot chose the area around what is now known as the Dead Sea because it was an area which was green and beautiful. We know this area today as Sodom and Gomorrah. Of course, the resultant judgment upon that land caused the utter desolation of this region that we see unto this day.

Hundreds of years later the country continued to be fruitful. We remember the cluster of grapes the size of a basketball that the twelve spies brought back to Moses after walking through the Land. Also we recall the thick forest that David and his men hid in while enduring Absalom's rebellion. The abundance of the region even allowed wild animals to reside there. Sampson came across the carcass of a lion and we discussed how David fought against both a bear and a lion.

Again, Old Testament Israel sounded a lot like Oregon.

Mountain lions, black bears, beautiful forests and lush meadows can all be found within ten minutes of my house. Yes, Oregon and Israel. They are a lot alike!

But then things changed. Israel fell into idolatry and powerful nations were allowed to conquer the walled cities. To accomplish this, wood was harvested from the countryside by the invading nations to build their engines of war. Also the enemy would destroy forest land to keep the people from hiding and mounting retaliatory campaigns. Thus, the lush forests of the mountains of Israel started to become a memory after the Assyrian and Babylonian invasions. It is important to note that in the climate we are discussing, if trees are clear-cut, it would take centuries for the forests to recover naturally. Only by systematic replanting by man could the forest hope to return for the unshaded heat of the summer would not allow a quick recovery of the wooded areas otherwise.

But the land was to suffer further degradation after our Lord's First Coming to the Promised Land. The Romans became so incensed with the Jews that they systematically destroyed the nation's ability to recover. They created a wasteland as was prophesied to happen so many times in the Old Testament. The remaining trees were cut down and the land was salted. This evil custom was very effective in keeping plant life from rebounding back for centuries.

The Arab occupiers of the Ottoman-Turk Empire continued to treat Palestine with disdain. It was so bad that by the late 19th Century, the famous author Mark Twain, in traveling to Palestine, was quoted as saying that he could not understand how any thing good could have happened in this land. He said it appeared to him to be the most GOD-forsaken place he had ever seen. A Land of jackals and scorpions, unfit for man or beast. Truly, Israel had become a wasteland. A testament to GOD's earlier displeasure.

But as we understand, GOD is faithful. He promised Abraham, Isaac, and Jacob that the Land would be their perpetual inheritance. And as we have seen, he promised to bring fruitfulness back to the countryside.

Indeed this has and is happening. About one hundred years ago, Jews started moving back to their ancestral Land. They began planting trees and harvesting crops in communes known as kibitzes. Later, after gaining their independence in 1948, they started a massive regeneration plan. Trees are being planted by the thousands and fields once salty and rocky are growing forth abundantly in the perfect climate. Even the desert is in bloom from irrigated land which is green with fruit!

The words of the prophets have come true in yet another beautiful way. A way in which GOD, through the nation of Israel, is again showing his sovereignty, mercy, and grace as we see the fig tree literally budding and blossoming as we march forward to the end of this present age!

This is wonderful, but what does this say to you and say to me? How do we keep in that fruitful place? That place of abundance and blessing where we don't have to get salted and then miraculously revived by the Lord to again be fruitful. The Gospel of John gives a key. Jesus said,

> I am the true vine, and my Father is the husbandman. Every branch in me that beareth not fruit he taketh away: [A better translation is that he lifts and cleans!] And every branch that beareth fruit, he purgeth it, [he prunes] that it may bring forth more fruit...Abide in me, and I in you. As the branch cannot bear fruit of itself, except it abide in the vine; no more can ye, except ye abide in me. I am the vine, ye are the branches: He that abideth in me, and I in him, the same bringeth forth much fruit: For without me you can do nothing.
>
> JOHN 15:1–2, 4–5

We cannot bring forth any fruit without being attached to the vine—that is, without belonging to the Lord. But more than that, the True Vine reveals that the believer who is not bearing fruit will be lifted up and cleaned by the Father and the one who bears a little fruit will be pruned so as to produce more fruit. To be lifted up and cleaned is a picture of the disciplining act of GOD that brings us to a place of fruitfulness. The pruning process pictures the point when a believer gives up needless energy and activity which may be holding him back from producing more fruit. Now the last person is the one who abides in the vine. This is the one who in the Lord produces *much* fruit.

Dear believer, get to that place of being with the Lord all of the time. That place where you walk and think alike—that Spirit-filled place. Then you will see a harvest of fruit in your life which will be apparent to all!

Can Dry Bones Live?

As we have seen, the prophet Ezekiel has much to teach us concerning the Day of the Lord and concerning the budding of the fig tree immediately prior. In the 37th chapter of his prophecy we are given a beautiful analogy concerning the revival of Israel which has partially come to pass in our life-time. The prophecy is given as a whole, for in GOD's reckoning, the events of this prophecy are simultaneous!

> The hand of the Lord was upon me, and carried me out in the spirit of the Lord, and set me down in the midst of the valley which was full of bones...and, lo, they were very dry. And he said unto me, Son of man, can these bones live?...Again he said unto me, Prophecy upon these dry bones, and say unto them, O ye dry bones, hear the word of the Lord. Thus saith the Lord GOD unto these bones; Behold, I will cause breath to enter into you, and ye shall live: And I will lay sinews upon you, and will bring flesh upon you, and cover you with skin, and put breath in you, and ye shall live; and ye shall know that I am the Lord. So I prophesied as I was commanded: And as I prophesied, there was a noise, and behold, a shaking, and the bones came together, bone to his bone. And when I beheld, lo, sinews and the flesh came upon them, and the skin covered

them above: But there was no breath in them. Then said he unto me, Prophesy unto the wind, prophesy, son of man, and say to the wind, Thus saith the Lord God; Come from the four winds, O breath, and breathe upon these slain, that they may live. So I prophesied as he commanded me, and the breath came into them, and they lived, and stood up upon their feet, and exceeding great army. Then he said unto me, Son of man, *these bones are the whole house of Israel:* (emphasis mine)

Ezekiel 37:1, 2B-3A, 4–11A

As we saw earlier, the nation would be born in one day; the fig tree would once again bud. We learned that the generation which witnessed the budding of the fig tree would not pass away until the Lord would return physically to the planet. These words of Ezekiel are just God's way of saying it in another manner!

"These bones are the whole house of Israel." We understand the scattered dry bones to be the people of the nation as they were scattered, without form or fruit in the nations of the world for the last two millennia.

Beautifully, in 1948 there was a loud noise and a shaking as the bones came together. Soon we will discuss the battle for independence that the Jews waged in that year and will see God's deliverance as nothing less powerful that when he delivered them in the days of Gideon or Jehoshaphat.

God states that along with bringing the bones back together, along with putting bone next to bone, that he would put muscle and flesh and skin upon the bones. When the Lord initially did this, Ezekiel noted that there was no breath in the revived body of Israel.

This is exactly the time in which we live today! Israel has been brought back to their Land. The bones are upon each other. They have a form. Muscle and skin are present as we see the fig tree turning green with forests and agriculture. Yet, spiritually they have no life. They have no breath. They understand not that Yeshua (Jesus) is their King.

But wonderfully, we see in Ezekiel's prophecy that God will breathe into them the breath of life. We know in Bible typology that breath (Greek: pneuma) and the Spirit are synonymous.

GOD will breathe the breath of the Spirit into them in the not to distant future.

When he does, Ezekiel went on to say,

> And I will make them one nation in the land upon the mountains of Israel; and one king shall be king to them all: And they shall be no more two nations, neither shall they be divided into two kingdoms anymore at all…And David my servant shall be king over them; and they shall have one shepherd…And they shall dwell in the land that I have given unto Jacob my servant, wherein your fathers have dwelt; and they shall dwell therein, even they, and their children, and their children's children for ever: And my servant David shall be their prince for ever.
>
> EZEKIEL 37:22A, 24A, 25

In that day, they will recognize David as their king, their shepherd and their prince. This means that they will recognize Jesus, the Son of David, as their King.

We also see that once the bones are revived, the people will dwell in the land of Jacob for ever. This tells me that the trouble we are witnessing today in Israel will *not* lead to the demise of the nation. For GOD's Word cannot lie. I wouldn't bet against Israel in these last days! Lastly, in considering the spiritual reawakening of Israel, we should look a few verses earlier to the dry bones analogy to learn what it will resemble.

> For I will take you from among the heathen, and gather you out of all countries, and will bring you into your own land. Then I will sprinkle clean water upon you, and you shall be clean [water, in typology, pictures the Spirit]…a new heart also will I give you, and a new spirit will I put within you…and I will put my spirit within you…and ye shall dwell in the land that I gave to your fathers, and ye shall be my people, and I will be your GOD.
>
> EZEKIEL 36:24–25A, 26A, 27A, 28

This is all so wonderful! The dry bones have come back and have flesh and skin upon them. We wait patiently, yet expectantly, for we know they will receive the breath of life as they recognize their King on that day not too far away!

. . . .

But there must be an application for you and me as we wait for the soon return of the Lord. We too, like Ezekiel, live in a valley of dry bones. We all know and see people who are dry, who appear alive but have no breath. Just as the Lord told Ezekiel to say to the wind, "O breath, come upon them that they may live." We too must speak to the dry bones, to the people we see in the valley of life who are in need of the Lord. We must breathe upon them the breath of life, the Word of GOD, for it is spirit and life. I need to tell people about Jesus the Christ with my words and also with my life. You do too!

A Cup of Trembling

We have seen that Israel will not again fall after her revival. The children of Jacob are to dwell in the land of their fathers for ever and ever. Yet in these days we know that Jerusalem is the flash point of a Holy War which has raged on since the revival of Israel in 1948.

As you might expect, GOD in his Word has told us this would happen.

> The burden of the word of the Lord for Israel, saith the Lord, which stretcheth forth the heavens, and layeth the foundation of the earth, and formeth the spirit of man within him. Behold, I will make Jerusalem a cup of trembling unto all people round about, when they shall be in siege both against Judah and against Jerusalem. In that day will I make Jerusalem a burdensome stone for all people: All that burden themselves with it shall be cut in pieces, though all the people of the earth be gathered together against it.
>
> ZECHARIAH 12:1–3

The context of this portion of Zechariah's prophecy is the end times. GOD's mouthpiece revealed that another sign that the

Day of the Lord was near would be that Jerusalem and Judah (Israel) would be a cup of trembling to the world.

The Lord also said that he would defend his people in that Day.

> And it shall come to pass in that day, that I will seek to destroy all the nations that come against Jerusalem.
>
> ZECHARIAH 12:9

And,

> Therefore all they that devour thee shall be devoured; and all thine adversaries, every one of them, shall go into captivity; and they that spoil thee shall be a spoil, and all that prey upon thee will I give for prey.
>
> JEREMIAH 30:16

Again,

> No weapon that is formed against thee shall prosper; and every tongue that shall rise against thee in judgment thou shalt condemn.
>
> ISAIAH 54:17A

This is indeed what we have witnessed since the birth of the nation in 1948.

Concomitant with Israel's inception on May 14, 1948 was the withdrawal of the occupying British army. As they retreated to their battleships in the port of Haifa the Arab League invaded and anticipated a quick and utter defeat of the outmanned and out-gunned Israeli freedom fighters. The Arab Grand Mufti predicted that his militia would push the Jews into the Mediterranean Sea within three days of the British departure. .

But GOD had another agenda!

Military historians to this day cannot adequately explain what happened next. After gaining the upper hand, the Arab leadership ordered a retreat from their strongholds back into Syria and

Jordan. Jewish historians tell us they were in a position to inflict a death blow to the new nation but they did not take it. This of course allowed the weaker Israelis to shore up their defenses and, as they say, the rest is history! This victory had the same ring to it as when Gideon and his three hundred men routed the Midianites in their midnight raid or the time Jehoshaphat had the priests lead his men to victory against the larger force of Edom with songs of praise. GOD was defending the children of Israel each time in a way that revealed it was by his power and will that Israel should prevail.

The next birth pang for Israel occurred in 1956. Egypt began a military buildup on Israel's frontier. The no longer passive Jewish nation invaded Egypt in response to this in the conflict known as the Suez Canal War. After the hostilities cooled to a simmer, a band-aid cease-fire was arranged by the United Nations.

An uneasy peace with many small local skirmishes along the Israeli-Syrian border followed over the next decade until 1967 when Egypt again postured against Israel by massing thousands of troops along their two borders. Again, Israel struck first in response to the threat and demonstrated this time to the world how militarily advanced she had become. Jordan mistakenly joined with Egypt and in the hugely one-sided Arab-Israeli Six Day War the two Arab nations were soundly defeated by the powerful Israeli air and ground forces. Israel took all of the Sinai from Egypt as well as the West Bank of the Jordan River from Jordan. This of course liberated all of Jerusalem into the control of the descendants of David.

An interesting aside to that campaign occurred when the Jews reached the Temple Mount in East Jerusalem which was under Jordanian control. As the men were racing to take the Mount, General Moshe Dayan ordered his men to stand down saying that One greater than he was intended to conquer that special place. This prophetic statement indeed is correct as the Temple Mount continues to be the hot spot between the two groups. Of course, one day soon the King of Kings and Lord of LORDS will ride in from heaven upon his white horse to take the site as foretold in the book of Revelation (Revelation 19:11).

In 1973, GOD again delivered his chosen people from a powerful birth pang which at the time many Christians hoped was the sign that the rapture of the church was imminent. The Egyptians and Syrians boldly attacked Israel in a masterfully organized surprise invasion on the Jewish high-holy day of Yon Kippur. The country was sleeping at the wheel with all governmental and private infrastructures at a standstill. The normally stronger Israeli army was caught off guard and nearly succumbed to the invaders. A bitter eighteen day battle with street fighting and much bloodshed ensued. Again, GOD miraculously delivered his people. Up north, in the Golan Heights, a single tank led to the retreat of an entire army of Syrian tanks and soldiers as they believed that the Jews were using a ploy with only one tank in view while thinking they were vastly outnumbered. GOD used misinformation that Syria's leaders were propagating to fool the officers on the front lines. The Syrian government, in order to gain U.N. favor, reported that Israel had advanced all the way to Damascus. This lie caused the tank commanders on the Golan to believe they were surrounded. They retreated laterally to the south which secured the victory for Israel and gained for her the strategic Golan Heights. With the Golan under her control, Israel is able to look down upon Damascus instead of having the Syrians peer into her living rooms! Meanwhile, the nations of the world feared that a nuclear exchange was imminent and much pressure was placed upon Syria and Egypt to disengage as it became clear that they had not won. It was apparent to the U.N. that Israel was prepared to take whatever means necessary to remain viable.

Disengagement agreements were signed in '73 and '74 and later in 1979 Menachem Begin and Anwar Sadat signed a peace treaty with America's President Jimmy Carter as the brokering agent. This, of course, did not please the other Arab nations. A few years later, Sadat was assassinated machine-gun style by Arab extremists during a motorcade procession in Cairo.

Meanwhile, in 1964 the Palestine Liberation Organization was formed with the express mission of the formation of an Arab state in the Land and the annihilation of the state of Israel. Their charismatic leader, Yasser Arafat, continued to stir the hatred between the people and many painful contractions persisted in the region under his charge.

Also the 70's felt three other birth pangs which continued to validate the words of Zechariah concerning Jerusalem's role as a cup of trembling to the world. First, an Israeli commercial airliner was hijacked by Islamic fighters and taken to the African nation of Uganda. The eyes of the world were focused upon the situation as the Arabs flaunted their catch. But Israel was in no mind to stand and negotiate from a position of weakness. The famous nighttime Entebbe airport raid by Israeli special-force commandos miraculously liberated her citizens while violently wiping out the hijacking militia. Again, those with eyes to see have noted that this attack was reminiscent of GOD's deliverance of his people in the Old Testament. Jonathan and his amour bearer's victory over the Philistine garrison jumps into my mind when I consider this miraculous Israeli victory!

In 1976, the Olympics were held in Munich Germany and the world witnessed a travesty against Israel by cowardly Arab extremists. While at the Olympic Village, the Jewish Olympic team was kidnapped and viciously murdered while the impotent world looked on from the Olympic stage. This event galvanized the Jewish perception that they indeed needed to stay in control of their destiny and not to count on the West for help in the defense of her people.

This mindset led to the Israeli air raid of an Iraqi nuclear facility soon thereafter and set the stage for retaliatory scud missile attacks upon Israel from Sadam Hussein during the Gulf War a decade later.

In our present day, the cup continues to tremble with suicide bombings becoming the preferred method of terror by the weaker Arabs against Zion. Also, in the near future it appears that Iran will be posturing itself against the children of Jacob. Hardly a day goes by that the conflict between Arab and Jew is not front page news. Indeed, this small strip of land (Israel) and this relatively small city (Jerusalem) have become the center of the world so to speak. In no other place are the eyes of the world so focused as leader after leader of the free world has tried to intervene to help relieve the quagmire.

We need to look again at the words of Zechariah when we consider this dilemma that the nations are trying to address. After the prophet said that Jerusalem and Judah would be a cup of trembling he also said these words of warning which seem to be going unheeded by our leaders.

> And in that day I will make Jerusalem a burdensome stone for all people: All that burden themselves with it shall be cut in pieces.
>
> ZECHARIAH 12:3A

In this context I would not relish the job as President of the United States or Secretary General of the United Nations. For all who burden themselves with the troubles of Jerusalem are destined to fail.

Later we will see that in this context, a world leader will come on the scene who will apparently have a solution to the Middle East problem. The Bible calls him "Bands" in Zechariah (Zechariah 11:7–17) and "the prince that shall come" in Daniel (Daniel 9:26b). We know him as Antichrist and he will, for a short time, seem to have an answer to the Arab-Israeli conflict.

But before that day, the Bible seems to indicate that two more birth pangs will happen prior to, or immediately with, the rapture of the church. In our analogy of GOD's dealings with mankind as a woman's pregnancy, these two events will be prior to, or concomitant with, the rupture of the membranes, the rapture, and the onset of true labor which is the Tribulation time period. Those two events are the fall of Damascus and the attack of Israel by a confederacy of nations led by Russia.

But also before I tackle these near future events I feel an application from GOD's Word is needed. GOD, in his Word, gives a blessing and a curse to all people and nations depending upon how they deal with his chosen people, Israel. It is a prophetic word for all time which I pray our nation will continue to heed. When GOD first spoke to Abram, he told him to leave his fathers house and go to a land which he would show him. He also said,

And I will make of thee a great nation, and I will bless thee, and make thy name great; and thou shalt be a blessing: *And I will bless them that bless thee, and curse him that curseth thee:* And in thee shall all families of the earth be blessed (emphasis mine).

GENESIS 12:2–3

We have seen this four thousand year-old blessing come to pass. Abraham continues to have a name that is great, and his nation has influenced the world more than any other. Of course, all of the families of the earth have been blessed because of Abraham's seed, Jesus Christ!

But of note is the blessing and curse stated in the promise to Abram. GOD said that any person or group of people that bless Abram, and by extension his descendants, would be blessed and any people who curse Israel would be cursed. Indeed, this has occurred. Throughout history, every nation that has dealt with Israel has received the rewards of their approach to the tribe of Jacob. We think of the end of the many ancient nations which have dealt harshly with Israel from Egypt to the Canaanites, Philistines and Edom to Assyria, Babylon and Persia and finally to Greece and Rome. All these early nations were clearly judged by GOD for their hatred of the Jews. In modern times we remember how Germany treated the Jews and cheered her total defeat for her many transgressions. Of course, the Arab nations continue to be cursed for their intense hatred of the Jews.

This brings me to the blessing. We recall in the days of Solomon how GOD blessed Hiram, the king of Tyre, for his willingness to help in the construction of the Temple (I Kings 5:11). Prior to that, Abimelech dealt kindly with Abraham after mistakenly thinking Sarah was only his sister. GOD blessed his people for his dealings with Abraham (Genesis 20:1–18).

In modern days we have seen this principle at work also. Great Britain was the nation that oversaw the World in the 19th Century. It was said that the sun never set upon the British Empire as she controlled nations and peoples on the four corners of the globe. She also loved the Jews in those days. The children of Israel were welcome in the lands controlled by Britain and, as a consequence, Britain flourished. God used the British foreign secretary Arthur Balfour in 1917 to facilitate the formation of Palestine as a national home for the Jews. This was called the Balfour Declaration. Thus Britain was blessed.

But unfortunately for her, she changed course!

With winds of war blowing in Europe in the late '30's, Britain, which controlled Palestine, sought to appease the Arabs by restricting Jewish immigration. During WWII she closed down the Land to the Jews of Europe allowing Hitler to run free with his "ethnic cleansing" of the Arian nations. This sin of Britain led to her downfall. Since WWII, Britain no longer is a world power. But the friend of the Jew, America, became the blessed nation. America, with all of her sins has been blessed beyond compare in the 20th Century. Most do not understand, but God's Word is clear, it's because she has blessed the Jew! America has never in its history had issues with the Jewish people. They have been embraced here and have thrived. Also, America has consistently backed the Jewish nation since it's formation in 1948. This the British did not do when they abruptly left the nation and people to the will and lust of the Arab League in 1948, as we have already discussed.

Yes, America, as she continues to stand with Israel, will be blessed. In fact, I will go on to say that because of her support of Israel, God has kept her from the destruction she otherwise would receive. Judgment due to the national disgrace of abortion, judgment due to the hedonistic lifestyle we live as we approve of things God hates such as evolution, homosexuality, pornography and tolerance of Islam while railing on the things he loves in these post-Christian days.

Unfortunately, though, we are starting to see a shift in our national approach to the Jew. Like Britain before, the influence of the enemies of Israel are beginning to have an affect. Our leaders want to please the Arabs as they control much of that commodity which we lust after. That being oil! I fear that in the days to come, America will continue to distance ourselves from Israel as we seek to appease the Arab-Islamic world in order to keep the flow of oil open to our energy consuming land! This will be to our detriment as America *will* be judged harshly once she loses GOD's protection and will likely become irrelevant as the world enters the last days!

The application for you and me? The first one should be clear! Love the Jew, pray for the nation of Israel, and pray for our nation that we continue to "get it right" in regards to our friendship towards David's descendants. And tell people who will listen, that GOD will bless us as we stand with Israel and we can expect to be cursed if we don't. Lastly, use your vote wisely. Along with a candidate's stance on abortion, also look at how he or she views Israel. It can make a difference!

As a second application, GOD told Abraham that he would bless and protect his progeny. But we understand that by faith in Jesus Christ, we too have become spiritual children of Abraham. We also can expect and have received that same blessing that GOD gave to Abraham and his clan! Like Israel, we believers in the Lord will go through tough times, for it's "not heaven till heaven" but we know that our Savior will see us through and be with us every step of the way! We can count on him for he is closer than a brother!

· · · ·

Now I promised you a look into the future as GOD tells us what soon will come to pass. That being the fate of Damascus (Syria) and the battle over oil. It will be a terrible battle between Russia and her confederates, against Israel.

The Latter Day Prophecy Against the Land of Magog

I certainly believe that the Lord could come at any time. For indeed, I see dimly and do not pretend to have GOD's timetable concerning the countdown to the rapture completely understood. But it may be that two other birth pangs still need to occur before the seven year Tribulation time frame occurs. That being the destruction of Damascus and the defeat of Russia on the mountains of Samaria, known as the West Bank. Of course, it also could be that these two events will occur nearly simultaneously with the onset of that wonderful day. Thus, I'm not going to stop looking up! Let's look at the upcoming events as the prophet Ezekiel tells the story.

We saw in chapter 36 of Ezekiel's prophecy that GOD would bring the Jews back to their homeland and that the people and the land would once again bear fruit. We have noted that this has partially come to pass as we see literal fruit growing forth on the many irrigated fields of the nation; yet, the spiritual fruit in the hearts of the people has yet to mature.

Next in chapter 37 of this wonderful book, we learned of the dry bones of Israel coming back together as a body and then receiving the breath of life. Of course, we remember that breath and spirit are synonymous in GOD's verbiage and understand that Israel will have a body before they are revived spiritually. Once again, this is the place where we are now in history. Israel has a body, they are a together and bearing literal food in abundance; however, they have not spiritually awakened to the plan of GOD for their lives.

Now we come to chapters 38 and 39 which deal with the spiritual awakening of Israel. That revival will come as they see and understand the mighty deliverance by their GOD from the hands of a powerful invader in the very near future. For we remember that in GOD's eyes these four chapters we are discussing from Ezekiel are all simultaneous end times prophecies. Again, we just find ourselves today right smack dab in the middle of the events as they unfold!

> And the word of the Lord came unto me, saying, Son of man, set thy face against Gog, the land of Magog, the chief prince of Meshech and Tubal, and prophecy against him, And say, Thus saith the Lord GOD; Behold, I am against thee, O Gog, the chief prince of Meshech and Tubal:
>
> EZEKIEL 38:1–3

The first thing GOD revealed to Ezekiel concerning this upcoming battle is the villain of our story. That nation, like Egypt before them whom GOD will use to show forth his power, is the land of Magog. We read that this Gog is the chief prince of Meshech and Tubal. What does this mean?

Well, Bible scholars have long understood this to mean the land of modern-day Russia. The word "Gog" simply means "the leader" or "the chief" and "Magog" is known to mean "the land of the far north," that of Russia. Meshech is the ancient name for Moscow and Tubal was the name for Moscow's little sister city of Tubolsk which is now called Tula.

Thus we have the major antagonist in this upcoming saga being Russia!

> And I will turn thee back, and put hooks into thy jaws, and I will bring thee forth, and all thine army, horses and horsemen,

> all of them clothed with all sorts of armor, even a great company with bucklers and shields, all of them handling swords:
>
> EZEKIEL 38:4

It's interesting to consider an ancient prophet trying to describe scenes of future events with words that didn't exist in his day. Words like tanks and rockets, AK-47's and gas masks did not exist. Thus we read of great horses and horsemen, bucklers and shields.

We learn that GOD will somehow put a hook in the jaw of the Russian leadership, Gog, and bring them forth to perform his will. It's interesting that in Old Testament days, when a nation would defeat another people, they would lead off the captives by stringing them in a line with hooks in their jaws to keep them from escaping. Truly the imagery is powerful as GOD will orchestrate this seemingly ruthless attack to show forth his glory and power as we will soon see.

Just what is this "hook" that GOD will use to mobilize Russia to attack the pleasant land? Many scholars feel the hook is oil! The people from the land of the north will seek to obtain that much needed black nectar and will conspire against Israel in order to have the enemies of the Jews, who control the oil, give that precious commodity to her!

Let's see who co-stars in this villainous plot.

> Persia, Ethiopia, and Libya with them; all of them with shield and helmet: Gomer, and all his bands; the house of Togarmah of the north quarters, and all his bands: And many people with thee.
>
> EZEKIEL 38:5–6

It's not surprising to see Persia listed. This of course is modern day Iran and Iraq. These two countries which otherwise have been enemies recently are united in their hatred for the Jews!

Ethiopia, as it is referred to in this verse, is not the poverty stricken little country in the horn of Africa, but the land south of Egypt in east-central Africa, known in our day as Sudan. In Sudan, we have another outspoken enemy of present day Israel.

Of course, it goes without saying that the Islamic nation of Libya, which today is led by its unpredictable despot Muammer Kaddaffi, will gladly join with Russia to destroy the children of Israel.

Now Gomer surprises me, but maybe it shouldn't. Gomer is Germany! What are they doing on the side of evil? Are they not in NATO? Aren't they an ally of Israel? Apparently not! In the days ahead we will see Europe, led by Germany, distance itself from Israel. Why will that be? Oil, of course! The last player mentioned is Togarmah. This speaks of modern-day Turkey.

When will this story unfold?

> After many days thou shalt be visited: In the *latter years* thou shalt come into the land that is brought back from the sword, and is gathered out of many people, against the mountains of Israel, which have always been a waste: But is brought forth out of the nations, and they dwell safely all of them (emphasis is mine).
>
> Ezekiel 38:8

Could it be any clearer? It's in the last days when this will occur. It will be in that day which we have spoken of. The time after the people have been gathered out of the nations and the land is no longer a waste. Dear reader, it's in our day today that this is going to happen! In case we missed it, God repeated himself in verse 16 as he proclaimed:

> And thou shalt come up against my people of Israel, as a cloud to cover the land; it shall be in the *latter days,* and I will bring thee against the land, that the heathen may know me, when I shall be sanctified in thee, O Gog, before their eyes (emphasis mine).
>
> Ezekiel 38:16

Apparently, this battle will open the eyes of many unbelievers after they witness the deliverance of God towards his children. Ezekiel continues with more detail.

Thou shalt ascend and come like a storm, thou shalt be like a cloud to cover the land.

EZEKIEL 38:9A

My mind pictures the locusts as they descended upon Egypt during the plagues in the days of Moses.

It shall also come to pass, that at the same time shall things come into thy mind, and thou shalt think an evil thought: And thou shall say, I will go up to the land of unwalled villages...To take a spoil, and to take a prey...

EZEKIEL 38:10B-11A, 12A

Is it a coincidence that in the dominant language of the end times that the word "spoil" rhymes with "oil?" I think not!

Sheba, and Dedan, and the merchants of Tarshish, with all the young lions thereof, shall say unto thee, Art thou come to take a spoil?

EZEKIEL 38:13A

These countries mentioned will protest this action by Russia and her allies. But that's all they will do. No help will be provided to Israel in this day of her calamity. No help that is, other than from the Lord!

So who are these impotent bystanders?

Linguists tell us that Sheba and Dedan are the nations of the Arabian Peninsula, specifically Kuwait and Saudi Arabia on today's map of the world.

Tarshish is believed to mean the isles to the far north and west, that of Great Britain. And by extension, the young lions thereof, the young lions of Tarshish, are likely an ancient Biblical reference to then unknown lion-like nation of the United States of America. A nation who we understood came forth from Tarshish. Yes, Israel's allies of Kuwait, Saudi Arabia, Great Britain and America will disapprove of this military endeavor, but apparently that's all the assistance they will provide.

Now that we have all the actors in this drama, isn't there one more major player on the world stage who is glaringly missing? That nation is Israel's modern-day enemy of Syria, known biblically as Damascus. Why is Syria not mentioned as joining with this evil confederacy? Could it be that because at the time of this invasion they no longer are relevant? Let's consider that possibility, for in Isaiah we read, "The burden of Damascus. Behold, Damascus is taken away from being a city, and it shall be a ruinous heap" (Isaiah 17:1).

This prediction, from the prophet who has hit the mark on so many other future events can also be trusted. Damascus, which brags to the nations that it is the world's oldest continuously inhabited city, will indeed become a ruinous heap. GOD told Isaiah to reveal this future event and thus we know beyond a shadow of a doubt that this will come to pass. Damascus will be destroyed.

It is very likely that somehow Syria will fade in prominence before the day of Russia's invasion of Israel. Thus, they are not included in the list of players in this end-times scenario.

Another theory as to what the "hook" is that GOD will use to bring in this Russian confederacy may be the destruction of Damascus at the hands of Israel. Could it be that Israel will somehow be forced to take out their ancient enemy? Could it be that the prophesied destruction of Damascus, as yet to be fulfilled from Isaiah's words, will be the hook that brings down the Russian coalition? I don't know! We'll just have to wait and see!

> And it shall come to pass at the same time when Gog shall come against the land of Israel, saith the Lord GOD, that my fury shall come up in my face.
>
> EZEKIEL 38:18

I would *never* want to see GOD's fury come up in his face!

> For in my jealousy and in the fire of my wrath have I spoken, Surely in that day there shall be a great shaking in the land of Israel...and I will plead [judge] against him with pestilence and with blood; and I will rain upon him, and upon his bands, and upon the many people that are with him, an overflowing

rain, and great hailstones, fire, and brimstone...and I will turn thee back, and will leave but the sixth part of thee...and I will smite the bow out of thy left hand, and will cause thine arrows to fall out of thy right hand. Thou shalt fall upon the mountains of Israel, thou, and all thy bands, and the people that is with thee.

Ezekiel 38:19, 22; 39:2a, 3–4a

When Russia and her minions cover the land like a storm, the Lord God reveals that there will be a terrible shaking in the land and that nearly 85% of the attacking army will fall in Israel as an overflowing rain of fire and brimstone overtakes that attacking army. Is this talking about a nuclear retaliation by Israel or is this describing an earthquake and heavenly judgment towards Russia in a vein similar to the fire and brimstone which Sodom and Gomorrah received? I don't know. But whatever scenario, Russia and her allies will be utterly defeated in a most dramatic manner!

It will be a demonstration of power which will also have two very positive effects.

First, it will cause the nations to acknowledge the Lord, and secondly the house of Israel will have the Holy Spirit poured upon them.

Let's look at the first of God's words.

Thus will I magnify myself, and sanctify myself; and I will be known in the eyes of many nations, and they shall know that I am the Lord.

Ezekiel 38:23

God will sanctify himself. That means he will set himself apart from other so-called Gods with his rescue of Israel. Those Gods on the scene today are nothing when compared to the God of the universe. Those Gods being the God of the crescent moon, Allah, and the God of prosperity, Wall Street!

The Lord stated that the nations will know that he is God. That he is the One who is in control of the fate of men and of nations.

This verse reminds me of the day that GOD's prophet to the backsliding nation of Israel in the Old Testament, Elijah, called down fire from heaven to consume the water-soaked sacrifice. What did the people do and say? "And when all the people saw it, they fell on their faces: And they said, The Lord, he is GOD; the Lord, he is GOD" (I Kings 18:39).

Secondly, along with GOD receiving the glory in the eyes of the heathen, this foretold event will be the time that GOD will pour his Spirit upon Israel. It will mark the time that the dry bones which we discussed earlier will receive breath.

> Then shall they know that I am the Lord their GOD, which caused them to be led into captivity among the heathen: But I have gathered them unto their own land, and have left none of them any more there. Neither will I hide my face any more from them: For I have *poured out my spirit upon the house of Israel*, saith the Lord GOD (emphasis is mine).
>
> EZEKIEL 39:28–29

In that day the entire nation will receive spiritual eyes. They will finally see with eyes which comprehend GOD's plan for their nation and their lives.

It will resemble the day when Elisha's servant had his eyes opened. That day when the Syrians were surrounding Dothan, the village where Elisha abode, and that servant feared how things would occur. Elisha prayed and asked GOD to open his eyes to see spiritually. And what happened? Instead of seeing the city compassed about only by Syrian horses and chariots, he saw that the mountain surrounding the Syrians was full of heavenly horses and chariots of fire (II Kings 6:8–17).

Yes, just as that servant pictures the nation, Israel will receive spiritual understanding of GOD's plan for them, his love for them, and his promised protection for them.

No, it's still not at this time that they understand Yeshua as their Messiah, that will come a few years later during the Tribulation time frame, but at this time they will understand that Jehovah's covenant with them cannot be broken!

So what does this say to me and to you when we find ourselves in a backslidden state? Look at Israel. They too were GOD's love. But they fell away and seemed to have been swallowed up by the world around them. They were seemingly without GOD in their lives. They were despondent and pathetic. Persecuted and beaten down. And then GOD intervened and rescued them. That's what he promises to you and me also. When you are that wondering little lamb that left the other ninety-nine, our Lord said that he, as the Good Shepherd, will seek you out. He will find you and bring you home!

Lastly, I would like to amplify upon the timing of this battle. It certainly sounds like something which would occur only during the terrible days of the Great Tribulation. I mean, come on! Blood flowing upon the mountains of Samaria, otherwise known as the Valley of Megiddo or Armageddon! Five sixths of the attacking army being wiped out by fire and brimstone! Could this really be a battle that occurs *before* the seven year Tribulation time frame?

Well, the narrative gives some information which makes it seem that if it's not before the Rapture and the Tribulation it most certainly will be at the very onset of this time. We are told that after the battle the people of Israel will be burning the contaminated weapons of their defeated enemy for seven years (Ezekiel 39:9).

We understand that the Lord will return from heaven seven years after the onset of the Tribulation. Thus, it would seem that this battle must at the onset of Jacob's Trouble, if not before, since it seems very implausible that the Jews will be concerned with cleaning up the mess of the Russian defeat after their Messiah comes to make things right in this world. Of course, this is only conjecture. It may be that this event is much later in the end-times scenario and that indeed the clean-up will continue into the Millennial Kingdom that Jesus will come back to set up.

• • • •

With our discussion of the battle over Jerusalem completed we leave the signs of the times that Israel reveals concerning the end of the age. We perceive that the world's thirst for oil may be the trigger of this latter-day military campaign. We understand that *we* are the generation that has witnessed the fig tree putting forth her leaves. We can comprehend that Israel has come back as a nation on the very day foretold by the prophets. We have witnessed the nation become agriculturally fruitful and that the dry bones now have a body. We have heard the pure language spoken in the land and we read every day in the news that, indeed, in these last days, Jerusalem has become a cup of trembling to all the people round about. But there are several more signs, birth pangs, if you will, which the Bible speaks of concerning the very soon Day of the Lord.

Let me tell you about the Days of Noah!

Like † he Days of Noah

But as the days of Noah were, so shall also the coming of the
Son of man be.

MATTHEW 24:37

The speaker, of course, was Jesus. He had just revealed to Peter,
James, and Andrew the parable of the fig tree and concluded that
truth with the statement that the *exact* day and hour of the end
is known only by the Father. But this very next statement is yet
another truth concerning the times of the end of this Age. The
Revealer of Secrets proclaimed that the days prior to his return
would resemble the days of Noah!

We need to turn back to Genesis chapter 6 to understand
just how the days of Noah appeared; however, I must warn you.
Even though this account was over four thousand years ago, it
will sound disturbingly like today! Four things will jump out of
the narrative which are present today and which have not been
present since those days of Noah. Those days prior to GOD's first
judgment of the world, otherwise known as the Flood!

First, there was a population explosion.

> And it came to pass, when men began to *multiply* on the face
> of the earth (emphasis is mine).
>
> GENESIS 6:1A

Genesis chapter 5 speaks of the generations of Adam. We are informed that humans lived long, long lives in those days. Thus, with a person's reproductive potential spread out over hundreds of years it is easy to see that over the next ten generations leading to Noah, literally many millions of people populated the planet. After the Flood the population has been much less. That is, of course, until the last century. We have been part of a skyrocketing population explosion that even has dwarfed the multiplication of people that occurred leading up to Noah's day. Indeed, in our day men are again multiplying on the face of the earth.

Secondly, in Noah's Day there was sexual confusion.

> There were giants in the earth in those days; and also after
> that, when the sons of GOD came in after the daughters of
> men, and they bare children to them, the same became mighty
> men which were of old, men of renown.
>
> GENESIS 6:4

This difficult verse needs a translator into modern English. I'll give it my best shot, but I'm sure there are nuances to it that I don't understand. The "giants" in the earth in those days is better translated "fallen ones." This chapter is talking about evil and rebellion, about judgment and salvation; the "giants" of Noah's day are better understood as fallen ones in wickedness!

Bible teachers are divided on the term "sons of GOD." Some have said that this is Seth's line or Seth's descendants. Along with that, they say that "the daughters of men" are the evil progeny of Cain. Thus, we have good and evil uniting in an unholy matrimony much like we discussed with the church in Pergamos. Believers and unbelievers being unequally yoked in marriage. We understand that GOD hates this type of union. No, the unbeliever doesn't often get lifted up, but the believer is nearly always taken down in this type of unholy marriage!

The second view I've heard from the pulpit is that the "sons of GOD" are devils and the "daughters of men" are human beings. Thus, in this interpretation of the verse, we have devils joining sexually with humans in a sort of Hollywood science fiction horror scenario creating a new race of "mighty men." These mighty men of renown are further translated to be mighty men of wickedness. In this interpretation, it is said that GOD clearly needed to destroy mankind as the mixing of unredeemable devils with redeemable mankind was unacceptable to the Creator.

Jude sheds some light to this second view as in verse 6 of his epistle he makes an illusion to these sons of GOD or fallen ones.

> And the angels which kept not their first estate, but left their own habitation, he hath reserved in everlasting chains under darkness unto the judgment of the great day.
>
> JUDE 6

Angels leaving their first estate seems to correlate with the theory of devils joining with women sexually. The resultant judgment from GOD was severe. Mankind was wiped out in the Flood and the devils involved in that fornication were and are kept in a dark and cramped place awaiting the judgment of the last day. It is taught that these extremely evil devils which were involved in this sexual aberration are not allowed to roam the Earth as do other devils. It is further taught that in the Tribulation time period these angels, under the command of one called Apollyon ("Destroyer," in English), will be released for a short time from the bottomless pit to cover and devour the Earth much like a swarm of locusts. (Revelation 9:1–11).

So, back to the Days of Noah. We can begin to see that in his day some sort of bizarre sexual activity occurred which had not been witnessed before. A new race may have been germinating which did not come from the union of man and woman. Certainly, it doesn't take much imagination to understand that a sexual deviation of unprecedented scale is present again today. This calls our generation in similitude to Noah's day. But also we now have a "new thing" in the modern picture. It's called cloning! Could it be that the cloning of humans is the thing that makes

our generation compare to the Days of Noah? A new and different line of men which resemble the mighty men of old! I don't
know, but it could be! After a population explosion and a time of
sexual depravity we come to the third similarity between our day
and Noah's.

> And GOD saw that the wickedness of man was great in the
> earth, and that every imagination of the thoughts of his heart
> was only evil continually.
>
> GENESIS 6:5

Wow! That sounds terrible. Every imagination and thought
was toward evil continually!

As bad as that sounds, we see this again today. Many have
become so dark and depraved that all their waking time is spent
considering evil. Whether due to the influence of drugs or of the
occult or due to the love of money or power, men and women
have given themselves over to every evil imagination in our day,
too! Just like the days of Noah!

The last similitude is the scope of violence upon the face of
the Earth.

> And GOD said unto Noah, The end of all flesh is come before
> me; for the earth is filled with violence through them; and
> behold; I will destroy them with the earth.
>
> GENESIS 6:13

In Noah's day they didn't just have pockets of violence here
and there but the Bible declares that the Earth was filled with
violence. It overflowed with violence. Of course, this is again
the case. Not since the days of Noah has the struggle of man
against man, tribe against tribe, nation against nation been so
pronounced. The violence present in our day also suggests that
these days are like the days of Noah!

Thus, Jesus' words should be clear. Just as judgment came in
the days of Noah, so too will judgment come upon this generation. The flood of Noah, as we have stated previously, is a picture
of the seven year Tribulation (II Peter 2: 4–9).

But as the days of Noah were, so shall also the coming of the Son of man be. For as in the days that were before the flood they were eating and drinking, marrying and giving in marriage, until the day that Noah entered into the ark, And knew not until the flood came, and took them all away; so shall also the coming of the Son of man be.

MATTHEW 24:37–39

Thankfully, Paul told us not to walk in the dark, but to walk in the light (I Thessalonians 5:4–6). Those who want to follow GOD's Word don't have to be in the dark concerning the times in which we live. We are to be sober, looking for our Savior's blessed return.

It's the last days little children! The Lord's coming is near!

Next, we come to the days of Lot. We will learn that our day unfortunately resembles his day also. And once again we will recall that judgment from our Maker was quickly sent forth as a result of the sins of the days of Lot. For just as the flood of Noah pictures the Tribulation, so does the judgment of Sodom and Gomorrah!

Like ✝ he Days of Lot

And when he was demanded of the Pharisees, when the
kingdom of GOD should come, he answered them and said...
Behold, the kingdom of GOD is within you. And he said unto
his disciples, The days will come when ye shall desire to see one
of the days of the Son of man and ye shall not see it...And as
it was in the days of Noah, so shall it be also in the days of the
Son of man. They did eat, they drank, they married wives, they
were given in marriage, until the day that Noah entered into
the ark, and the flood came, and destroyed them all. Likewise
also as it was in the days of Lot; they did eat, they drank, they
bought, they sold, they planted, they builded; But the same day
that Lot went out of Sodom it rained fire and brimstone from
heaven, and destroyed them all. Even thus shall it be in the day
when the Son of man is revealed.

LUKE 17:20A, 21B-22, 26–30

The setting of these famous words of our Lord is different than
the location of his words given in our previous chapter. For in
the last chapter, when the Prophet spoke of the days of Noah,
he was only speaking to Peter, James, John, and Andrew from
the Mount of Olives after leaving the temple during the week of
his Passion (Mark 13:38). Here, he is on his way to Jerusalem as

the first part of chapter 17 notes, and he was challenged to speak of the end times by some Pharisees who were traveling along with the entourage going up to that fateful Passover feast. In this discourse, not only did Jesus compare the time leading up to the end to the days of Noah, but he also likened the pre-Tribulation period to the days of Lot.

As we remember, Lot was the nephew of Abraham. He, along with Abraham and Abraham's father, Terah, left the land of the Chaldees (modern-day Iraq) and traveled to the Promised Land (Genesis 11:31–32; 12:4–5). There, both Abraham and Lot prospered to the point where they needed to separate. It seemed that their flocks were unable to coexist together. The Bible tells us that Abraham allowed his nephew to pick between the land of Canaan (Israel) and the land of the plain of Jordan (the land on the east side and adjacent to the Dead Sea). We learn that Lot chose the latter as he saw that it was a beautiful land which was lush and well watered (Genesis 13:5–13). We are told that in the time before GOD destroyed the area that it was as the garden of the Lord. It was like Eden! Certainly, since the destruction of Sodom and Gomorrah, the area around the Dead Sea can no longer be called lush and green. Such is the result of losing GOD's blessing and protection. Beauty to ashes, abundance to poverty, as the result of sin!

So Lot pitched his tent toward Sodom and soon we find that he was sitting in the gate of Sodom. For when the angels came to destroy the cities, as described in Genesis 19, they found Lot at the gate. This means that Lot became a leader in the community.

Unfortunately for Lot, after stating that the plain of Jordan was beautiful, the Bible has nothing good to say about Sodom.

> But the men of Sodom were wicked and sinners before the LORD exceedingly.
>
> GENESIS 13:13

It got so bad that after GOD told Abraham that he intended to destroy Lot's home of Sodom, Abraham challenged the Creator of the universe to spare the city if only ten righteous could be found. God said he would if there were but ten in the city. Of course, we learned as chapter 18 concluded that there were not even ten righteous souls in the doomed city.

After Lot met the two angels at the gate of the city he constrained them to lodge with him for the night as was the custom in that day.

> But before they lay down, the men of the city, even the men of Sodom, compassed the house round, both old and young, all the people from every quarter: And they called unto Lot, and said unto him, Where are the men which came in to thee this night? Bring them out unto us, that we may know them.
>
> Genesis 19:4–5

The Bible is not stating that all the men, both young and old wanted to meet the visitors. What this means is that they wanted to have sexual intercourse with these two new men from out of town! Men having sex with men. Men raping men! This is how sickening the city had become!

But no, it gets even worse.

> And Lot went out at the door unto them...And said, I pray you, brethren, do not so wickedly. Behold now I have two daughters which have not known man; let me, I pray you, bring them out unto you, and do ye to them as is good in your eyes: Only unto these men do nothing, for therefore came they under the shadow of my roof.
>
> Genesis 19:6A, 7–8

Lot was willing to sacrifice his two virgin daughters to appease the lust of the men of Sodom. How terrible was that! But in that day the protection of a guest was considered of greater importance than the protection of one's own family.

We read in the next verse that the sexually enraged men would not accept the sacrifice of Lot's daughters but only wanted to satisfy their lust in having sex with the men visiting Lot. At this point Lot would have been injured had not angels used their heavenly powers to pull him back into the house while simultaneously smiting the attackers with blindness.

So we understand that the men of Sodom, and by extension the men of Gomorrah, had come to the point that sex with other men was the preferred outlet for their sexual tension. The term for this act, sodomy, of course is derived from this biblical account.

Now, before we compare the days of Lot to our day we should establish what GOD has to say about sodomy.

> Thou shall not lie with mankind, as with womankind: It is an abomination.
>
> LEVITICUS 18:22

And,

> If a man also lie with mankind, as he lieth with a woman, both of them have committed an abomination: They shall surely be put to death;
>
> LEVITICUS 20:13A

GOD is clear in proscribing against sodomy. He states that the sodomite will surely die. And, indeed, that is what always happens. When men leave their natural desire for women, something dies within.

Paul put it this way in the Book of Romans.

> Professing themselves to be wise, they became fools...Wherefore GOD also gave them up to uncleanness through the lusts of their own hearts, to dishonor their own bodies between themselves...For even their women did change the natural use into that which is against nature: And likewise also the men, leaving their natural use of the woman, burned in their lust one toward another; men with men working that which is unseemly, and receiving in themselves that recompence of their error which was meet.
>
> ROMANS 1:22, 24, 26B-27

So we learn that homosexuality is the result of pride! Professing to be wise they became fools. The same original sin that brought Lucifer down to hell is able, when properly germinated, to bring men and women to the place of losing their desire for heterosexual relationships!

Thus, in considering the sin of Sodom, that of homosexuality, why does the Lord single it out as such a major indicator of his soon return? After all, homosexuality has always been with us! The Bible is full of references to sodomy in the Old Testament as are ancient secular historical accounts. So what's so different about today?

Well in the past, except for this account of perversion from Sodom that we've just reviewed, sodomy was something that generally was done behind closed doors. It was an embarrassment at the least and completely taboo at the most. No man or woman wanted others to know of their lifestyle. All cultures inherently understood that sodomy was wrong. Often, homosexuals suffered terrible inner strife as the lust of their flesh continued to take them to that awful place.

Not so today! In our day, the term sodomy, which of course is associated with evil, is the embarrassment and is taboo, not the act! We call it an alternate lifestyle or a non-heterosexual relationship. It's not so bad! It's sanitized! It's tolerated, accepted, and in most large cities it's even embraced!

That's why our day is like the days of Lot. Not because we have rampant homosexuality everywhere...that's always been the case. But because we embrace the gay lifestyle as being equal to heterosexuality, just as they did in Sodom.

And just as GOD was quick to judge Sodom and Gomorrah, he will be quick to judge this world. For we understand that the days of the Son of Man include the Great Tribulation—that time when GOD pours out his wrath on a Christ-rejecting, sinful world in an attempt to have many wake up and call upon Jesus as their Lord.

• • • •

But there is more to this analogy than just the sin of sodomy. For Jesus stated that, as in the days of Lot, the people were eating and drinking; they were buying and selling, they were planting and building.

At no time in history have humans enjoyed so much abundance. Truly we are gluttons in eating and drunkards from drink. At no time in the world's history has the economy been so huge! More wealth is exchanged on the stock markets of the planet in a single day now than even existed one hundred years ago. Indeed, we are buying and selling to a degree that is remarkable!

And planting and building. Well, the earth has never brought forth so abundantly. Science has taken agriculture to a new level that is only matched by the incredible building boom that is occurring on every inhabitable continent on Earth.

Yes, Jesus' words, which on the surface seem so benign, actually are pregnant with meaning!

But Ezekiel reveals another set of problems which Sodom had which should be considered when we compare that day to today.

> Behold, this was the iniquity of thy sister, Sodom, pride, fullness of bread, and abundance of idleness was in her and in her daughters, neither did she strengthen the hand of the poor and needy. And they were haughty, and committed abomination before me: Therefore I took them away as I saw good.
>
> EZEKIEL 16:49–50

Along with the abomination we have discussed, the inhabitants of Sodom were haughty, had no want for food, were lazy and had no compassion. Again, as Paul pointed out in Romans, one direction pride can take the soul down is the road to depravity.

The phrase "fullness of bread" is important when I consider Jesus as he is the bread of life. When I am full with the food of the world I am not hungry for Jesus. Sodom had lost all desire for spiritual food.

GOD told Adam that the ground would be cursed for his own sake (Genesis 3:17). That is, GOD was stating that working the "cursed" ground would ultimately be a blessing in light of man's sin nature which entered into all of us at the time of Adam's sin. In other words, due to our sin nature, working would help keep my mind from evil imaginations. It would help us from taking the road to depravity. Here in Sodom, it would appear that the land was like the garden of the Lord. It brought forth abundantly and the men became idle. This, of course, contributed to their demise spiritually.

Lastly, the people of Sodom did not strengthen the hand of the poor and needy. It is said that if you walk a mile in my shoes you will better understand my plight. There is a fellowship among sufferers. When I come to that place of gluttonous abundance, I can lose my empathy and compassion for those less fortunate. Truly, in the flesh, the place that the men of Sodom found themselves in was a very dangerous place!

As I look at Europe and America, I see the same set of variables present. In the West, our haughtiness and pride overflows. We are the "me" generation. It's rule by the individual as individual's rights take precedence over the will of the majority. Idleness is the goal now. We have four-day weekends and airport gridlock as we all indulge in our abundant free time. Those less fortunate have become invisible. Swept aside and out of our conscience as we continue to eat, drink and be merry! It's just as Jesus said: They did eat, they drank, and they married right until the time Noah entered the ark.

And that's really the point of our Lord's comments to his listeners on that road to Jerusalem. Just as in the days of Noah and Lot, many will be unaware of the upcoming judgment. Millions of lost souls today have no idea that we are living in the last days! My heart cries out as I consider their upcoming demise as our world enters the labor pains that will invariably come before the delivery of the baby!

Note also, the Teacher clearly makes the association in both of these stories that on the *very* day that Noah entered the ark and the *very* day that Lot was pulled out of Sodom judgment came down. So too, I believe that on the very day that we are called home, that day of the rapture of the church, the Tribulation time frame will begin. Can I be dogmatic? Of course not! But it would seem when looking at these two pictures of the Tribulation that as soon as the righteous were delivered out of harms way, rains of water and fire came down.

Next we come to the great wisdom of the world. It too is a powerful sign of the Lord's imminent return!

Professing themselves to be wise, they became fools.
ROMANS 1:22

Knowledge Shall Be Increased

Many would agree that the Prophet Daniel may have received the most abundant and wide ranged revelation of any man other than the God-man, Jesus the Christ. Daniel's interpretation of King Nebuchadnezzar's disturbing dream introduced the world to the four world powers which would sequentially reign from his day forward until the God of Heaven will set up a kingdom which will have no end (Daniel 2:1–49). He also correctly interpreted the terrifying handwriting upon King Belshazzar's palace wall during that sacrilegious feast the night before the Medes and Persians toppled Babylon (Daniel 5:1–31). Later in Daniel's life, he was given several dreams of his own which have spoken prophetically. He dreamt of those same four world powers of Nebuchadnezzar's dream, not as body parts of a huge statue, but as four carnivorous animals. Daniel lived to see the first two world powers, that of Babylon and of Medio-Persia. Those two were the head and arms of Nebuchadnezzar's dream and the lion and the bear of his own, but chapter 11 of his inspired book gives incredible detail of the next world power to come. That third world power was Greece. The Greek dynasty of Alexander the Great as well as the four lesser kings after Alexander and the subsequent Ptolemaic and Seleucid reigns are given in such prophetic detail that the skeptic scholar of ancient history can only conclude that Daniel must have been written in New Testament times!

Daniel spoke extensively of the first coming of the Messiah. Indeed, in chapter 9 we discussed how the Jews were told that there would be four hundred eighty-three years from the command to restore and rebuild Jerusalem until Messiah, the Prince, would come. As we noted, the Jews missed this prediction causing our Lord to weep over the city as they understood not the day of their visitation which Daniel had so accurately prophesied.

Thus, with so much documented accuracy concerning prophetic events predicted by Daniel, through the Spirit of GOD, which have already happened, we can be assured of his words concerning the things of which he spoke which are still to come. Specifically, Daniel has much to say about the evil exploits of a yet future king, the one we understand to be Antichrist. Thus, when we come to mankind's time of travail, that of the Tribulation time period, we will look at Daniel's words concerning this satanically-possessed ruler. Also in chapter 12, Daniel gave a timetable for some of the events of the Tribulation leading up to the return of Messiah again for his people. Hopefully, the children of Israel will not miss the prophetic word this time when the day of its fulfillment arrives.

Lastly, though, near the end of Daniel's revelation we are given a clue to the appearance of the days leading up to the end-times prophecies of which he spoke so extensively. In one verse, Daniel encapsulates how the days before the Tribulation will appear. In other words, Daniel reveals yet another aspect of the days in which we live in right now! Those days of false labor, the days of the budding of the fig tree and the days of Noah and of Lot which we have considered.

Let's look at his words,

> But thou, O Daniel, shut up the words, and seal the book, even to the time of the end: Many shall run to and fro, and knowledge shall be increased.
>
> DANIEL 12:4

The Lord revealed to Daniel that the words of his prophecy

would not be understood until the time of the end. This is indeed what has happened. Ancient scholars understood little of Daniel's words, yet scholars today can see the marvelous prophetic detail just as God said would happen in this verse.

The revelation that in the days leading up to the end, that many would run to and fro, is very interesting. In Daniel's day, people would travel on foot or, if they were wealthy, they would ride a horse. Most people would never venture more than five or ten miles away from the home of their birth. Things remained pretty much the same as time marched on to Jesus' day. Travelers were still walking on foot with the occasional trip of thirty or forty miles to celebrate in Jerusalem. Over the next nineteen hundred years transportation improved but would still be considered a snail's pace by today's standards. To travel to a far country would take weeks and months by boat or over land. And those weeks and months were often times filled with danger and tragedy!

Not so today! In our day, if I want to go the Jerusalem, I can get on a plane. In less than 24 hours, I'm standing in front of the Western Wall! Hawaii is just five hours away and I can go to Chicago in three! Indeed the speed of travel over this last generation has logarithmically increased. We are running just as Daniel predicted.

A logarithmic increase in the number of travelers can also be understood as fulfilling Daniel's prophecy. One hundred years ago, only the very wealthy and those wanting to start a new life somewhere else were hitting the road. Not so in our day. The masses are traveling from here to there in search of pleasure, the pursuit of work or just to visit relatives. Many are running to and fro! Certainly Daniel could not have understood just what he was speaking of when he predicted this but as we look upon it with hindsight it is wonderfully full of richness for us to consider!

Next, we are told that knowledge shall be increased in the last days. But just what is knowledge? Is it the same as truth or wisdom? Of course not! Knowledge is the same as facts. It's different from truth, which is wisdom applied. Truth is eternal, knowledge is temporal.

Indeed, educators tell us that the body of knowledge remained static for most of the world's history. Pockets of increased knowledge were seen in the ancient Orient, as well as Egypt and Greece. Of course, the Jews were given more than knowledge from the Revealer of Secrets, but, for the most part, little increase in the facts of the world was noted. A doubling of the planet's knowledge occurred in the second half of the second millennium after Christ. Science started to be taken seriously as the likes of Galileo and Newton were speaking forth. Then the twentieth century arrived and the collective knowledge of the world took off like a rocket! Industry arrived, mathematics and physics blossomed and then the computer chip was introduced. The doubling time of the knowledge of the world is now measured in decades, years and months instead of centuries and eras. We all lament that the things we learned just a few years ago are often out of date and irrelevant as the explosion of knowledge just marches forward!

Also along with the explosion of knowledge has come a revolution in the access to information in our century. First it was radio, then TV and now it's the Internet and CNN. Everyone has instant access to news and information! In fact, now that the world-wide network is in place, the entire planet is ripe to be controlled by that charismatic false leader which will hypnotize the world with his charm and words of peace and safety in the days to come! Yes, knowledge has increased just as Daniel so accurately predicted.

Unfortunately, though, a high price has been paid for this increase in knowledge. There is so much material for our youth to learn and absorb that they often miss out on the important "facts" of life. The wisdom that only comes from slowing down and learning truth!

Yes, our world has created an educational monster which can blind us from noting truth as we fill our minds with temporal and trivial pursuits. Again, Paul noted it well when he said of those who do not understand GOD's eternal truth: that they are ever learning but never coming to the knowledge of the truth!

I pray that that not be true for you, dear reader. Take time to smell the roses, to hear that still small voice of the Lord. Slow down and get quiet. The Lord will not often shout at you. If you want to know the truth you won't find it on Leno or at Tinsel Town. It won't be found on the Internet or seen on World News Tonight. But it is present on the pages of the greatest book ever written, and it will come to your heart and mind as you meditate upon the words that you read and which are spoken to your heart.

Don't settle on being a fact finder but become a "true" knowledge seeker!

We are now at our last stop before the water breaks. Yes, we are about to examine the rapture of the Church which will bring in the labor and delivery of our world. But first we should understand how the people of the world will view those followers of the Lord Jesus Christ in the days leading up to the end.

Scoffers in The Last Days

Knowing this first, that there shall come in the last days scoffers, walking after their own lusts, And saying, Where is the promise of his coming? For since the fathers fell asleep, all things continue as they were from the beginning of creation.

II PETER 3:3–4

The third chapter of Peter's 2nd epistle is pregnant with truth for the man or woman who desires to consider the days in which we live as well as the days to come. But the very first thing Jesus' fiery disciple reveals about the end times is that there will be scoffers. He tells us that there will be naysayers who will taunt those of us looking to and longing for our Lord's return by pointing out that since the beginning of time everything has been the same. And, of course, that is exactly what the world and even some of the church is saying. They laugh, thinking the Evangelical Christians must be crazy. Those fundamentalists Christians of every century since Christ have been telling us he would return soon, and look, everything just stays the same!

Indeed, those mocking words can affect the believer's faith! I've been looking to meet the Lord in the air since 1973 when I first came to realize the signs of the times which were present in that decade. After I learned that I needed a Savior in March of that year, Israel was invaded by Syria and Jordan in the Yom Kippur War. Christians everywhere were hoping that Jesus would come in the clouds in those days. After all, many of the things we have discussed had occurred. Israel had returned as a nation, the fig tree had budded, and she certainly was a "cup of trembling" to the nations. I was just *so* thankful that I had learned of Jesus before it was too late for me. I really believed at that time that it was going to be any day!

Then the Lord didn't return that year. Furthermore, he didn't come back during the Gulf War of the early '90's when Saddam Hussein's SCUD missiles were raining down on Jerusalem. Nor did he come to get us at the start of the new millennium! No, things have pretty much stayed the same in my lifetime. Maybe I don't really understand GOD's prophetic words concerning the end! Woe is me!

But, praise be to GOD, as I read these words of the Apostle Peter! He tells me that these *very* scoffers are also a sign that the Day of the Lord is near! By their scoffing at the belief that the rapture of the church is near, they indeed are fulfilling prophecy.

Jude states the same truth in these words,

> But, beloved, remember ye the words which were spoken before of the apostles of our LORD Jesus Christ; How they told you there should be mockers in the last time, who should walk after their own unGODly lusts.
>
> JUDE 17–18

Jude uses the exact same Greek word as Peter did in describing those who would decry the eminent return of the Lord in the last days. They are "empaiktes." Interestingly, these two uses of "empaiktes" are the only two times in the entire Bible that this word is used! I wonder if GOD wants to make a point here in reserving this word for only this topic. You may remember that the number two in the Bible signals GOD's emphasis. When GOD repeats himself, he is establishing a truth. Whether it be Pharaoh's dream which was doubled (Genesis 41:32) or the truth that in the last days there will be scoffers, that there will be mockers!

The reason Jude says the world will mock the believer who hopes for the soon return of his Lord is so that they can continue to walk in their unGoᴅly lusts! That's it! If I am looking forward to Jesus' soon return it gets a bit harder to walk in sin—to follow hard after my flesh. A man is not very likely to sleep with his neighbor's wife if he knows the husband is due to return at any minute! So it is for me. As I continue to look towards the Lord's eminent return it cleanses my fallen mind from many of those evil desires which would otherwise pop in there! Unfortunately, those who have decided to let the flesh rule in their lives must deny the soon return of the Lord as a protective mechanism for their own mental health. They want to walk in their own unGoᴅly lusts and, thus, cannot accept that they may soon be held accountable for their choices. That's why they scoff and mock!

Paul has important words to be considered as he shares his heart to his young protégé Timothy,

> Now the Spirit speaketh expressly, that in the latter times some shall depart from the faith, giving heed to seducing spirits, and speaking doctrines of devils; Speaking lies in hypocrisy...
>
> I Tɪᴍᴏᴛʜʏ 4:1–2ᴀ

Also to Timothy,

> This know also, that in the last days perilous times shall come. For men shall be lovers of their own selves, covetous, boasters, proud, blasphemers, disobedient to parents, unthankful, unholy, without natural affection, trucebreakers, false accusers, incontinent, fierce, despisers of those that are good, traitors, heady, highminded, lovers of pleasure more than lovers of Goᴅ; Having a form of Goᴅliness, but denying the power thereof: From such turn away.
>
> II Tɪᴍᴏᴛʜʏ 3:1–5

Truly, the heart condition of those who will mock will not be good! They have departed from the faith and are listening to, and speaking forth, a doctrine that is from hell itself. They love themselves and their pleasure more than Goᴅ and this leads to the seventeen other evil traits that they display.

Indeed, in our day we have seen these prophecies come to pass! From inside and outside of the so called "church" we see the New Age philosophy that we are all Gods. This is the same lie that the Serpent told Eve—that she could be like God!

We also see a form of Godliness displayed in this latter day religion and philosophy but sadly there is no power.

Paul's words of exhortation apply to you and me. "From such turn away," he says. Realize what is going on in our day as we approach the End but don't get sucked in to this mentality that is so pervasive in our day. Turn away from it! Don't look at it!

· · · ·

Next consider with me, the words of Peter after he proclaims the coming of the latter day scoffers.

> For this they willingly are ignorant of, that by the word of God the heavens were of old, and the earth standing out of water and in the water: Whereby the world that was then was, being overflowed with water, perished:
>
> II Peter 3:5–6

He correctly points out that something similar to the end times has *already* occurred and they willingly have dismissed this sign! Peter correctly reveals that the flood of Noah typifies the judgment which will come upon the world on the Day of the Lord.

Everyone has heard of the Flood. But do the scoffers believe it really happened? Of course not! If they did, then they would have to accept that something like that could happen again. Something like what those fundamentalist teach could actually happen!

Peter goes on to say that indeed it will. Only this time it won't be water doing the cleaning, it will be fire!

> But the heavens and the earth, which are now, by the same word are kept in store, reserved unto fire against the day of judgment and perdition of unGodly men.
>
> II Peter 3:7

So there it is, dear mocked believer. In the last days there will be those who laugh at you for the hope that is within your heart. Don't let it bring you down! Feel sorry for the scoffers and keep speaking truth in grace as did our Lord. But rejoice when you hear the naysayers as they are fulfilling Bible prophecy!

Lastly, before we leave Peter's wonderful words of comfort for those who look for the Lord's Return, we must consider *why* it seems that the Lord is taking his time in coming back for us.

> But, beloved, be not ignorant of this one thing, that one day is with the LORD as a thousand years, and a thousand years as one day.
>
> II PETER 3:8

It's only been two days since he was here! In GOD's economy, it hasn't been very long.

Look also at the grace the Lord has demonstrated by his delay.

> The LORD is not slack concerning his promise, as some men count slackness; but is longsuffering to us-ward, not willing that any should perish, but that all should come to repentance.
>
> II PETER 3:9

Jesus has taken his sweet time so that you and I can live with him for eternity. Think of all the saved souls in the last few decades. If the Lord would have come back in 1967 during the Six Day War between Egypt and Israel, I would have been lost. Maybe you too! No, it's by GOD's grace and mercy that he has delayed, wanting all that will, to come to repentance and to receive that life-saving gift of eternal life through faith in Jesus the Savior.

•   •   •   •

Well, dear reader, we have come to a milestone in our book. We have concluded our study of "the beginning of sorrows" which Jesus spoke of to his disciples and are now ready to consider the Rapture of the Church, the Tribulation time period and the Return of Jesus Christ.

We will see that there are many things in place today which will fulfill the prophecies foretold of those difficult days to come. We will be reminded that today, the European Common Market is poised to become the ten toed image of Daniel's prophecy as well as the ten horned beast of his and John's revelation. We will consider that China already has a two hundred million man army that could easily march from the East for the battle of Armageddon. We will reflect on the Arab League as Daniel's King of the South and of course speak of computer chip technology which has the means for the Mark of the Beast to become a reality.

In the obstetrical analogy we have considered, the false labor is over and the water is about to break signaling the onset of true labor and the subsequent delivery of the baby! For the rapture of the church can be typified as the rupture of membranes. With that event, a series of labor pains the degree of which the world has never before experienced will begin. And with that labor, the world will birth something wonderful and it will be called the 2nd Coming of Jesus Christ!

Birth Pangs: ✝he Future

✝he Rapture of the Church as the Rupture of Membranes

Words of Comfort

Just as the rupture of membranes is the most unexpected and unique event in all of pregnancy, so too, the Rapture of the Church will be the most surprising and matchless event in the history of the world. And just as the breaking of the water begins the onset of labor, so too, the departure of the believers in Jesus Christ will signal the onset of the Great Tribulation.

> But I would not have you be ignorant, brethren, concerning them which are asleep [those who have died], that ye sorrow not, even as others which have no hope. For if we believe that Jesus died and rose again, even so them also which sleep in Jesus [those who are born again, those who belong to Jesus] will GOD bring with him. For this we say unto you by the word of the LORD, that we which are alive and remain unto the coming of the LORD shall not prevent [proceed] them which are asleep. For the LORD himself shall descend from heaven with a shout, with the voice of the archangel, and with the trump of GOD: And the dead in Christ shall rise first: Then we which are alive and remain shall be caught up together with them in

the clouds, to meet the Lord in the air: And so shall we ever be with the Lord. Wherefore comfort one other with these words.

I Thessalonians 4:13–18

In my opinion, these are about the most wonderful words in all of Scripture. This is the hope which I have in my heart. That one day I will be caught up to be ever with the Lord! This is what "turned me on" to the Lord those many years ago in 1973 when I first saw through the fog of life and realized that there was "oh, so much more!"

That was the past. In the present, this hope of hearing the voice of the archangel is what puts everything in perspective for today in my life. For without the hope of heaven, then as Paul the apostle states, "we are of all men most miserable" (I Corinthians 15:19b). When I live for eternity, with my life with Jesus in the equation, then the sacrifices in my job, the letting go of my stuff, and the pain and tragedies of life make sense. But without this comfort, then those same things will make me miserable instead of building me up as they presently do! Without the promise of the Lord's return for me I may as well do what Paul also suggested in this same context. "If after the manner of men I have fought with beasts at Ephesus, what advantageth it me, if the dead rise not? Let us eat and drink; for tomorrow we die" (I Corinthians 15:32).

Paul is saying, why put up with all the sacrifices of the Christian walk if there is no hope of the resurrection in Christ. It's not worth it, man! I'm just going to party, for tomorrow I die!

Jesus spoke of accepting voluntary sacrifices in this life in the context of the next one with these words.

And he said to them all, If any man will come after me, let him deny himself, and take up his cross daily, and follow me. For whosoever will save his life shall lose it: But whosoever will lose his life for my sake, the same shall save it.

For what is a man advantaged, if he gain the whole world, and lose himself, or be cast away? For whosoever shall be ashamed of me and my words, of him shall the Son of man be ashamed,

306

> when he shall come in his own glory, and in his Father's, and
> of the holy angels.
>
> LUKE 9:23–26

Our Lord said for me to take up *my* cross. If I lose my life,
then I will find it. Taking up my cross is not suffering for the
Lord those things which I cannot avoid, like the pain of a broken
leg or the grief of the loss of a loved one. No, it is sacrificially and
voluntarily choosing to walk daily in the steps of the Lord. It's
keeping that promise to mentor that little boy of the single mom
down the street when times are tough instead of chucking it. It's
joyfully giving ten percent and even more to the work of the Lord
instead of keeping it for my earthly pleasure. Or, it can be waking up at night and delivering that baby when it would be better
for my flesh to sleep and let the on-call doctor attend the birth!
That's taking up my cross and it's the blessed hope of hearing the
trump of GOD and meeting the Lord in the air which puts it all
into perspective. When I live for eternity, life makes sense. But
when I forget about the promise of heaven, then I can become
most miserable!

•　•　•　•

Let's look at our hope verse by verse for it truly is too good to
be true. No, it is so good it must be true!

> But I would not have you ignorant, brethren, concerning them
> which are asleep, that ye sorrow not, even as others which have
> no hope.
>
> I THESSALONIANS 4:13

Paul says for the believer not to be ignorant of the hope of
the resurrection. He says not to sorrow as the world sorrows concerning those who have gone before us, for unlike the man or the
woman of the world who has no hope, we should know that there
is much, much more.

Paul, as GOD's mouthpiece, says not to be ignorant concerning the rapture. This is the fifth time in the New Testament that

he has said that we are not to be ignorant of an important spiritual truth. The other four are as follows.

1. We are not to be ignorant of Israel's place in GOD's plan. (Romans 11:25)

2. We are not to be ignorant of biblical typology. (I Corinthians 10:1–11)

3. We are not to be ignorant of spiritual gifts. (I Corinthians 12:1–11)

4. We are not to be ignorant of spiritual warfare, of Satan's devices. (II Corinthians 1:8; 2:11)

The word "ignorant" is an interesting choice of words by the Author. It implies a total lack of knowledge about a subject or a concept. GOD tells the believer not to be ignorant of his, yet to be realized, redemptive plan for Israel and not to be ignorant of how the Old Testament pictures Jesus and New Testament principles. He teaches his children not to be ignorant of the gifts of the Spirit and not to be ignorant of the wiles of the devil in tripping up the believer. And lastly, he proclaims words of comfort in telling the believer to not be ignorant about that future day when he or she meets the Savior in the clouds. As I reflect upon these five truths I can see why GOD chose the word "ignorant," as indeed throughout New Testament history, Christians have generally been ignorant to these five important keys to the abundant life that Jesus came to give.

Don't let that happen to you, dear reader. Remember that GOD is not through with the Jew. Recall his promises to Abraham, Isaac, and Jacob and understand that during the time of Jacob's Trouble, all Israel will be saved. Realize that the Old Testament is a picture book showing us prophetic aspects of our Lord as well as typifying New Testament principles. Understand that the gifts of the Spirit are for today to empower you to be a witness for our dear Redeemer and that we wrestle not against flesh and blood but against evil principalities and powers. And lastly, remember to look to the hope of our Lord's soon return for your soul!

> For if we believe that Jesus died and rose again, even so them also which sleep in Jesus will GOD bring with him.
>
> I THESSALONIANS 4:14

This is the gospel, dear reader. This is the Good News!

We must look again at our main text from Book II of *A Woman's Silent Testimony* entitled Death, Burial, and Resurrection when we consider this wonderful verse.

> Moreover, brethren, I declare unto you the *gospel,* which I preached unto you, and wherein ye stand; By which also ye are saved, if ye keep in memory what I preached unto you, unless ye have believed in vain. For I delivered unto you first of all that which I also received, how that Christ *died* for our sins according to the scriptures; And that he was *buried,* and that he *rose again* the third day according to the scriptures: (emphasis mine)
>
> I CORINTHIANS 15:1–4

Belief in the death, burial, and resurrection of Jesus Christ is the Good News. And here in 1st Thessalonians we see a wonderful reason why it is such wonderful news. Because those who have died believing in the reality of Jesus Christ, believing in the redemptive work of the Cross of Calvary and of his subsequent resurrection, will also be resurrected one day by GOD.

> For this we say unto you by the word of the LORD, that we which are alive and remain unto the coming of the LORD shall not prevent them which are asleep.
>
> I THESSALONIANS 4:15

Paul cannot emphasize this truth enough!

"I am saying this to you by the *Word of the* Lord." He is yelling at us to pay attention to this truth! Don't be ignorant of this truth, no, not for one minute! The word is that we who are alive and are remaining unto the coming of the Lord will not precede those who have died.

Since Paul was alive when he wrote this passage, he included himself in the "we" group. Obviously in retrospect, he is in the sleeping group. As you and I will be also if we die before this blessed day arrives! For we remember that Jesus told us that no man, or any angel in heaven, knows the exact day we are presently discussing, only his Father in heaven (Matthew 24:36).

The phrase "shall not prevent them which are asleep" makes sense if I lived in England in the 1611 when the King James Version of the Bible was translated. But in modern English, the word "proceed" gives the proper meaning. For we see in the next two verses that the dead in Christ will rise first, followed by those who are alive on that day. Those who are alive will not precede those who have died.

I discussed in Book II of *A Woman's Silent Testimony* concerning the death, burial, and resurrection of Lazarus, that in GOD's eyes, sleep and death are the same. Jesus said that he would go to Lazarus and wake him up, for he was sleeping (John 11:11). We also recall that every night when we fall asleep it typifies our death and every morning when we wake up it is a wonderful picture of our resurrection. We, on this side of eternity, see death as such a "big deal." But GOD sees it as just a good night's sleep!

> For the LORD himself shall descend from heaven with a shout, with the voice of the archangel, and with the trump of GOD: And the dead in Christ shall rise first:
> I THESSALONIANS 4:16

Three audible signs will simultaneously occur which will signal our departure. Upon Jesus' descent from heaven to greet his bride we will hear a shout, an angelic voice and the trump of GOD. I think it's significant, of course, that once again GOD uses the number three very precisely in picturing the completeness of the resurrection of the saints on that day!

The shout, the voice of the friend of the groom, and the trump are all seen on the night of a Jewish wedding ceremony. In Book X of *A Woman's Silent Testimony,* entitled the "Marriage of the Lamb," we developed the beautiful picture of the rapture of the bride of Christ which has perfect analogies to traditions present in the Jewish wedding ceremony.

Also, later in this section, we will discuss the "trump of GOD." This is very significant for we will make the point in that discussion that mankind has heard the trump of GOD before. That day, over three thousand years ago, was also a very significant day, one which had far reaching consequences as we shall see.

Lastly, though, before leaving this verse we see that it's the dead *in Christ* who will rise first. This is not the resurrection seen late in the book of Revelation where all who have died will rise. On that terrible day the books will be opened and those who know not the Lord will be judged according to their works (Revelation 20:12). As we understand, all have sinned and fall short of the glory of GOD. Thus, without the covering of the blood of the Lamb any judgment according to our works will turn out very badly for us. It will also be on that day, that *every* knee will bow and *every* tongue confess that Jesus is Lord just as Isaiah and Paul predicted will happen (Isaiah 45:23, Romans 14:11 and Philippians 2:10). But this resurrection is not about judgment but about reconciliation. Jesus will bring those belonging to him to the "mansion" he has been preparing for us for over two thousand years (John 14:1–3).

> Then we which are alive and remain shall be caught up together with them in the clouds, to meet the LORD in the air: And so shall we ever be with the LORD.
>
> I THESSALONIANS 4:17

Do you miss the Lord? Do you long to be with him? On that day we shall ever be with him! This verse clearly states that there will be some who will be alive and not suffer the curse of physical death. We will see in a moment that this too has happened before. Just ask Enoch and Elijah!

We learn that we will be "caught up." This phrase is the Greek word "harpazo" and the Latin word "raptuso." Of course, in English we have used the term Rapture to describe this event of being caught up. Some have sarcastically said that the word "rapture" is not in the Bible. Well, technically they are correct, for the New Testament was written in Greek, not Latin. Somehow though, the "catching up" or the "harpazo" do not have that certain ring to it that the word "rapture" has in describing this blessed event. I'm going to stick with the term "rapture" and believe that you know what I'm talking about!

Paul spoke of his own rapture in type in II Corinthians 12. He recalled in that epistle that fourteen years earlier he was "caught up" to the third heaven. Two verses later he repeated that he was "caught up" to paradise (II Corinthians 12:2, 4).

Truly, the Rapture will be extraordinary, but it will not be unique!

> Wherefore comfort one another with these words.
> I THESSALONIANS 4:18

Do you want to be a comfort to people? Do you want to have a way to bless people? Then keep speaking of our blessed hope. Remind your brothers and sisters that we will soon meet our beautiful Savior in the clouds and be ever with him. No more pain, no more sorrow. Only love, peace, light and beauty!

What a day that will be!

The Witness of History

As I mentioned in the last chapter, the rapture has happened twice before. Both Enoch and Elijah were taken up to heaven without experiencing death. Let's look at their accounts.

Jude tells us that Enoch was the seventh generation from Adam (Jude 14). Seven of course, is that perfect number. And we learn from the Book of Genesis that, "And Enoch walked with God: And God took him" (Genesis 5:24) The book of Hebrews sheds more light upon what this means.

> By faith Enoch was translated that he should not see death; and was not found, because God had translated him: For before his translation he had this testimony, that he pleased God.
>
> HEBREWS 11:5

The picture is perfect. Not everyone who has had faith and has pleased God in the Old Testament was raptured. In this example it was only Enoch. Likewise, not every believer throughout the Church Age gets to avoid the sting of death. But for those for whom Enoch typifies, the living Gentile believers who hear the shout, the voice and the trump, they will be translated to God just as he was!

Yes Enoch is a powerful picture of the church of Christ.

He was before Abraham, he was not a Jew, yet he had faith and he pleased GOD. These two go together, for without faith it is impossible to please GOD (Hebrews 11:6).

Elijah, on the other hand, was a man of Israel who had great faith and pleased GOD. He, of course, pictures those Jewish believers in the Messiah who will not see death on that day of his return to meet us in the air. Yes, the Church of Christ is made up of Jews and Gentiles. Believers in Christ from both groups will be caught up on that day as Enoch and Elijah typify.

Let's read together the account of Elijah's departure.

> And it came to pass, as they still went on [Elijah and Elisha], and talked, that, behold, there appeared a chariot of fire, and horses of fire, and parted them both asunder, and Elijah went up by a whirlwind into heaven.
>
> II KINGS 2:11

Elijah took an extraordinary ride to heaven just as we also will on that wonderful day. Note also that just as Elisha was left behind, so too will the unbeliever be left behind as a witness to our departure.

Jesus put it this way,

> Then shall two be in the field; the one shall be taken, and the other left. Two women shall be grinding at the mill; the one shall be taken, and the other left.
>
> MATTHEW 24:40–41

So we see that we have two Old Testament pictures of the New Testament reality of the rapture of the church. And we remember that when GOD repeats himself, when he states something twice or demonstrates something twice, he is emphasizing the point he wants to make. Enoch and Elijah demonstrate to us that GOD is able to do what he says he will do. That is, some will meet him without experiencing death!

Wha✝ About Jesus?

Jesus himself, as the Son of Man, also had a dramatic departure.

> And when he [Jesus] had spoken these things, while they beheld, he was taken up [he was lifted up, he was exalted, he was raptured]; and a cloud received him out of their sight.
>
> ACTS 1:9

But unlike the believer who will not have to experience death, our Redeemer suffered the death we all deserve. I cannot even begin to fathom how terrible that last statement is! He died the death of billions so that those who call upon his name will live!

Yes, our Lord as the Son of Man pictures those who have died, those who are asleep. He died, he was buried, he rose again, and he went to be with his Father in heaven. Just as the dead in Christ have died, were buried, will rise again, and will go to be with the Father in heaven!

Indeed, as Paul so eloquently proves in chapter 15 of First Corinthians, Jesus is the first fruits of the resurrection.

> But now is Christ risen from the dead, and become the first fruits of them that slept.... For as in Adam all die, even so in

315

Christ shall all be made alive. But every man in his own order: Christ the first fruits; afterward they that are Christ's at his coming.

I CORINTHIANS 15:20, 22–23

Lastly, in considering our hero, the book of Revelation uses wording which the believer may find comforting. "And she brought forth a man child, who was to rule all nations with a rod of iron: And her child was caught up [harpazo] unto GOD, and to his throne" (Revelation 12:5).

GOD uses the same word to describe Jesus' ascension to heaven that he uses to teach of yours and mine! I hope you are starting to see that this is really going to happen!

✝he Two Witnesses of Revelation

The book of Revelation gives the account of two very special men who will give testimony to the truth of the departure of the church to those who are left behind during the Tribulation time frame.

In chapter 11 of Revelation we learn that power will be given to the two men to witness in Jerusalem for 1,260 days during the middle of that seven year labor and travail. During the time of their testimony they will not be able to be harmed by men and they will have power over heaven and earth to demonstrate God's potency. You may remember we developed this story in greater detail in Book II of *A Woman's Silent Testimony* when we considered the death, burial, and resurrection of Moses. We saw in that discussion that these two witnesses, the ones Jesus calls *my* two witnesses, are likely Moses and Elijah.

After they complete the work God will give them, the Bible states, "the Beast that ascendeth out of the bottomless pit shall make war against them, and shall overcome them, and kill them" (Revelation 11:7b). Their bodies will lie in the street of the city where our Lord was crucified, i.e. Jerusalem. The fooled of the world will rejoice at their demise, but then, suddenly, after three and a half days, the spirit of life will enter into their bodies. They will stand upon their feet and great fear will come upon the scoffers witnessing this event.

Next we read in GOD's own words,

> And they heard a great voice from heaven saying unto them, Come up hither. And they ascended up to heaven in a cloud; and their enemies beheld them.
>
> REVELATION 11:12

Yes, the Bible states that the Devil has the power of death (Hebrews 2:14). Here we see the Beast once again seemingly victorious. But the Word also states that Jesus was victorious over death and thus those who are his witnesses will also be victorious on that day!

I too want to hear those words..."Come up hither!"

Come Up Hi✝her

After this I looked, and, behold, *a door was opened in heaven:* And the first *voice* which I heard was as it were *a trumpet* talking with me; which said, *Come up hither,* and *I will show thee things which must be hereafter* (emphasis mine).

REVELATION 4:1

Revelation 4:1 is another one of those wonderful verses of the Bible. It's a diamond!

And there again are those exact same words in English and in Greek, "Come up hither."

You may remember, as I have heard Pastor Jon state many times, that the book of Revelation is not a hard book to understand. For it is the only book in the Bible that comes with its own divine outline. That outline is found in Chapter 1:19.

John was told to, "Write the things which thou hast seen, and the things which are, and the things which shall be hereafter" (Revelation 1:19). You will remember that the *things which thou (John) hast seen* was the risen Christ. That's chapter one of the Revelation where we saw the glorious Savior with the countenance of the Sun!

The second point of the divine outline is *the things which are.*

That's chapters 2 and 3 where we learn of the seven epic Christian churches which populate the Church Age. The Age of Grace in which we and the Apostle John have resided.

Chapter 4 begins with *the things which shall be hereafter.* Chapter 4 begins with the Rapture! John heard those wonderful words, "Come up hither," for the catching up of the saints is *the* event which signals the end of the Church Age, that age of false labor, that age of the things which are, and the beginning of the Tribulation, the day of true labor, the time of the things which shall be hereafter.

Again to summarize, chapters 4 and 5 describe in some detail how heaven will appear to the believer during the seven year honeymoon we have with the Lord. Next, chapters 6–19 tell of the Tribulation upon planet Earth where the epic battle between Satan and GOD is concluded. At the same time GOD will be waking up the unbeliever to call as many as would be saved during that very tumultuous time. In chapter 19, we read of heaven being opened again with the second coming of Christ then the Millennial Kingdom is foretold in chapter 20. Lastly, chapters 21 and 22 teach, in very limited detail, of the New Heaven and the New Earth in which we will all live happily ever after!

So, back to this wonderful verse that describes the Rapture. Once again, we hear a sudden voice and a trumpet. We remember in Paul's description that it was a voice, a shout of the archangel and the trump of GOD. Also, earlier in chapter one of this revelation given to John, he told us, "I was in the Spirit on the Lord's day, and I heard behind me a great voice, as of a trumpet" (Revelation 1:10).

So we understand that whenever a man tries to describe what the rapture will be like, he proclaims that the voice will be loud like a trumpet. Later we will also learn of it's suddenness as Paul will teach that it will be in the twinkling of an eye!

Also note in verse one of chapter four that a door was opened in heaven. This is significant as only three verses earlier Jesus said that he stands at the door and knocks. If any man will open that door, he will come in unto him and sup with him. So we see that when and man or women open the door of their heart to Jesus, he will open the door of heaven to them. The door will also open again in chapter 19 when Christ returns in victorious battle as we read:

> And I saw heaven opened, and behold a white horse; and he that sat upon him was called Faithful and True, and in righteousness he doth judge and make war.
>
> REVELATION 19:11

Oh, dear reader, GOD uses words *so* precisely and yet we in our puny little minds often miss it totally! Voices, trumpets and doors opening. It all fits so beautifully!

Next, after the trumpet-like voice spoke to John saying "come up hither," he said, "And I will show thee things which must be hereafter" (Revelation 4:1b). This should ring a bell once again in our little minds as it's very similar to the third point of the divine outline verse, Revelation 1:19.

Predictably and wonderfully it's the *same* word in Greek, "metetauta." We would expect nothing less from GOD since he is talking about the same thing! The things which shall (must) be hereafter all start with the rapture just as true labor starts with the rupture of membranes!

So we see that the beginning of the next age starts with the door of heaven opening and a voice of a trumpet calling us to come up hither. To come and be with our Groom!

What a day that will be!

Our next stop will be Paul's oft quoted words of promise which speak of a mystery, the twinkling of an eye and of the last trump.

Behold, I Show You a Mystery

Behold, I show you a *mystery:* We shall not all sleep, but we shall all be changed, In a moment, in the twinkling of an eye, at the last trump: For the trumpet shall sound, and the dead shall be raised incorruptible, and we shall be changed. For this corruptible must put on incorruption, and this mortal must put on immortality. So when this corruptible shall have put on incorruption, and this mortal shall have put on immortality, then shall be brought to pass the saying that is written, Death is swallowed up in victory (emphasis mine).

I Corinthians 15:51–54

In First Corinthians 15, Paul powerfully proves the truth of the resurrection. These last verses are the summary statement of his great discourse. And, noticeably, this man of God concludes by stating that this is a mystery!

In the Bible, a mystery means that God is revealing a truth that, up until that point in time, was unknown by man or sometimes even by angels. It doesn't mean that it is a new truth that God has come up with, but it is an aspect of God's plan that previously was not revealed. It's much like truths children learn as they grow and mature. Just because I didn't understand romance or physics when I was a boy doesn't mean that they weren't a reality. Those things were just a mystery to me!

As far as I can tell there are seven mysteries revealed in the New Testament. Of course, multiple mysteries await us to discover during the Millennial Kingdom of Revelation twenty and the New Heaven and New Earth time frame of chapters twenty one & twenty two. As I study these chapters, it is clear that very little detail is given to us by GOD at this point in our walk with him.

The seven mysteries which you may reflect upon and study if you chose are as follows:

1. The mysteries of the Kingdom of Heaven
(Matthew 13:11, Mark 4:11 and Luke 8:10).

2. The mystery that blindness in part has happened to Israel until the fullness of the Gentiles be come in (Romans 11:25).

3. The mystery of the Rapture (I Corinthians 15:51–54).

4. The mystery that the Gentiles should be fellow-heirs, of the same body, and partakers of GOD's promises in Christ by the Gospel (Ephesians 3:1–11 and Colossians 1:26–27).

5. The mystery of iniquity (II Thessalonians 2:7).

6. The mystery of the seven prophetic churches (Revelation 1:20).

7. The mystery of the world-wide false religion based in Rome (Revelation 17:5, 9, 18).

Jesus told his disciples that they were being taught the mysteries of the Kingdom directly while he spoke to the multitude in parables. Since the disciples were in a position of relative maturity compared to the mere curious followers, they were given deeper truths which only they, who were with the Teacher continually, could comprehend. Again, the child-like example is illuminating. When I was a child, I was not ready for adult topics; I needed stories, not lessons. The masses were given parables as they were not ready for mysteries!

Secondly, Paul revealed in his epistle to the Romans that Israel's general rejection of the Gospel of Christ was partly due to that fact that this administration of time that we are presently living in is the Age of the Gentiles. The time GOD is using to bring the Gentiles into his family. When the "fullness of the Gentiles be come in" (Romans 11:25), then the eyes of Israel will be opened and they will recognize Jesus as their Messiah.

Thirdly, Paul is telling us here in our present study that these many aspects of the rapture were not previously known. They were a mystery!

Some may say, what gave Paul the audacity to proclaim this? It sounds like a new religion. Did Paul start a cult!

Three important verses in the Book of Galatians give the answer.

> Paul, an apostle, (not of men, neither by man, but by Jesus Christ, and GOD the Father, who raised him from the dead;)... But I certify you, brethren, that the gospel which was preached of me is not after man. For I neither received it of man, neither was I taught it, but by the revelation of Jesus Christ.
>
> GALATIANS 1:1, 11–12

When I consider the many mysteries that Paul brought to the church, I need to decide if Paul had the credentials to do this. Here it proves to me that he does!

Paul didn't add to our religion by his great learning and imagination. No, he was directly tutored by the Lord Jesus Christ himself. After seeing Jesus on the road to Damascus, the Bible tells us that Paul dropped off the radar scope and went to the desert of Arabia. There, Jesus gave him the many revelations which are now part of our faith and are generally new when compared to the Old Testament. Yes, these mysteries can be found, veiled in the Old Testament, but Paul expounds upon them in the New Testament.

The fourth mystery is one of my favorites. Paul calls this mystery, that the Jews and Gentiles are fellow-heirs with Christ, the mystery of the Gospel (Ephesians 6:19) and the mystery of Christ (Colossians 4:3). He teaches in Ephesians chapter three that this mystery is an entire administration or era of God which was given to him to proclaim (Ephesians 3:3–4). He states that it was not made known to men in the past (Ephesians 3:5). He writes that the grace given to the Gentiles was previously unsearchable or untraceable in the Old Testament (Ephesians 3:8). He states that since the beginning of the world this mystery was hid in God (Ephesians 3:9). Beautifully, he announces that this mystery is the eternal purpose of God (Ephesians 3:11). Think of that, we Gentile believers are the eternal purpose of God! Truly, God's love has no bounds!

So, you may ask, why did God need to hide the revelation of this mystery of the Jews and Gentiles being fellow-heirs? Why did he need to keep this mystery unsearchable in the Old Testament?

First Corinthians gives the answer.

> Howbeit we speak wisdom among them that are perfect [mature]: Yet not the wisdom of this world, nor of the princes of this world [devils], that come to naught: But we speak the wisdom of God in a *mystery*, even the *hidden* wisdom, which God ordained before the world unto our glory: Which none of the princes [Satan and his minions] of this world knew: For had they known it, they would not have crucified the Lord of glory.
>
> I Corinthians 2:6–8

The Bible teaches that Satan is the God of this world (II Corinthians 4:4). Here we incredibly learn that this mystery was hid in God because had Satan and his henchmen, the princes of the world, known about it they would not have crucified the Lord of Glory! Paul teaches that Satan would rather have let Jesus live if he had only understood what Jesus' death would bring forth. Because Jesus died for our sins, Satan lost his grip upon mankind. He gave the title deed of Earth back to God. He lost everything by his lack of comprehension of God's ultimate plan. By his lack of understanding of God's eternal purpose!

Colossians chapter 1 tells of the riches of this mystery which Satan failed to grasp. It's wonderful!

Whereof I am made a minister, according to the dispensation of GOD [administration or era] which is given to me for you, to fulfill the word of GOD; Even the *mystery* which hath been *hid* from ages and from generations, but now is made manifest to his saints: To whom GOD would make known what is the riches of the glory of this mystery among the Gentiles; which is *Christ in you,* the hope of glory: (emphasis mine)

COLOSSIANS 1:25–27

Christ in me...Christ in you! No wonder this mystery needed to be hid. If Satan, whose intelligence makes Einstein look like an idiot, had known that you or I would have Christ in us, he would have never mobilized Pilate and the Jews to crucify the Lord of Glory! Satan would rather have had one Jesus, one perfect man among so many failures, walking his planet, than the millions of "little christs" which now cover the landscape because of his blunder!

The fifth and seventh mysteries, those of the mystery of iniquity and of the Mystery Babylon Religion will be spoken of later in this book. You may also remember that the sixth mystery spoke of Jesus' prophetic words to the seven churches in chapters 2 and 3 of Revelation and was covered in great detail earlier in this book. So now it's time to check out another aspect of this third mystery. That aspect being the catching up—the Rapture—will be in the twinkling of an eye!

In the ✝ Twinkling of an Eye

> Behold, I show you a mystery: We shall not all sleep, but we shall all be changed, In a moment, *in the twinkling of an eye,* at the last trump: for the trumpet shall sound, and the dead shall be raised incorruptible, and we shall be changed. For this corruptible must put on incorruption, and this mortal must put on immortality. So when this corruptible shall have put on incorruption, and this mortal shall have put on immortality, then shall be brought to pass the saying that is written, Death is swallowed up in victory.
>
> I Corinthians 15:51–54

Jesus told his followers to be ready, for we know not when he will return. Paul adds that it will be quick. I mean really fast! It's going to be in the twinkling of an eye.

Do you know how fast the eye can blink?

Neither do I!

But I do know that it's measured in nanoseconds. God made the eye so responsive to invasion that at the very instant of an insult the eyelid will close to protect itself. That's how fast it will be. One instant we are going about our business and the next moment we will hear the shout, the voice, and the trump of God and will be meeting Jesus in the air!

There will be no preparation. That's why I want to be ready all the time. I fear how embarrassing it will be to be in the middle of some sin when the Lord returns.

Jesus said that just as lightning flashes from the east to the west...that's how fast will be his return (Matthew 24:27)! He stated that he would come quickly as he spoke to the church in Philadelphia (Revelation 3:11). That statement didn't necessarily mean that he was going to come in John's lifetime. No, it meant that when he did come, it would be fast, it would be rapid, it would be quick!

So here is the application for you and me. Keep the hope of the return of Christ alive in our minds. Don't be like the five virgins who were not ready for the Groom's return in Jesus' parable of the ten virgins (Matthew 25:1–13). Don't be in the dark about the rapture as Jesus predicted would happen to the church in Sardis (Revelation 3:3). Don't let his return overtake you like a thief in the night. But be sober, be vigilant, be ready. It will be sooner than you think!

> But ye, brethren, are not in the darkness, that that day should overtake you as a thief. Ye are all the children of light, and the children of the day: We are not of the night, nor of darkness. Therefore let us not sleep, as do others; but let us watch and be sober...putting on the breastplate of faith and love; and for an helmet, the hope of salvation.
>
> I THESSALONIANS 5:4–6, 8A

At ✝ he Last Trump

Behold, I show you a mystery: We shall not all sleep, but we shall all be changed, In a moment, in the twinkling of an eye, *at the last trump:* For the trumpet shall sound, and the dead shall be raised incorruptible, and we shall be changed. For this corruptible must put on incorruption, and this mortal must put on immortality. So when this corruptible shall have put on incorruption, and this mortal shall have put on immortality, then shall be brought to pass the saying that is written, Death is swallowed up in victory (emphasis mine).

I CORINTHIANS 15:51–54

The last trump is an interesting choice of words. It certainly implies that there must have been a first trump. Indeed, there was! Let's listen for it as it can still be heard in Exodus 19 by those with ears to hear.

In the third month, when the children of Israel were gone forth out of the land of Egypt, the same day came they into the wilderness of Sinai...and Moses came and called for the elders of the people, and laid before their faces all these words which the LORD commanded him. And all the people answered together, and said, All that the LORD hath spoken we will do...and the

LORD said unto Moses…Be ready against the third day: For the third day *the LORD will come down in the sight of all the people… when the trumpet soundeth long, they shall come up* to the mount… and it came to pass on the third day in the morning, that there were thunders and lightnings, and a thick cloud upon the mount, and the *voice* of a *trumpet* exceeding loud…and Moses brought forth the people out of the camp to meet with GOD… and mount Sinai was altogether on a smoke, because *the LORD descended* upon it in fire: And the smoke thereof ascended as the smoke of a furnace, and the whole mount quaked greatly. And when the *voice* of the *trumpet* sounded long, and waxed louder and louder, Moses spake, and GOD answered him by a voice…and GOD spake all these words, saying, I am the LORD thy GOD, which have brought thee out of the land of Egypt, out of the house of bondage. Thou shalt have no other GODS before me. Thou shalt not make unto thee any graven image… thou shalt not take the name of the LORD thy GOD in vain… remember the sabbath day, to keep it holy…honor thy father and thy mother…thou shalt not kill. Thou shalt not commit adultery. Thou shalt not steal. Thou shalt not bear false witness…thou shalt not covet…(emphasis is mine)
EXODUS 19:1, 7–8A, 10A, 11A, 13B, 16A, 17A, 18–19; EXODUS 20:1–
4A, 7A, 8, 12A, 13–16A, 17A

That, my friends, was the first trump! It was just as incredible as the last trump will be. When GOD descended down into the air above Mount Sinai a trumpet blew exceedingly loud and *all* his people came up to the mount. In that we see a picture of the Rapture!

The first trump and the last trump both portray the important truth that when GOD meets with his children it's something for heaven to shout about, something to blow its trumpet about! The first trump was the day GOD spoke the Ten Commandments. The last trump will be the day we are delivered from the curse of our inability to obey those Commandments!

• • • •

Between the first and the last trump are many other trumpet

blasts in the Bible. Let's look at a two of them as they too give insight into the last trump.

Leviticus 23 speaks of the seven feasts of the Lord. The fifth one is very germane to this discussion.

> Speak unto the children of Israel, saying, In the *seventh* month, in the *first* day of the month, shall ye have a Sabbath, a memorial of blowing of *trumpets,* an holy convocation (emphasis mine).
>
> LEVITICUS 23:24

This is the Feast of Trumpets. As GOD so precisely does, once again the numbers he uses tell a story. Five is the number of grace and we see that on the first day of the seventh month the trumpets are sounded as a day of joy, celebration and holiness. In a moment we will see that the sixth and seventh feasts also occur in the numerically significant seventh month.

The seventh month is called Tishiri and later in their history GOD had the Jews change the seventh month to the first month. Thus the Feast of Trumpets, which was on the first day of the seventh month, became the first day of the first month. It became the Jewish New Year!

Indeed, the Feast of Trumpets typifies the rapture of GOD's children. On the first day of the "Day of the Lord," the trumpet will sound and all of GOD's children will feast and celebrate a most holy convocation!

Now you may be thinking, *that's a bit of a stretch, doctor!*

Well, actually not, as all seven of the feasts of the Lord picture GOD's Plan. Let me briefly show you what I've been taught by my mentors.

GOD gave the seven feasts to both commemorate the past and to reveal the future. They celebrated what GOD had done for Israel as well as prophetically reveal what he would do for the nation. In Hebrew, the word "feast" actually means "appointed times" and also "times that point to."

Four of the feasts are in the Spring and three in the Autumn. In our picture of prophetic implications, the first four typify

Christ's first coming and the last three portray truths concerning the Second Coming.

Let me put it together for you now.

1. Passover: This occurred on the 14th day of the original first month (the month of Nisan) and speaks of the blood of the lamb. Israel was delivered from the angel of death by the blood on the doorpost and prophetically would be delivered from everlasting death by the blood of the One John the Baptist called the Lamb of GOD.

2. The Feast of Unleavened Bread: This was the seven-day feast which started on the 15th of the first month, the day after Passover. It commemorated the rapid departure from Egypt without taking leaven and it remembered the manna which GOD gave to sustain his children in the Wilderness. The unleavened bread is stripped and pierced and pictures Jesus' sacrifice prophetically in that way. Also of incredible interest to me is the practice of the modern day sadir by the Jewish family. It occurs over the Feast of Unleavened Bread and is a powerful picture of Christ and the Trinity. At a sadir, three loaves of unleavened bread are taken. The middle one is broken, wrapped in a white linen called the afekommen and hidden for three days. Remarkably, afekommen means "I came!" Yes, along with Passover which speaks of Christ's death, the Feast of Unleavened Bread speaks of Christ's burial.

3. The Feast of Firstfruits: This celebration occurred on the morrow after the Sabbath during the week-long Feast of the Unleavened Bread. Thus it was always on a Sunday. It celebrated the barley harvest which came to fruition in the Spring. Of course we remember that Paul in 1 Corinthians 15 told us that Jesus is the firstfruits of the resurrection. Jesus' resurrection on the Sunday after Passover is beautifully portrayed in the Feast of Firstfruits!

4. Feast of Weeks: This celebration occurred seven weeks after the Feast of Firstfruits. It commemorated the giving of the Law and looked with anticipation to the upcoming wheat harvest at the end of the year. Prophetically, Pentecost occurred on the Feast of Weeks. That, of course, was the day that the

Holy Spirit was given to the church. In the Bible, believers are pictured as wheat and with the Holy Spirit in their hearts look forward to the harvest at the end of the age.

5. The Feast of Trumpets: As mentioned before, this feast occurred in Fall. The Jews celebrated the soon to be realized Autumn wheat harvest at the time of this feast. We, of course, see the promise of the rapture of GOD's wheat to be with him as the prophetic fulfillment of The Feast of Trumpets! We will also soon see that GOD used the blowing of trumpets for three important reasons. To proclaim a celebration, to convocate together, and to mobilize for battle. All three reasons to blow the trumpet have ties to our departure on that special day.

6. The Day of Atonement: Directly on the heels of the Feast of Trumpets, on the 10th day of Tishiri is Yom Kippur. This is the day of repentance. It is the day when the Jews afflict their soul. They are reminded and reflect upon their sins of the year. Clearly, this day prophetically depicts the time of Jacob's Trouble. Yes, the Day of Atonement typifies the Tribulation and will be a time shortly after the rapture of the believers.

7. The Feast of Tabernacles: Also known as the Feast of Booths. This seven day feast beginning upon the 15th day of Tishiri recalled the time of Israel's wanderings in the Wilderness and specifically the day that GOD caused water to gush forth out of the rock. It celebrated the final wheat harvest which, by that time of the year, was now complete. During that celebration, a giant menorah was lit on a high hill in Jerusalem and Josephus tells us that the light from it could be seen from over sixty miles away during the nights of this feast. This day has prophetic ties to both the first and second coming of our LORD. Of course, Jesus, as quoted in John 7, proclaimed on the last day of the Feast of Tabernacles in his day that those who came to him would have torrents of living water gush forth. He also said on the next day, found in John 8, after the menorah had been extinguished marking the end for the feast, that he was the light of the world. Lastly, as the final in-gathering of the wheat harvest this wonderful feast pictures the second coming of Christ! The day when the wheat harvest will be complete and the day that, according to Jesus' parable of the wheat and the tares, the two groups, the children of the Kingdom and the

children of the devil, will be gathered up and separated. One group to everlasting life and the other to everlasting destruction.

Thus we see GOD's Plan beautifully wrapped in the holidays he gave to Israel.

Also, did you notice what occurred upon each of the four feasts which spoke of Jesus' first coming? The very event each prophesied of actually occurred upon its same corresponding feast day! Jesus' death occurred on Passover. He was buried over the Feast of Unleavened Bread, he rose on the Feast of Firstfruits and the Holy Spirit came on the Feast of Weeks. Thus, with the Father being such a GOD of order, it would not surprise me at all if the events portrayed concerning the Second Coming will *actually* occur also on their corresponding days! That is, the Rapture will likely occur on a Feast of Trumpets in a year not to far away, the Tribulation will start on the subsequent Day of Atonement ten days after the Rapture and the Second Coming will occur on the Feast of Tabernacles seven years after that! I must admit, every year in September as the Feast of Trumpets draws near, I get a little antsy and excited as this little theory which I have makes a lot of sense to me!

• • • •

Let's look at another set of two trumpets to learn more of GOD's plan.

In Numbers, the Lord spoke unto Moses, saying,

Make thee *two trumpets* of *silver*...that thou mayest use them for the *calling of the assembly,* and for the *journeying of the camps...* . When ye blow an alarm, then the camps...shall go forward...and if ye *go to war* in your land against the enemy that oppresseth you, then ye shall blow an alarm with the trumpets...also in the *day of your gladness,* and in the *solemn days,* and in the *beginnings of your months,* ye shall blow with the trumpets...(emphasis mine)

NUMBERS 10:2A, C, 5A, C, 9A, 10A

These two trumpets picture our salvation. Silver in the Bible is associated with redemption. The redemption price of a slave was measured in silver as well as the betrayal money given to Judas for our Lord. The two silver trumpets speak of the First and the Last Trump very wonderfully. Both times GOD was and will call his people together for a journey with him. He was mobilizing them for travel, first to the Promised Land and still in the future to heaven. The First Trump announced the war against sin and the last one will announce the beginning of the last great war against Satan during the Tribulation. Lastly, the First Trump marked the solemnness of Israel's beginning in the receiving of the Ten Commandments while the Last Trump will proclaim the joy we will experience on that wonderful day of gladness not too far away!

Now you may be saying, that's great that you are so excited about the Lord's return, but I'm not so sure. I haven't been living as I should. I'm afraid I will be left behind. I'm not sure he won't just leave me here as I'm not at the place I know I should be.

Well, I have good news for you!

In all of these analogies, the Lord called *all* of his children. It didn't matter if they were in particularly good standing in the nation or not! When the First Trump sounded, the entire nation ascended up to the mount. When the silver trumpets were blown, the entire nation convocated, mobilized, and celebrated.

Wonderfully, Jesus said in John 6, "And this is the Father's will which hath sent me, that of *all* which he hath given me *I should lose nothing*, but should raise it up again at the last day" (John 6:39, emphasis mine).

Be at peace, dear believer, if the Father has given you to Jesus, if you have confessed and believed Romans 10:9, saying Jesus is Lord and you believe that the Father raised him from the dead, then he will *not* lose you! You *will* be raised up again at the last day.

See you there!

A Day of Peace and Safety

But of the times and the seasons, brethren, ye have no need that I write unto you.

For yourselves know perfectly that the Day of the LORD so cometh as a thief in the night. For when they shall say, Peace and safety; then sudden destruction cometh upon them, as travail upon a woman with child; and *they* shall not escape (emphasis mine).

I THESSALONIANS 5:1–3

Dear believer, these verses are talking about "they" not "you." We note that these words of Paul come directly upon the heels of his words of comfort concerning the day when we hear the shout, the voice and the trump of GOD. Paul is teaching that leading up to that day the unbeliever, the one who does not call Jesus Lord, will be caught off guard. That poor soul will be enjoying a time of peace and safety when the labor pains of the Tribulation overtake him just as the onset of hard labor comes upon a pregnant woman immediately after the rupture of membranes!

Again, GOD's Word clearly states that "we" are not appointed to see this day. A few verses later Paul states, "For GOD hath not appointed us to wrath, but to obtain salvation by our Lord Jesus Christ" (I Thessalonians 5:9).

The Tribulation is the time of GOD's wrath, the time of the Wrath of the Lamb (Revelation 6:16–17; 11:18). Paul states in Romans and earlier in I Thessalonians that we are saved from the wrath to come (Romans 5:9; I Thessalonians 1:10).

Now as I reflect upon this day in which we live, I see this prophecy playing out most dramatically! Never before in the history of the world has it been so "comfortable" for so many. The masses of the Western World, and now even many in the Orient, have it made in the shade. Peace, prosperity, good health, you name it. Stock portfolios, life insurance, modern health care, a nice car, a big home, a good school for the kids...the list goes on and on. Truly, to the one who will be caught off guard, to the one who does not see the many false labor signs which are marking the end of the age, never has there been a time of peace and safety like today!

Eerily it was also the same at the onset of those two other days when GOD poured out his wrath and judgment upon the world. Those two days, of course, were the flood of Noah and the day fire rained down upon Sodom and Gomorrah.

In Peter's second epistle, he speaks much of the end times. And in the second chapter he tells us that both the Flood and the judgment of Sodom were examples to the unGODly of the future Tribulation.

Thus, we understand that these two events foreshadow the judgment of the Tribulation time period. We also saw earlier in this book that the days leading up to the end will be as the days of Noah and as the days of Lot. They were days of peace and safety right up to the day that Noah entered into the ark and right up to the day the angel took Lot and his family out of Sodom. But the point I want to show you here in these days of peace and safety is what GOD did with his children immediately before those judgments arrived.

In Noah's case, as soon as GOD shut the door of the ark the rains came. And as you read Lot's story, the rain of fire could not come until the angel rescued Lot, his wife, and his daughters.

These two examples give me much comfort. It once again reveals to me that GOD will rescue you and me *before* the rain of judgment is poured out upon planet Earth.

Peter succinctly summarizes this principle, "The Lord knoweth how to deliver the GODLY out of temptations [tribulation], and to reserve the unjust unto the day of judgment to be punished" (II Peter 2:9).

Lot's story is particularly comforting. Look at him, he was a mess! He pitched his tent before Sodom! He was connected heavily into the carnal world's system of Sodom, and yet GOD in Hebrews 11 called him righteous!

You see, it's not about my righteousness, but about my Savior's. If I am clothed with the Lord's righteousness—and I am, if I belong to him—then GOD will call me righteous even while at the same time I know I'm not! Once again, it all about GOD's wonderful matchless *grace!* GOD's Riches At Christ's Expense.

✝he Fullness of the Gentiles

For I would not, brethren, that ye should be ignorant of this mystery, lest ye should be wise in your own conceits; that blindness in part is happened to Israel, until the *fullness of the Gentiles* be come in.

ROMANS 11:25

You may recall from the discussion in the chapter entitled, "Behold, I Show You a Mystery," that one of the mysteries given to Paul from Jesus was to reveal that even though it looked like GOD had given up on the Jews after they rejected and crucified Christ, he had not. In fact, in reading this verse closely, it is clear that Paul is warning us Gentile Christians not to become conceited in our own puny minds, thinking that now *we* are the chosen of GOD instead of the children of Jacob.

Paul is preaching to the Gentile believer to rejoice in GOD's grace to us but to realize that he is not through with Israel. He proclaimed that the blindness the Jews have toward the Old Testament pictures of Jesus are in part to bring the millions of Gentiles into GOD's family. Earlier in verse eleven, Paul stated that the salvation of the Gentiles was to jealously provoke the Jews back to him.

Here Paul proclaims that Israel's blindness will end at the time of the fullness of the Gentiles.

So what does the phrase, "the fullness of the Gentiles," mean?

It is understood that the Day of the Lord is not just a single day but a time period. It is the time that the Lord will rule and reign. But in this present dispensation, before the Day of the Lord, GOD has allowed man to have his way to a great degree. Of course, man's rule is tainted greatly by the GOD of this world, Satan. As the Day of the Lord proceeds forth, Satan will lose control.

Now the Day of the Lord starts with the rapture of the church of Christ. The rapture is for the Church. Seven years later will be the Second Coming of Christ. This event is for the Jew. The intervening seven years, called the Tribulation, is spoken of greatly in the Old Testament as we shall discuss in the next section of this book. Also, after Satan is put down, the Day of the Lord will proceed into the Millennial Kingdom which also is given in great detail by nearly all of the Old Testament prophets. It is this time that the Jews are looking to as their Scriptures clearly promise to them that there will be a day when the lion will lay down with the lamb. A day when all is made right and they will be free to worship Jehovah during a time of peace and prosperity.

Thus since the rapture is for the church, the phrase "the fullness of the Gentiles" is relating back to the rapture. Paul is teaching that when the *last* Gentile destined to be saved during our present administration of Grace calls upon the Lord, then the rapture will occur! Not a moment sooner or a moment later! When the church of Christ, made up of Jews and Gentiles, receives its last Gentile convert, then we will meet the Lord in the air. That will signal the fullness of the Gentiles. The membranes will rupture and the labor will begin. The time that GOD will use to call Israel to him will birth forth. Now it is important to understand, though, that millions of Gentiles will also come to the Lord during the Tribulation time frame. Revelation 7:9–14 clearly teach this fact, but the Lord will directly use the time of Jacob's Trouble to wake the Jews out of their sleep.

Now, as we have emphasized over and over again in this book, the Day of the Lord is at hand. The fullness of the Gentiles is very near. So let's look at another verse which sounds familiar to our text in this chapter in order to see something wonderful.

> ... and Jerusalem shall be trodden down of the Gentiles, until the times of the Gentiles be fulfilled.
>
> LUKE 21:24B

Our Great Prophet, in his discourse concerning the times leading up to the End, concerning the days of false labor which we have discussed in detail, stated that Jerusalem would be trodden down by the Gentiles until the times of the Gentiles be fulfilled.

Now the question is...are the phrases "the fullness of the Gentiles" and "the times of the Gentiles" the same? The answer is no! We know this because today, in our day, the times of the Gentiles has already been completed while the fullness of the Gentiles has not.

You see, since the day that Nebuchadnezzar's army conquered Jerusalem in 586 b.c., the city of the Great King has been trodden down, or under the control of a foreign government. Babylon, then the Medes and Persians, followed by Greece and then Rome dominated over the city of David. After that, the Arabs and Turks for fifteen hundred years until the 19th Century when Britain came into control of Jerusalem. As we have discussed, in 1948 Britain withdrew from Palestine and the Jews won their war for independence. But noticeably, they still did not control Jerusalem. The city remained under Jordanian rule until the Six Day War of 1967. It was on that June day when General Moshe Dyan and his army marched into the Old City and took it back under Jewish control. On that day the "times of the Gentiles" were fulfilled! Jerusalem was no longer ruled by a foreign country. After over 2,500 years the Jews finally reclaimed their holy city!

This is so relevant to our discussion because in reading Luke

24 we see that the division between the days of false labor and the days of true labor is made with this statement of our Lord's. That is, the very next verse speaks of signs in the sun and the moon, etc. Things that clearly occur during the Tribulation time frame. Thus, according to this division of God's Word by our Lord, the rapture of the Church can occur anytime after the "times of the Gentiles" be fulfilled, any time after the Jews take back Jerusalem!

Well dear reader, this happened four decades ago. *We're in overtime!* Everything is in place for the Lord to call us home, all we need is for that last Gentile believer to call upon Jesus and we're outta-here! So what is the Lord waiting for?

Peter gives the answer in his discourse concerning the end times.

> The Lord is not slack concerning his promise, as some men count slackness; but is longsuffering to us-ward, not willing that any should perish, but that all should come to repentance.
>
> II Peter 3:9

That's it! Once again it's only by the Lord's grace and mercy that we haven't heard the voice, the shout and the trump of God. He is waiting for all that will, to come to repentance. When that happens, in a day not far away, then the water will break and the labor will begin.

The Tribulation as a Laboring Woman

The Epidural

Thus far in this book which compares God's dealings with Israel, the nations and all of creation to the course of a woman's pregnancy, we have seen the Creation as a conception, the Flood as a miscarriage, and God's work with Old Testament Israel as the first and second trimesters of pregnancy, complete with many Braxton-Hicks contractions. Next we came to a time of preterm labor which was typified by Christ's first coming. After that, the third trimester ensued. We saw that the third trimester was time of false labor which will crescendo up to our present day as we wait for the rupture of membranes and the true labor to begin.

So, continuing into the time of labor, it is important to understand what a pregnant woman would be thinking as she considered her upcoming labor in days gone by. In the past, women feared for their lives as they considered their time of travail. In addition, there was no hope of any pain relief for that time. Indeed, many attempts were made to relieve that terrible agony of the birth process. Unfortunately, most were placebo concoctions which would help the mind through the pain but really didn't provide much, if any, relief. Then along came the 20th Century and modern medicine. Today, women really have no concept of the birth ordeal as it was from the time of Genesis to about sixty years ago. That's because pain relief in those days was not adequate, and women understood that they could even die during the process of birthing their children. But since that time, the maternal mortality rate has fallen so precipitously that pregnant women today do not even consider the possibility of death that was so present in the minds of those women in the days before. Also they understand that if things get "too tough" they can have an epidural to relieve the terrible agony of labor. So it is for the believer in Christ Jesus!

The Jews, the nations, and creation itself are heading for labor. They are steaming toward that seven year time of trial and travail while the man and woman who have put their faith in Jesus will be spared the pain of labor. If you will, the believer will receive an epidural from the Great Physician! Revelation chapters four & five tell us of the wonderful pain relief we will experience while at the same time the world is laboring in pain to bring forth the child! Let's look at this pain relieving time before we delve into the hard labor of the Tribulation on Earth.

The Apostle John, after hearing the voice of a trumpet saying "Come up hither," reveals the "things which must be hereafter." And it starts with an incomprehensibly wonderful heavenly scene.

> And immediately I was in the spirit: And, behold, a throne was set in heaven, and one sat on the throne.
>
> REVELATION 4:2

"Immediately I was in the spirit." We saw this before when we looked at First Corinthians 15. In the twinkling of an eye this corruptible must put on incorruption and this mortal shall put on immortality. There will be no further fleshly tendencies to deal with any more. We will immediately be in the spirit! Praise GOD!

Look at our first impression of heaven...It's the *Father* sitting upon the throne! GOD the Father, GOD Almighty, El Shaddai... he's the first One we will see!

> And he that sat was to look upon like a jasper and a sardine
> stone:
>
> REVELATION 4:3A

We call a jasper stone a diamond. The sardine stone we call a ruby. Yes, GOD is white like a diamond—he is light. And GOD is red like a ruby—he is love.

It's interesting that we have seen these two stones before in the Bible. The High Priest in the Old Testament wore a breastplate with twelve stones upon his chest representing the twelve tribes of Jacob. The first stone, remembering the firstborn son, Reuben, was jasper, and the last stone representing the youngest son, Benjamin, was a sardine. The significance becomes clear when we consider the meaning of the two boy's names. Reuben is translated "Behold My Son" and Benjamin means "Son of My Right Hand." Of course, both of the names refer to titles given to the Second Person of the Trinity, Jesus Christ. Thus we see that Jesus, the First and the Last, the Alpha and Omega, is intimately tied together with the Father in this first impression of heaven which we will see.

> And there was a rainbow round about the throne, in sight like
> unto an emerald.
>
> REVELATION 4:3B

In the Bible, the rainbow is a picture of GOD's covenant of grace towards man. After the flood of Noah, GOD gave the rainbow as a reminder that he would not again judge the world by a flood. That promise is truly by his grace as nothing done by mankind since the Flood would merit our release from such judgment!

Yes, the throne of GOD is covered in grace. Consider the words found in the book of Hebrews, "Let us therefore come boldly unto the throne of grace, that we may obtain mercy, and find grace to help in time of need" (Hebrews 4:16). Think how wonderful it is that today by faith we can come before the same heavenly throne of grace which we will one day see with our very eyes!

> And round about the throne were four and twenty seats: And upon the seats I saw four and twenty elders sitting, clothed in white raiment; and they had on their heads crowns of gold.
> REVELATION 4:4

John witnesses twenty-four elders who were clothed in white and wore golden crowns. Can we know who these elders are? GOD does give us some clues in his Word such that we can make an educated guess!

First of all the number twenty-four is germane. We remember that twelve is the number of Israel, thus a multiple of twelve will pertain to Israel in some way. In this case the doubling of twelve represents heavenly or spiritual Israel. We understand that GOD promised Abraham that his children would be as numerous as the stars in the sky and as numerous as the sand on the seashore. GOD also told him that he would be the father of many nations. Thus, twenty-four is the number of heavenly Israel, those children of Abraham from all nations, both Jew and Gentile. That is, the twenty-four elders picture the church of Christ!

We can know this because we are told that they are wearing white raiment and crowns of gold. We understand that in the New Testament, Paul told us that we too would wear white because of the blood of the Lamb and that we will receive everlasting crowns of gold because of our walk with the Lord in this life. Also, earlier in Revelation, Jesus promised the overcomers in Smyrna that they were to receive a glorious crown of life and he revealed to the church in Sardis that their overcomers would wear white raiment (Revelation 2:10; 3:5a). Thus, the twenty-four elders seem to be the heavenly way of speaking of the church of Christ.

Thus far, in this picture of heaven which John is given and is sharing with us, we have the Father sitting upon the throne of grace, radiating light and love and surrounded by those who have called upon his Son as their Savior!

And out of the throne proceeded lightnings and thunderings and voices:

REVELATION 4:5A

Lightnings and thunderings typify GOD's judgment. For we know that just as our GOD is full of grace and mercy, full of light and love...he is also a just GOD. He is a consuming fire!

And there were seven lamps of fire burning before the throne, which are the seven Spirits of GOD.

REVELATION 4:5B

Once again, we read of the perfect number, seven. This time it's in speaking of the Holy Spirit, the third Person of the Trinity.

But you may be thinking, three persons in one is hard enough to comprehend, now you're telling me that the Holy Spirit is actually seven Spirits!

Well, not exactly. This likely is an illusion to the seven-fold nature of the Spirit of GOD. Let's look in Isaiah for some illumination of this idea.

And there shall come forth a rod out of the stem of Jesse, and a Branch shall grow out of his roots: And the spirit of the LORD shall rest upon him, the spirit of wisdom and understanding, the spirit of counsel and might, the spirit of knowledge and of the fear of the LORD.

ISAIAH 11:1–2

Jesus told us that just as a father would not withhold a piece of bread or a fish from a child who asked, so too would not GOD the Father withhold the Holy Spirit from one who asked (Luke 11:11–13).

Look at what he gives the one who asks for the Spirit! It's the Spirit of the Lord. It's wisdom and understanding. It's counsel and might. It's knowledge and the fear of the Lord! It's a good deal! Now look at the way the Spirit operates practically in the next verse from Isaiah's revelation to us.

... and he shall not judge after the sight of his eyes, neither reprove after the hearing of his ears: But in righteousness shall he judge the poor, and reprove with equity for the meek of the earth:

ISAIAH 11:3B

You see the Spirit of GOD is *not* like the spirit of man. We judge and reprove by what we see and hear. Not so with the Spirit of GOD. His wisdom, understanding, counsel, and might come not by the five senses but revelation from GOD. That's why in this first scene of heaven the Spirit is before the throne. Yes, the Holy Spirit also is prominent in this holy place. Also, this seven-fold nature of the Spirit is seen as seven lamps of fire.

Do you remember the first time the Holy Spirit was given to the believers in the book of Acts on that first Pentecost after Jesus' ascension? It came as tongues of fire! The picture is perfect!

And before the throne there was a sea of glass like unto crystal:

REVELATION 4:6A

Wow, that's going to be beautiful!

In the Old Testament, Moses and the elders of Israel also recalled this impression of heaven which they were given. "And they saw the GOD of Israel: And there was under his feet as it were a paved work of a sapphire stone, and as it were the body of heaven in his clearness" (Exodus 24:10).

And in the midst of the throne, and round about the throne, were four beasts full of eyes before and behind.

REVELATION 4:6B

The revelation continues by telling us that each of the beasts has a different face. One like a lion, another like a calf, the third appears with the face of a man, and the fourth resembles an eagle. They have six wings and it is repeated that they are full of eyes!

They don't need any rest and proclaim before GOD's throne of his holiness. In fact, they sound out that heavenly prayer which many of us by faith have also joined in with at one time or another. They say (sing), "Holy, holy, holy, Lord GOD Almighty, which was, and is, and is to come" (Revelation 4:7–8). They sing of GOD's wholeness! He's everything we need! They sing of his power and might. He is the Almighty! They sing of his eternalness. He was before time began and is after time ends. He is the GOD who was, and is, and is to come!

The Prophet Ezekiel also spoke of these beasts in chapters 1 and 10 of his prophecy. He too was given a glimpse of heaven which he has shared. In his revelation these beasts are none other than living creatures. He also calls them cherubims. They are angels! As I read his vision, he too saw the One sitting upon the throne with the glassy sea of sapphire before him and the rainbow over the throne. So, continuing with John's revelation, these four cherubims are full of eyes. In the Bible, eyes typify wisdom. It is with their great wisdom that they realize that GOD is so holy!

• • • •

After John speaks of how Heaven will appear we learn of the heavenly drama for the ages in chapter five of the book of Revelation.

> And I saw in the right hand of him that sat on the throne a book written within and on the backside, sealed with seven seals.
>
> REVELATION 5:1

John saw GOD holding a book, better translated a scroll, with writing on both sides. It also had seven seals holding it closed.

In our day this imagery is difficult to understand, but not to the reader in John's time. A scroll with writing on both sides was the title deed to a piece of property. If it was sealed, it meant that the property was about to be foreclosed! It needed to be redeemed or it would be lost to the family. So here we see GOD holding the title deed for a piece of property about to be bought at a bargain price from him.

Where is this property? Why, it's the third rock from the Sun. It's planet Earth and it's about to be taken in foreclosure by the GOD of this world, Satan!

> And I saw a strong angel proclaiming with a loud voice, Who is worthy to open the book, and to loose the seals thereof?
> REVELATION 5:2

Note the angel doesn't ask who is willing, as many from Nimrod to Hitler have been willing to be the potentate, he asks who is worthy!

> And no man in heaven, nor in earth, neither under the earth, was able to open the book, neither to look thereon. And I wept much, because no man was found worthy to open and to read the book, neither to look thereon.
> REVELATION 5:3–4

The Bible clearly states that all have sinned and fall short of the glory of GOD (Romans 3:23). No man by his works, wisdom, good deeds, or intelligence is worthy to save the planet from foreclosure to Satan. This made John weep.

But one of the twenty four elders has good news for John,

> Weep not: Behold, the Lion of the tribe of Judah, the Root of David, hath prevailed to open the book, and to loose the seven seals thereof.
> REVELATION 5:5B

A mere few days after being formally rejected by the leaders of the nation, the Lion of the tribe of Judah, Jesus from the house of Judah, prevailed. He went to the cross and died for the sins of mankind. GOD then raised him from the dead, taking back the title deed of the planet. He is the Root of David, for he was before David. He is the Lion which became a Lamb!

And I beheld, and, lo, in the midst of the throne and of the four beasts, and in the midst of the elders, stood a Lamb as it had been slain, having seven horns and seven eyes, which are the seven Spirits of GOD sent forth into all the earth.

REVELATION 5:6

Now we see the second Person of the Trinity at the throne. He is Jesus the Christ. He is the Lamb who was slain. He has seven horns and seven eyes representing his immense spiritual power and insight and we again see that he is filled with the seven-fold nature of the Holy Spirit as Isaiah has prophesied. Beautifully, he has sent the seven Spirits of GOD forth into all the earth. After he died for us, he sent the Spirit of truth, the Holy Spirit, which has spoken of him, glorified him, guided us into all truth and spoken of things to come (John 16:13–14).

And he came and took the book out of the right hand of him that sat upon the throne.

REVELATION 5:7

This is the *best* news I can think of! He, Jesus, came and took the scroll. We were about to be the permanent the property of Satan, yet Jesus was willing to pay the price. He was worthy, certainly, but he was also willing to go to the cross on Mount Moriah and redeem you and me back to the Father.

The Bible says that for the joy set before him, he willingly endured the cross (Hebrews 12:2). We are that joy. He died for his bride!

Thus, this beautiful chapter ends with the angels and the saints singing a new song. They (we) sing with a loud voice,

Worthy is the Lamb that was slain to receive power, and riches, and wisdom, and strength, and honor, and glory, and blessing.

REVELATION 5:12B

Seven praises. Just what you would expect from a heavenly song. It's perfect!

• • • •

We now come to the end of this heavenly drama which we will live to be a part of if we believe in Jesus. We will see in the next chapter that the Lord will open the seals of this property deed and the Tribulation will begin. For in opening these seals, the Lord will call to him those who will come in a most dramatic way!

But, as I opened this chapter, considering this wonderful time from an obstetrical point of view, so I feel we should close it. Indeed, I have witnessed thousands of women get incredible relief from the otherwise intense and seemingly unremitting pain of labor and delivery. But in every case, the woman asks for the epidural. I don't insist that she must have this pain relief. So it is with the Lord. He doesn't force himself upon us. He doesn't insist that we call out to him for salvation from the upcoming labor. He has given us free will to chose, just as all my patients have the free will to choose to receive an epidural or to go through tribulation. It's their choice!

But an important point I want to make, and the application to this analogy, is that just as I would almost never withhold an epidural from a woman asking for one I do not want to withhold the Good News of Jesus Christ from a man or a woman wanting to know him. Not telling people who are seeking GOD about the Good News of Jesus Christ, how he died for their sins, gave them a new life, and will some day take them to be with him in heaven is like withholding an epidural from a woman asking for it in labor! It should not be done.

Lord, help us to share the Good News!

The Four Horsemen of the Apocalypse

It is now time to consider the hour of labor and travail upon planet Earth. As we mentioned at the opening of this book, labor is the time when the pains are regular in frequency and increasing in intensity. Like a vice tightening, so is labor. And lest we forget, let me remind you why labor is so painful. We were warned about birth pangs in the first book of the Bible.

> Unto the woman he said, I will greatly multiply thy sorrow and thy conception; in sorrow thou shalt bring forth children.
> GENESIS 3:16A

The agony of labor is the result of sin in the world, sin in our lives. Originally, GOD did not intend for the birth process to be so incredibly intense. The pain of labor is part of the curse mankind received through Adam and Eve, as we all have inherited their sin nature.

Thus, it should not be surprising that the sinful world of the end times should experience labor in order to bring forth new life. For, indeed, GOD will use this time to get the attention of millions of unsaved souls. People who otherwise would remain without him in their lives will instead birth something wonderful in their hearts as a result of the travail they and the world around them will experience.

Let's look at some of the obstetrical imagery that GOD uses to describe this time.

> And these are the words that the LORD spake concerning Israel and concerning Judah. For thus saith the LORD; We have heard a voice of trembling, of fear, and not of peace. Ask ye now, and see whether a man doth travail with child? Wherefore do I see every man with his hands on his loins, as a woman in travail, and all faces are turned into paleness? Alas! For that day is great, so that none is like it: It is even the time of Jacob's trouble...
>
> JEREMIAH 30:4–7A

First and foremost, this time of travail, this time when it appears that even men will experience the pain of labor, is for the Jew. It's called Jacob's Trouble and it's the time when the Lord will reveal himself to his brothers just like Joseph before him when he tested his brothers to learn what was in their hearts before he revealed himself to them. Yes, GOD has many promises to Israel which have yet to be fulfilled. He will use the time of Jacob's Trouble to call them to the place of repentance so that he can bless them with his grace and mercy. So that they can be in a place to receive all the promises peppered throughout the Word concerning their fate. "For I know the thoughts that I think towards you, saith the Lord, thoughts of peace, and not of evil, to give you an expected end" (Jeremiah 29:11).

Secondly, this time of labor and travail will be to get the attention of the entire world as Isaiah and Paul speak,

> Howl ye; for the Day of the LORD is at hand; it shall come as a destruction from the Almighty. Therefore shall all hands be faint. And every man's heart shall melt: And they shall be afraid: Pangs and sorrows shall take hold of them; they shall be in pain as a woman that travaileth:
>
> ISAIAH 13:6–8A

And,

> But of the times and the seasons, brethren, ye have no need
> that I write unto you.
> For yourselves know perfectly that the Day of the LORD so
> cometh as a thief in the night. For when they shall say, Peace
> and safety; then sudden destruction cometh upon them, as tra-
> vail upon a woman with child:
>
> I THESSALONIANS 5:1–3A

The prophet Micah, along with Isaiah, used obstetrical imagery to shed light upon when this day will be.

Let's compare their two texts to learn when the birth pangs
will hit.

> But thou, Bethlehem Ephratah, though thou be little among
> the thousands of Jacob, yet out of thee shall come forth unto
> me that is to be ruler in Israel; whose going forth have been
> from old, from everlasting. Therefore will he give them up,
> until the time that she which travaileth hath brought forth:
> Then the remnant of his brethren shall return unto the chil-
> dren of Israel.
>
> MICAH 5:2–3

This well-known verse, which clearly speaks of Jesus Christ,
reveals that there will be a time that he will give them up. We
understand that after he was rejected by the nation, our Lord
ascended to the Father. But he promised to come back and here
we learn that the time of his return will be when she which travaileth hath brought forth.

Isaiah told us about that time when he told us who the woman
would be.

> Before she travailed, she brought forth; before her pain came,
> she was delivered of a man child. Who hath heard such a thing?
> Who hath seen such things? Shall the earth be made to bring
> forth in one day? Or shall a nation be born at once? For as soon
> as Zion travailed, she brought forth her children.
>
> ISAIAH 66:7–8

Isaiah taught us that Israel would be birthed in one day as we have discussed previously. In comparing theses two obstetrical allegories, we understand that the Ruler from Bethlehem will come to govern when Zion travailed and birthed in one day. That day of course was May 14, 1948, the day that the fig tree blossomed. We remember that the generation that witnesses the birth of Israel would also see the One whose going forth is from everlasting! Dear reader, look up, we are in the Last Days!

• • • •

With that introduction, it is now time to study the various labor pangs Israel and the world will experience as there is much truth to discuss. And let me again remind you of the blessing we receive as we read this special book which was given by Jesus to the Apostle John, "Blessed is he that readeth, and they that hear the words of this prophecy, and keep those things which are written therein: For the time is at hand" (Revelation 1:3).

Just like labor, this first pang of the Tribulation time frame is not very intense. In fact, many, including the Jews, will see this first labor pain as a blessing.

> And I saw when the Lamb opened one of the seals...And I saw, and behold a white horse: And he that sat on him had a bow [rainbow]; and a crown was given unto him: And he went forth conquering and to conquer.
>
> REVELATION 6:1A, 2

Remarkably, here in the first two verses of the Tribulation, we are introduced to a conquering hero. This world leader is covered by a rainbow. We know that in the Bible a rainbow signifies a covenant relationship. In this case, this world leader will broker a peace treaty between Israel and the Arab world. He will promise that under his direction Jerusalem and the world will be able to climb out of the quagmire of the Middle East tumult as well as recover from the recent disappearance of the millions of people who seemingly have vanished overnight!

He will wear a crown. But this crown is not like the gold crowns that we saw the twenty four elders wearing in chapter 4 of the Revelation. No, this crown is a temporary crown made of garland. It is what the Olympic champions of old wore. Aptly, it is what the Caesars wore!

This conqueror, of course, is Antichrist. Paul has explained when he will be revealed. It will be after we, the saints, can no longer can hinder his coming.

> Now we beseech you, brethren, by the coming of our LORD Jesus Christ, and by our gathering together unto him, That ye be not soon shaken in mind, or be troubled, neither by spirit, nor by word, nor by letter as from us, as that the day of Christ is at hand. Let no man deceive you by any means: For that day shall not come, except there be a falling away [departure] first, and that man of sin be revealed, the son of perdition.
> II THESSALONIANS 2:1–3

In the first century, as in our day today, people were and are confused as to when the day of Christ will be. Paul taught that that day cannot happen until after the departure, until after our gathering together. In the vernacular of our day, we understand that the man of perdition cannot be revealed until after the Rapture!

The next few verses tell us why this is so;

> And now ye know what withholdeth that he might be revealed in his time. For the mystery of iniquity doth already work: Only he who now letteth [hinders] will let, until he be taken out of the way. And then shall that Wicked be revealed...
> II THESSALONIANS 2:6–8A

This old English language is difficult at first to understand, but when broken down we can learn that the departure Paul is speaking about, the thing that is hindering the revelation of Antichrist is GOD's Spirit working in the world through his children, holding "that Wicked" back. When we, who have the Holy Spirit, are taken out, then the mystery of iniquity is free to reign without constraint. That Wicked one will be revealed!

Unfortunately, the world will make him their king, as will Israel. Jesus had some words about this day as he spoke to the Pharisees concerning their lack of faith in him.

> Search the scriptures; for in them ye think ye have eternal life: And they are they which testify of me. And ye will not come to me, that ye might have life.... . I am come in my Father's name, and ye receive me not: *If another shall come in his own name, him ye will receive* (emphasis mine).
>
> JOHN 5:39–40, 43

Jesus gave this prophecy which we will see fulfilled at the beginning of the Tribulation. On that day when this seemingly man of peace rides in on a white horse he will be embraced by Israel and the world as a man in which they can put their confidence. As a man they can trust. They will see him as their salvation!

Oh, and one little postscript. We believers know him as the man of sin and the son of perdition. He is called Antichrist, that Wicked and the Beast. In the Old Testament he is pictured as Adonizedek in the book of Joshua and as Abimelech the Bramble in the book of Judges. In the New Testament he is typified by Herod the Great and the Caesars. But to those blinded souls of Jacob's Trouble he will not come on the scene as an ugly evil monster. Quite the contrary, he will be remarkable. He likely may have the charisma of JFK, the looks of Brad Pitt, the oratory skills of Winston Churchill and the brains Albert Einstein. He will seem wonderful. He will seem formidable. He will seem to be a GOD!

Next, chapter six continues with the opening of three more seals. We are introduced to the riders of the red, black, and pale horses of the Apocalypse. These riders carry war, famine, and death in their hands and begin the painful rhythmic contractions which characterize true labor. It is likely that the invasion of Israel by Russia as described in Ezekiel 38–39, and as previously discussed in great detail earlier in this book, will ride in with the red horse of war. The black horse of famine and poverty and the pale horse of death, with the demise of one fourth of the world's population will follow closely. Then after the learning of the four horsemen, the opening of the fifth seal takes the reader back to heaven for a very interesting question presented to the Lord:

"How long, O Lord?"

The Martyrs' Question of Suffering

And when he had opened the fifth seal, I saw under the altar
the souls of them that were slain for the word of GOD, and for
the testimony which they held: And they cried with a loud
voice, saying, How long, O LORD, holy and true, dost thou not
judge and avenge our blood on them that dwell on the earth?
And white robes were given unto every one of them; and it
was said unto them, that they should rest yet for a little season,
until their brethren, that should be killed as they were, should
be fulfilled.

REVELATION 6:9–11

This fifth seal is very interesting to me, for the focus shifts back
to heaven and we see the millions of slain martyrs from centuries
past until this time crying out to the Lord for justice. Crying out
for revenge, if you will.

It's also intriguing to me as I look at GOD's numerology. For
I expect to find some nugget of truth imbedded in the number
GOD uses. In this case, we have the number five. We remember
that five is the number of grace, but here in this fifth seal we have
the slain souls asking GOD, not for grace, but to move in judgment. What's up with that?

The answer to grace lies in where they are found. They are

under the altar. They are no longer on the altar of sacrifice but now are safely ensconced beneath the altar. They are no longer in a place of persecution but in a place of rest. And it's by GOD's grace that they, or any of us, will be found in heaven, for GOD clearly tells me that the wages of sin is death. We all deserve death, even those slain in Christ. Only One has led a perfect life! Thus, it's by GOD's grace that we have received the free gift of eternal life through Jesus Christ our Lord (Romans 6:23).

As I reflect upon this heavenly scene further I should not be surprised to see how many souls are there. Since the death of our Savior, millions have died throughout the centuries and across the globe for the Word of GOD and for the testimony which they held. Tradition teaches that, with the exception of John, the Lord's disciples died a martyr's deaths. Christians in the Roman Empire were slaughtered by the hundreds of thousands, as we discussed when we spoke of the persecuted church of Smyrna. Later, the Reformation time period, which included the Inquisitions of Europe and the French Revolution, took millions more home to be with the Lord due to their stand of faith against the Roman Church. Missionaries of the last two hundred years often have died for their love of Jesus, and today in China countless numbers are hiding out and dying as the Communist government does not allow belief in the only name GOD has ordained unto salvation. But Jesus and other writers told us this would happen, both in our lifetimes and in the Tribulation era.

Let me remind you of some of the many passages which speak of our persecution, which speak of tribulation for faith in the Messiah.

> These things I have spoken unto you, that in me ye might have peace. In the world ye shall have tribulation: But be of good cheer; I have overcome the world.
>
> JOHN 16:33

The Lord clearly tells us to look to him for peace. That's the key in overcoming the tribulation we *will* experience.

Yea, and all that will live GOD ly in Christ Jesus shall suffer persecution.

II TIMOTHY 3:12

Yes, it's clearly wrong to think that life in Christ will always be smooth!

Beloved, think it not strange concerning the fiery trial which is to try you, as though some strange thing happened to you: But rejoice, inasmuch as ye are partakers of Christ's sufferings; that when his glory shall be revealed, ye may be glad also with exceeding joy.

I PETER 4:12–13

We must not be surprised by trial and travail in life, Peter states. It's all in GOD's plan. So rejoice, for when we are persecuted for the Lord we partake in his very sufferings!

Peter also spoke of the glory and joy in store for the believer.

Blessed be the GOD and Father of our LORD Jesus Christ, which according to his abundant mercy hath begotten us again unto a lively hope by the resurrection of Jesus Christ from the dead. To an inheritance incorruptible and undefiled, and that fadeth not away, reserved in heaven for you, Who are kept by the power of GOD through faith unto salvation ready to be revealed in the last time.

Wherein ye greatly rejoice, though now for a season, if need be, ye are in heaviness through manifold temptations: That the trial of your faith, being much more precious than gold that perisheth, though it be tried with fire, might be found unto praise and honor and glory at the appearing of Jesus Christ.

I PETER 1:3–7

Wow! We have this lively hope through the Christ which is perfect and will not fade away! Ever!

I find it remarkable that we can rejoice in our seasons of heaviness "if need be!" I feel that's me. My life is so easy that I often feel guilty that I have it so good when I look around the world and into the past and future and see it so tough for the believer. I'm definitely in the "need be" group, that's for sure. It's only by GOD's mercy as he knows I'd probably fold under the pressure of real persecution! Look at what I'm missing. The trial of one's faith is *more* precious than gold! Let me repeat that...The trial of one's faith is *more* precious than gold!

Paul revealed to us yet another benefit of the labor pangs of life.

> Blessed be GOD, even the Father of our LORD Jesus Christ, the Father of mercies, and the GOD of all comfort; Who comforteth us in all our tribulation, that we may be able to comfort them which are in any trouble, by the comfort wherewith we ourselves are comforted by GOD.
>
> II CORINTHIANS 1:3–4

GOD uses our tribulation so that we can relate to others going through tribulation and thus be a comfort to them in their fiery trials. GOD is actually partnering with you in your travail so that you can help other souls navigate their struggles!

Thus, we understand that tribulations and persecutions are part of the life of the believer. Therefore, I believe the Lord may be saddened by this question he is asked by the multitude of martyrs as this fifth seal is opened. For he told us to expect persecutions, as we have discussed. Consequently, I believe he is gently reprimanding this group of wonderful believers by telling them to rest yet for a little season and then he graciously explains the reason why they needed to wait. It is because many more of their fellow servants are going to be martyred as the Tribulation time frame evolves.

This explanation by our Lord is truly redundant as Jesus, through the gospel writers, clearly teaches that intense persecution awaits the believer, and especially the believing Jew, during Jacob's Trouble. Let me show you the reference from Mark as it is very enlightening to this fifth seal. Also, Matthew and Luke cover the same material as they discuss the Olivet Discourse given by our Lord (Matthew 24:9; Luke 21:12–19).

But take heed to yourselves: For they shall deliver you up to councils; and in the synagogues ye shall be beaten: And ye shall be brought before rulers and kings for my sake, for a testimony against them... . But when they shall lead you, and deliver you up, take no thought beforehand what ye shall speak, neither do ye premeditate: But whatsoever shall be given you in that hour, that speak ye: For it is not ye that speak, but the Holy Ghost. Now brother shall betray the brother to death, and the father the son; and children shall rise up against their parents, and shall cause them to be put to death. And ye shall be hated of all men for my name's sake: But he that shall endure unto the end, the same shall be saved.

MARK 13:9, 11–13

Speaking to disciples of all time but specifically to those believers in the Tribulation Era, Jesus unloads the harsh truth of that day. Believers will be beaten and killed. They will be judged before rulers and kings and incredibly, the truth of the Gospel will be so upsetting that families will be separated to the point of betraying each other—brothers turning in brothers, fathers turning against sons and children rising up against their parents.

Why will the Good News be so upsetting to people? Well, somebody has to take the blame for the waves of labor pangs hitting the planet. Antichrist and those millions in his web will blame the believers in Christ for all of the problems they are suffering, both Jewish and Gentile Christians. The person who calls Jesus Lord will become a total outcast!

But just as we saw before, persecution has a good side. We see in the words of Jesus, that the Holy Spirit will give the martyr special revelation as to what to speak in that day. It will be a testimony against them. The unsaved will not be able to say that they didn't know.

Paul shares why this testimony to the unbeliever is so important to GOD.

Seeing it is a righteous thing with GOD to recompense tribulation to them that trouble you; And to you who are troubled rest with us, when the LORD Jesus shall be revealed from heaven with his mighty angels, In flaming fire taking vengeance on them that know not GOD, and obey not the gospel of our LORD Jesus Christ: Who shall be punished with everlasting destruction from the presence of the LORD, and from the glory of his power; When he shall come to be glorified in his saints...

II THESSALONIANS 1:6–10A

You see, GOD is a loving One, but also a very just GOD. Paraphrasing that wonderful line in C.S. Lewis' book, *The Lion, the Witch and the Wardrobe,* speaking of Aslan the Lion, who typifies Jesus Christ in Lewis' allegory: "No, Lucy. The Lion is *not* tame...but he is very good!" GOD is not tame, but he is very good! Being a just GOD, he will not banish a soul to outer darkness, to everlasting destruction, to a place out of his presence, without giving a person a true choice to decide between what he has to offer and what the GOD of this world has offered. By speaking the truth with the words of the Holy Spirit, the martyrs throughout the centuries and into the Tribulation will be offering the Good News to countless unsaved souls as they stand for their Master. This will lead many to fall in love with Jesus and come to salvation! Those who do not, unfortunately for them, will receive the reward for their sins as they are without the covering of the blood of the Lamb. This judgment that Paul speaks of here in Second Thessalonians is apparently what the slain martyrs are asking for as the Tribulation period starts. "We want the revenge you promised, Lord!" Jesus loving says to wait and rest, more of your fellow servants will be offered on the altar of sacrifice in order to give countless others the chance to repent!

As you can sense, I am bothered by their question as it seems extraordinary to me that these wonderful martyrs are calling for revenge while partaking of their glorious and heavenly rest! Why can't they just let it go! Why can't they forgive their persecutors from their heavenly vantage point? After all, the Savior asked for forgiveness upon his killers. Why are they even asking this question!

I can't say I know the answer to this question other than what we have just covered. That is, that the Word clearly teaches that Jesus *will* take revenge during the Tribulation era and, thus, maybe they are just asking if the time of the seal judgments is that time. Anyway, it reveals to me what is in their hearts and that's what bothers me about this question. It exposes the dark side of my own heart for it's what I would be asking also!

As I extend this thought into an application, our words reveal what is in our hearts. As James states, the tongue is able to bless GOD and curse one's neighbor. As we speak, so we are. I'm bothered that they are calling for revenge instead of forgiving and forgetting. For that's what I would be doing too! I want to know how does one forgive and forget.

> These things I have spoken unto you, that *in me* ye might have peace. In the world ye shall have tribulation: But be of good cheer; I have overcome the world.
>
> JOHN 16:33

WWJD...What would Jesus do? That's the answer. Well, he would forgive, wouldn't he? But that's not so easy, he's Jesus and I'm me. He's good and I'm not!

There must be more. And there is! To be like Jesus, I must first *like* Jesus. And to like Jesus, I must *look* at him. Dear reader, it's *in Jesus* that we find our peace. I will find myself forgiving and being like Jesus as I first like Jesus. And to like Jesus I must look at him. So the key to forgiveness is to not neglect the Word of GOD, for in it you will be looking at Jesus!

✝he Wrath of the Lamb

The next labor pang of the Tribulation is quite intense as in it the righteous anger of the Lord is revealed. It is a contraction that takes the reader back to Earth for the great day of the wrath of the Lamb.

> And I beheld when he had opened the sixth seal, and, lo, there was a great earthquake: And the sun became black as sackcloth of hair, and the moon became as blood;
>
> REVELATION 6:12

As we have discussed, Jesus told us that in the last days there would be an increase in earthquakes as well as famine, pestilence and war, but this earthquake is called a great one. The magnitude of it will be something that has never before occurred on our little sphere. It will effect planet Earth from east to west in a most dramatic and profound way. As we will see, every mountain and island will be displaced and all those who are left will wonder and question at what is going on!

We also remember that our Lord told his disciples that in that day there would be signs in the sun and the moon. Most likely, this cataclysmic earthquake will trigger multiple volcanic eruptions from the various active volcanoes worldwide which will inundate the atmosphere with dust and debris. This, of course, will darken the sun and give the moon a red hue.

> And the stars of heaven fell unto the earth, even as a fig tree casteth her untimely figs, when she is shaken of a mighty wind.
>
> REVELATION 6:13

In the Bible, a mighty wind often speaks of GOD's judgment. Indeed, judgment has come upon man as this sixth seal, the number of man, is opened.

The falling stars also intrigue me. Could this be fallout from the many volcanoes that may simultaneously erupt with this great quake or is it something entirely different? As I look forward to chapter twelve of this Revelation, I see that a third part of the stars of heaven were cast down to the earth. In this section of Scripture, these stars are the fallen angels that are cast out of heaven. Could it be that here at the time of the sixth seal, GOD is also beginning his final judgment upon those rebellious angels who have sided with Lucifer? I think it very possible!

> And the heaven departed as a scroll when it is rolled together; and every mountain and island were moved out of their places.
>
> REVELATION 6:14

When the Indonesian earthquake of December 2004 occurred, it was so massive that seismologists told us that the entire planetary surface moved a few millimeters out of position. But with this great earthquake, every mountain and island will palpably feel the effects of this birth pang. The people of the world will not need scientists to tell them that a change has occurred. It will be obvious to all!

> And the kings of the earth, and the great men, and the rich men, and the chief captains, and the mighty men, and every bondman, and every free man, hid themselves in the dens and in the rocks of the mountains; And said to the mountains and the rocks, Fall on us, and hide us from the face of him that

sitteth on the throne, and from the wrath of the Lamb: For the
great day of his wrath is come; and who shall be able to stand?

REVELATION 6:15–17

It is very interesting to me that all the people of the world,
from the least to the greatest, all seven groups listed in this Scripture, realize that this judgment is coming from the One who sits
upon the throne and from the Lamb.

Paul tells us in the first two chapters of the book of Romans
that all men understand that there is a GOD by his work of creation and by their conscience. Everyone intuitively realizes that
there is a GOD. But many choose to not recognize him in order
that they can continue to live in their unGODly ways. At this
point in history it will no longer be possible to do that. There
will no longer be any atheists! All will recognize that there is a
GOD in heaven and that the day of his wrath has arrived. Unfortunately, as we shall see, many will stubbornly continue to refuse
to call him Lord. But again, it will no longer be possible to refuse
to acknowledge his existence! That still small voice that speaks
to the quiet and listening heart has now become a shout that all
will hear!

As we continue to discuss this great quake, Isaiah has some
prophetic words for us to consider.

> Enter into the rock, and hide thee in the dust, for fear of the
> LORD, and for the glory of his majesty. The lofty looks of man
> shall be humbled, and the haughtiness of men shall be bowed
> down, and the LORD alone shall be exalted in that day...and
> the idols he shall utterly abolish. And they shall go into holes
> of the rocks, and into caves of the earth, for fear of the LORD,
> and the glory of his majesty, when he ariseth to shake terribly
> the earth. In that day shall man cast his idols of silver, and his
> idols of gold, which they made each one for himself to worship,
> to the moles and to the bats; To go into the clefts of the rocks,
> and into the tops of the ragged rocks, for fear of the LORD, and
> for the glory of his majesty, when he ariseth to shake terribly
> the earth.
>
> ISAIAH 2:10–11, 18–21

Later Isaiah would say,

Behold the Day of the LORD cometh, cruel both with wrath and fierce anger, to lay the land desolate: And he shall destroy the sinners thereof out of it. For the stars of heaven and the constellations thereof shall not give their light: The sun shall be darkened in his going forth, and the moon shall not cause her light to shine. And I will punish the world for their evil, and the wicked for their iniquity; and I cause the arrogancy of the proud to cease, and will lay low the haughtiness to the terrible...therefore I will shake the heavens, and the earth shall remove out of her place, in the wrath of the LORD of hosts, and in the day of his fierce anger.

ISAIAH 13:9–11, 13

Indeed this labor pain has been foretold.

And it also has been pictured previously in Scripture for us. You may remember the battles that Joshua and his men engaged in while taking the Promised Land also typify the Tribulation time frame as we pointed out earlier in the book. Specifically, the seven year campaign to take back the Promised Land is an Old Testament picture of the seven year Tribulation campaign where the greater than Joshua, Jesus Christ, will take back the world which belongs to him. Remember early in that campaign, Joshua and the Israelites took on a coalition of nations headed by the charismatic Adonizedek. As you may recall, Adonizedek means "Lord of righteousness" and his position was as the king of Jerusalem. This king of the Canaanites with the lofty title as Lord and king is a perfect allegory of the Antichrist who will also seek to be Lord and king over GOD's children in his day. You may also remember that chapter 10 of the Book of Joshua tells us that the Lord discomfited those men before Israel by raining down great stones from heaven. Of course, that also was the day in history when another great sign in the sun and the moon was demonstrated as a preview of coming attractions in this picture GOD was painting. For Joshua called out for the sun and the moon to stand still. GOD answered that proclamation by granting that request so that Israel could mop up their enemies. Later in the story we are told that the five kings of Adonizedek's coalition had hid themselves in the cave at Makkedah as a preview of those future kings who will also hide themselves from the One whom Joshua typifies! They hid from the wrath of Joshua as the kings and great men of the world will try to hide from the wrath of the Lamb!

Now, there is one point and one application I would like to make at this juncture in the narrative. If one does a word study on the word "wrath," the student of the Bible will note that many times when this word is used it relates to this time of judgment upon the Earth. It relates to the Tribulation. At other times "wrath" is associated with GOD's judgment on a smaller scale. But we can count on the word "wrath" being associated with the reaction of a just GOD in relation to his dealing with sin which has persisted unchecked.

Thus, thanks be to GOD that we who have called upon the Lord are covered by the blood of the Lamb and thus are saved from the Wrath of the Lamb. Otherwise, we too would come face to face with the judgment that a just GOD must pronounce upon the many sins that have marred our lives! As Paul has taught us concerning this day;

> ... how ye turned to GOD from idols to serve the living and true GOD; And to wait for his Son from heaven, whom he raised from the dead, even Jesus, which *delivered us from the wrath to come* (emphasis mine).
>
> I THESSALONIANS 1:9B-10

Thank you, Lord, that we will be heaven, in your presence, while this seven year time of trial and travail is meted out upon the Earth. Thank you that when this great earthquake shakes the very foundations of the planet, signaling the great day of your wrath, that we who have followed after the narrow way of your Son will be safely ensconced with you in heaven!

Indeed, it is a narrow way, for only by the name of Jesus can a man or woman be saved (John 14.6). But it is available to any and all who would choose (I Timothy 2:3–4). The way is narrow but it is not exclusive!

. . . .

What is it that makes the Lord angry? We may reflexively say that it must be the rejection of Jesus as the Lord of a person's life. For GOD does say that there is on only one unforgivable sin (Matthew 12:31). Well, that grieves him but it doesn't bring anger to his face. We remember that our Lord asked his Father to forgive his murders not to condemn them. Also you may recall what the Savior said to those two Sons of Thunder, James and John, when they asked Jesus to call down fire from heaven upon that Samaritan village that did not receive him. Jesus rebuked them and said that he had come to save men's lives, not destroy them (Luke 9:51–56).

No, Jesus is not angered when men reject him. But when I study the life of Jesus, he was angered whenever men would keep *others* from coming to him, from receiving him. This is what angers the Lord. This is what brings the wrath of GOD upon the children of unbelief. It's keeping others, who would, from coming to him. It can be the Pope in Rome in 1600, or Stalin in Russia in 1930. It could be the Pharisees who were casting out those from the synagogue who believed in Jesus or the Dad who won't let his kids go to Sunday school. In the Lord's eyes, it's all the same. It brings anger to those eyes that we saw earlier to be a flame of fire!

In Jesus' own words concerning what angers him, he said,

> It is impossible but that offences will come: But woe unto him, through whom they come! It would be better for him that a millstone were hanged about his neck, and he cast into the sea, than that he should offend one of these little ones.
>
> LUKE 17:1B-2

The thing that really ticks off Jesus, the thing that gets his righteous blood boiling, is to keep a little one away from him. A little one can be a child but it also can be any one who in simplicity wants to know Jesus as Lord but is kept away from that truth. Woe to that man, that leader, that religion, or that nation that blocks the way to Jesus! For the wrath of the Lamb has and will fall heavy on any person or providence that would keep the little ones from coming to the Master! In fact, I would suspect that the fall of most nations and monarchies, the fall of most religions and philosophies throughout history has been a direct or an indirect result of how that entity suppressed the truth!

Certainly, this thought is a word of warning for America as we head into the 21st Century. Is America going to continue to make it difficult for people to come to Jesus by outlawing the truth of the Bible while elevating an irrational 19th Century theory of our origins? Are the Ten Commandments and school prayer going to continue to be suppressed or will we wake up before it's too late for judgment to rain down? Unfortunately, I fear we have gone past the point of no return.

But on a personal level, it's not too late! Don't anger the Lord, dear reader. And stop angering him if you suspect you are! Don't stifle a conversation you hear in front of a "little one" out of embarrassment. Don't put up roadblocks for your wife and children to go to Sunday or Wednesday night services. Don't condone a religion that confuses the truth about salvation by professing that all roads go to Chicago! They don't! And don't support a leader who suppresses the truth in order to stay in power or to get votes. Don't keep the little ones from seeking him! Don't kindle God's Wrath!

✝he Greatest Revival

And after these things...I saw another angel ascending from the east, having the seal of the living GOD: And he cried with a loud voice...saying, Hurt not the earth...till we have sealed the servants of our GOD in their foreheads. And I heard the number of them which were sealed: And there were sealed an hundred and forty and four thousand of all the tribes of the children of Israel...After this I beheld, and, lo, a great multitude, which no man could number, of all nations, and kindreds, and people, and tongues, stood before the throne, and before the Lamb, clothed with white robes, and palms in their hands; And cried with a loud voice, saying, Salvation to our GOD which sitteth upon the throne, and unto the Lamb...and one of the elders answered, saying unto me, What are these which are arrayed in white robes? And whence came they? And I said unto him, Sir, thou knowest. And he said to me, These are they which came out of great tribulation, and have washed their robes, and made them white in the blood of the Lamb.

REVELATION 7:1A, 2A, 3A, C–4, 9–10, 13–14

Chapter 7 of the Book of Revelation documents the greatest revival the world will ever see. Multitudes in Israel and in the nations will wonder about these things they have witnessed and will be ready to receive GOD's seal upon their foreheads. They will question the wisdom of the one who rode in upon the white horse as they consider the other three riders that have also come to visit bringing war, famine, and death. After that they felt the terrible earthquake and saw the signs in the heavens which accompanied that event. Thus between the sixth and seventh seal judgment will come a time of choosing sides. It will be a time when people will decide their eternal fate. Will they align with the True and Living GOD and with the Lamb or will they continue to follow the one the Bible calls the Beast.

We learn of the result in this seventh chapter. The Bible states that 144,000 Jews will call upon Messiah and become the greatest evangelistic force the world will ever see. John tells us wonderfully that a "great multitude" which no man can number will come out of the Tribulation having their robes washed in the garments of salvation. They will be washed by the blood of the Lamb.

Elsewhere, the Bible reveals how and when this will occur.

> For the children of Israel shall abide many days without a king...Afterward shall the children of Israel return and seek the LORD their GOD, and David their king and shall fear the LORD and his goodness in the *latter days* (emphasis mine).
>
> HOSEA 3:4A, 5

At the time of the End, Israel will call upon David their king. This, of course, refers to the greater than David, the Son of David, Jesus the Christ!

Hosea next focuses upon the timing of this revival in Israel with the following prophecy, "I will go and return to my place, till they acknowledge their offence, and seek my face: In their affliction they will seek me early" (Hosea 5:15). Jesus proclaimed to the men of Jerusalem: "Behold, your house is left unto you desolate. For I say unto you, Ye shall not see me henceforth, till you say, Blessed is he that cometh in the name of the Lord" (Matthew 23:38–39).

Indeed, Hosea's words are speaking of the Messiah! Jesus told the leaders of the nation that due to their rejection of him, they would no longer see him until they realized he is Lord. Hosea reveals that they will seek him "early in their affliction." Early in the Tribulation time frame, early during the time of Jacob's Trouble the Jews will call out to Jesus. And as we have seen, 144,000 will have a special anointing.

What Hosea reveals next is remarkable.

> Come, and let us return unto the LORD: For he hath torn, and he will heal us, he hath smitten, and he will bind us up. After *two days* will he revive us: In the third day he will raise us up, and we shall live in his sight (emphasis mine).
>
> HOSEA 6:1–2

We remember that with the Lord, a day is as a thousand years. Thus this prophecy proclaims that after two thousand years, Israel will be revived. In the third day they will rise up!

Well, dear reader, this is the third day! We are *in* the third day. Two thousand years ago Jesus told the Pharisees that they would not see him again until they acknowledged their offense. This is the day they will do that very thing!

One generation after Hosea, the prophet Joel revealed how this evangelistic anointing will appear,

> Fear not, O land; be glad and rejoice: For the LORD will do great things...Be glad then, ye children of Zion, and rejoice in the LORD your GOD...And I will restore to you the years that the locust hath eaten...And ye shall know that I am in the midst of Israel...And it shall come to pass afterward, that I will pour out my spirit upon all flesh; and your sons and your daughters shall prophesy, your old men shall dream dreams, your young men shall see visions: And also upon the servants and upon the handmaids in those days will I pour out my spirit.
>
> JOEL 2:21, 23A, 25A, 27A, 28–29

Jesus put it this way in speaking of this end time revival, "And the gospel of the kingdom shall be preached in all the world for a witness unto all nations; and then the end shall come" (Matthew 24:14).

C.S. Lewis has been widely quoted saying, GOD whispers to

us in our pleasure but he shouts to us in our pain. Here, early in the Tribulation, we see the eternal benefit of the labor pangs the people of the world have undergone thus far. Millions will come to know the Lord who otherwise would have dismissed the Gospel as irrelevant to them. From a spiritual perspective, that's a main reason for tribulation in our lives, both today and in that future time period.

I think of the story in the book of Daniel of Shadrach, Meshach, and Abednego to illustrate this principle. We read that after those three young men were thrown into the fiery furnace that their bonds were broken and another "like the Son of GOD" walked in their midst. This speaks of the literal Son of GOD who *was* in their midst. Yes, it is in that time of tribulation, that time of intense labor, that we cry out to the Lord. In the world's case, it will be that type of travail that will lead many will cry out to Jesus and receive the message of salvation.

I see this often in a woman's travail. During that time of concentrated rhythmic labor pain, many women who are not really very close to GOD will cry out to him for relief and support. Indeed, a woman's labor is a spiritual time for her just as the Tribulation will be a very spiritual time for those left behind.

Jesus said speaking of these things, "Come unto me, all ye that labor and are heavy laden, and I will give you rest" (Matthew 11:28). It is when I come to him that I find rest. Paul adds these words concerning tribulation,

> ... but we glory in tribulations also: Knowing that tribulation worketh patience;
> And patience, experience; and experience, hope: And hope maketh not ashamed;
>
> ROMANS 5:3B-5A

Tribulations refine the soul like fire refines a sword. Paul teaches that it is by the tribulation of life that I develop that important fruit of the spirit called patience. Then as I patiently wait on the Lord's deliverance I gain the experience that he always is there when I need him. This experience is most valuable the next time a trouble occurs in my life. For now I have the hope that no matter what, he will be there for me. Thus, I am not ashamed for I have lost my natural unbelief that I had before the refining fires came into my life.

Lastly, concerning this pain of labor, we must always remember that there is nothing that we go through in this life that our Savior has not also felt and experienced. He has literally felt our pain. When I consider the GOD of the Universe, leaving his place as Lord of angels and galaxies and becoming confined to a man's body—it blows me away! Not only that, he first became a baby and had himself birthed in a stable by a teenage woman. Then, he went through the process of submitting to those young and inexperienced parents before beginning a ministry, not as an upper echelon rabbi, but as an uneducated teacher from the other side of the hierarchal fence. He was rejected at every turn and ultimately was tortured and killed in a manner that closely resembled a laboring woman's course as we discussed in Book VI of *A Woman's Silent Testimony* called "Of Blood and Water." No, our GOD is not one that is remote and out of touch. In all things he was tempted and tried just as you and I are. Indeed, our GOD is full of compassion and he feels our pain!

So to conclude, we read how wonderful this time will be. In that day, millions who will be left behind will seek and call upon Jesus as Lord. They will be clothed in white and will ever be with the Lord. But the Tribulation will bear on! Some will be miraculously protected as we will later see, but many will be martyred for their new faith as the Beast and the GOD of this world will attack relentlessly in an ethnic cleansing that will make Hitler's Holocaust look like a schoolboy's prank in comparison.

But first, there will be silence in Heaven as the terrible seventh seal is opened!

Chernobyl

And when he had opened the seventh seal, there was silence in heaven about the space of half an hour. And I saw the seven angels which stood before GOD; and to them were given seven trumpets.

REVELATION 8:1–2

The seventh seal to the title deed of planet Earth contains seven trumpets. I must remind you that in the Bible, trumpets are associated with release from bondage. They are associated with freedom, with victory, with jubilee! So it should not be surprising that as the Lord is taking back the planet from Satan that trumpets will sound.

These trumpets also herald an increase in the intensity of the birth pangs the Earth will experience. As with a laboring woman, as the end approaches, the pains become closer and more intense.

Let's listen to their sound.

The first angel sounded, and there followed hail and fire mingled with blood, and they were cast upon the earth: And a third part of the trees was burnt up, and all green grass was burnt up.

REVELATION 8:7

I recall the plagues of Egypt as GOD was delivering his people from Pharaoh as I read of some of these trumpet judgments. And in reflecting upon those plagues, I remember that in some of them the children of Israel felt their effects as did the Egyptians. While in others, they were shielded. This phenomenon we will see again. Not all of these trumpet judgments will affect the believer during the time of their sounding.

Hail and fire mingled with blood cast down from above. Could this be a 1st century description of a nuclear exchange? Quite possible!

And the second angel sounded, and as it were a great mountain burning with fire was cast into the sea: And the third part of the sea became blood.

REVELATION 8:8

Scientists tell us that the Earth is riddled with meteor impacts. We can look up into the night sky as see the effects of numerous celestial collisions which our satellite moon has endured. Here, this second trumpet sounds like a massive meteor landing in the sea. We understand that the devastation from such an event will be incredible as the earth and sea will rock to and fro like a drunken sailor on the deck of a wind tossed sea. Coastal areas will be inundated with tsunamis and blood will flow.

In our day today, NASA and the government talk about developing the technology that would deflect such a meteoric event from occurring. In reading the Bible, I learn the result of this search will not be successful!

And the third angel sounded, and there fell a great star from heaven, burning as it were a lamp, and it fell upon the third part of the rivers, and upon the fountains of waters; And the name of the star is called Wormwood: And the third part of the waters became wormwood; and many men died of the waters, because they were made bitter.

REVELATION 8:10–11

Like the fiery mountain before, which will taint the sea, this burning star will make one third of the rivers, one third of the fresh water, bitter and deadly. In considering what exactly this falling star could be we find a powerful clue in its name. The Apostle John reveals that the star is called Wormwood.

Wormwood is rotten worthless wood which is not suitable for building. Its only use is to be burnt in a fire. C.S. Lewis, in his wonderful book, *The Screwtape Letters,* named one of the tempting devils, Wormwood. Could it be that this falling star called Wormwood is a powerful devil which will fall to Earth much like Lucifer had fallen earlier? Well, as much as I like Lewis, I don't think that's where the clue is found. No, the meaning is found by traveling north, to Russia. Specifically to a little city, which until the 1970's, no one outside of the Ukraine had even heard of. The city is called Chernobyl.

Chernobyl became infamous in the 70's because the energy producing nuclear reactor located nearby suffered a terrible uncontained meltdown. This accident contaminated the downwind area for many miles with radioactivity. Thousands suffered and died and the local area became uninhabitable. To use biblical terminology, the waters were made bitter! Now you are wondering, that's interesting, but how do you make the leap from a falling star called Wormwood to what happened in Chernobyl?

The answer is found in the Russian dictionary. Chernobyl means "wormwood!" I believe GOD in his foreknowledge was smiling when he told John to name this falling star Wormwood. For indeed, he knew that in time the notable event in Chernobyl would reveal the future meaning of Wormwood!

Thus, this falling star is most likely a radioactive event which will ruin one third of the fresh water of our planet and cause many to die from radioactive poisoning. We remember that the first trumpet was also likely associated with nuclear energy, so it may be that these two are tied together in that way. Obviously, I cannot be dogmatic on these things as they are yet to occur!

And the fourth angel sounded, and the third part of the sun was smitten, and the third part of the moon, and the third part of the stars; so as the third part of them was darkened, and the day shone not far a third part of it, and the night likewise.

REVELATION 8:12

Darkness will cover the Earth like a blanket. Again, in our modern scientific understanding we have learned that as dust and debris inundate the atmosphere after multiple nuclear exchanges and/or a horrific meteoric collision that light from the sun, moon and stars will be blocked. The Bible is very accurate as an ancient science manual and this verse, to me, is clearly a 1st century way of describing the phenomenon we understand as nuclear winter. GOD reveals that this judgment will not be so catastrophic as to completely blot out the sun, leading to an ice age, but it will cause enough atmospheric havoc that for one third of the time, likely for a time after sunrise and before sunset, when the sun is low, that its light will not be seen due to the blanketing effect of this trumpet blast.

Other writers using GOD's pen have also shared this information with us. First, Mark quotes Jesus:

> But in those days, after that tribulation, the sun shall be darkened, and the moon shall not giver her light.
>
> MARK 13:24

The prophet Joel is next,

> And I will show wonders in the heavens and in the earth, blood, and fire, and pillars of smoke. [This could this be the earliest description of a mushroom cloud!] The sun shall be turned into darkness, and the moon into blood, before the great and terrible Day of the LORD come.
>
> JOEL 2:30–31

And lastly, Isaiah,

> Behold, the Day of the LORD cometh, cruel both with wrath and fierce anger, to lay the land desolate: And he shall destroy the sinners thereof out of it. For the stars of heaven and the constellations thereof shall not give their light: The sun shall be darkened in his going forth, and the moon shall not cause her light to shine.
>
> ISAIAH 13:9–10

And,

> The earth is utterly broken down, the earth is clean dissolved, the earth is moved exceedingly. The earth shall reel to and fro like a drunkard...And it shall come to pass in that day...Then the moon shall be confounded, and the sun ashamed, when the LORD of hosts shall reign in mount Zion, and in Jerusalem, and before his ancients gloriously.
>
> ISAIAH 24:19–20A, 21A, 23

Indeed, the first three trumpet blasts, that of the hail and fire, the great mountain cast into the sea and Wormwood seem to have brought about this fourth angelic trumpet.

> For we know that the whole creation groaneth and travaileth in pain together until now.
>
> ROMANS 8:22

Without a doubt, at this point of future history which we are considering, Planet Earth will not be in false labor as Paul was describing in the First Century, but it will be in hard travail, it will be in active labor! Next, we are taken from these natural calamities as we are in wonder of this time of progressive labor, to the description of supernatural and demonic events which the Bible calls the three "Woes."

Apollyon's Locus✝s

And the fifth angel sounded, and I saw a star fall from heaven
unto the earth: And to him was given the key of the bottomless pit. And he opened the bottomless pit; and there arose
a smoke out of the pit, as the smoke of a great furnace...and
there came out of the smoke locusts upon the earth: And unto
them was given power...and it was commanded them that they
should not hurt the grass of the earth, neither any green thing,
neither any tree; but only those men which have not the seal
of God in their foreheads. And to them it was given that they
should not kill them, but that they should be tormented five
months...and in those days shall men seek death, and shall not
find it; and shall desire to die, and death shall flee from them...
and they had tails like unto scorpions, and there stings were in
their tails: And their power was to hurt men five months. And
they had a king over them, which is the angel of the bottomless
pit, whose name in the Hebrew tongue is Abaddon, but in the
Greek tongue hath his name Apollyon. One woe is past; and,
behold, there come two woes more hereafter.

REVELATION 9:1–2A, 3A, 4–5A, 6, 10–12

At this point, the Tribulation time period shifts gears dramatically. Yes, as we have seen, the people of the world intuitively

understand that the difficulties they find themselves in are due to the wrath of the Lamb. But these same terrors which have befallen will likely be explained away as unfortunate natural disasters by those with hardened hearts. Not so anymore. Now we are entering a time of demonic activity which will continue to plague those left behind in new and devilish ways. No longer will the events of the day have an apparent rational explanation.

We first learn that with the sound of this fifth trumpet, John saw a star fall from heaven to earth. Is this a literal star? Of course not! Like the star called Wormwood in our last chapter, this star is speaking about something bright and remarkable. But interestingly, this star must be a person as we are told that "to *him* was given the key to the bottomless pit."

I recall that Jesus told his disciples that he had beheld Satan fall as lightening from heaven. And then he said something very interesting immediately thereafter,

> Behold, I give you power to tread on serpents and scorpions, and over all the power of the enemy: And nothing shall by any means hurt you.
>
> LUKE 10:18–19

Indeed this account we are studying seems to refer back to Jesus' words as given in Luke. We will see that just as our Lord said, these demonic entities will have no affect upon his followers.

Most likely, this star is Lucifer, the brightest of GOD's angelic creation who rebelled by wanting to be a star himself. He was kicked out of heaven and now, in the narrative, he is given the key to the bottomless pit.

Of course, there is an application that is staring us in the face here. It's the "lose my life to gain it verses the try to hang onto it to lose it" scenario. As I try to be a *star*, I will fall like lightning. Don't be a star, for all good gifts come from GOD and to him belongs all glory and honor. As I grab the glory for myself I will fall just as Satan did.

So to the serpent was given the key to the bottomless pit. We remember that early in this Revelation we were told that the One whose eyes were as a flame of fire, whose voice was as the sound of many waters and whose countenance was as the sun held the keys of Hell and death. Indeed, it is Jesus, the GOD-man, who as possessor of this particular key gives it to our Enemy so that he can release those who have been locked away in that terrible smoky place.

We read that these interned devils are as terrible locusts which pour out upon the earth and begin a plague which makes the locusts of Egypt look like fruit flies in comparison! They are hopping mad and upon their release they are going to take out their anger upon the men of the Earth. But once again, like some of the plagues of Egypt, they are not allowed to hurt the one who has the seal of GOD on his forehead, the one who has GOD on his mind, the one who has Jesus' blood covering and protecting him. They are not allowed to hurt GOD's children!

Now the Bible gives us some clues as to how these demonic locusts, with their leader Apollyon, ended up in the pit in the first place. Jude, in speaking of fallen angels starts the discussion,

> And the angels which kept not their first estate, but left their own habitation, hath he reserved in everlasting chains under darkness unto the judgment of the great day.
>
> JUDE 6

Jude informs us that certain angels did something extraordinarily evil and were banished to the bottomless pit until this day we are presently discussing. He prophesies that indeed these angels will be released just as John is describing. Peter tells us that these imprisoned spirits were punished in the days of Noah and that the Lord revealed the finished work of salvation to them after his death on the cross (I Peter 3:19–20).

So what did these particular angels do in the days of Noah which caused them to be sent to the bottomless pit while others, including Satan himself, have had continued power over the affairs of the world? Genesis chapter 6 gives the answer. There we learn that certain sons of GOD, otherwise known as fallen angels, saw that the daughters of men were fair and took them as wives. Thus, in that unholy matrimony devils were having sex with humans and creating a race of unredeemable children. We are told that the offspring were "mighty men, men of renown." More correctly, in modern vernacular, they were mighty in wickedness.

Thus, GOD immediately judged those angels who participated in Apollyon's lust as they left their first estate as Jude revealed. They left the bounds that GOD had allowed them to operate in by joining sexually with the daughters of men.

We learn that after their release they are allowed to torment the unbeliever for five months but that those unfortunate ones cannot die. Indeed, they want to commit suicide, as the Bible tells us they will seek death, but death will flee from them for some reason.

Thus, after five months, we come to the end of the first woe. The angels that led to the miscarriage of the flood of Noah are back on the scene. The Earth is not a safe place now. One woe is past, but behold, two more will follow!

✝he Fire and Brimstone of Idolatry

And the sixth angel sounded, and I heard a voice...saying... Loose the four angels which are bound in the great river Euphrates. And the four angels were loosed, which were prepared for an hour, and a day, and a month, and a year, for to slay the third part of men.

REVELATION 9:13A, 14A, C-15

As the sixth angel blasts his trumpet we see GOD's sovereignty over the demonic principalities and powers. I am comforted as I read that these four murderous angels have been prepared for this time, in GOD's mind, from eternity past!

It's also very interesting that they have been kept in the great Euphrates River. We remember this river was first mentioned in the book of Genesis as one of the four rivers which flowed out of the Garden of Eden. Indeed, Adam and Eve's wonderful garden was no doubt near the lush and beautiful Euphrates River valley! Now you may be thinking, lush and beautiful! Not quite! Have you seen Iraq on the news? It's dry and dusty! It's brown and hot. But that's the point! The Euphrates River, along with the Tigris River, outlines a valley in Iraq which was once called the Fertile Crescent. It's is my contention that Iraq, called the land of Shinar in the Bible, became cursed because of it's heavy demonic activity which has been present there throughout the ages.

You see, after Satan tricked Eve in Eden, along came an evil man named Nimrod to settle in the land. The Bible states in Genesis 10 that he was a mighty hunter against the Lord. He founded the kingdom of Babel and his rebellion led to the infamous Tower of Babel which was erected there.

Later, this area became known as Babylon, and a religion which has persisted as an alternative to GOD's truth was born called the Babylon mystery religion. Without a doubt, this false religion, which is at the root of all of the mythologies which followed, was inspired by the demonic powers which ruled the land.

The Book of Daniel also gives much strength to this argument of the strong demonic presence found in the Euphrates River Valley. In chapter 10 we read that Daniel purposed to fast and pray to understand from GOD of the things to come. We read incredibly that an angel was dispatched at the time of Daniel's initial request but was blocked for twenty-one days by "the prince of the kingdom of Persia!" It was not until "Michael, one of the chief princes" came to help his comrade that he could deliver the message from GOD to Daniel. This tells me that Daniel was living in the heart of the GOD of this world's kingdom. And this explains much of the past, as well as much of the predicted future events which have and will occur in Iraq.

Thus, these four powerful demons are released and they raise an army of two hundred million horsemen. The Bible tells us next that they kill a third of the remaining citizens of the planet with an issue of fire and brimstone which proceeds forth from horses' mouths.

It is interesting to reflect upon the numbers used once again. Four is the number of Earth and in this case this planet-wide disaster initiated by these four demons will make World Wars I and II look childish by comparison. Also, this being the sixth seal shows the tie between man and the demons who have inspired us. Lastly, when I jump forward to the sixth vial judgment of chapter sixteen, I see that the great river Euphrates is dried up so as to prepare the way for the kings of the East. Thus the sixth trumpet judgment seems to be closely aligned with the sixth vial judgment.

Now as we have seen already, these prophecies of the end times are not isolated to the book of the Apocalypse, Joel in the Old Testament, gives a parallel prophecy to John's.

> Alas for the day! For the Day of the LORD is at hand, and as a destruction from the Almighty shall it come...Blow ye the trumpet in Zion, and sound an alarm in my holy mountain: Let all the inhabitants of the land tremble: For the Day of the LORD cometh, for it is nigh at hand. A day of darkness and of gloominess, a day of clouds and of thick darkness, as the morning spread upon the mountains: A great people and a strong; there hath not been ever like, neither shall be any more after it, even to the years of many generations. A fire devoureth before them; and behind them a flame burneth: The land is as the garden of Eden before them, and behind them a desolate wilderness; yea, nothing shall escape them. The appearance of them is as the appearance of horses: And as horsemen so they run. Like the noise of chariots on the tops of mountains shall they leap, like the noise of a flame of fire that devoureth the stubble, as a strong people set in battle array. Before their face the people shall be much pained: All faces shall gather blackness. They shall run like mighty men; they shall climb the wall like men of war...When they fall upon the sword, they shall not be wounded...The earth shall quake before them.
>
> JOEL 1:15 2:1–7A, 8B, 10A

Scholars are not clear just what these horses and riders will be. Are they 1st Century depictions of tanks and cannons, of jeeps and hummers? Or are they otherworldly forces under the command of the four rulers of the Euphrates River?

I don't know! But I can't help but think that there is a tie between this army, as the sixth trumpet, and the two hundred million man army of the kings of the East coming forth over the dried up Euphrates River when the sixth vial is poured out. As an aside, in speaking of the kings of the East, in speaking of the

Orient, China recently boasted of the ability to mount an army of, you guessed it, two hundred million men!

So we'll just have to wait and see from which dimension comes this army!

Next we read,

> And the rest of the men which were not killed by these plagues yet repented not of the works of their hands, that they should not worship devils, and idols of gold, and silver, and brass, and stone, and of wood: Which neither can see, nor hear, nor walk.
>
> REVELATION 9:20

Here we learn of the root cause of man's problem—the root cause of these plagues: man will not repent from worshiping the *works of their hands!*

GOD thundered in the first commandment that he is the Lord and he would not tolerate other GODS before him. Not because he's insecure, but because he knows what will give us the most eternal satisfaction. When you or I put the works of our hands before him, we suffer a separation that can have eternal consequences. The Bible tells us that GOD is a jealous GOD. Again, this means that he is jealous for us. He doesn't want us to be courted by other GODS!

When we worship the works of our hands, that job, that hobby, that portfolio, instead of trusting GOD for our sufficiency and satisfaction we learn from the text that we are really worshiping devils! We learn that we are suffering from a case of idolatry!

And what a rip off it is! These six idols (there is that number six again) cannot deliver me. They cannot see and hear for me and they cannot walk with me. They are worthless!

That's how I'll feel about my job, my golf game or my portfolio in they day of trouble and in the Day of the Lord. Those things that I may worship from time to time will be without value to me in that day!

So how do we tell if we are worshiping the works of our hands? How do we tell if we are worshiping idols?

There are three easy questions to ask ourselves:

1. What do we turn to in the time of trouble? Who do we look to in the day of despair? Is it the LORD or is it my idol? Do I seek the LORD, or do I run out to work or to the golf course to find relief?

2. Where do we turn for our satisfaction? Again, do I long to dwell in the house of the LORD? Do I enjoy his Word and his presence in my life or would I rather sit in front of the latest sitcom or work on my stock investments than spend time with my Savior? Now I am not saying that working my investments, caring about my job, enjoying golf, and snowboarding are bad in themselves. I'm only saying, like the First Commandment, that when they become more important than my relationship with my Father, then I've got a problem.

3. Idolatry causes me to become what I worship! Am I known as a Jesus guy who happens to be a doctor and like golf? Or do others see me as passionate investor with eyes focused like lasers on the non-eternal goals of my life?

The Psalmist has some important words to consider,

The idols of the heathen are silver and gold, the work of men's hands. They have mouths, but they speak not; eyes have they, but they see not; They have ears, but they hear not; neither is there any breath in their mouths. *They that make them are like unto them: So is every one that trusteth in them* (emphasis mine).
PSALM 135:15–18

So, dear believer, ask yourself these three questions from time to time and then make the necessary adjustments to give your life the proper balance. GOD's Word clearly states in our text here that the blinded of the world would not *repent* of their idolatry. Know that it's always *pride* that gets in the way of repentance. Look at the passions and loves of your life, and if they are before your Maker, then swallow your pride and repent of the pedestal you have placed them on. And the great thing about it is, for the most part, if those passions are not wrong in themselves, you don't have to give them up! Just put them in their proper place.

Next we come to chapters ten through fifteen of the book of Revelation. As we have discussed, this prophecy is given in chronological order, yet many events will occur simultaneously. This is the case for the next five chapters leading up to the vial judgments of chapter 16. It is my belief that the things we will study leading up to these next seven judgments will occur concomitantly as well as overlap with some of the seal and trumpet plagues which we have just reviewed.

So off we go to the very interesting next section of Revelation. Five chapters telling of a mighty angel, two powerful witnesses, celestial battles, a more complete revelation of Antichrist, his ten nation confederacy and his sidekick, the False Prophet.

The Seven Thunders and the Little Book

The World now is in the middle of the Tribulation time frame. In our labor analogy, the cervix is dilated to five or six centimeters and the pains are very intense each being only a couple of minutes apart now. Things are moving forward with rapidity and the birth of the baby is only a few hours away! But what a few hours they will be.

> And I saw another mighty angel come down from heaven...
> and he had in his hand a little book open...and he cried with a
> loud voice...and when he had cried, seven thunders had uttered
> their voices. And when the seven thunders had uttered their
> voices, I was about to write: And I heard a voice from heaven
> saying unto me, Seal up those things which the seven thunders
> uttered, and write them not.
>
> REVELATION 10:1A, 2A, 3A, C-4

What is this? John knows a secret that no one else, since this revelation was given to him, comprehends. He heard what the seven thunders uttered but he's not telling! That's because he was instructed by the voice from heaven to seal up this part of the revelation. So unlike the seven seals, the seven trumpets and soon the seven vials, we won't know in advance any details of the seven thunders.

And that's the way many things are in spiritual life. We walk by faith and not by sight. God is not in the business of giving me all the details. Sure, he speaks to me. But he's not always a chatterbox! When Peter asked for an explanation of why the Master was washing his feet, look at what Jesus said: "What I do thou knowest not now; but thou shalt know hereafter" (John 13:7b).

Later, Peter understood of the importance of service in regards to leadership. But at that time he was scandalized by what he perceived Jesus was doing. That is, the greater washing the feet of the lesser.

So it is for us here. Certainly, important truths were revealed to John which the voices of the seven thunders uttered, but they are truths that we must wait to hear and understand. Likely it is that I cannot even appreciate their message this side of their future occurrence, but on that day when they are uttered again, I will!

Moses, in the Torah spoke of this principle also, "The secret things belong unto the Lord our God: But those things which are revealed belong unto us and to our children for ever" (Deuteronomy 29:29a). There are many things the Lord has revealed to mankind, but other truths remain a secret. The sum total of this principle is as follows: The blessing is not in knowing, the real blessing is in knowing the One who knows!

Stay close to Jesus, dear believer, that's all the information you really need to know!

> And the voice which I heard from heaven spake unto me again, and said, Go and take the little book which is open in the hand of the angel...and I went unto the angel, and said unto him, give me the little book. And he said unto me, Take it, and eat it up; and it shall make thy belly bitter, but it shall be in thy mouth sweet as honey. And I took the little book out of the angel's hand, and ate it up; and it was in my mouth sweet as honey: And as soon as I had eaten it, my belly was bitter. And he said unto me, thou must prophesy again before many peoples, and nations, and tongues, and kings.

Revelation 10:8a, 9–11

We understand from the first verse in chapter one of this Revelation that this Word was given, sent, and signified by Jesus to his angel unto John. A further understanding of the word "signified" is that it was written in sign language, it was written in code. One of the reasons a type of sign language was used was to stimulate passion in the reader. For example, which gives you a better mind picture of Jesus' righteous anger as his judgment begins to fall? To say, Jesus will judge the world or to call it "the wrath of the Lamb"? You can think of many other examples that we have studied thus far. The code is always found in the Bible and so it is in concluding what is this little book John was told to eat.

Jeremiah stated,

Thy words were found and I did eat them."

Jeremiah 15:16

David said,

The law of the Lord is perfect, converting the soul: The testimony of the Lord is sure, making wise the simple...More to be desired than gold, yea, than much fine gold: Sweeter also than honey and the honeycomb.

Psalms 19:7, 10

Of course, the little book is none other than the Word of God. I can see why eating this little book would be sweet to the taste, for the Word is wonderful. The Good News that I have a Savior that died taking my sins to his Cross and who will come back to take me to be with him is as tasty as can be. But why then is the Word bitter in my belly?

That's because the Word also reveals what happens to the man or woman who rejects the Good News, who rejects the Gospel of salvation, who rejects our Lord's brutal sacrifice which atoned for that man or woman's sins. They will be banished to outer darkness. They will suffer eternal destruction. They will be sent to hell and whatever unimaginable place that statement implies. Thus, the Word, the little book, will be bitter as I contemplate the message of death it delivers to those who reject it.

And that's why the angel told John that he was to again prophesy to the peoples, nations, tongues, and kings. For it's the truth of the Word concerning people who are dying that motivates me, that motivates us, to keep witnessing to the lost.

・　・　・　・

Now before we move on to the next chapter there is an application to be found in examining the mighty angel which held the little book. We are further told in the text of chapter ten that the mighty angel was clothed with a cloud, he had a rainbow upon his head, his face appeared as the sun and his feet were as pillars of fire. Also, when he spoke his loud voice sounded like a lion.

Wow, that description sounds like GOD, it rings of Jesus. Certainly, many times when GOD appeared in the Old Testament it was in a cloud. Examples of the cloud upon Mt. Sinai, the cloud before the tabernacle, and the cloud which appeared when Jesus was transfigured come to mind. Also, we remember John's description of Jesus from Chapter one so very well. There Jesus' countenance appeared as the sun and his feet burned as fine brass. In that heavenly scene described in chapter four, we saw the One who sat upon the throne with a rainbow over his head. And lastly, we remember in chapter five that Jesus is called the Lion of the tribe of Judah. Is this mighty angel Jesus? The answer is no!

This angel we are told is seen standing with one foot upon the land and the other in the sea. He's on the earth. But, in the book of Acts, we are told that Jesus would come back as he had left (Acts 1:11–12). He is coming back to Jerusalem and specifically he will come back to the Mount of Olives as also Zechariah prophesied (Zechariah 14:1–4).

No, this angel just looks an awful lot like Jesus. And that's the application! This angel has been sitting in the presence of his Lord and, thus, has taken on the appearance of the Lord. Remember when Moses was glowing after spending time with GOD on Mount Sinai. So it is with this mighty angel. He looks like Jesus because he has spent time with Jesus. And that's what I want for me. That's what can happen in your life also. As I (as we) spend time with the Lord, as we seek him hour after hour, day after day, we begin to look like him. We take on his mannerisms and we begin to reflect his glory. That's what this mighty angel did, and that's what we can do, too!

Thus, after John heard the seven thunders and ate the little book he was taken to Jerusalem and to the Temple Mount. That will be our next stop also as the labor ensues in preparation for the birth.

✝ he Temple of God and the Court Given Unto the Gentiles

And there was given me a reed like unto a rod: And the angel stood, saying, Rise, and measure the temple of God, and the altar, and them that worship therein. But the court which is without the temple, leave out, and measure it not; for it is given unto the Gentiles: And the holy city shall they tread under foot forty and two months.

REVELATION 11:1–2

You may recall as the time of Jacob's Trouble began we witnessed a man ride in on a white horse. Remember that he had a rainbow and wore the crown of Caesar. He went forth conquering and to conquer. This introduction of the future world leader who will become the Antichrist will occur under the guise of peace. The rainbow signifies a covenant relationship and here in our text we learn how he initially gains power and prestige. It's because he is able to seemingly solve the Middle East problem after so many before him have failed. He will be able to somehow successfully bring both Arab and Jew together and for a time they will appear to dwell side by side in peace.

Yes, this charismatic "peacemaker" will bring about the construction of the Jewish Temple, on Mount Moriah, the only place it can be, without offending the Arabs. Our text tells us how he will do it.

John was told to take a reed. This was a ten foot rod which was a type of yardstick used to measure architecture. He was to measure the temple and the altar but not to gauge the court which is without. You may recall from the Old Testament descriptions of the Tabernacle, and later of the Temple, that the house of God consisted of three distinct areas. They were known as the Outer Court, the Holy Place, and the Holy of Holies. Any Jew could enter the Outer Court but only the priests who were sanctified were allowed to go into the Holy Place. As for the Holy of Holies, just the High Priest could enter and that was on one day each year which was the Day of Atonement. Well, John is told that at this point in history that the Temple is rebuilt and he was to measure it. But he was to only gauge the Holy Place and the Holy of Holies. That's because the Outer Court is given over to the Gentiles. It will still belong to the Arabs! That's how this so-called man of peace will broker the peace between Arab and Jew. He'll get them both to compromise! You see, now that the Jews control Jerusalem, they desperately want to have their Temple rebuilt. Since they do not accept Jesus as Messiah they understand that they are still living in their sins. They understand, as the Torah clearly states, that only by the shedding of blood are their sins forgiven. And they see that this is not occurring. They fear for their spiritual lives and desire their Temple to be rebuilt so that the yearly sacrifice can begin anew.

But their politicians understand the roadblock to this dream. It's called The Dome of the Rock. This Islamic holy site was erected in the late 7th Century and is the fourth most holy site in all of the Islamic world. It was built by Omar on the site which was held to be the Holy of Holies. The jagged rock in the midst of Dome is believed to be the site where Abraham went to sacrifice his son. Only, to the follower of Allah, that son was Ishmael, the father of the Arab nations, not Isaac, one of the three Hebrew patriarchs.

Thus, today's Jewish leaders understand that to raze the Dome of the Rock to build the Temple would lead to World War III. They just can't risk it, as they know that the entire Islamic world would unite in a way that would lead to much bloodshed and death. It would be a fierce battle that Israel, even with all her modern military might, would not want to initiate.

But wait! Maybe there can be both the Dome of the Rock *and* the Temple on Mount Moriah. That's the deal Antichrist will broker. That's the covenant which will cause him to begin to glow like the Messiah in the eyes of the Jews as he allows for the construction of the Temple without feeling the wrath of the Arab world. And he'll have help from the Hebrew scholastic community.

That's because in the early 1980's a Hebrew scholar, Dr Asher Kaufman, concluded that the Dome of the Rock is not really built upon the ancient site of the First and Second Jewish Temples. He had concluded that another piece of exposed bedrock, approximately one hundred meters to the north of the Dome of the Rock, is the true site of the Temple. This flat piece of bedrock, which would have been much more suitable for animal sacrifice, does have a small shrine erected over it by the Arabs called the Dome of the Tablets. A second name for this little memorial is the Dome of the Spirits. Originally those names where bestowed upon this modest shrine as it is believed that the Arabs initially understood that it was on that piece of bedrock where the Ark of the Covenant holding the two tablets upon which were inscribed the Ten Commandments resided. Likewise, they understood that it was upon this site that the Spirit of GOD hovered over the mercy-seat. Also Kaufman concluded through archaeological means that the Dome of the Tablets was directly west of the ancient Eastern Gate of the city. This was an important discovery, for the Mishna, that Hebrew book of oral tradition, had long stated that when the High Priest stood in the Holy of Holies, he could look directly out through the Eastern Gate and see the Mount of Olives. This visual relationship is not present when one stands near the Dome of the Rock. Since the Dome is to the south of the true site, if one were to look through the Eastern

Gate he would see Mount Scopus, the mount to the north of the Mount of Olives, which presently is the site of Hebrew University.

Thus, many Jews have already concluded that the Dome of the Rock is not on the site of the Temple, but one hundred meters to the south. Antichrist will grab hold of this fact and offer the construction of the Temple without an Outer Court. For the Outer Court would extend into the Dome and thus cause a deal-breaker. The Jews will take the offer and a Temple without an Outer Court will indeed be constructed just as the Bible tells us here in our text! We are even told how long the two will co-exist together. It will be for forty two months. For three and a half years. It will last for half of the seven year time of Jacob's Trouble!

Now we must ask ourselves if this will be such a good idea. That is, should the Jews compromise with the Arabs at the suggestion of the charismatic leader to come and build their Temple without an Outer Court? After all, we have all learned from our parents very early in life that compromise is a good thing!

Well, in this case, compromise will not be good. And that's because the leaders of Israel will be asked to compromise on the Word of God! You see, II Timothy 2:15 tells us that all Scripture is inspired. The Jews certainly know that their Scriptures always include an Outer Court when speaking of either the Tabernacle or of the Temple. When God told Moses how he wanted his earthly house to be constructed he included the Outer Court. After Moses, when the revelation of the heavenly Temple was given to Ezekiel it also included an Outer Court. Thus, for the men of Israel to concede to build a Temple without an Outer Court, well that's *no* Temple at all. No wonder it will only stand for forty two months!

The application to you and me should be clear. Compromise is fine if it doesn't involve stepping over God's Word! But when it does, then I must look to another avenue for conflict resolution. When the Word tells me that Jesus is the only way to the Father, that homosexuality and adultery are bad, well, then I must decide if I will compromise upon these truths when the world asks me to accept its doctrines! It's very subtle, dear reader. Don't fall for it! Always remember that *all* scripture is "GOD breathed," is inspired. Embrace GOD and his Word and you will know when to compromise and when to respectfully decline the offer!

•   •   •   •

Next, after learning of the apostate Temple, John is given revelation of the two witnesses and their 1,260 day ministry to the people of Israel. As we developed earlier in Book II of *A Woman's Silent Testimony,* entitled "Death, Burial and Resurrection," these two powerful men are likely none other than Moses and Elijah. Those two men who were with Jesus on the mount of Transfiguration will likely again powerfully appear as a witness to the Jews. They will witness of the Law (Moses pictures the Law) and of the Prophets (Elijah typifies all of the Prophetical writings) as they speak of Jesus, the One of whom the Law and the Prophets reveal.

When their testimony is finished they will be murdered by the man the Bible calls the Beast, and will then be resurrected, before the world to see, three and one half days later. There will be a great earthquake which will occur in the same hour of their resurrection and that will cause the remnant of Jews who are spared to give glory to GOD.

This will mark the end of the second woe and will immediately be followed by the blast of the seventh trumpet. In heaven it will be a beautiful sound while on Earth the sound will not be so sweet.

And David Shall Be King

And the seventh angel sounded; and there were great voices in heaven, saying, The kingdoms of this world are become the kingdoms of our Lord, and of his Christ; and he shall reign for ever and ever.

REVELATION 11:15

This is the second coronation of Jesus as king. Earlier in chapter five of Revelation, we witnessed the first coronation of our Lord. On that day shortly after the rapture of the church, the Bible proclaims that ten thousand times ten thousand will be surrounding him and singing the heavenly song of his kingship and authority. We will sing worthy is the Lamb that was slain to receive power, riches, wisdom, strength, honor, glory, and blessing.

The third coronation, of course, will occur in chapter nineteen of Revelation as Jesus returns to the Earth as King of Kings and Lord of Lords. The Bible tells us in Zachariah fourteen that all of the nations will come up to Jerusalem to worship and honor him yearly during the Feast of Tabernacles.

We remember that three is the number of completeness and here in his coronations we see the complete progression of Jesus' anointing as King. The first ceremony occurs in heaven before his family, if you will. The Father and Spirit are present along with the cherubims and the church, as we discussed in a prior chapter. This second coronation is now in heaven a few years later. The Tribulation saints who have died by this point are now also in heaven praising their Savior. They now are joining in and witnessing this second ceremony. You might say that we have progressed from the family to the tribe as the scope of the Messiah's reign widens. Of course, the entire world will partake in the King's last coronation. On that day he will be recognized by *all* as the only and true King.

We have seen this pictured before for us in the Old Testament. The Bible teaches that King David was a powerful picture of the future King of Israel, Jesus Christ. Jesus, as a descendant of David, will on that day claim his right to the throne of David.

Let's look at the name that the prophets gave the One who would ascend to the throne on that latter day.

> But they shall serve the Lord their God, and David their King, whom I will raise up unto them.
>
> JEREMIAH 30:9

And,

> David my servant shall be king over them; and they shall have one shepherd…and my servant David shall be their prince for ever.
>
> EZEKIEL 37:24A, 25B

Also,

> For the children of Israel shall abide many days without a king, and without a prince, and without a sacrifice, and without an image, and without an ephod, and without teraphim: Afterward shall the children of Israel return, and seek the Lord their God, and David their king; and shall fear the Lord and his goodness in the latter days.
>
> HOSEA 3:4–5

The prophets, by revelation, see the connection between

David, whom they have known historically, and the future King. Thus they are free to call him David. As you may have guessed by now, David also had three coronation ceremonies which picture perfectly the future kingdom of the Lord. And of course, the progression is the same.

David first was anointed by Samuel in the company of his father and brothers (I Samuel 16:3). At that point no one else in the tribe of Judah or the nation of Israel recognized him as King. As we saw at Jesus' first coronation, only the family, so to speak, were present.

Later, after Saul's death on Mount Gilboa, David was anointed King over Judah (II Samuel 2:4). But the men of Israel still did not recognize him as the rightful King. Abner, Saul's mighty general, proclaimed Ishbosheth, the son of Saul, king over Israel. This is analogous to Jesus coronation here in our text as now the family and the tribe have come to see him as King but those of the world still are rejecting him.

Lastly, David was elevated to king of the entire nation after the deaths of Abner and Ishbosheth (II Samuel 5:3). Finally, after his enemies were put down, did all see David as their rightful King. Of course, when Jesus returns as defeats his enemies on that day, all will also understand just who he is. He is the King!

Here at this time of the second heavenly pronouncement of Jesus' kingship, the nations continue to be angry and rage. They are still against the King. They continue the process of active labor. The birth pangs are most brutal now. The sound of the seventh trumpet, which will be so sweet to you and me in heaven will not be so pleasant to those laboring away in unbelief upon planet Earth.

The Bible teaches that at this time the temple of God will be opened in heaven and the ark of his testament will be seen (Revelation 11:19). I picture Indiana Jones in that classic Hollywood scene at the end of the movie, *Raiders of the Lost Ark*. Remember, when the ark was opened that deadly power proceeded forth. Likewise at this point, the Revelation testifies that lightnings, and voices, and thunderings, and an earthquake, and great hail will issue forth as yet another power labor pang will seize upon the Planet (Revelation 11:19).

Thus, after the sounding of the seventh trumpet we come to the next section of Jesus' Revelation to us concerning his plan. It is one of my favorites. The imagery is powerful as GOD pictures past and future events in a way that is remarkable. For who can forget a woman clothed with the sun and the moon under her feet!

✝he Day Christ was Born

And there appeared a great wonder in heaven; a woman clothed with the sun, and the moon under her feet, and upon her head a crown of twelve stars: And she being with child cried, travailing in birth, and pained to be delivered.

REVELATION 12:1–2

Scholars have debated over the years as to the meaning of these and the other upcoming verses which speak of both a celestial and earthly battle. Very interesting conclusions have been put forth and as such I won't say that I have the final answer to the question. But I will give you my understanding of these descriptive words and I will suggest to you that GOD, in his immense command of poetry and prose, can assign more than one meaning to this section. For indeed, that is what I believe he has done. Like peeling an onion, layer by layer, GOD has placed in code more than one truth for the student of Scripture to peel off and understand.

The most common interpretation, and the one that is most important towards studying the flow of this Revelation, is that the woman is the nation of Israel and of course the child is the coming Messiah which Israel births. In several places, most notably in Isaiah, Israel is called the wife of Jehovah. "For thy Maker is thine husband; the Lord of hosts is his name" (Isaiah 54:5a).

Also, we read in the story of Joseph found in the book of Genesis concerning the sun, the moon, and the twelve stars, that in Joseph's dream, Jacob, who typifies Israel, was pictured as the Sun while his wives typified the Moon and his sons were analogous to the stars (Genesis 37:9–10). Lastly, we remember that twelve is the number that GOD has attached to the nation of Israel. Thus it's easy to conclude, after comparing Scripture with Scripture, that the woman in this imagery is Israel. We will be told concerning the child in a couple of verses that he is the one who will rule all nations. Thus it's not too hard to get the identity of the child as Jesus the Christ.

But a second meaning is much more deeply imbedded in the onion. For we see a labor and delivery occurring in this heavenly scene and as an obstetrician I must ask myself, could this be an actual delivery? Could this be talking about the actual, literal delivery of the Christ?

Let's consider that possibility!

All would agree that Jesus was not born on December 25th. It's been understood for centuries that the day of his birth was not really known. Thus the early Christians accepted the incorporation of Christ's birthday into the Roman winter celebration of Saturnalia after the Empire was Christianized by Constantine. But could this second meaning of these verses actually give us the day of Jesus' birth? With a little help from modern calculus and physics, I think it can!

You see others have stated that this heavenly woman is the Virgin Mary and she is laboring to bring forth the Messiah. And indeed, that can be part of this understanding, for that interpretation also directs us to the birth of the child who will rule all nations. But there is another woman in heaven who has on her head a crown of twelve stars. That woman...Her name is Virgo!

Scholars have taught us that GOD has revealed his plan in the stars. E.W. Bullinger's book, *The Witness of the Stars,* is the classic text describing how GOD's plan for salvation is revealed night after night in the sky above. Ancient people understood some of this revelation and yet the devil, also having some understanding of these things, directed the corruption of these truths into the occultic "science" of astrology.

Nonetheless, as David declared,

> The heavens declare the glory of GOD: And the firmament showeth his handiwork. Day unto day uttereth speech, and night unto night showeth knowledge. There is no speech nor language, where their voice is not heard.
>
> PSALMS 19:1–3

Truly, GOD has written his Word in the firmament above. This is the clue we need to grasp in order to see this woman spoken of here in our text as the Queen of the Zodiac, known as Virgo.

The zodiac, of course, is that line in the night sky made up of twelve constellations which are coursed by the Sun during each of the twelve months of the year. Virgo has historically been designated as the head of the twelve constellations and our text here in Revelation would tend to confirm that as we see her wearing the crown of twelve stars.

But it's the celestial association with the Sun and the Moon which may give us the day of Christ's birth.

You see, Virgo is viewed during the night in the springtime. But she is clothed with the Sun in September. Thus, in working through this possible interpretation of our text we can conclude that the month of Jesus' birth was the month that Virgo was clothed with the Sun, i.e. September.

This would make much more sense when we consider the birth of our Lord. Everyone agrees that shepherds would not have been grazing their sheep outside of Bethlehem on December 25th. It was far too cold at that time of the year in Israel, but in September it would not have been. September is also important biblically. For in it we have the Jewish New Year called the Feast of Trumpets, the Day of Atonement and the Feast of Tabernacles. Certainly, GOD who loves to have things work out, might have his Son arrive on the planet at this time as it would add further meaning to his Word and his plan. So September looks good. What about the actual day?

That's where we need to have some help from mathematics. You see, scientists today can calculate what the sky looked like on any day in past history because they can calculate the stars motion mathematically. The paths of the stars are predictable into the future and can be retraced back into the past. Mathematicians can tells us when and where the next eclipse of the sun will be as well as calculate when the next pass of Halley's Comet will come. So it is with the night sky in the year of Jesus' birth. Astronomy has suggested to us that 3 b.c. was the actual year of our Lord's birth because in that year a conjunction between Jupiter, known as the king planet, and Regulus, the most prominent star in the constellation of Leo the Lion, occurred several times. It was understood that the constellation of the Lion represented the people of Jacob, and a few biblical scholars believe that it was this very unique celestial event, occurring on numerous occasions that revealed to the Magi that a King had been born in Israel. This would explain why so few other people were cognizant of the Christ star. It's because it wasn't necessarily so bright and beautiful but because it had such meaning only to those who understood the language of the stars.

So back to 3 b.c., the year of the Messiah's birth. In that year, Virgo was clothed with the Sun from August 27th to September 15th. Those were the days the Sun appeared to track through the constellation of Virgo. But our text also tells us that the Moon was under her feet. Now that's more like it for now we have just one day to pick from. Remember, the Moon orbits the Earth on a twenty eight day course. One week the Moon will seem full and then we note it waxing and waning. Also for one week out of the month the Moon is not seen well because it is on the same side of our planet as the Sun. This type of moon is called a new moon and it is only seen just before daybreak or just after sunset. But just because we can't see it doesn't mean it isn't there. That's how the Sun and the Moon were aligned on the day of Jesus' birth. The woman wearing the twelve stars, Virgo, as head of the twelve constellations, was clothed with the Sun and the Moon was under her feet. The Moon was just below the constellation as we would look at it. That alignment can only occur on one day per year and in 3BC that day was September 11th! [1]

So there you have it! September 11th 3 b.c. was the day I believe that Jesus Christ was born. Can I be dogmatic? Of course not! But it is interesting to consider.

Also, two other pieces to the puzzle. What was the first thing you thought of when I mentioned September 11th? Why, the World Trade Center attacks, of course. What an irony if our Lord's true birthday occurred on the anniversary of the day that will live in infamy in our national conscience! But the second piece to the puzzle is just something GOD would love to ordain. September 11th 3 b.c. was Tishiri 1st on the Jewish calendar.

Now that's incredible! Remember that's the Jewish New Year, that's the Feast of Trumpets. That's the day that the trumpets were blown from sunrise to sunset to celebrate Jehovah's reign over the entire world. How symbolic it is that his Son would be born on the Feast of Trumpets!

• • • •

Okay, that's the hidden meaning which many of you skeptics may not believe. I accept that. It's okay. I realize that it's a little far out there also. But it's important to remember that we don't know all of GOD's ways and we don't understand all of his revelation. So it seems very likely to me that there are some things on the edge of our comprehension, like this, that will come to light in the ages to come. On that day when we see and understand things more clearly!

Next, it's time to dig into the more accepted interpretation of these interesting verses. The spiritual cause for the battle which has affected our planet for eons will be explained. In other words, we will learn of the spiritual reason for birth pangs!

V.P. Wierwille: Jesus Christ Our Promised Seed

✝he Battle of the Ages

> And there appeared a great wonder in heaven; a woman clothed
> with the sun, and the moon under her feet, and upon her head
> a crown of twelve stars: And she being with child cried, travail-
> ing in birth, and pained to be delivered.
>
> REVELATION 12:1–2

Remember, by comparing this imagery with other Scripture we
can conclude that the woman is the nation of Israel and she is
birthing forth the Messiah—the Child who will rule forever.

We see that the woman is suffering the travail of labor.
Indeed, that has been the lot that the nation of Israel has received
throughout her history in her role as the mother of the Christ.
The clan, and later the nation, has been laboring since their
beginning. Up next, we learn of the reason for their suffering as
we are introduced to the villain of the story.

> And there appeared another wonder in heaven; and behold a
> great red dragon, having seven heads and ten horns, and seven
> crowns upon his heads.
>
> REVELATION 12:3

The woman giving birth was the first great wonder. Next we see another great wonder. We see an ugly, multi-headed red dragon who is a king, or more correctly, he is seven kings as he has seven heads all wearing kingly crowns.

Now, if we skip ahead to verse nine we learn that this dragon is none other than the Serpent, the devil. This dragon is Satan. Paul in his 2nd letter to the Corinthians calls him the GOD of this world (II Corinthians 4:4). Here we read that he has a seven-headed kingship.

Pastor & Teacher Jon Courson, and others in the Calvary Chapel denomination have said that this seven-headed manifestation of the dragon is seven kingdoms which have been directed by Satan to dominate Israel throughout her history. Those kingdoms being, Egypt, Assyria, Babylon, Medio-Persia, Greece, Rome and, last but not least, the still to come seventh kingdom which will intimidate Israel during the Tribulation time frame. That seventh kingdom, of course, will be ruled by Antichrist and will be the ten nation confederacy of the revived or new Roman Empire.

Now let's see what the dragon, the GOD of this world, causes to happen.

> And his tail drew the third part of the stars of heaven, and did cast them to the earth:
>
> REVELATION 12:4A

This is speaking of the rebellion in heaven which occurred in prehistoric time past. You see, as we read the Bible, we note that angels are often referred to as heavenly lights. They too are called stars. They were seen as the heavenly host when they announced the birth of Jesus to the shepherds that night over Bethlehem and they are called the hosts of heaven when those fallen angels are spoken of. Thus, we learn here that Satan conspired with one-third of the stars in heaven, one-third of the angels, and by their rebellion they were cast to the earth.

As a digression, Ezekiel reveals why this occurred,

Son of man, take up a lamentation upon the king of Tyrus, [Lucifer] and say unto him, thus saith the LORD GOD; Thou sealest up the sum, full of wisdom, and perfect in beauty. Thou hast been in Eden the garden of GOD; every precious stone was thy covering...the workmanship of thy tabrets and of thy pipes was prepared in thee in the day that thou wast created. [Incredibly, Lucifer was created as heaven's worship leader.] Thou art the anointed cherub that covereth; and I have set thee so: Thou wast upon the mountain of GOD; thou has walked up and down in the midst of the stones of fire. Thou wast perfect in thy ways from the day thou wast created, till iniquity was found in thee. By the multitude of thy merchandise they have filled the midst of thee with violence, and thou has sinned: Therefore I will cast thee as profane out of the mountain of GOD: And I will destroy thee, O covering cherub, from the midst of the stones of fire. *Thine heart was lifted up* because of thy beauty, thou hast corrupted thy wisdom by reason of thy brightness: I will cast thee to the ground, I will lay thee before kings, that they may behold thee. Thou hast defiled thy sanctuaries by the multitude of thine iniquities...therefore will I bring forth a fire from the midst of thee, it shall devour thee, and I will bring thee to ashes upon the earth in the sight of all them that behold thee. And they that know thee among the people shall be astonished at thee: Thou shalt be a terror, and never shalt thou be any more (emphasis mine).

EZEKIEL 28:12–13A, 13C–18, 18C–19

Remember these prophetic words as we discuss what Satan has been doing in the course of world events we are considering. He was the anointed cherub. He was created as the perfect musical minstrel. He was able to lead all of the heavenly hosts in praise and worship of their Creator by reason of his tabrets and pipes. We would say, that man could sing!

He walked with GOD in the midst of the stones of fire! I'm not sure what that means but I do comprehend that it was something special! But then he sinned. And what was Lucifer's sin? What was the sin that caused GOD to change his name from Lucifer, meaning "morning star" to Satan, which means "hostile opponent?" His heart was lifted up! His wisdom was corrupted by reason of his beauty. The thing that wiped out God's most perfect created being was pride!

That's the sin that was found in his heart and that's the same sin that we humans, who are born in sin, also suffer from. Our pride is killing us! It's killing me. Oh Lord, please forgive us of our prideful hearts, for when we consider you, we have nothing to be proud of. Only holy fear as we consider the result of Satan's elevated heart and his very fate.

Thus, the dragon was able to pull one-third of the other angels into his web of deception as apparently they too became jealous of their Creator as pride filled their hearts also. Consequently, they were cast out of heaven as Ezekiel revealed and as John confirms here in this section of the Revelation.

But at this point, even though they have been cast out of heaven, by comparing Scripture with Scripture it is apparent that Satan still has access to God. He is still free to have an audience with Jehovah. The Bible calls him the accuser of the brethren. I picture him standing before God pointing out our flaws and shortcomings. I also hear the Father say in response to Satan that he only sees us covered by the blood of his Son. He proclaims to Satan that we are not guilty, for we have been made righteous by the redemptive work of Calvary. Thank the Lord for the Cross!

We remember that Satan stood before God and desired to test Job and we recall the words of Jesus when he told Peter that Satan had demanded to sift him like wheat. Yes, up to this point in history Satan has been cast out of heaven but he still has access to God. We will soon see that that access to God will be closed down.

So, just what does it mean then when we are told in Ezekiel and here in the Revelation that Satan was cast out of heaven, when we consider that he can still stand before Jehovah?

Well, consider that God lives outside of the space–time continuum. He is outside of the box, if you will. I believe that before Satan and his minions fell into the sin of pride they too were present with the Father outside of the dimension of time. And that's the change that happened to the fallen angels when they were cast out of heaven. They left that place of time and space eternal and where thrown into the dimension of linear and progressive time and of finite space. Satan and his leagues were banished into time and space. They lost the ability to move freely above time and space as the Lord does. Satan became much more limited. Soon we will see that he will become even more grounded as later in this chapter he will be unable to leave planet Earth and will no longer have any access to God or to heaven. Now he is in time and space, soon he will be banished geographically as well. Banished to the earth, waiting for the end-game that will send him to the lake of fire!

Thus, the dragon is mad!

> And the dragon stood before the woman which was ready to be delivered, for to devour her child as soon as it was born.
>
> REVELATION 12:4B

Satan, knowing that time is now against him has made it his top priority to kill the child that the woman would deliver. He concluded that if he could keep the child, the Messiah, from coming to rescue mankind, he could salvage a victory out of the jaws of the defeat he had suffered in being cast out of heaven.

Thus, as we look at the history of the woman, at the history of Israel, we see the evidence of Satan's intense attack. Story after story in the Bible illustrates the world's displeasure with Israel. From Cain killing Abel, to Esau wanting to take Jacob's life, to the cruel bondage under Egypt, to battles with the Amorites and the Midianites and the Philistines, we see Satan's inspired efforts at destroying the Jews and thus keep the prophesized Messiah from arriving. When he wasn't successful at taking out the entire nation he would go after the line of David for he knew of the prophecy that the Anointed One would come from the loins of David. More than once the dragon nearly decimated the Christ line, only to have God miraculously intervene with a rescue.

Later, the kingdoms of Babylon, Persia, Greece, and Rome all took their best shots at total extermination of the Jews. We remember the biblical account of Herod and his murderous rampage against the children of Bethlehem after he first learned of the Messiah's arrival from the Magi. Of course, the dragon was behind all of these activities from his seat as GOD of this world!

After Satan's unsuccessful attempts at stopping the Redeemer's initial arrival, you may remember from an earlier chapter that he thought he had won the battle when he successfully crucified the Messiah. How insanely mad he must have been when he learned of the Christ's resurrection three days later followed by the outpouring of the Holy Spirit upon those the Savior came to rescue!

His anger then spilled into our present era. World leader after world leader, both secular and religious, have persecuted, tortured and killed the Jews. I think of the Caesars, the Popes of the Middle Ages, Ferdinand and Isabella during the Spanish Inquisition, the Ottoman Turks, followed by Hitler and Stalin. In our day, the Arab World as well as the religion of Islam desire to see the destruction of Israel and the Jew. All inspired by the dragon in his zeal to devour the child as it was born!

> And she brought forth a man child, who was to rule all nations with a rod of iron: And her child was caught up to GOD, and to his throne.
>
> REVELATION 12:5

Of course, the man child is Jesus; after fulfilling his Father's will he was caught up (raptured) to GOD just as the Bible prophesied! The anger of the dragon toward the woman, toward the Jews, will culminate with his inspired world potentate which the Bible reveals is Antichrist. This Satanically possessed despot will relentlessly desire the annihilation of the children of Jacob. Of course, GOD will not let that happen.

> And the woman fled into the wilderness, where she hath a place prepared of GOD.
>
> REVELATION 12:6A

Isaiah and Zechariah prophesied of this same protection from the Lord.

In that day shall this song be sung in the land of Judah: We have a strong city; salvation will GOD appoint for walls and bulwarks. Open ye the gates, that the righteous nation which keepeth the truth may enter in.

ISAIAH 26:1–2

And,

Send ye the lamb to the ruler of the land of Sela [Petra]...Let mine outcasts dwell with thee, Moab; be thou a covert to them from the face of the spoiler: For the extortioner is at an end, the spoiler ceaseth, the oppressors are consumed out of the land.

ISAIAH 16:1A, 4

Isaiah reveals that the place of protection will be the ancient, famous rock city and fortress of Petra. Petra is that city built into a narrow rift in the earth's crust in modern-day Jordan, just southeast of the Dead Sea. It is so narrow that historically it was easily defended against otherwise superior attackers. In the future that same thing will happen as the Jews will hole-up in the land of Sela, in Petra. By GOD's grace and mercy he will keep Antichrist from destroying them.

As I alluded to, Zechariah adds the following information to the story.

And it shall come to pass, that in all the land, saith the LORD, two parts therein shall be cut off and die; but the third shall be left therein. And I will bring the third part through fire, and will refine them as silver is refined, and will try them as gold is tried: They shall call on my name, and I will hear them: I will say, It is my people: And they shall say, The LORD is my GOD.

ZECHARIAH 13:8–9

GOD will deliver the remnant. One third of those Jews alive during Antichrist's reign of terror will be delivered by GOD to Petra. There they will be safe and will call Jehovah their GOD!

... that they should feed her a thousand two hundred and threescore days.

REVELATION 12:6B

For 1,260 days the children of Israel will be protected in Petra. That's three and one half years. It will be half of the seven year time of Jacob's Trouble that the Jews will be safely ensconced in Petra. Next, while war is raging here on Earth, Revelation tells of a brutal heavenly conflict which will occur simultaneously as the dragon tries one last time to defeat his Creator.

And there was war in heaven: Michael and his angels fought against the dragon; and the dragon fought and his angels, And prevailed not; neither was their place found any more in heaven. And the great dragon was cast out, that old serpent, called the Devil, and Satan, which deceiveth the whole world: He was cast out into the earth, and his angels were cast out with him.

REVELATION 12:7–9

Don't think for a minute that Satan is on opposite, yet equal footing with GOD. No, the Devil is on the same footing as Michael and the other angels, but not on par with GOD. GOD has allowed Satan to roam heaven and earth to accomplish his will in allowing man the free choice that love requires. But now that time is near its end he graciously allows Michael and his forces to once and for all boot Satan and his doomed followers out of heaven. No longer will heaven have to suffer the accusations of the evil one.

And I heard a loud voice saying in heaven, Now is come salvation, and strength, and the kingdom of our GOD, and the power of his Christ: For the accuser of our brethren is cast down, which accused them before our GOD day and night.

REVELATION 12:10

The next verse is a parentheses which describes how the brethren, how we believers, overcome the dragon.

> And they overcame him by the blood of the Lamb, and by the word of their testimony; and they loved not their lives unto the death.
>
> REVELATION 12:11

We overcome our Adversary in three ways. First, the blood of the Lamb frees us from the legal grip that Satan had over us. Secondly, the word of their testimony, that is, the Word of GOD washes our mind of the dirt that Satan would seek to cover us in. Lastly, as we die to this world and live for heaven, we complete the process and are truly set free. It's the blood covering my heart, the Word in my mind, and my eyes looking to heaven. That's the winning combination. That's how the brethren overcome their accuser.

> Therefore rejoice, ye heavens, and ye that dwell in them. Woe to the inhabiters of the earth and of the sea! For the devil is come down unto you, having great wrath, because he knoweth that he hath but a short time. And when the dragon saw that he was cast unto the earth, he persecuted the woman which brought forth the man child.
>
> REVELATION 12:12–13

This persecution of the Jews, and the other followers of the man child, the Tribulation Christians, will be the most intense siege of cruelty and bloodshed that the world will ever see. Not because of GOD's wrath, but due to Satan's! He will attack GOD's people in a blind rage as his time is short. He is a cornered animal. As Ezekiel stated earlier, a fire will come forth from within him and will devour him.

Again, GOD promises to come to the rescue.

> And to the woman were given two wings of a great eagle, that she might fly into the wilderness, into her place, where she is nourished for a time, and times, and half a time, from the face of the serpent.
>
> REVELATION 12:14

GOD essentially repeats himself as this verse is nearly identical to verse 6 which we read earlier in this chapter.

Israel will fly to her desert enclave where she will be protected for two and one half times. A "time" in the Bible is five hundred four days. Doing the math we see that five hundred four plus five hundred four plus two hundred fifty two equals 1,260 days.

Yes, GOD states this same truth of his protection of the remnant again. We remember that when GOD repeats himself it is an important key to understanding what this Author wants to emphasize. In this case, he is telling Israel, once again that he will never leave or forsake them. That's the same promise I have, that you have, from Yahweh!

> And the serpent cast out of his mouth water as a flood after the woman, that he might cause her to be carried away of the flood.
>
> REVELATION 12:15

I see this flood as a great army of men and military materials sent by Antichrist, under the serpent's direction, in an attempt to annihilate the Jews. We remember that Zechariah tells us that two thirds will indeed be taken out. But look at the result of the attack!

> And the earth helped the woman, and the earth opened her mouth, and swallowed up the flood which the dragon cast out of his mouth.
>
> REVELATION 12:16

We remember the earth swallowing up Korah, Dathan, and Abiram and their rebellious company of confederates in the Book of Numbers (Numbers 16:1–33). Of course, that story was a near perfect picture of this rebellion by the serpent. Likewise on this future day, the armies of Antichrist will be swallowed up miraculously by the earth.

Could this be an actual rift on the surface which will engulf the armies of the beast? Possibly. Or it could be that in this area of desert sand, that a supernatural sand storm may engulf the attacking leagues.

Whatever it is that GOD uses to defend the remnant of the children of Israel, it will be a birth pang of tremendous intensity which will swallow up the flood which the dragon cast out of his mouth. This will intensify the dragon's anger against the Jews as well as their compatriots, the Tribulation saints.

> And the dragon was wroth with the woman, and went to make war with the remnant of her seed, which keep the commandments of GOD, and have the testimony of Jesus Christ.
>
> REVELATION 12:17

GOD told Abraham that he would be the father of many peoples and nations. Along with that, Paul told us that we who have called Jesus, Lord, are children of Abraham. Indeed, we will see very soon in Revelation that Antichrist, in association with the one the Bible calls the False Prophet (Revelation 19:20), will relentlessly seek to kill and destroy those who have the testimony of Jesus Christ, those who are related to Abraham through faith in the Messiah. How will they do this? Read on...it called the Mark of the Beast. It's the one world government and the one world currency. It's the number 666!

✝he Beast

Revelation now is ready to describe the Antichrist in all of his infamy. But he has been present in the story from the very beginning of the Tribulation. We remember that Paul told us in Second Thessalonians that the man of sin, the son of perdition, would be revealed after the Rapture. You may also recall that when Jesus opened the very first seal on the title deed of the world in Revelation chapter six that it brought the first of four horsemen. Of course, that first horse was white and carried one wearing a temporary wreath. He was a man who conquered through peace and diplomacy. He was the Antichrist who came to power early in the seven year Tribulation.

But now we have crossed into the Great Tribulation. That three and a half year period, that forty two month period, that 1,260 day period, which is the second half of the seven year time of Jacob's Trouble. It is characterized by Antichrist's entering into the Jewish Temple and declaring himself to be GOD! The Bible calls this the Abomination of Desolation. We will discuss this certain future event in some detail in a bit.

Also, in considering the analogy that this book has carried forth throughout its course, that of a woman's pregnancy, this time of the Great Tribulation is late in the active phase of labor.

The contractions are very close together now and are extremely intense. The baby will soon be born!

Of importance, though, Jesus told the men of Israel in Matthew 24 that when they saw their Temple being desecrated by Antichrist, then immediately all in Judah and Jerusalem should flee. As we saw in the last chapter, they will flee to Petra in nearby Jordan where they will be protected by GOD for the duration of the Great Tribulation, for forty two months.

Let's look at our Lord's words concerning the flight of the Jews,

> When ye therefore shall see the abomination of desolation, spoken of by Daniel the prophet, stand in the holy place... Then let them which be in Judea flee into the mountains: [to Petra] Let him which is on the housetop not come down to take anything out of his house: Neither let him which is in the field return back to take his clothes.
>
> MATTHEW 24:15A, 16–18

The Prophet is saying that as soon as the Abomination of Desolation occurs, Antichrist will begin his attempt to destroy the Jews. We saw in our last chapter that the dragon will be very wroth with the woman and Zechariah revealed that only one third of the Jews, the remnant, will be able to make it to Petra and thus be protected from the flood that Antichrist will unleash. Jesus is lovingly warning the Jews that if they want to be included in Zechariah's surviving remnant they better not go back home to get their things but immediately high-tail it to the mountains. As chapter twelve of Revelation described, they need to get on the wings of a great eagle and go to the place prepared for them in the wilderness.

I think the days leading up to Hitler's consolidation of power in Germany illustrate this well. There was a brief time in those days when many Jews departed Germany, Poland, and Austria before those countries were closed down. After that, the wrath of the Devil's man, Adolph Hitler, fell upon those Jews who remained under his domain.

Jesus next summarized how bad the days after the Abomination of Desolation will be.

> For then shall be *great tribulation,* such as was not since the beginning of the world to this time, no, nor ever shall be. And except those days should be shortened, there should no flesh be saved: But for the elect's sake those days shall be shortened (emphasis mine).
>
> MATTHEW 24:21–22

And because the days will be so bad, people will be looking for salvation. Jesus said to beware of this,

> Then if any man shall say unto you, Lo, here is Christ, or there: believe it not.
> For there shall arise false Christs, and false prophets, and shall show great signs and wonders; insomuch that, if it were possible, they shall deceive the very elect.
> Behold, I have told you before. [Before it happens!] Wherefore if they shall say unto you, Behold, he is in the desert; go not forth: Behold he is in the secret chambers; believe it not. For as lightning cometh out of the east, and shineth even unto the west; so shall also the coming of the Son of man be.
>
> MATTHEW 24:23–27

Jesus emphasized to his listeners not to leave their place of refuge in seeking after the Messiah. Don't leave Petra looking for him in the desert or in the secret chambers. That's because the Antichrist and the False Prophet will have supernatural powers to deceive, if possible, even the very elect.

Jesus is stating emphatically not to leave the place of protection looking for salvation elsewhere. And that's what he says to you and me also. "Don't leave the place of safety that I have provided through faith in me," he would say. Don't look for salvation, satisfaction, fulfillment and meaning to life in false Messiahs, in false doctrines, in false philosophies. He would say to you and me that he is the door to the sheepfold, he is the bread of life, and he is the way and the truth and the life. It's Jesus and no other. "You don't have to look for me," he would say. "When I come back it will be obvious! It will be as bright and sudden as lightning. There will be no doubt about it!"

The Apostle John had much to say about this false spirit of anti-christ in his epistles also. For he too wanted to emphasize that even though the Antichrist will be the ultimate expression of a false Messiah, there will be many little antichrists which will come and go before the return of the True Christ.

John, indeed, gives the key in deciphering the counterfeits which would come. "Little children, it is the last time" (I John 2: 18a). Remember we have been in the last time ever since that day the two angels told Jesus' disciples that he would return in the same manner that they saw him leave (Acts 1:11). Thus far, the last time has lasted two thousand years, two days in GOD's reckoning. If you will, the last time is pictured as these days of false labor which we have spoken of in this book, *Birth Pangs*. The last time has been the last two thousand years of false labor!

> And as ye have heard that antichrist shall come, even now are there many antichrists; whereby we know that it is the last time...Who is a liar but he that denieth that Jesus is the Christ. He is antichrist, that denieth the Father and the Son.
>
> I JOHN 2:18B, 22

And,

> Beloved, believe not every spirit, but try the spirits whether they are of GOD: Because many false prophets are gone out into the world. Hereby know ye the Spirit of GOD: Every spirit that confesseth that Jesus Christ is come in the flesh is of GOD: And every spirit that confesseth not that Jesus Christ is come in the flesh is not of GOD: And this is the spirit of antichrist, whereof ye have heard that it should come; and even now already is it in the world.
>
> I JOHN 4:1–3

Again,

> For many deceivers are entered into the world, who confess not that Jesus Christ come in the flesh. This is a deceiver and an antichrist.
>
> II JOHN 7

John clearly and repeatedly states that the spirit of antichrist is already at work and can easily be identified. For it denies the Christ, it denies the Son. It states that the Christ, the Messiah, did not come and in proper grammatical usage that deceiving spirit of antichrist proclaims that the Christ *will not come again* in the flesh! You see, in John's two usages of the phrase "Jesus Christ is come in the flesh," the word "come" is used as a present participle. Thus it is better translated; "Every spirit that confesseth not that Jesus Christ is *coming* in the flesh is not of GOD."

Now that makes perfect sense, for Antichrist will say that he is GOD, that he is the Christ. Thus the spirit of antichrist cannot and will not confess that Jesus the true Christ will come back again in the flesh.

So for the application...When I live like Jesus is not coming back, when I become "master" of my own universe so to speak, I better look out, for that's the spirit of antichrist at work in my life. For the Spirit of GOD always speaks of Jesus, that Spirit looks to his soon return!

•   •   •   •

Thus with that introduction, it is time to let the Revelator show us the Beast in all of his darkness.

> And I stood upon the sand of the sea, and saw a beast rise up out of the sea...
>
> REVELATION 13:1A

In Bible typology, the sea represents the Gentile nations. The beast will come forth from the Gentiles.

Later on we will see that the False Prophet, Antichrist's high priest, will rise up out of Israel. For the Bible will soon tell us that John saw that deceiver rise up out of the earth. The earth in Biblical allegory speaks of Israel.

> ... having seven heads and ten horns, and upon his horns ten crowns.
>
> REVELATION 13:1B

Bible scholars state that there will be some combination of seven and ten Gentile nations which will be the power base of Antichrist. Seven heads and ten horns. In Bible typology horns speak of authority. Ten horns, ten seats of authority in some manner will oversee this beast. (Again, allegories which I have discussed earlier in this book which have *already* happened are a lot easier to be dogmatic about. These many allegories in this future section I cannot be so precise with in regards to their interpretation).

... and upon his heads the name of blasphemy.
REVELATION 13:1C

Again this seven and/or ten nation confederacy of Antichrist will vehemently deny the Son, they will be unified by the spirit of antichrist that the true Christ will not come again in the flesh!

And the beast which I saw was like unto a leopard, and his feet were as the feet of a bear, and his mouth of a lion.
REVELATION 13:2A

The student of Scripture may recognize these animals in relationship to the conquering Gentile nations of the past, for they have been spoken of before. Daniel, that great prophet who received so much revelation concerning future events, dreamed of these three predatory animals as found in chapter seven of his book.

Looking at Daniel's words will bring illumination as we consider the beast.

In the first year of Belshazzar king of Babylon Daniel had a dream and visions of his head upon his bed: [The year is 553B.C, not New Testament times as skeptics would suggest considering the accuracy of Daniel's other words!]...I saw in my vision by night, and, behold, the four winds of the heaven strove upon the great sea. [Remember the sea represents the nations in Bible typology]. And four great beasts came up from the sea, diverse one from another. The first was like a lion, [Babylon]...And behold another beast, a second, like to a bear, [Medio-Persia]...After this I beheld, and lo another, like a leopard, [Greece]...

After this I saw in the night visions, and beheld a forth beast, dreadful and terrible, and strong exceedingly; it had great iron teeth: It devoured and brake in pieces, and stamped the residue with the feet of it: And it was diverse from all the beasts that were before it; and it had ten horns. [This fourth beast is the Roman Empire, both past and one still to come as a revived entity!] I considered the horns, and, behold, there came up among them another little horn, before whom there were three of the first horns plucked up by the roots: And, behold, in this horn were eyes like the eyes of man, and mouth speaking great things.

DANIEL 7:1A, 2B-4A, 5A, 6A

I must stop and comment upon these verses which are pregnant with prophetic implications and predictions. The ten horns represent ten nations of a revived Roman confederacy. We also recall that in Daniel chapter two, when we read of Nebuchadnezzar's dream, that the fourth image had ten toes. Again, this is a reference to a ten nation alliance. As I look at today's geopolitical world, the European Union may be the entity that will morph into this confederacy which Daniel is revealing.

The fourth beast is different because this little horn is a man and not a nation. This horn has eyes like a man and a mouth which will speak great things. A better translation of the phrase "great things" is that he will speak great *lies!* Three of the horns, or three of the nations, will be plucked up by the roots, taken out, in other words, when the little horn is manifested. The little horn, of course, is the Antichrist! When he comes to power he will speak great lies and three nations of the Roman Confederacy will be toppled.

Continuing with the prophet's words,

I beheld till the thrones were cast down, and the Ancient of days did sit, whose garment was white as snow, and the hair of his head like the pure wool: His throne was like a fiery flame, and his wheels [feet] as burning fire.

DANIEL 7:9

Daniel reveals that the four kingdoms will be cast down. And look who's sitting upon the throne in the fifth and last kingdom. It's the Ancient of Days, the Father. And note that his description is like the appearance of Jesus we saw in Revelation chapter one. The One John also told us had hair like wool and feet like unto fine brass as if they burned in a furnace. The Father and the Son obviously look alike!

> I beheld then because of the voice of the great words which the horn spake: I beheld even till the beast was slain, [There it is! The little horn and the beast are one and the same!] and his body destroyed, and given to the burning flame. As concerning the rest of the beasts, they had their dominion taken away: Yet their lives were prolonged for a season and time. I saw in the night visions, and, behold, one like the Son of man came with the clouds of heaven, and came to the Ancient of days, and they brought him near before him. And there was given him dominion, and glory, and a kingdom, and all people, nations, and languages, should serve him: His dominion is an everlasting dominion, which shall not pass away, and his kingdom that which shall not be destroyed.
>
> DANIEL 7:11–14

Thus, GOD summarizes his dealings with the nations in this succinct vision given to the great prophet Daniel. Four kingdoms will sequentially dominate the world, only two of which Daniel actually saw in his lifetime (those being Babylon and Medio-Persia). The fourth kingdom, likened to a dreadful ten-horned beast made of iron will see another horn in the body of a man come upon the scene. He will speak great lies, take down three nations upon his rise to power and will ultimately be sent to the Lake of Fire. All four beastly kingdoms will have an end and will be replaced by a kingdom headed by the Son of Man. That wonderful kingdom will have no end!

In considering this fourth beast of Daniel's dream let's look at his power base.

... and the dragon gave him his power, and his seat, and his great authority.

REVELATION 13:2B

This beast, this little horn, is given his power from the dragon. We remember that Paul taught us that Satan is the GOD of this world so it doesn't take much faith to realize that Satan can pull this off. The interesting thing to me is that GOD openly predicted Satan will do this without any apparent worry that his revelation would tip the adversary's hand!

And I saw one of his heads as it were wounded to death; and his deadly wound was healed: And all the world wondered after the beast.

REVELATION 13:3

The head that will be wounded is the little horn. It's the Antichrist. Scholars believe that this charismatic future leader may be assassinated or at least be wounded and near death and yet be revived. This will lead to an outpouring of sympathy and love towards this deceiver. Imagine those of you who were alive when JFK was brutally gunned down, if he had recovered. Or even better, if he had died and then was resurrected back to life. How would have the world reacted? Why President Kennedy would have been elevated to the place that this future world leader will reach. JFK would have been crowned the king!

Zechariah speaks of this injury in his prophetic book. Chapter eleven of Zechariah tells us of two shepherds. One called Beauty, that's Jesus, the Good Shepherd, and the other called Bands. Bands is the one Zechariah calls the idol shepherd. He's the Antichrist. But here I want to point out again the idol shepherd's injury,

For, lo, I will raise up a shepherd in the land, which shall not... nor heal that which is broken, nor feed that that standeth still: But he shall eat the flesh of the fat, and tear their claws in pieces. Woe to the idol shepherd that leaveth the flock! The sword shall be upon his arm, and upon his right eye: His arm

shall be clean dried up, and his right eye shall be utterly darkened.

ZECHARIAH 11:16A, C-17

Among other things this speaks of concerning the Antichrist,
it may also be revealing that his mortal injury involves severe
trauma to his arm and right eye. And it's inflicted by a sword.
That is, by a personal military weapon. In today's arsenal the
implication is that this deadly wound will be inflicted most likely
by a gun!

And they worshiped the dragon which gave power unto the
beast:

REVELATION 13:4A

This is incredible to me. Even in these last days, only a
minority of unsaved people actually worship Satan. But somehow, after this seemingly wonderful world leader is resurrected
from the dead, Satan will receive the glory he has for so long
craved. The people of the planet will actually understand that
Satan, the GOD of this world, is behind the scenes running the
show. And they will worship him! Unbelievable, but the Bible
states that this *will* happen! Later, in the next chapter, Daniel
will reveal that Antichrist will be heavily immersed in the occult.
Indeed, Satanism will become a viable religion during the second
half of the Tribulation.

And they worshipped the beast, saying, Who is like unto the
beast? Who is able to make war with him?

REVELATION 13:4B

We who know the King of Kings and Lord of LORDS recognize the answer to this question! Yet the blinded of the world
will sadly see Antichrist as Messiah. He will receive their worship along with his father, the dragon! The Dragon and the Beast
seek to take the place of the Father and the Son. Soon we will
see that the one the Bible calls the False Prophet will complete

this unholy trinity as he will counterfeit the ministry of the Holy Spirit!

> And there was given unto him a mouth speaking great things and blasphemies; and power was given unto him to continue forty and two months.
>
> REVELATION 13:5

This reign of terror will last three and one half years. A short period of time when compared to the duration of time given to the reigns of many other evil leaders the world has known.

Yet Jesus put the time frame in perspective with these words,

> For then shall be great tribulation, such as was not since the beginning of the world to this time, no, nor ever shall be. And except those days should be shortened, there should no flesh be saved: But for the elect's sake those days shall be shortened.
>
> MATTHEW 24:21–22

Jesus spoke of the importance of these days being brief. For it will be so dark and evil that the days will need to be short for the elect's sake. Those whose names are written in the Lamb's Book of Life will suffer tremendous pressure to lose their faith as they see powerful demonstrations of the adversary's dominion. They will also be in constant danger of losing their heads for their continued belief in Jesus as Messiah.

> And he opened his mouth in blasphemy against GOD, to blaspheme his name, and his tabernacle, and them that dwell in heaven.
>
> REVELATION 13:6

This is the Abomination of Desolation spoken of by Daniel the prophet and confirmed by Jesus.

Indeed, the Temple in Jerusalem, which has been longed for by the Jews, will be rebuilt, prior to, or during the first half of the Tribulation. Most likely, this apparent man of peace will broker a deal with the Arabs, as we have previously discussed, which will allow the Temple and the Dome of the Rock to co-exist together.

Now, here in the second half of the Tribulation, the Antichrist will enter the Temple, proceed to the Holy of Holies, and declare that he is God! It will appear to the fooled of the world that indeed it must be true. Remember he has just demonstrated by his miraculous recovery that he has the power over death. They will believe it to be true!

Now, one reason this is such an abomination is that according to Old Testament law, only the High Priest was to enter into the Holy of Holies. Thus it is sacrilege for one who is not the High Priest to enter that unique place.

In the next chapter, we will see that this has happened before. The Grecian, or more specifically, the Seleucid Emperor, Antiochus Epiphanies, was a near picture of the future potentate we have been discussing. He too entered the Temple and desecrated it. Thus when our Lord spoke of the Abomination of Desolation to his followers they would have understood what he meant since it had occurred in their history only two centuries earlier.

Before leaving this verse, though, I would like to show you Paul's description of what this abomination of desolation will look like and then make an application.

> Let no man deceive you by any means: For that the day shall not come, except there come a falling away first, and that man of sin be revealed, the son of perdition; Who opposeth and exalteth himself above all that is called God, or that is worshipped; so that he as God sitteth in the temple of God, showing himself that he is God.
>
> II Thessalonians 2:3–4

In the middle of the Tribulation time frame, at the beginning of the second half called the Great Tribulation, this famous and immensely popular world leader we understand as the Antichrist will enter the rebuilt temple of God in Jerusalem and declare that he, not Yahweh, is God. He will essentially be saying that the Jewish faith is passé and the only true faith is one which worships him!

This will unleash a backlash from the Jews who will now begin to understand the true nature of the Beast for the first time. As we saw in the last chapter, a war will break out when the Jews refuse to recognize Antichrist's claim to deity. We understand that one third of the Jews will flee to Petra and be spared as we have discussed previously.

Jesus' words about this bear repeating,

> When ye therefore shall see the abomination of desolation, spoken of by Daniel the prophet, stand in the holy place, (whoso readeth, let him understand:) Then let them which be in Judea flee into the mountains.
>
> MATTHEW 24:15–16

The application I would like for us to consider concerning this abomination of desolation is an easy one when we remember where Paul in these New Testament times tells us that the Temple is located. For Paul repeatedly states that *we,* our bodies, are the Temple of GOD (I Corinthians 3:16–17; 6:19; II Corinthians 6:16; Ephesians 2:21). GOD, by way of the Holy Spirit, resides in our hearts. And to the degree that we crown him King in our lives, is the degree that we elevate him to Lord in our minds. Paul tells us that the riches of the mystery of Christ is that we have *Christ in us,* the hope of glory (Colossians 1:27). He proclaimed that this truth was so wonderful that if Satan had understood the implications of it, had he known that there would be "little christs" running around the planet, he would not have crucified the Lord of Glory (I Corinthians 2:8).

Thus, just like the Antichrist's desire is to sit in the Holy of Holies and declare himself to be GOD, so the spirit of antichrist wants to sit in my mind, in the holy of holies, if you will, and rule and reign! You see, the spirit of antichrist wants to take the throne of our minds. He wants to sit in that holy place! I need to be aware of this type of attack. For the only real cure for tribulation is to have the Lord sit on the throne of my mind. Then I will have joy and peace. Then will the Kingdom of Heaven be near to my heart. For then I will experience righteousness peace and joy in the Holy Ghost (Romans 14:17).

✝he Shadow of Antichrist

Daniel had predicted and history has documented that a Grecian ruler named Antiochus Epiphanies came on the scene in the second century b.c. as a shadow of the Beast to come. Let's study Daniel's prophecy from chapters eight, nine, and eleven concerning this man and as we do we will learn of additional aspects of the future evil despot which will become apparent to those alive during his reign as they open their eyes to see!

We pick up in chapter eight. Belshazzar, the last king of Babylon was on the throne. You may remember that in chapter 5 of Daniel's prophecy Belshazzar held a great feast for thousands in his kingdom. The wine was flowing and much debauchery was occurring when he foolishly called for the golden vessels of the Lord's Temple. Those were the vessels the priest's drank from which had been taken out of the Temple when Belshazzar's father, Nebuchadnezzar, had conquered Jerusalem. As a result of this blunder, the finger of GOD wrote upon the wall, in front of all the guests, that his kingdom had been judged and found wanting. That very night, in 539 b.c., the Medes and Persians entered the city and overthrew Babylon.

Well, it was eleven years earlier that Daniel received the revelation about the next two world powers. That's incredible to me, as I will hopefully convey. Daniel will tell us in minute detail about two kingdoms which didn't even exist when he first wrote about them! When Daniel lifted up his eyes he saw a ram with two horns. One was higher than the other and that was the one which came up last. History documents that Xerses, also known as Ahasuerus from the Book of Esther, was this last notable horn.

Daniel saw Xerses pushing westward and northward and southward and becoming great as the book of Esther so beautifully documents. But next, Daniel saw a he goat from the west come with great speed and fierceness and completely take out the ram, stomping him into the ground. Truly a brutal scene! Of course, this was Alexander the Great, the first and greatest Emperor of Greece. In 333 b.c. Alexander's army defeated Xerses and the Medes and Persians were no more!

Next, Daniel saw that the great horn of the he goat was broken at the height of its power and four other horns took its place. We know historically that this is exactly what happened! Alexander died shortly after consolidating power and four lesser kings, four of Alexander's generals, vied for supremacy.

Daniel then predicted of a little horn which arose out of one of the four horns.

> And out of one of them came forth a little horn, which waxed exceedingly great, toward the south, and toward the east, and toward the pleasant land.
>
> DANIEL 8:9

I find it very interesting that again the phrase "a little horn" is used. Not surprising though since this man is the pre-figure of the little horn of the book of Revelation which we understand will be Antichrist. The little horn in this portion of Daniel's vision is the Seleucid king known as Antiochus I, or Antiochus Epiphanies.

The pleasant land, of course, is Israel. Daniel reveals that Antiochus would magnify himself to the prince of the host. In other words he was a worshipper of Satan! We are told that he would take away and cast down the daily sacrifice in the Temple and replace worship of Jehovah with occultic practice. Daniel finally reveals that the Temple will be desecrated for 2,300 days, or nearly seven years.

Here in chapter eight we have the first mention of the Abomination of Desolation. History tells us that Antiochus butchered pigs, that un-kosher animal, in the Temple and forced the priest's to drink their blood! Needless to say, that birth pang was one of the lowest points in the history of Israel!

The next section of this chapter gets even more interesting. The Angel Gabriel, whose name means "strongman of GOD," appeared to Daniel and explained the vision. He then skipped a few millenniums and revealed of a fierce king which will come forth in the spirit of Antiochus and reign in the latter time.

We are told that this king, who is Antichrist, will be mighty, but not in his own power. For as we saw Antichrist's power emanates from the dragon, from Satan. Daniel teaches that this one will practice in the occult and will destroy the mighty and the holy. In other words, he will overcome the mighty of the world as well as the holy ones. He will temporarily overcome those Jews and Gentiles who will be the saved of the Lamb during the Tribulation. Lastly, verse 25 proclaims that this future king will magnify himself, not GOD, and by peace he will destroy many. Indeed, Antichrist will come on the scene as an apparent man of peace but as time marches on his true colors will emerge!

> He shall also stand up against the Prince of princes; but he shall be broken without hand.
>
> DANIEL 8:25B

Happily, the end of Antichrist is predicted as the chapter comes to a conclusion.

• • • •

Next, our discussion comes to Daniel chapter nine. You may remember we looked into this chapter as we discussed mankind's pre-term labor earlier in this book. Recall that Palm Sunday, the day our Lord stood over Jerusalem and wept because the leaders of the nation did not recognize the day of their visitation. The

Daniel A. Tomlinson, M.D.

reason they should have known was given in Daniel chapter nine. There the predicted four hundred eighty-three years from the decree to rebuild Jerusalem to Messiah was given by Daniel. It was the important sixty-nine weeks prophecy of Daniel. The last two verses speak of the seventieth week. That seven year time period we understand as the Tribulation which is yet to occur. It is very important to us now in our discussion as it speaks of Antichrist and the Abomination of Desolation.

> And...Messiah shall be cut off...and the people of the prince that shall come [Antichrist] shall destroy the city and the sanctuary and the end thereof shall be with a flood, and unto the end of the war desolations are determined.
>
> DANIEL 9:26A, C, E

Daniel declared that after the leaders of Israel rejected Messiah, after Messiah was cut off, that the people of the prince that should come will destroy the city and the sanctuary. In other words, he prophesied that after Christ was crucified that the people of the coming world leader would destroy Jerusalem and the Temple. We understand that the prince to come is Antichrist. Who are his people? Why the Romans, of course! Remember, Antichrist was described as a little horn which came forth in the latter days of the revived Roman Empire.

In 70 a.d. the Romans, under the command of General Titus, conquered and razed Jerusalem and the Temple. Jesus predicted earlier that not even one stone would be left upon another at the Temple site after that utter defeat (Matthew 24:1–2).

But here over five hundred years earlier, Daniel described the who, the when, and the what of this historical event and then he stated that the destruction would occur *unto the end*. He stated that unto the time of the end desolations would be the fate of Jerusalem. Of course, we understand that since 70 a.d. until 1948, indeed, that has been the fate of Jerusalem and of the Jews. Now that we are at the time of the end the next verse, the seventieth week prophecy will have immense interest to us as we consider the seven year Tribulation and the Antichrist.

And he shall confirm the covenant with many for one week:
And in the midst of the week he shall cause the sacrifice and
the oblation to cease, and for the overspreading of abominations he shall make it desolate, even until the consummation,
and that determined shall be poured upon the desolate.

DANIEL 9:27

Daniel reveals for the first time that this coming world leader
will confirm a seven year peace treaty with many. He will get
the Jews and the Arabs to agree to live in peace for seven years.
The Temple will be rebuilt and the Jews will once again be able
to offer sacrifice and oblation to Jehovah. But then, in the midst
of the week, in the very middle of the seven year covenant we
understand to be the Tribulation, the prince that shall come will
cause the sacrifice and the oblation to cease. Jesus called this the
Abomination of Desolation! This abomination would last until
the judgment which is predetermined will be poured upon the
desolate. In other words, the Temple would remain in its desolate
state until that evil prince is judged.

Thus, to summarize Daniel's seventy week prophecy, the
prophet predicted that four hundred eighty-three years would
intervene between the proclamation to rebuild Jerusalem until
the arrival of Messiah. Then, the Christ would be cut off, he
would be killed, and the people of the coming evil world leader
would destroy Jerusalem and the Temple. Israel and the Temple
would remain anonymous until the end and then would reappear.
That brings us to today. Soon the seventieth week will start when
the end-times prince confirms a seven year covenant which he
will violate in the midst of that time frame. That abomination
will last until he is judged and consumed by GOD's righteous and
holy wrath!

• • • •

Now we will conclude by looking at chapter eleven where in
539 b.c. The very year that Babylon was defeated by the Medes
and Persians, GOD revealed to Daniel in very minute detail the
course of the future third world power, that of Greece. In this

chapter we obtain more information on the shadow of antichrist, Antiochus Epiphanies, and on Antichrist himself.

Verses one through thirty-five of this wonderful chapter tell of the foretime. That is, these verses speak of the time prior to Daniel's seventieth week. The remainder of the chapter and to the end of the book tell of the Antichrist and of the end times.

Read verses one through thirty-five with the following background information in mind: The king of Persia was Xerses and the mighty king which stood up against him was Alexander. His four generals took control after Alexander's untimely death and the empire was broken into a much weaken state. These four entities coalesced into two kingdoms which we historically understand to be the Ptolemaic Dynasty, the king of the south, and the Seleucids, the king of the north. Verses five through twenty give incredibly detailed prophetic information about future battles between these two family dynasties. Marriage arrangements which occurred were foretold. Wars were predicted and victories were accurately prophesied. Then in verses 21–35 we learn of the shadow figure. The Bible calls him a vile person. Detailed information of Antiochus' exploits, his victories and defeats and his evil indignation against the holy covenant and the covenant people are predicted. His defeat by the ships of Chittim, which we understand to be his defeat in Cyprus by the Roman navy, is foretold and the uprising by the Maccabeans is hinted at in verse thirty-two.

In verse thirty-five we are told that Greece will have influence until the end times and we comprehend that the Greek worldview has been the dominant thinking of the Western World even to our day today. Then we come to verse thirty-six unto the end of the book of Daniel where we are given some detailed information about the last world leader which is so germane to our story of mankind's labor and delivery.

And the king shall do according to his will; [Contrast that to Jesus who always did his Father's will!] and he will exalt himself, and magnify himself above every GOD, and speak marvelous [unbelievable and untrue] things against the GOD of GODS, and prosper till the indignation be accomplished: For that that is determined shall be done. Neither shall he regard the GOD [Elohim] of his fathers, [He likely will be an apostate Jew who has rejected Elohim or Jehovah]. nor the desire of women, [He likely will be homosexual or asexual, having no desire for women] nor regard any GOD: For he shall magnify himself above all.

But in his estate shall he honor the GOD of forces: A GOD whom...shall he honor with gold, and silver, and with precious stones, and pleasant things.

DANIEL II: 36–38A, C

The Antichrist will honor the GOD of forces, or as your margin reads, he will honor the GOD of munitions with gold and silver and precious stones. In other words, he will spend much money in building up his arsenal! The revived Roman Empire which he is leading will be a superpower which will make modern-day America look like a third-world country as far as military might is concerned!

Chapter eleven concludes by saying that Antichrist will divide Israel in verse thirty-nine. The end times kings of the south and north, understood to be the Arabs and Russia, will come against him in verse forty. Tidings out of the East will trouble him in verse forty-four. This is understood to be China. And lastly, in great fury he will go forth to the land between the seas in the glorious holy mountain, better known as the Valley of Megiddo or Armageddon, where he shall come to his end with none to help him.

Thus we come to the end of what has been revealed aforetime concerning the shadow and the real Antichrist. Both worship and serve Satan. They attempt to consume the Jews and they horrify GOD's children as they pollute the Temple. In the case of Antichrist, he will likely be a homosexual or asexual apostate Jew who will be mortally wounded on his right shoulder and right eye and yet be revived. The world will worship him, as will the Jews, until he declares himself to be GOD and outlaws the faith of Abraham. In his short and brutal reign he will battle the Arabs and Russians as well as meet the mighty Chinese in the last battle, known as Armageddon. There he will be defeated not by these Earthly kings, but as we shall see when we reach Revelation nineteen, he will be utterly destroyed by the King of Kings, Jesus the true Christ!

. . . .

So as we close this section let me give one more application and then we'll proceed to the next section of the book of Revelation where we will encounter the False Prophet and consider the mark of the beast.

You see, this one who exalts himself above all that is called GOD we call the Antichrist. His title literally means "one who is against Christ." But it can also mean "one who has taken the place of Christ." It is that particular meaning which I would like to explore for a moment.

When we put someone or some thing on the throne of our lives, we are really letting the spirit of antichrist have control. That's because we are letting that person or thing be in place of Christ, on the throne of our life. Jesus told us that he is the vine and we are the branches. Apart from him we can do nothing. What this means is that apart from my Lord, nothing I do has any *eternal* value. Thus, when I put an antichrist, that person or thing "in place of Christ" on the throne, well, then anything I do will have absolutely no value or worth at all. I will have wasted my time doing things which amount to nothing.

Let it not be that way for you, dear reader. Keep Christ on the throne of your heart and mind. Then, and only then, will the things you accomplish in life have eternal value. Oh…if you are saved you'll still get to heaven, but those things done without the Spirit of Christ will not. Once again, as Jesus said, "for without me ye can do nothing" (John 15:5b).

✝he False Prophet

> For there shall arise false Christs, and false prophets, and shall show great signs and wonders; insomuch that, if it were possible, they shall deceive the very elect. Behold, I have told you before.
>
> MATTHEW 24:24–25

Indeed, the true Prophet has warned the world of the False Prophet we are about to consider!

> And I beheld another beast coming up out of the earth: And he had two horns like a lamb, and he spake as a dragon.
>
> REVELATION 13:11

This second beastly creature is like the first beast but he arises from the earth not the sea as we saw in the case of the Antichrist. As mentioned previously, the False Prophet will have ethnic ties to Israel as the earth typifies the nation of Israel while the sea speaks of all other nations. Thus, Antichrist will crop up from a Gentile nation whereas the False Prophet will hale from Israel.

His two horns like a lamb speak of his religious authority. The False Prophet will be the spiritual leader to the doomed souls of the Tribulation time frame. He will seem pious and religious but will really be a wolf in sheep's clothing! As I reflect upon the world's history, I can think of many who have come before, many other false prophets who have duped the world. I'm sure you can too, the list is long! Here are a few to get you started. I think of Mohammed and Buddha, the Popes of the Middle Ages as well as Jim Jones and Charles Manson!

> And he exerciseth all the power of the first beast before him, and causeth the earth and them which dwell therein to worship the first beast, whose deadly wound was healed.
>
> REVELATION 13:12

This religious leader will also be charismatic and will direct praise and worship to the one who seemingly was resurrected from the dead. He will cause those dwelling upon the Earth to fall in love with pure evil. He will direct them to, figuratively speaking, sleep with the Antichrist.

Also, it's important to remember that Christians will no longer dwell upon the Earth. Those who call upon Jesus by this time of Jacob's Trouble will be hunted, persecuted, and butchered to the point that it cannot be said that they "dwell therein" upon the Earth!

> And he doeth great wonders, so that he maketh fire come down from heaven on the earth in the sight of men.
>
> REVELATION 13:13

In the eyes of Israel, this will bring to mind the fire that Elijah called down from heaven. Before Antichrist claims to be GOD in the Temple, the Jews will be completely duped by the first and second beast into believing that they are seeing a re-visitation of the power of GOD as described in their Scriptures!

To the Gentile people left behind, this display of fiery power from the False Prophet will be used to counter the fire that will be seen to proceed forth from the mouths of the two witnesses in Jerusalem. Indeed the people of the world will be confused as they on the one hand hear the gospel from the potent witnesses but on the other hand see the powerful and seemingly valid demonstrations from Antichrist's co-conspirator.

So what's the answer for those left behind? Which fire is the real one?

That's easy. It's the fire that points me to Jesus, that's the real fire of GOD. Any other fire is "strange fire!" Thus, not only in this time frame we are speaking of, but also for me today, I must beware of people with a "new fire." I must ask myself, does this thing that seems so hot direct me to Jesus or does it take the focus off of my Lord? My analysis of that question tells me by which fire to stay warm.

> And deceiveth them that dwell on the earth by the means of those miracles which he had the power to do in the sight of the beast; saying to them that dwell on the earth, that they should make an image to the beast, which had the wound by a sword, and did live. And he had power to give life unto the image of the beast, that the image of the beast should both speak, and cause that as many as would not worship the image of the beast should be killed.
>
> REVELATION 13:14–15

When this was first written, undoubtedly the reader would not be able to understand how an image could appear to live. No problem now though. All I have to do is turn on my TV to understand how this prophecy will play out. The image of Antichrist will be everywhere! And those who do not worship it, those who look away from his image, when they are caught, will be murdered.

Turn in your Bible to Daniel chapter 3 to see what this was like when it occurred previously. Do you remember that charismatic and supreme ruler by the name of Nebuchadnezzar? Recall how he commissioned an image of gold to be made of him which was sixty six cubits in height (don't fail to take note of that number!). It was big, at ninety nine feet by our measure. He placed it in the plain of Dura in the province of Babylon and proclaimed that whenever the six musical instruments were played (there is that number again) all were to fall down and worship the golden image. Those who did not were to be cast into a fiery furnace. Well, you know the story. Daniel's three friends refused to bow before the image and indeed where given a baptism by fire! They were rescued and walked with the One Nebuchadnezzar understood to be the Son of GOD. Likewise, those who refuse to worship the image of this latter day Nebuchadnezzar will also be rescued by Jesus. No, maybe not literally rescued from physical death, but they will be rescued from spiritual death by their faith in the true Christ.

One last point, then I will move on. In our day, there are many distractions and choices. I can worship Jesus, I can worship myself, I can worship my wife, my job or my hobby. The list goes on and on. Not so in this day we are considering. In that day there are only two choices. I must worship either the coming World Leader or the King of Kings. The line will be drawn in the sand and everyone will have to choose!

> And he caused all, both small and great, rich and poor, free and bond to receive a mark in their right hand, or in their foreheads.
>
> REVELATION 13:16

It's interesting to me, and likely not a coincidence, that this mark of the Beast sounds so similar to a practice with which the Jews can already identify. In Deuteronomy 6 we find the Great Shema. That wonderful prayer often recited by the Orthodox Jew.

> Hear, O Israel: The LORD our GOD is one LORD: And thou shalt love the LORD thy GOD with all thine heart, and with all thy soul, and with all thy might. And these words, which I command thee this day, shalt be in thine heart: And thou shalt teach them diligently unto thy children, and shalt talk of them when thou sittest in thine house, and when thou walkest by the way, and when thou liest down, and when thou risest up. And thou shalt *bind them for a sign upon thine hand,* and they shall be as *frontlets between thine eyes* (emphasis mine).
>
> DEUTERONOMY 6:4–8

The children of Israel were directed by Moses to keep the Word of God as an integral part of their daily lives. So much so that it would appear that God's Word was embedded in their hands and foreheads!

Of course Satan, being the great counterfeiter, will use the forehead and the hand to determine those who will follow him. Spiritually speaking, the God of this world wants the works of our hands and the thoughts of our minds to be placed upon things of this world and not upon things eternal as the Great Shema proclaims.

For those who do not receive the mark upon their foreheads, God has a promise.

> And their shall be no more curse: But the throne of God and of the Lamb shall be in it; and his servants shall serve him: And they shall see his face; and his name [nature] shall be in their *foreheads* (emphasis mine).
>
> REVELATION 22:3–4

The choice is clear. Receive the mark of the beast and present comfort will be available, or receive the name of God and have short-term discomfort with the hope of eternal blessing. As for the mark itself, in the past, like the image of Antichrist we discussed previously, Bible teachers could not really comprehend this type of technology. Again, no problem now. Smart cards, bar codes and implantable chips are already in existence and ready for mass production.

And remember, this mark won't be called the mark of the Beast! It will have a Wall Street type of market appeal and will seem to make perfect sense. Let me explain to you why it will seem to be the answer.

> And that no man might buy or sell, save he that had the mark, or the name of the beast, or the number of his name.
>
> REVELATION 13:17

Do you know that people are tired of money! It's a big hassle and much easier to use a credit card without having to worry about having enough cash. And it's nice to not have to worry about getting my cash ripped off. But in the last decade my credit card has become a liability. Pirates are ripping us off as identity theft is a major problem. One that is hard to overcome for a person once the information is loose. So when the coming World Leader announces a cashless marketplace, without the worry of credit card fraud, it will be embraced widely.

Also of great appeal will be the security this future system affords. The government will be able to track the location of all its citizens. No more kidnapping little children. And criminals better look out because they won't be able to flee the scene of the crime! Yes, this technology will sound great! And as the problems of the Tribulation time frame bear on it will be welcomed by the masses as a way to get things under control, both economically and domestically. But what about the spiritual consequences?

We have seen that the False Prophet will demand that the Beast be worshiped. One very clear way of offering worship is by receiving the mark with his name. You see, this mark will not be able to be procured unless a man or a woman declares total allegiance to the Potentate. By doing that, the poor soul will clearly be rejecting the true Savior and receiving Antichrist, if you will, as savior and Lord. Remember, by this time in the Tribulation, the birth pangs are so close that the baby is near. Sides are drawn and people will know when they take the mark what the implications are. It's not as though they will find out later that this mark caused their eternal destruction. They will know the implications of taking the mark and choose to believe that the Word of GOD is untrue and irrelevant. Thus, they will seal their doom not because they received the mark but because they have rejected Jesus. Taking the mark is just the outward sign of that rejection.

In John's Gospel we see a foretaste of the kind of pressure those who refuse to take the make will undergo. Chapter 9 gives the details.

Jesus had just healed a man born blind by anointing his eyes with clay and spittle. The Pharisees were incensed since the miracle occurred on the Sabbath. Thus, they tracked down the blind man's parents in order to get some more information against

Jesus. They asked the parents if their son was really born blind and if they believed Jesus healed the boy.

Their answer reveals what it's like to be ostracized.

> His parents answered them and said, We know that this is our son, and that he was born blind: But by what means he now seeth, we know not: He is of age; ask him: He shall speak for himself. These words spoke his parents, because they feared the Jews: For the Jews had agreed already, that if any man did confess that he was Christ, he should be put out of the synagogue.
>
> JOHN 9:20–22

Being put out of the synagogue is not the same as getting kicked out of your church today. The implication is that to be put out of the synagogue meant that they were rejected by the nation. It was exile. It was economic and social murder!

That's what it will be like for the Tribulation saints. They will become invisible as the rest of the world continues to buy and sell. There will be no place to interface with society without being identified as a traitor and suffer the mortal consequences of that decision. In the truest sense of the phrase, they will be living off the land, without any access to the infrastructure of the world's system.

Now many other examples of this type of economic blackmail have occurred throughout the ages. This is one of the favorite strategies that the devil gives to the evil leaders he has employed over the centuries. For instance, I think of the monetary chaos those suffered who lived under the indulgence system of the Medieval Catholic Church. Believers were tricked into thinking that they could purchase the salvation of loved ones already departed and stuck in Purgatory. Billions of dollars flowed into Rome while the peasants of Europe went without food and clothing. Of course, the opulence of those days is still very apparent to any and all who travel to the Vatican. Gold is everywhere! Or, how about Hitler's 3rd Reich? European Jews were segregated in ghettos and shipped off to concentration camps simply because they were not born with Hitler's mark—that being of Arian descent!

Jesus said to let the children come to him and that it was better to have a millstone tied around a man's neck and he be cast into the sea than to cause a little one to stumble. In other words, the thing that really makes our Lord mad is keeping others from him. The mark of the Beast is the culmination of that devilish desire as it forces people to choose death over life! And it will get Jesus' righteous anger boiling!

> Here is wisdom. Let him that hath understanding count the number of the beast: For it is the number of a man; and his number is Six hundred threescore and six.
>
> REVELATION 13:18

There it is! That infamous number that even the most ignorant atheist understands is associated with evil. Six-six-six, the number of a man!

I have been told that the numerical values of the letters which make up the name of the Antichrist will add up to six hundred sixty-six. I'm not so sure about this but it is interesting to think about. I guess it wouldn't surprise me as GOD in his foreknowledge knows who the Antichrist will be and thus he knows his number.

I am also told that Caesar Nero's name adds up to six hundred sixty six. You may want to remember this little tidbit as its significance will come up again!

In taking a different direction with this verse though, you may recall that GOD uses numbers in Scriptures very exactly. Volumes have been written about the precision of GOD's numerology which is beyond the scope of this book. But I would be remiss if I did not again refer you to E.W. Bullinger's book entitled, *Number in Scripture,* for a complete review of this topic.

Nonetheless, six is the number always associated with man and especially man working in is own efforts apart from GOD. Check out Bullinger's book for numerous examples of this. You will be impressed with the Lord in a new and fresh way as you catch a glimpse of the incredible wisdom it would take for a Being to author a book which is so precise in ways that a mere mortal could never duplicate.

Continuing, three is the number of completeness. Thus, three sixes in a row is the number of man in complete folly apart from GOD. Six-six-six is complete separation from GOD. It's not a good number!

That's why the mark of the beast is called six-six-six. As we have suggested, taking the mark of the beast will be the sign that a person has rejected GOD via a clear and conscious decision. It's rejecting the grace of GOD through Jesus and taking the "I can do" mentality of man. You certainly recall Jesus' words concerning this world view. He said in John 15 that he is the vine and we are the branches, apart from him we can do nothing! Paul amplifies the proper perspective when he taught in his letter to the Philippians, "I can do all things through Christ which strengtheneth me" (Philippians 4:13).

Thus, the insight for you and me from six-six-six is clear. It's a complete mess when I try to work in my own power. Whether it's writing this book, delivering a baby, or spending time with my family, when I'm doing my own little thing and not relying upon the Spirit of GOD through Jesus Christ I am moving in the six-six-six mentality.

• • • •

One last contrast between good and evil that this section teaches.

As we accept, GOD is unique in an incomprehensible way in that he is one GOD yet manifested in three Persons. The devil, in his desire to be like GOD, will attempt to imitate this truth. Instead of Father, Son, and Spirit, Satan will offer the world Dragon, Antichrist, and False Prophet. These three counterfeits will copy the three ministries of the GODhead. Satan, as the Dragon, will oversee his kingdom but without mercy and grace as we see in our Father. Antichrist will offer himself as the Messiah and will appear to resurrect from the dead to authenticate his claim. Lastly, the False Prophet will copy the work of the Holy Spirit but in a devilish way. The only similarity between the work of the Spirit and the work of the False Prophet is that just as the Spirit speaks of and points people to Jesus, the False Prophet will elevate Antichrist. That's where the similarities end. The Holy Spirit is like Christ, while the False Prophet is like Antichrist. The Spirit is kind while this man of evil is cruel. The Spirit is benevolent, this false one is malicious. The Spirit enlightens, this prophet deceives. The Spirit gives life, this apostate one will kill. The Spirit is light to men, this possessed one lies to men. The Spirit teaches, but Antichrist's man enforces. Lastly, the Spirit seals men with GOD while the False Prophet seals men with the mark!

✝he Harvest of the Earth

As was mentioned at the beginning of this book, the time immediately prior to the birth of the baby is called the transition phase.
This is a sanitized term which really doesn't give the process the
credit it deserves. It should be called the "horrific" phase or the "I
wish I would die" phase, as this short time immediately prior to
birth is intensely terrible. So it will be on planet Earth at this time
immediately prior to the Second Coming of Christ. Chapters 14
through 19 of Revelation describe the transition phase of this
picture we have been discussing. The events of these six chapters
really happen nearly simultaneously. So many birth pangs occur
though that it takes the next section of Revelation to tell of them.
My feeling from studying these times is that chapters 14 through
19 will occur over a thirty to sixty day period at most. So let's dive
in and discuss mankind's transition phase. The time immediately
prior to the birth of the baby!

> And I saw another angel fly in the midst of heaven, having
> the everlasting gospel to preach unto them that dwell on the
> earth...
>
> REVELATION 14:6A

The everlasting gospel! Truly, the good news of Jesus Christ, his death for my sins and his resurrection to defeat death, is news I will never grow tired of hearing. But look who is doing the preaching now! It's an angelic evangelist!

You see, by this point in the Tribulation, the saints who are still alive are on the run. They are hiding and are ineffective in spreading the Gospel as Antichrist and the False Prophet have declared all out war upon those who do not take the mark because of their faith. Thus GOD in his grace will send a mighty angel to take over the ministry of reconciliation which up until that point has been given to man (II Corinthians 5:18–20).

> ... and to every nation, and kindred, and tongue, and people.
>
> REVELATION 14:6B

The number four is GOD's number for the Earth. Four seasons, four corners of the Earth, etc. Thus we again can comprehend the majesty of GOD's authorship as he describes this preaching to those upon the earth with four adjectives.

> Saying with a loud voice...
>
> REVELATION 14:7A

People are not going to miss this angel's message!

> Fear GOD...
>
> REVELATION 14:7B

In the Proverbs we are taught that the fear of the Lord is the beginning of wisdom (Proverbs 9:10a). Also, we have learned the opposite of this truth. That is, the fear of man will bring a snare (Proverbs 29:25a).

The first thing this angel proclaims is to remind mankind that true fear should be in GOD and not in man. For to fear the Dragon, Antichrist, and the False Prophet and what they can do is wrong if it causes me to dismiss the fear of the Lord. The Bible states emphatically that our GOD is a consuming fire! (Hebrews 12:29). The Lord is a man of war (Exodus 15:3a). Jesus told us not to fear them which can kill the body but not the soul, but rather to fear him which is able to destroy both soul and body in hell! (Matthew 10:28). Just as people are being forced to choose death over life as the mark of the Beast is revealed, this angel is lovingly reminding those still undecided of the obvious spiritual truth. Don't let your fear of man blind you to the fear of GOD!

> ... and give glory to him; for the hour of his judgment is come: And worship him...
>
> REVELATION 14:7C

This wonderful angel implores in a loud and clear voice to give glory to GOD and to worship GOD.

The hour of judgment is now! Don't worship the Beast!

> ... that made heaven, and the earth, and the sea, and the fountains of waters.
>
> REVELATION 14:7D

This enlightened angel clearly states what GOD told us in the very first verse of the Bible...that GOD created the heaven and the earth.

Also, look how many ways he uses to describe GOD's creation. There is that number four again, the number of the Earth!

> And there followed another angel, saying, Babylon is fallen, is fallen, that great city, because she has made all nations drink of the wine of the wrath of her fornication.
>
> REVELATION 14:8

We will see when we come to chapter 18 of this Revelation of the fall of the city of Babylon. Again things are happening simultaneously now. GOD has to pick which topic to tell us about first in these remaining chapters, but when it's all said and done we will see that it all came crashing down together!

But note, immediately on the heels of the first angelic evangelist comes another with the message not to trust in the world's economic system. For we will see the world's greedy economic system is what this Babylon is of which the second angel is speaking. Babylon is fallen. He is saying that the mark of the Beast is like Confederate money! It's worthless!

> And the third angel followed them...
> REVELATION 14:9A

Remembering again that three is the number of completeness we are not surprised that GOD dispatches three angels to deliver his warning against taking the mark of the Beast.

I hope you are seeing how great this book is! How utterly incomprehensible it is that it could be written by man!

> ... saying with a loud voice, If any man worship the beast and his image, and receive his mark in his forehead, or in his hand, The same shall drink of the wine of the wrath of GOD, which is poured out without mixture into the cup of his indignation...
> REVELATION 14:9B-10A

I will stop there. The rest of the verse is so bad that I don't even want to write what the angel said next to those who take the mark and reject the Lord. You can look it up on your own if you choose.

So we see that GOD uses three heavenly messengers to tell those wavering souls still undecided why they must not worship the Beast but put their faith in Jesus. And I use the term "faith" very loosely, for when a person sees and hears an angel proclaiming GOD's Word, I'm not sure it takes all that much faith to believe that what he is saying might be true!

Again the first angel said to fear GOD, the creator of all things. Don't fear man. The second angel proclaimed that the mark of the Beast is passing anyway as Babylon is about to fall. And the third bluntly stated that worshiping the Antichrist will lead to eternal destruction! Three excellent reasons to buck the establishment and think about the decision you are making.

Now I must stop for a moment and consider this for myself! These are the same three reasons that I have today in choosing life in Jesus over enjoying the pleasures of carnality apart from the Lord for a short season. First, the fear of the Lord is the beginning of wisdom. He created me and knows what is in my best interests. Secondly, the world's system is an illusion. It's not real. I must remember to store up treasure in heaven and not be consumed with my earthly kingdom! Lastly, I must remember that my GOD is a consuming fire. Without the covering of the blood of the Lamb, I am toast. I mean, man...I am burnt toast!

> And I looked, and behold a white cloud, and upon the cloud one sat like unto the Son of man, having on his head a golden crown, and in his hand a sharp sickle.
>
> REVELATION 14:14

Clouds symbolize GOD's presence as you read through the Word. Here the Son of Man, Jesus himself, is wearing not a crown of thorns but a golden crown. And he has in his hand that instrument of harvest. He is holding a sickle!

> And another angel came out of the temple, crying with a loud voice to him that sat on the cloud, Thrust in thy sickle, and reap: For the time is come for thee to reap: For the harvest of the earth is ripe.
>
> REVELATION 14:15

Jesus told his followers that only the Father knows the day and the hour of the end (Matthew 24:36). To fulfill this prophecy, he waits for instructions from the Father, who is in the temple, as to when the proper time is to begin the harvest.

> And he that sat on the cloud thrust in his sickle on the earth; and the earth was reaped.
>
> REVELATION 14:16

The next four and a half chapters tell of this reaping. The seven vial judgments, the fall of religious and economic Babylon and the inevitable march toward the battle of Armageddon with the subsequent Second Coming of Christ and the separation of the sheep from the goats all begin at this point! These events, which we will consider in detail, for they are all terrible birth pangs which the world will experience, all are part of the reaping process of the Earth which is beginning at this point in history!

> And another angel came out of the temple which is in heaven...
>
> REVELATION 14:17A

As an aside, the reason the earthly tabernacle and temple needed to be constructed according to a strict pattern is that there is also a heavenly temple which those earthly temples pictured.

> ... also having a sharp sickle. And another angel came out from the altar, which had power over fire; and cried with a loud cry to him that had the sharp sickle, saying, Thrust in thy sharp sickle, and gather the clusters of the vine of the earth; for her grapes are fully ripe. And the angel thrust in his sickle into the earth, and gathered the vine of the earth, and cast it into the great winepress of the wrath of GOD.
>
> REVELATION 14:17B-19

Jesus has told us about this harvest by the angels previously. Look with me in Matthew's Gospel.

> Another parable put he forth unto them, saying, The kingdom of heaven is likened unto a man which sowed good seed in his field: But while men slept, his enemy came and sowed tares among the wheat, and went his way. But when the blade was sprung up, and brought forth fruit, then appeared the tares also. So the servants of the householder came and said unto him, Sir, didst not thou sow good seed in thy field? From whence then hath it tares? He said unto them, An enemy hath done this. The servants said unto him, Wilt thou then that we go and gather them up? But he said, Nay; lest while you gather up the tares, ye root up also the wheat with them. Let both grow together until the harvest: And in the time of harvest I will say to the reapers, Gather ye together first the tares, and bind them in bundles to burn them: But gather the wheat into my barn
>
> MATTHEW 13:24–30

The disciples didn't understand this parable and thus they asked for further illumination upon what the Teacher meant. This was his reply,

> He answered and said unto them, He that soweth the good seed is the Son of man; The field is the world; the good seed are the children of the kingdom; but the tares are the children of the wicked one; The enemy that sowed them is the devil; the harvest is the end of the world; the reapers are the angels. As the tares are gathered and burned in the fire; so shall it be in the end of the world. The Son of man shall send forth his angels, and they shall gather out of his kingdom all that offend, and them which do iniquity; And shall cast them into a furnace of fire:
>
> MATTHEW 13:37–42A

Jesus followed up this teaching by repeating its truth only the second time using fish instead of wheat and tares as the objects.

> Again, the kingdom of heaven is like unto a net, that was cast into the sea, and gathered of every kind: Which, when it was full, they drew to shore, and sat down, and gathered the good into vessels, but cast the bad away. So shall it be at the end of the world: The angels shall come forth, and sever the wicked from among the just, And shall cast them into the furnace of fire:
>
> MATTHEW 13:47–50A

Later, during the week of his Passion, our Lord again reminded his disciples of this truth as part of a discussion they were having concerning end-times events.

> And then shall appear the sign of the Son of man in heaven: And then shall all the tribes of the earth mourn, and they shall see the Son of man coming in the clouds of heaven with power and great glory. And he shall send his angels with the great sound of a trumpet, and they shall gather his elect from the four winds, from one end of heaven to the other.
>
> MATTHEW 24:30–31

Jesus reinforces the idea that the Second Coming and the reaping by his angels are simultaneous events. For we have the Second Coming and the harvest of the Earth occurring together in our Lord's description of the events. He sees these events as all part of a flow that occur together without any separation or demarcation. Lastly, before we leave this verse, we must consider an Old Testament verse which also foretold of these days.

The prophet Joel has much to say concerning these times. And we will hear more from him in a few chapters hence. But consider these words proving this same point from a man who received revelation from GOD nearly three thousand years ago.

> Assemble yourselves, and come, all ye heathen, and gather yourselves together round about: Thither cause thy mighty ones to come down, O LORD. Let the heavenly be awakened, and come up to the valley of Jehoshaphat: For there I will sit to judge all the heathen round about. Put ye in the sickle, for the harvest is ripe: Come, get you down; for the press is full, the fats overflow; for their wickedness is great. Multitudes, multitudes in the valley of decision: For the Day of the LORD is near in the valley of decision.
>
> JOEL 3:11–14

When we come to chapter 19 of Revelation, we will see the Lord gathering the heathen before him in the Valley of Jehoshaphat, which is also known as the Kidron Valley. It is there, in that valley between the Mount of Olives and Mount Moriah that our Lord will judge in righteousness the sheep from the goats as Matthew 25:31–46 describe in detail. Again, please note in Joel's prophecy that the harvest, the Second Coming, and the judgment are all events which are closely linked.

> And the winepress was trodden without the city...
>
> REVELATION 14:20A

This reminds me of Jesus. Before I let my mind wonder why the reaping of the world is described as a winepress which was trodden without the city, I must recall that that's exactly what

Jesus did for you and me, and what he has offered to the whole world! He too was trodden without the city! He went to Gethsemane, which means "olive press" and there he sweat blood as he considered the sacrifice he was about to make. Soon thereafter he was taken outside of the city walls where he was brutally tortured and murdered as the alternative to what we are considering here in this section of the book of Revelation.

> ... and blood came out of the winepress, even unto the horse bridles, by the space of a thousand and six hundred furlongs.
> REVELATION 14:20B

Taking this verse literally reveals some interesting information. The height of a horse's bridle is approximately four feet high. The length of 1,600 furlongs is one hundred eighty miles. Thus, I believe that as the winepress is trodden without the city, blood will flow from four feet above the ground for a distance of one hundred eighty miles. Four feet is the approximate height of a man's heart as he stands upright. One hundred eighty miles is the distance from the entrance to the Valley of Armageddon down to Jerusalem and the Dead Sea and from there further south to Petra where the Jewish remnant will be safely protected from Antichrist. You see, I feel this verse is talking about the Battle of Armageddon! It's talking about the last battle. It's talking about the second coming of Christ!

Now hold on, you may be thinking! That's not until chapter 19. This is chapter 15! That's right! Chapter 16 through 19 is basically a parenthetical which gives us more detail about the end-time scenario. GOD could have skipped that additional detail had he wanted and continued with the next verse being Revelation 19:11, the verse we commonly associate with the Second Coming of Christ. I'm glad he didn't though as we will gain much insight as we consider the seven vial judgments, the fall of religious and economic Babylon and look at the wonderful marriage of the Lamb prior to reaching that most wonderful section of scripture.

✝he Seven Vials of God's Wrath

And I saw another sign in heaven, great and marvelous, seven angels having the seven last plagues; for in them is filled up the wrath of God.

REVELATION 15:1

The Bible emphatically tells us that, "Vengeance is mine; I will repay, saith the Lord" (Romans 12:19b). God is not quick to judge as is man, yet he will judge in righteousness and truth. At this point in history, the Almighty has had enough! His anger towards the Dragon, Antichrist, and the False Prophet will come up his neck and into his eyes. You may remember what makes God mad from our previous study. Recall that whenever men keep others from the Lord...well, that really ticks God off! So we see that these last seven plagues are the direct result of the wrath of God.

But first, before we feel the birth pangs of God's wrath, we are treated to a heavenly song sung upon a glassy sea by those who had obtained victory over the Beast, and over his image, and over his mark.

They sang the song of Moses, singing,

Great and marvelous are thy works, Lord God Almighty; just and true are thy ways, thou King of saints. Who shall not fear thee, O Lord, and glorify thy name? For thou only are holy: For all nations shall come and worship before thee; for thy judgments are made manifest.

REVELATION 15:3B-4

Immediately after hearing this beautiful witness of God's works and ways, John looked and saw seven angels clothed in white linen and girded with golden breastplates coming forth from the heavenly temple. They were given vials full of the wrath of God.

And the temple was filled with smoke from the glory of God, and from his power; and no man was able to enter into the temple, till the seven plagues of the seven angels were fulfilled.

REVELATION 15:8

No man was able to enter into the temple for the glory of God was present. This reminds me of the earthly temple and specifically of the Holy of Holies. Only once per year, on the Day of Atonement, could the High Priest enter into this part of the temple which contained the glory of the Living God. And that was to sacrifice to God for the sins of the nation in order to appease the wrath of their Maker. That Old Testament picture is what is being illustrated in this New Testament reality. The Temple is closed, for God's wrath is being poured out upon a Christ-rejecting, sinful world. Only the High Priest, Jesus Christ, can enter the Temple at this point.

In a moment, I will show you how these seven vials full of God's wrath tell of what our Lord did for you and me so that we now *can* enter boldly into the Temple and specifically stand before the Throne of Grace—the very throne where the Bible states we find grace to help in time of need (Hebrews 4:16). The way to God is open because Jesus took the seven vials of God's wrath as atonement for the sins of those who would be saved. Unfortunately, for those who refuse the High Priest's offering, the literal seven vials of GOD's wrath are now ready to fall upon them!

> And I heard a great voice out of the temple saying to the seven angels, Go your ways, and pour out the vials of the wrath of GOD upon the earth. And the first went, and poured out his vial upon the earth; and there fell a noisome and grievous sore upon men which had the mark of the beast, and upon them which worshipped his image.
>
> REVELATION 16:1–2

I am reminded of the grievous boils which fell upon the Egyptians during the time of the Exodus as I read of the account of this first vial judgment. But I am also reminded of the words of Jeremiah the prophet as I consider this birth pang.

> Thine own wickedness, will correct thee, and thy backslidings shall reprove thee: Know therefore and see that it is an evil thing and bitter, that thou hast forsaken the LORD thy GOD, and that my fear is not in thee, saith the LORD GOD of hosts.
>
> JEREMIAH 2:19

Those who have taken the mark are now receiving the correction due from their own wickedness as they have forsaken the Lord their GOD. What Jeremiah through the Spirit is saying is that often GOD doesn't have to punish sin, for the repercussions of sin itself will ultimately come back to hurt the sinner and will be punishment in itself!

I wonder, though, what this noisome and grievous sore is whereby only those who have received the mark of the beast are plagued. Could it be that the mark which is implanted either in the hand or the forehead will cause a terrible reaction which was not anticipated by its developers?

> And the second angel poured out his vial upon the sea; and it became as the blood of a dead man: And every living soul died in the sea.
>
> REVELATION 16:3

This catastrophe will make the accident of the Exxon Valdez look like a glass of spilt milk by comparison! Every living soul in the sea will die! Every fish, every dolphin, every whale will succumb. The oceans will be cisterns of death!

We read that the waters will become as blood. I have been told that this may be the result of a tremendous red plankton overgrowth choking out the oxygen from the world's oceans and thus lead to the demise of every living creature therein.

> And the third angel poured out his vial upon the rivers and foun-tains of waters; and they became blood. And I heard the angel of the waters say, Thou art righteous, O LORD, which art, and wast, and shalt be, because thou hast judged thus. For they have shed the blood of the saints and prophets, and thou hast given them blood to drink; for they are worthy. And I heard another out of the altar say, Even so, LORD GOD Almighty, true and righteous are thy judgments.
>
> REVELATION 16:4–7

We see in the second and third vials the result of mankind's rejec-tion of Jesus' blood of forgiveness. Just like the Nile River in Moses' day but on a grander scale, all waters are turned to blood. Amazingly, the angel declares that this is a righteous judgment! Seems pretty harsh to me! That is, until I consider the Cross of Calvary. When I put Jesus into the equation, and remember of the wrath he received on my account, then this carnage makes sense as I look at the result of spitting into the face of such a sacrifice!

This is a key for my life today. When I want to get down and consider why bad things happen to good people, I must remember that there are *no* good people!

No, that's not right! There was one good person, and he died brutally for my sins! He died for yours, too!

> And the fourth angel poured out his vial upon the sun; and power was given unto him to scorch men with fire. And men were scorched with great heat, and blasphemed the name of GOD, which hath power over these plagues: And they repented not to give him glory.
>
> REVELATION 16:8–9

This totally blows my mind! Just like Pharaoh in days of old, the people of this future day understand that the plagues they are suffering are coming from GOD. There is no one claiming global warming or any other such nonsense. All understand that GOD is in control and they understand that he is the One who is shaking things up. Yet, with this knowledge they choose to blaspheme his name rather than change their direction. Blasphemy over repentance…no wonder the lake of fire awaits these foolish people. If a man or a woman is continually unrepentant, then the only option GOD has left to him is to grant their request and send them away from his presence. Of course, that means eternal destruction, for without GOD we have no hope of survival.

> And the fifth angel poured out his vial upon the seat of the beast; and his kingdom was full of darkness; and they gnawed their tongues for pain, And blasphemed the GOD of heaven because of their pains and their sores, and repented not of their deeds.
>
> REVELATION 16:10–11

Total darkness will be the physical manifestation to the world of the spiritual state of their leader. While people once saw him as charismatic and wonderful, a man possessed with ability far above mere mortals, now they see the true state of his heart: complete darkness and depravity. Like Adolph Hitler before him, this evil dictator's kingdom is crashing down. But once again, instead of turning to GOD and drinking of the water of life, men will continue to thirst terribly and will continue to blaspheme their Creator.

> And the sixth angel poured out his vial upon the great river Euphrates; and the water thereof was dried up, that the way of the kings of the east might be prepared. And I saw three unclean spirits like frogs come out of the mouth of the dragon, and out of the mouth of the beast, and out of the mouth of the false prophet. For they are spirits of devils, working miracles, which go forth unto the kings of the earth and of the whole world, to gather them to the battle of that great day of GOD

Almighty...and he gathered them together into a place called in the Hebrew tongue Armageddon.

REVELATION 16:12–14, 16

This is very interesting. The Euphrates River will cease to flow giving the kings of the East (China and possibly Japan) a straight run into the Middle East. GOD in his sovereignty will oversee this unholy trinity as they release miracle working devils to call the world to the battle. This is something GOD is very good at. He uses events in life to accomplish his purposes. In this case, these devil spirits will be used by GOD to bring the world to that one hundred eighty mile-long valley called Armageddon where the final judgment will be pronounced.

Zephaniah spoke of this gathering in his book.

Therefore wait ye upon me, saith the LORD, until the day that I rise up to the prey: For my determination is to gather the nations, that I may pour upon them mine indignation, even all my fierce anger: For all the earth shall be devoured with the fire of my jealousy.

ZEPHANIAH 3:8

The Psalms speak of this gathering from mankind's point of view. As I read it, it would be comical if it weren't so true.

Why do the heathen rage, and the people imagine a vain thing? The kings of the earth set themselves, and the rulers take counsel together, against the LORD, and against his anointed, saying, Let us break their bands asunder, and cast away their cords from us. He that sitteth in the heavens shall laugh: The LORD shall have them in derision. Yet I have set my king upon my holy hill of Zion. I will declare the decree: The LORD hath said unto me, Thou art my Son; this day have I begotten thee. Ask of me, and I shall give thee the heathen for thine inheritance, and the uttermost parts of the earth for thy possession. Thou shalt break them with a rod of iron; thou shalt dash them in pieces like a potter's vessel.

PSALM 2:1–9

Now, briefly, as a digression concerning the work of the three froglike devil spirits, notice that these spirits will work miracles. This tells me once again that miracles are not proof of holiness or GoDliness. Both GoD and Satan have, and will use miracles to influence the affairs of men. Whenever I witness or hear of a miracle, I must ask myself of where this has originated. Is it from GoD or is it from the GoD of this world? The answer will be apparent when I note the following. What is the fruit produced from the miracle and does the Lord get the glory? If no eternal fruit is seen, if the Lord is not glorified, well then I know where this power originated and I will *not* be impressed.

> And the seventh angel poured out his vial into the air; and their came a great voice out of the temple of heaven, saying, It is done.
>
> REVELATION 16:17

That's it! It is finished!

This is essentially the excruciating pain a woman experiences as the baby is being delivered! The head is crowning and as we will see from the next few verses, the pain will be incredible. Understand, we have all of the nations at Armageddon and the last judgment has begun. Remember, when we talk about chapters 17 and 18 of the Revelation in the next two chapters of this book, they are events which are happening simultaneously with the birth pangs we are reviewing now.

> And there were voices, and thunders, and lightnings; and there was a great earthquake, such as was not since men were upon the earth, so mighty an earthquake, and so great. And the great city was divided into three parts...
>
> REVELATION 16:18–19A

When we come to chapter 17 of John's vision we will learn that the great city is Rome (Revelation 17:9, 18).

> ... and the cities of the nations fell: And great Babylon came into remembrance before GoD, to give unto her the cup of the

wine of the fierceness of his wrath. And every island fled away, and the mountains were not found. And there fell upon men a great hail out of heaven, every stone about the weight of a talent [100 lbs.]: And men blasphemed GOD because of the plague of the hail; for the plague was exceedingly great.

REVELATION 16:19B-21

Let's look back to the book of Leviticus. In it we will find something very interesting as we consider this account.

And he that blasphemeth the name of the LORD, he shall surely be put to death, and all the congregation shall certainly stone him.

LEVITICUS 24:16A

Remarkably, the penalty for blasphemy in the Old Testament is stoning! No wonder stones the weight of a talent will be falling. For in this entire account, men have continued to blaspheme the Name!

• • • •

Thus we have come to the end of the age. We have come to the second coming of Christ chronologically. The seven vials of GOD's wrath have been poured out and the Lord is poised for his return with the armies of heaven behind him. But we still want to discuss the fall of the two Babylons and speak of our wonderful marriage feast before we see him riding upon the white horse. And as promised, I would like to show you how our Lord also took these vials of wrath in our place on that day nearly two thousand years ago.

The first vial caused a noisome and grievous sore to fall upon those with the mark of the Beast. Jesus had spikes driven through his hands and feet yet he said, "Father, forgive them, for they know not what they do!"

The second vial turned the sea into blood. Of course, Jesus was reduced to a bloody pulp both on the scourging floor of the Antonio Fortress of Pilate and on the Cross of Calvary. Isaiah said, "His visage was marred more than any other man" (Isaiah

54:14). It is that same blood that in GOD's economy provided the atonement for my sins.

After the third vial was poured out upon rivers we heard a voice from the altar say, true and righteous are thy judgments O Lord. Likewise, in the Eastern translation of "Eli, Eli, lama sabachthani" (Matthew 27:46b) we read that Jesus proclaimed from the cross, "My GOD, my GOD, for this purpose was I reserved."

The fourth angel poured his vial upon the sun and men were scorched with fire. Of course, the picture of hell is one of fire and heat. Jesus went to that kind of hell in my place as he received the heat of his Father's wrath against my sin.

The fifth vial caused men to gnaw their tongues for pain. Similarly, the terrible thirst Jesus experienced as he hung on that Cross must have been unbearable! Psalm 22 speaks of that thirst with these words, "my tongue cleaveth to my jaws" (Psalm 22:15b).

Near the end of his passion he said, "I thirst." In this Jesus fulfilled prophecy as Psalm 69:21 predicted would occur.

Yes, our Savior was parched so that I wouldn't have to go thirsty. In fact, he said on the last day of the Feast of Tabernacles, that day which commemorated GOD's deliverance of the nation from the dry and dusty wilderness and into the Promised Land,

> If any man thirst, let him come unto me, and drink. He that believeth in me, as the scripture hath said, out of his belly shall flow rivers of living water.
>
> JOHN 7:37B-38

He was terribly thirsty...I am refreshed!

The sixth vial released devil spirits which will speak into the ears of kings. Jesus, as the King of kings, endured the taunting of devils as he hung upon the cross on that day.

Psalm 22 describes it in these words,

> Many bulls have compassed me: Strong bulls of Bashan have beset me round.

They gaped upon me with their mouths, as a ravening and a roaring lion.

PSALM 22:12–13

The bulls of Bashan were Canaanite idols which, of course, were under demonic control. And you may also remember that Peter in his epistle described the Devil as a roaring lion. Yes, the King of the universe listened as the sixth vial was poured upon him, yet he did not succumb to the hellish advice as the kings of the earth will when they are called to gather on that day in the Valley of Armageddon.

The seventh and last vial will cause a great earthquake. Of course, as Jesus died upon the cross, there too was an earthquake. It was a quake which caused the centurion at the foot of the Cross to exclaim, "Truly this man was the Son of GOD" (Mark 15:39b).

Also with the last vial we will hear a voice from heaven saying, "It is done." Immediately prior to our Savior's death, what did he say?

His final words were, "It is finished."

What was finished?

It was the work of our salvation which was completed. The veil in the Temple was rent from top to bottom and the way to GOD was open.

Yes, as I read of these terrible seven vials of GOD's wrath being poured out, I am sorry for the lost of the world. But on the other hand it makes me love my Lord even more. For in them I see the fulfillment of the Scripture. "For we have not an high priest which cannot be touched with the feeling of our infirmities; but was in all points tempted like as we…" (Hebrews 4:15).

Truly, Jesus knows my pain. What a wonderful Friend he is!

✝ he Woman Arrayed in Purple and Scarlet

I have heard it taught that the Bible is a tale of two cities. The first is the city of the Great King, the City of GOD, i.e. Jerusalem. The second city is the headquarters for the GOD of this world, it is the center of operations of Satan. That city is Babylon. Jerusalem means "peace," for GOD gives peace. Babylon appropriately means "heaven's gate," as those caught up in the Babylonian religion are trying to enter heaven via a gate of their own making instead of entering by the true door to the sheepfold, i.e. faith in Jesus Christ (John 10:7–10).

So, as we come to chapter 17 of Revelation we will learn of the judgment of Mystery Babylon. We will hear of the judgment of the woman arrayed in purple and scarlet! In it will be found much insight, not only about the end of the Tribulation time frame, but also we will gain understanding about the past as well as make application for our lives today.

> And there came one of the seven angels which had the seven vials, and talked with me, saying unto me, Come hither; I will show unto thee the judgment of the great whore that sitteth upon many waters.
> REVELATION 17:1

GOD is not going to pull any punches here! He tells us the

true state of this false religious system. It's a whore. And it sits upon many waters. Remember the waters, or the sea, is analogous to the nations while the land, or the earth, is analogous to Israel. The great whore sits upon many nations. It's pervasive. It has gone throughout the world and has existed from nearly the beginning.

Don't doubt this analogy for soon we will see that it is confirmed in verse 15.

> With whom the kings of the earth have committed fornication, and the inhabitants of the earth have been made drunk with the wine of her fornication.
>
> REVELATION 17:2

We understand that religion and politics have been in bed together. The kings of the earth have been sleeping with this false religion for eons. UnGodly world rulers have used this false religion to control the inhabitants of the world, keeping them drunk and thus sedated from the true nature of their reigns.

We remember the words of our Lord against the third church in chapter 2 of Revelation. That church was in the city of Pergamos. Recall that Pergamos means "objectionable marriage" and their sin was that they allowed those in their midst who held to the doctrine of Balaam. Balaam, of course, was that false prophet seen in the book of Numbers who caused Israel to stumble by bringing Gentile women into the camp which were looking for sex. Also, the prophetic picture which Pergamos foretold was of the days after Constantine when the Christians merged with the Roman Empire and by that fornication lost much of the truth which came down from the early church before them.

Yes, the kings of the earth have been making love with this harlot from the days of Nimrod in the original Babylon to our day today as well as on into the future, until the day this unholy woman will be judged!

> So he carried me away in the spirit into the wilderness:
>
> REVELATION 17:3A

The whore is found in the desert. She is dry. She offers no life. No water. No refreshment!

> And I saw a woman sit upon a scarlet colored beast, full of names of blasphemy, having seven heads and ten horns.
>
> REVELATION 17:3B

We remember from our pervious study that this beast full of names of blasphemy and having seven heads and ten horns is the revived Roman Empire which is headed up in the last days by the little horn called the Antichrist. On the day of her judgment the whorish woman will be riding the Antichrist. This religion will deeply kiss the Beast!

> And the woman was arrayed in purple and scarlet color, and decked with gold and precious stones and pearls, having a golden cup in her hand full of abominations and filthiness of her fornication.
>
> REVELATION 17:4

Purple is the color of royalty. This woman has been a queen over the earth for centuries! Scarlet is the color of sacrifice. This religion is all about sacrifice. Only it's not the Savior's sacrifice which is emphasized but the sacrifice needed by man in order to enter heaven's gate, which is the core of her doctrine. This woman has unlimited prosperity. She is decked with gold and precious stones and pearls. She has more wealth than she knows what to do with! She has stolen her money over the ages from those foolish inhabitants of the earth who were made drunk with the wine of her fornication!

Lastly, this verse informs us that she is holding a "golden" cup. In the Bible, silver is the metal of redemption. Gold symbolizes her unholy passion. This woman has no ability to save. All she can do is eat, drink and be merry, unaware that soon she will be judged and found desolate and naked!

And upon her forehead was a name written, MYSTERY,

Daniel A. Tomlinson, M.D.

BABYLON THE GREAT, THE MOTHER OF HARLOTS AND ABOMINATIONS OF THE EARTH.

REVELATION 17:5

GOD calls this evil woman Mystery. She is known as Babylon the Great. She is the mother of harlots and abominations.

Truly this royal religion which is decked in riches is mysterious. She is great and she is not what she seems. She is a prostitute who is full of lies while pretending to be holy. Who is GOD talking about here in this chapter? Is this woman the Catholic Church? The Seventh Day Adventists say the Pope is the Antichrist. Is the Roman Church Babylon the Great? The answer to that question is both "yes" and "no."

You see, Mystery Babylon really is much bigger than just the unsaved historical leadership of the Catholic Church. It started with Nimrod in Genesis chapters 10 and 11 as he attempted to build a tower which would reach to the heavens, it continued into the Canaanite religion of Abraham's day, advanced in mystery with Nebuchadnezzar's Babylon, then came to full blossom with the Greek and Roman deities of John's era.

Then, after the true gospel was revealed in Jesus Christ, the GOD of this world corrupted the message by the unsaved hierarchy of the Catholic Church. Yes, the despoiled leadership of the Roman Church is part of Mystery Babylon. But she does not make her up in totality.

What is the doctrine which this opulent woman propagates? Well, the Babylonian religion has always taken the original promise of GOD, given to Adam and Eve, and has twisted it so as to confuse men from the truth of the Gospel. This religion, at times, is a subtle counterfeit in order to keep men from seeing the simple truth of Jesus Christ. The good news is that we have a Savior who loves us enough to die for our sins. This news says that we don't have to work for our salvation, for it is a gift from GOD!

The promise found in Genesis 3:15 told of One who would come from the seed of a woman and would bruise the head of the serpent. It also foretold that the serpent would bruise his heel.

I have learned from Pastor Jon and others in the Calvary Chapel movement that the original lie stated that Nimrod impregnated a woman named Simeramis who miraculously delivered a baby named Tamuz. Tamuz died but was resurrected and the Canaanites celebrated this miracle with eggs, a Yule Log, and a decorated tree. These symbolized the birth, death, and resurrection of the child Tamuz. It's not hard to see the similarities to the Gospel and that's why GOD hates this religion. Once again we see that it keeps people away from the truth by its confusing subtlety. Remember, keeping poor souls from him is the one thing that really makes GOD angry!

Later, other cultures changed the names but the counterfeit remained intact. Simeramis is also known as Ashteroth, as Venus, as Eros, and as Iris. She has always been an ultra feminine character which has led men and women away from GOD's Law in the area of adultery and towards Satan's goal of lust and debauchery. In the Roman Church, Mary has been elevated in a royal sense. She has been deified as the Mother of GOD and legends, which are not at all biblical, have been circulated about her life with Jesus as well as her subsequent "appearances" to men and women in more recent times.

Not forgetting the baby, though. Tamuz has been given other counterfeit names as cultures changed. His story is told in Baal, Cupid, Aphrodite, and in Horace. It's always the same. We learn of a wonderful woman and a miracle baby. A baby who was resurrected and deserves our worship. Only it's not Jesus! But it's enough like Jesus that people are duped.

You know, Satan's not an idiot! In fact, he's a lot smarter than me. He's smarter than you, too! He's not going to make up some religion that is so unlike GOD's promise of salvation that nobody will fall for it. Remember, he knows he is going to lose, he understands that he is going down, that he's going to hell. But he wants to take as many people as he can with him!

Satan is going to try and weave a lie which sounds reasonable so that larger numbers of souls will fall for the story. Sure, he will use the "far out" stuff for the few. Like those who committed suicide in order to hitch a ride on the comet which appeared a few years ago or the ones in South America who drank poison in order to die with Jim Jones, their Messiah figure! But for the masses, our adversary has chosen Mystery Babylon as his agent of deception.

Okay, but what about the Eastern religions of Buddhism, Hinduism, Islam and so forth? Are they Mystery Babylon also?

Yes, they are variants of the lie we have been discussing. The truth of Jesus as the Way, the Truth and the Life is not elevated in any of these false religions. They, too, are ultimately under the control of the GOD of this world.

So, the sum total of the Babylon Mystery Religion is that Satan is a liar. He is the father of lies. Now is the time for this lie to be fully exposed!

> And I saw the woman drunken with the blood of the saints, and with the blood of the martyrs of Jesus: And when I saw her, I wondered with great admiration [great horror].
>
> REVELATION 17:6

This is really a gross vision that John endured. I picture this boisterous woman, one who is loud and obnoxious and over done with makeup. She is lying on her side, partially clothed upon a couch with blood dripping down the side of her mouth. What a sight!

Of course, this false religion has always attacked the true followers of GOD. Babylon, Greece, and Rome all had little or no tolerance for the people of Israel. Nebuchadnezzar and Caesar oversaw the destruction of the first and second temples. And we recall how the Greek Seleucids, under Antichious Epiphanies, desecrated the Temple in his day.

In New Testament times, the Romans were especially cruel. Caesars Nero and Hadrian were most notable in their brutality as they drank the blood of Jews and Christians alike. After these came the universal "Christian" church based in Rome. Her evil leaders did not tolerate any doctrine which spoke against her totalitarian rule. Believers in Europe were especially oppressed as thousands were butchered and burned at the stake during the centuries of her absolute power.

Yes, when I consider the history of Babylon as she has related to the people of GOD, I too see a smiling harlot with blood dripping from the side of her mouth!

> And the angel said unto me, Wherefore didst thou marvel? I will tell thee of the mystery of the woman, and of the beast that carrieth her, which hath the seven heads and ten horns.
>
> REVELATION 17:7

Pay attention! In the next several verses the angel is going to reveal much about the Beast as well as expose who this mystery woman is. But first, notice that the beast is now carrying her. This is always the case. Evil leaders have used false religion throughout history to accomplish their agenda. Antichrist is no different. The irony here, though, is that the whorish woman believes she is dominating over the Potentate while all along he is using her to see his work completed! In a few verses we will see that, after he is finished with her, he will cast her aside. Oh, the sexual parallel between fornicators is jumping out of the story, isn't it? I recall in David's story after his son Amnon raped his beautiful half-sister Tamar, he too hated the woman after he used her to fulfill his lust.

> The beast that thou sawest was, and is not; and shall ascend out of the bottomless pit, and go into perdition: And they that dwell on the earth shall wonder, whose names are not written in the book of life from the foundation of the world, when they beheld the beast that was, and is not, and yet is.
>
> REVELATION 17:8

This verse gives much insight. Here we see that the beast comes up from the bottomless pit. Remember, earlier in Revelation we read of Apollyon, the Destroyer, as he was released from the bottomless pit at the sound of the fifth trumpet. Yes, the Beast is from the pit as are all that have pre-figured him before. Figures like Nimrod, Adonizedek, Abimelech, Antichious Epiphanies, Herod, Nero, and Hadrian have all received their power from the GOD of this world. They have figuratively ascended out of the pit!

But again, notice that the Beast was, and is not, and yet is. This speaks of his mortal wound which we discussed when Antichrist was introduced to us in Chapter 13 of the Revelation. Also you may remember Zechariah's report in chapter 11 of his book how Bands, known to us as Antichrist, would have his right eye and right arm severely injured.

Unfortunately the ones dwelling upon the earth whose names are not written in the book of life will be wonderfully impressed with the apparent "resurrection" of the Beast. As we recall from chapter 13, they will worship the dragon, they will worship Satan, the one who had the power to raise their leader from the dead!

> And here is the mind which hath wisdom. The seven heads are seven mountains, on which the woman sitteth.
>
> REVELATION 17:9

The seven heads the woman is sitting on is seven mountains. What? Seven mountains? Is this a code? Yes! In fact, much of the Revelation is a code. It's a code based on the Bible. You see, the Apostle John wrote Revelation to seven real churches which he oversaw in Asia Minor. They were being persecuted by the Romans. He understood that this work would be circulated and in order to keep some of the information out of the hands of the Romans he used imagery which the Christians would understand while their oppressors would not. In this case, the seven mountains likely speak of the city of Rome itself! Throughout history, Rome has been known as the city of seven hills.

Yes, the angel revealed to John that it is wise not to follow any religion which is based in Rome. That would certainly include the false religion which corrupted Christianity after Constantine's conversion as well as the errant doctrine of the Catholic Church which followed during the Middle Ages. In the future, that will include a warning not to follow after the Mystery Religion which is carried by the Beast from his headquarters in Rome.

Recall that we stated earlier that the Bible is a tale of two cities: Jerusalem and Babylon; the city of GOD and the city of the GOD of this world. Well, there is a bit more to the analogy. Babylon and Rome are the two cities which come up time and time again as instruments of the Adversary. Two cities, but in GOD's eyes they are synonymous. Both are Babylon!

> And there are seven kings: Five have fallen, and one is, and the other is not yet come; and when he cometh, he must continue a short space. And the beast that was, and is not, even he is the eighth, and is of the seven, and goeth into perdition.
>
> REVELATION 17:10–11

When John was given this revelation, there had already been five Caesars who had fallen. Either by assassination or by suicide. The sixth was in power during the time of his writing and he foresaw yet another king before the arrival of the Beast. We are told in this passage that the Beast that was and is not is actually the eighth Caesar! Well, the eighth Caesar was the infamous Caesar Nero! You remember him. He was the one who burned Rome and blamed the Christians. He was the evil butcher who perfected torturous methods in his lust to kill Christians. Nero is the eighth!

Is Nero the Antichrist? Will he ascend again at the end of time from out of the bottomless pit? I don't know for sure if that's the interpretation here but it is interesting to consider. The Caesar's all typify the Antichrist, and Nero's full name I am told does add up to six hundred sixty six. Also, he was the eighth Caesar. You may recall that in GOD's Biblical numerology, eight is the number of new beginnings. Could it be that Nero, as the eighth Caesar, will have a new beginning at the end of the age as the devil's agent for death and destruction? Was and is Nero the Antichrist? We'll just have to wait and see!

> And the ten horns which thou sawest are ten kings, [the revived Roman Empire] which have received no kingdom yet; but receive power as kings one hour with the beast These have one mind, and shall give their power and strength unto the beast. These shall make war with the Lamb, and the Lamb shall overcome them: For he is LORD of LORDS, and King of kings: And they that are with him are called, and chosen, and faithful.
>
> REVELATION 17:12–14

Check out Daniel 7:7–9 to read of this same event prophesied hundreds of years earlier! But look who overcomes with the Lamb. Those who are with him! They are called, they have been chosen and they are faithful. That's what I want! Thank you, Lord, for calling and choosing me and please help me to be faithful! That's a prayer I can pray which I know he will answer!

> And he saith unto me, The waters which thou sawest, where the whore sitteth, are peoples, and multitudes, and nations, and tongues.
>
> REVELATION 17:15

Four is the number of the earth and once again we see GOD using four adjectives to tell us that the waters are the nations of the world. Indeed, the woman as the false Babylonian religion has gone over the four corners of the Earth with her unholy passion!

> And the ten horns which thou sawest upon the beast, these shall hate the whore, and shall make her desolate and naked, and shall eat her flesh, and burn her with fire.
>
> REVELATION 17:16

And thus we see the end of the Mystery Babylonian religion. The kings of the revived Roman Empire will cast her aside as a naked and desolate prostitute is thrown aside after her lover is finished satisfying himself.

The worldwide religion based in Rome will be replaced by a religion that looks only to Antichrist as GOD. Thus, the false portion of the Catholic Church as well as unbelieving Protestant groups and all of the Eastern mystical religions and philosophies will be revealed as naked after Antichrist "resurrects" and declares himself to be GOD. Of course, as we have mentioned earlier, the Jews will not accept the abolishment of their faith as do all the aforementioned other groups. This will lead to backlash from Antichrist which was portrayed to us in chapter 12 of Revelation.

Now, an application for me jumps out of the page at this

point. First, we saw the woman sitting upon the beast. It seemed she was in control. But soon thereafter we were told that the beast was carrying her. His tolerance of her as well as his usage of her is revealed in this picture. Lastly, we see that the beast's ten horns actually hate the woman and ultimately reveal her desolation and nakedness. This is the way of sinners. Partners in sin will actually grow to hate each other. Ultimately there is no getting along. Sinners in bed with each other will always end up destroying each other. It's just a fact of spiritual life.

But the application can also be taken a step farther! We see here that Antichrist will turn upon this false religious system and oversee her dismantling. Likewise that's the way it is with any sin I try and control. When you or I believe we have some wrong act under control, watch out, for it's going to come back and get you. Anytime I try and control a sin in my life, that I know is wrong, it will come back and turn on me. It's just a matter of time. As the Bible so eloquently, yet simply, proclaims, "And be sure your sin will find you out" (Numbers 32:23b).

> For GOD hath put in their hearts to fulfill his will, and to agree, and give their kingdom unto the beast, until the words of GOD shall be fulfilled.
>
> REVELATION 17:17

There you have it! Even though the GOD of this world seems to have things going his way, behind the scenes GOD is in control. GOD is sovereign. He will take bad and turn it to good. He will take the messes that we make in life and turn it in to something beautiful. GOD is the GOD of the second chance. He is the Redeemer. In this case, he is overseeing the evil Potentate and his henchmen to accomplish his purpose. That purpose being the exposure of the garish woman for the whore that she is. After the fall of Mystery Babylon, there are now only two choices for mankind. The smorgasbord of religions and philosophies has gone away and in this last day the question is clear. Who will a man or a woman serve?

And the woman which thou sawest is the great city, which reigneth over the kings of the earth.

REVELATION 17:18

John can only mean one city with this statement. Rome is that city. Rome was the city that had conquered the known world and her empire reached far and wide. Rome was the city that John understood to rule over the other lesser kings of the earth. The woman is Rome! And Rome has been the center of Satan's operations since the time of our Lord's death and resurrection.

So, Mystery Babylon is now exposed and judged. Soon, that other city will be reinvigorated as the King of Kings and Lord of LORDS will come to Jerusalem to rule and reign for ever and ever! Yes, two cities, Babylon and Jerusalem. Babylon will die while Jerusalem will live on into eternity.

✝he Merchandise of Babylon

In the last chapter we learned of the downfall of the religious system which has fooled mankind since the dawn of time. Next, it will be revealed to us through John of the fate of the economic system which has enslaved mankind for nearly as long. It's a system that you might not think is so bad on the surface, but underneath it's a tyrant. For throughout history, when it has gone unchecked, it's only driving force has been man's greed. The system I am speaking about is capitalism.

Capitalism is the system which states that I will work for you and you will pay me for my service. So far, so good. But it also takes it to the next level. It also says, "My money will work for you so you can pay me more!" It worships money and its only fuel is the lust for wealth. That's the problem. There is no love! Instead of love, the economic system of the world encourages men to covet. The American mantra of "keeping up with the Jones'" says it well. Capitalism enslaves people to worship money, thus taking their eyes off of their Maker and placing those eyes upon temporal things.

Paul put it well when he said, "For the love of money is the root of all evil" (I Timothy 6:10a).

Jesus also had a warning against worshiping this economic system,

Lay not up for yourselves treasures upon earth, where moth and rust do corrupt, and where thieves break through and steal: But lay up for yourselves treasures in heaven, where neither moth nor rust doth corrupt, and where thieves do not break through nor steal: For where your treasure is, there will your heart be also.

MATTHEW 16:19–21

My treasure is what is most important to me. If that treasure is centered in economic Babylon, then I will lose it. But if my treasure is in things eternal, then it will not be corrupted and stolen. I am told that Jim Elliot has said, "Wise is the man that gives what he cannot keep in order to gain what he cannot lose!"

•   •   •   •

With these words of introduction, let us look into chapter 18 to learn of GOD's judgment of the system we live under.

And after these things I saw another angel come down from heaven...saying, Babylon the great is fallen...For all nations have drunk of the wine of the wrath of her fornication, and the kings of the earth have committed fornication with her, and the merchants of the earth have waxed rich through the abundance of her delicacies.

REVELATION 18:1A, 2B, 3

After the fall of religious Babylon, John is shown the fate of the second Babylon. Note, too, that this entity is also called Babylon the Great. But it is not given the prefix, "Mystery." No mystery with economic Babylon. Only greed! Also here in our text we see the completeness of mankind's fornication with her as once again the number "three" pops up in GOD's writing. He includes the nations, kings, and merchants as engaging in intimacy with this "other woman!"

And I heard another voice from heaven, saying, Come out of her, my people, that ye be not partakers of her sins, and that ye receive not her plagues.

REVELATION 18:4

I want you to highlight this verse in your Bible! This verse is a key to the abundant life in Jesus Christ. GOD is calling his people to not make their lives centered in the woman called Babylon the Great. Yes, we live in this world, but we are not to make our life in this world. I want to remember the old hymn as I consider this verse. We sing, "This world is not my home…I'm just a passing through!"

Just as our spiritual father Abraham was a sojourner, we too need to recognize that heaven is our true home. I need to live for the life which is much bigger and infinitely more permanent than the short-lived pleasures of what our present economic system has to offer.

Now I am not saying that you should sell all of your assets and move to the backwaters of northwest Idaho. But it is clear that GOD does not want us to join in the fornication that the nations, kings, and merchants are committing with economic Babylon. GOD's people are to come out of her. The temple of my mind should not and cannot prosper when it's living for the merchandise of Babylon.

So how do I do this? How do I keep the balance of living in the world but not living for this world? That's easy. Remember the pneumonic K.I.S.S: "Keep it simple, stupid!"

That's it! Slow down…Take a breath…Don't be in such a hurry! Look at Jesus. When did you ever read about him rushing off to take care of this thing or that? Well, if the Savior of the world wasn't in a hurry with the work he needed to accomplish, why should I be?

And be generous. Don't tightly grip your money and other blessings GOD has given you. Give some of it away. It will free you up in ways you won't even imagine.

So that's the secret. K.I.S.S. and be generous. It's a winning combination and as I said, it's a key to the abundant life we have in Jesus.

Unfortunately, though, this verse speaks against the country we live in, doesn't it? America the Great, the country which has been blessed with an economic prosperity which has never before been attained in all of the world's history is indicted as I consider this command to GOD's people. America, the Land we call home, the great nation which calls herself "Christian" is really deeply in bed with Babylon the Great. No wonder we are told that in the last days, the love of many will grow cold. We believers in the West are having an affair with another woman. As we covet for the things of this world our love for our true husband, Jesus the Christ, is chilled. We are pursuing after the lust of our flesh and after the lust of our eyes!

Ezekiel spoke some ominous words to his people which should be considered at this point.

> Behold, this was the iniquity of they sister Sodom, pride, fullness of bread, and abundance of idleness was in her and in her daughters, neither did she strengthen the hand of the poor and needy. And they were haughty, and committed abomination before me: Therefore I took them away as I saw good.
>
> EZEKIEL 16:49–50

These verses apply to our world today. In place of the city of Sodom, I can place the name of nearly all of the modern Western nations and the verses will still apply. America, France, Netherlands, Germany, Japan, and on and on. Read the verses again but place the name of America in the place of Sodom. Ouch! The verses still are true!

> For her sins have reached unto heaven...
>
> REVELATION 18:5A

I recall that first tower in Babylon. Its goal was to reach to the heavens also. It was thwarted. But this tower, this economic edifice, well, her sins do reach to heaven!

> How much she hath glorified herself, and lived deliciously... for she saith in her heart, I sit a queen, and am no widow, and shall see no sorrow.
>
> REVELATION 18:7A AND C

Oh, how we are all fed the line that the stock market will never fail; how we are told that our economic system is so wonderful! Everything is just going to go forward, on and on into more and more prosperity. I especially want to gag every January when the sitting President tells us how wonderful we are! What a bunch of ripe bananas! This system we are worshiping is really a house of cards. It's intricate, and it's beautiful. But oh, how easily it will fall. If you doubt that, just ask your grandparents to tell you about Black Tuesday in October of 1929!

The next verse describes her rapid demise!

> Therefore shall her plagues come in one day, death, and mourning, and famine;
>
> REVELATION 18:8A

Three plagues tell of her complete destruction.

Note, though, that in this end-times judgment of Babylon the Great, her death will occur in one day! Like the fall of King Belshazzar's ancient Babylon before, as noted in Daniel chapter five, Babylon the Great will quickly fall down to utter destruction, right in the middle of the party!

> And the kings of the earth, who have committed fornication and lived deliciously with her, shall bewail her, and lament for her, when they shall see the smoke of her burning, Standing afar off for the fear of her torment, saying, Alas, alas, that great city Babylon, that mighty city! For in one hour is thy judgment come.
>
> REVELATION 18:9–10

These verses show that this woman whom the kings of the earth love is not the same woman we learned of from chapter 17 of Revelation. The woman named Mystery Babylon. For you may recall that the kings of the earth hated that woman. And it was they who made her desolate and naked. Here in this section, the Babylon being judged is loved by the kings of the earth.

Both Babylons, the religious and the economic are translated "Heaven's Gate." Both are counterfeits of Satan. They both are "stairways to heaven" which really can lead towards hell. For they can keep a man or a woman from walking with the true way to heaven; that is, they can keep a person from wanting to walk with Jesus.

> And the merchants of the earth shall weep and mourn over her; for no man buyeth their merchandise any more: The merchandise of gold, and silver, and precious stones...and cinnamon, and odors, and ointments, and frankincense, and wine...and horses, and chariots, and slaves, and souls of men.
> REVELATION 18:11–12A, 13A, C

In all, there are twenty-eight things mentioned by the Revelator that the merchants of the earth shall weep and mourn over. Twenty-eight is yet another number that GOD uses very precisely in his Word. For twenty-eight is seven times four. Seven is the number of perfection and four is used in association with the Earth. We see that Babylon produces twenty eight things. Earthly perfection of things, but nothing which will go on into eternity!

And look at the progression of the list. It starts out with things considered most valuable in our system. Those being "gold and silver and precious stones." But then we see more trivial items like cinnamon and ointments and wine. Near the end of the list we come to commodities like horses and chariots (cars and SUV's we would say today.) Lastly, the list ends with the heart of the problem: slaves and the souls of men!

That's what the world's economic system does. It enslaves men and women in debt. You know how the line goes, "It's okay to buy that thing you 'really' want. Just charge it!" Or how about the pitch that sounds like this, "If you buy today, we will finance it and you will pay no money down for an entire year." They conveniently forget to tell you that when next year comes around, the item you purchased will have lost most of its value while you still owe the full price. Talk about slavery! This type of trickery is worse than an outright lie because a lie is easy to expose. This system, on the other hand, is embedded in our collective minds as something inherently good!

Next, after men and women become slaves, they then give their souls away. That is, they only worship the GOD of prosperity to an even greater degree. They work harder and harder and live for the weekend. They forget GOD as they serve their task-master!

So what should you do, dear Christian? How do you come out of Babylon in this area?

That's also an easy one. Don't go into debt. Don't live beyond your means. Save some money and remember what we said a moment ago. Give some of it away!

Now I'm not saying you shouldn't buy a home and have a mortgage. The government practically partners with you in that area with the tax implications of a home purchase. But I am saying that to go deeper and deeper into debt is not a wise thing to do.

> And the fruits that thy soul lusted after are departed from thee...For in one hour so great riches is come to naught... Alas, alas, that great city, wherein were made rich all that had ships in the sea by reason of her costliness! For in one hour is she made desolate. Rejoice over her, thou heaven, and ye holy apostles and prophets; for GOD hath avenged you on her.
> REVELATION 18:14A, 17A, 19B-20

With these words, that of the judgment of Babylon the Great, we have come to the end of mankind's trial and travail. We have come to the end of the brutal labor called the Tribulation and we have come to the end of the figurative pregnancy itself. For now we have come to the wonderful chapter nineteen of the book of Revelation. We have come to the birth of the baby. For the return of Jesus Christ *is* the birth of the baby! He will come back in this awesome account we are about to consider.

But also, just like in every birth I have ever attended, there is some crying and some difficulty as the baby tries to orient to his new surroundings. Likewise, we will see at the onset of the Kingdom reign, some strong after-pains as the Lord sets up his kingdom on that day when the lightning flashes from the East to the West. On that day not very far away!

Birth Pangs: The Future Glory

✝he Second Coming of Christ as the Birth of the Baby

The Second Coming of Jesus Christ

There are certain days in our lives that exude GOD's blessing. You know, the days when we can palpate GOD's glory and presence. Your wedding day is a good example, but the day of the birth of your baby may be the best! Everyone intuitively understands that a birthday is most sacred.

For a woman who calls Jesus her Lord, the delivery of her baby is *the* most wonderful moment of her life. For it's a spiritual moment she will never forget! In a similar vein, I see this spiritual phenomenon come to light for the unbelieving woman also at this time. For in that moment of delivery, the unbelieving woman will often sense her Maker, even in her unbelief. Indeed, it's a holy time, for in the birth process is embedded a moment of the miraculous!

Even after seeing thousands of births, the joy I derive from my vocation has not dimmed. It fact, I've only become more addicted to my calling as an Obstetrician as time goes forward. Of course, that's because a birth is more than a new physical life coming into the world. It's an intense spiritual moment that we all crave to experience! Thus, I hope you can see that this picture I have developed, that of God's dealings with mankind as a woman's pregnancy and delivery, is a true divine portrait. For just as the birth of a child is the most momentous event in a woman's life, so too the Second Coming of Jesus Christ will be the most awesome moment in the history of the world!

> And I saw heaven opened, and behold a white horse; and he that sat upon him was called Faithful and True, and in righteousness he doth judge and make war. His eyes were a flame of fire, and on his head were many crowns; and he had a name written, that no man knew, but he himself. And he was clothed with a vesture dipped in blood: And his name is called the Word of God. And the armies which were in heaven followed upon white horses, clothed in fine linen, white and clean. And out of his mouth goeth a sharp sword, that with it he should smite the nations: And he shall rule them with a rod of iron: And he treadeth the winepress of the fierceness and wrath of Almighty God. And he hath on his vesture and on his thigh a name written, KING OF KINGS, AND Lord OF Lords.
>
> REVELATION 19:11–16

As I mentioned, this day will be without compare! These verses are so pregnant with truth and meaning that I must break them down as we discover aspects of our King which are herein revealed. But first I should comment upon what John alluded to immediately prior to his vision of the Second Coming. For he heard a voice out of heaven speak of that other spiritual day that many of us have already experienced this side of eternity. That of our wedding day!

> And a voice came out of the throne, saying, Praise our God, all ye his servants... And I heard as it were the voice of a great multitude, and as the voice of many waters, and as the voice of mighty thunderings, saying, Alleluia: For the Lord God omnipotent reigneth. Let us be glad and rejoice, and give honor to him: For the marriage of the Lamb is come, and his wife hath made herself ready.... And he saith unto me, Write,

Blessed are they which are called unto the marriage supper of the Lamb.

REVELATION 19:5A, 6–7, 9

It's just like Jesus to save the best until last! Here at the end of the Tribulation. Immediately before he is to return to planet Earth to rule and reign as King of Kings and Lord of LORDs, we see that the Lamb is getting hitched! And who's the lucky lady?

Why it's you and me! We are the bride and we are going to be married to Jesus on that day at the end of our seven year honeymoon with him. Remember, we will be with the Lord in heaven for seven years after the Rapture, before the Second Coming while the Tribulation is occurring upon Earth. Earlier we called this the epidural as the believer in Jesus Christ will be spared the wrath of true birth pangs which will occur during that awesome seven year time of trial and travail!

But you may be asking, "What do you mean having the marriage feast *after* the honeymoon?" That's because you are thinking from the world view of a person immersed in Western civilization. In the Eastern world, in the culture of the people of Israel, this is very natural. You may remember Book X of *A Woman's Silent Testimony* entitled "The Marriage of the Lamb." In it we read of the wonderful symbolism which is occurring at this very moment in history which has its roots in the Jewish wedding ceremony. We spoke how the marriage feast of the Lamb is exactly replicated at the time of a Jewish man's wedding. Despite what the book *The DaVinci Code* propagated, Jesus was *never* married during his first visit to Earth nearly two thousand years ago. That's because he has been saving himself for his one and only bride which he will present to the world when we come back with him on that day not too far away!

So the timing of marriage of the Lamb is indeed right where we are studying now. It occurs with the birth of the baby. It's immediately prior to the wonderful 2nd Coming of our Lord.

He is Called Faithful and ✝ rue

And I saw heaven opened...

REVELATION 19:11A

You may recall the first time John saw heaven opened earlier in this Revelation. It was in chapter four and it read as follows, "After this I looked, and, behold, a door was opened in heaven: And the first voice which I heard was as it were of a trumpet talking with me; which said, Come up hither" (Revelation 4:1a).

The first time John saw heaven opened was for the rapture, this second time it is speaking of the 2nd Coming!

> ... and behold a white horse; and he that sat upon him was called Faithful and True...
>
> REVELATION 19:11B

Do you remember that the first of the four horsemen of the Apocalypse also was riding white horse. That man was the Antichrist, this is the True Christ! In fact, in the East, conquering kings often would victoriously enter into a defeated city riding upon a white horse. The white horse symbolizes the power and potency of the conqueror. As I consider this entrance, my mind races back to that day two thousand years ago when the humble suffering servant, the Rabbi from Nazareth, rode into Jerusalem, not upon a powerful white stallion, but meekly upon a donkey just as prophecy dictated would happen.

On this day, though, Faithful and True will indeed enter into the city in power and majesty! Jesus himself described the scene with these wonderful words, "And then shall appear the sign of the Son of man in heaven...and they shall see the Son of man coming in the clouds of heaven with power and great glory" (Matthew 24:30a, c).

He prophesied this moment to the high priest on the day of his passion with these awesome words, "Hereafter shall ye see the Son of man sitting on the right hand of power, and coming in the clouds of heaven" (Matthew 26:64b).

This moment will be like no other! For the only thing that can picture it is the birth of a baby!

• • • •

His name is Faithful and True.
He is Faithful.

Indeed, Jesus, as the pure and perfect Lamb of God, is the only One who has faithfully lived among us and yet was without sin. And as Isaiah so graphically described in chapter fifty-three of his book, Jesus faithfully endured the cross to win back you and me as his runaway bride!

And he is True.

In him there is no guile. There is no shadow or turning. There is no respect of persons. But wonderfully for us enslaved sinners, John tells of the balance to the "white light" of his truth. That light which only reveals how dark we are in our fallen and sinfully pathetic state. John told of Jesus with these words,

> And the Word was made flesh, and dwelt among us, (and we beheld his glory, the glory as of the Father,) full of grace and truth...For the law was given by Moses, but grace and truth came by Jesus Christ.
>
> JOHN 1:14, 17

Standing in the light of our Lord's truth is so blinding that I can't even fathom how awesomely terrible that will be! Until I remember that he also is full of *grace*. His amazing grace, which saved a wretch like me is what allows me not to fear that day when the Truth is revealed!

So take heart, dear believer. You may even be in the midst of tribulation in your life right now as you are reading this. But know this, one day, not far away, heaven will open up and the One called Faithful and True will be embraced! It will be the day you have waited so patiently for.

In Righ✝eousness He Doth Judge and Make War

> ... and in righteousness he doth judge and make war.
>
> REVELATION 19:11C

We have seen earlier from Daniel chapter eleven as well as from the Revelation chapters 14 and 16, that the kings of the south (the Arabs of Islam), the king of the north (Russia) and the kings of the east (China and Japan) will meet in the Valley of Armageddon to battle Antichrist's forces as well as to annihilate the Jews. Revelation chapter 16 tells that the three frog-like devil spirits will go forth to the kings of the Earth and cause them to gather together to the battle of the great day of GOD Almighty (Revelation 16:12–14).

On that day, the winepress of the wrath of GOD will be trodden as Jesus will appear over that great battlefield in the event we are now discussing. Antichrist and the kings of the world will simultaneously turn their guns away from each other and take their futile aim at the One now being revealed.

Revelation goes on to tell us that the birds of the air will eat the flesh of kings and of captains and of mighty men as the Lord will destroy them with the sword of his mouth (Revelation

19:17–19, 21). In other words, Jesus, who is the Word of GOD, will speak the Word, and his enemies will die! The Word he speaks *is* the sword of his mouth. For I know I needn't to remind you that Paul in the book of Ephesians calls the Word of GOD a sword (Ephesians 6:17b).

Isaiah paints this same prophecy with these words,

> For, behold, the LORD will come with fire, and with his chariots like a whirlwind, to render his anger with fury, and his rebuke with flames of fire. For by fire and by his sword will the LORD plead [judge] with all flesh: And the slain of the LORD shall be many.
>
> ISAIAH 66:15–16

In the New Testament, Paul speaks of this extraordinary day with words of restraint to those who have been persecuted, promising that this day will be the day of reckoning for those who have rejected the Son.

> And to you who are troubled rest with us, when the LORD Jesus shall be revealed from heaven with his mighty angels, In flaming fire taking vengeance on them that know not GOD, and that obey not the gospel of our LORD Jesus Christ: Who shall be punished with everlasting destruction from the presence of the LORD, and from the glory of his power;
>
> II THESSALONIANS 1:7–9

Also, Zechariah and Ezekiel share some insight that we should look at concerning this day of war.

> Behold the Day of the LORD cometh...For I will gather all nations against Jerusalem to battle; and the city shall be taken, and the houses rifled, and the women ravished; and half of the city shall go forth into captivity, and the residue of the people shall not be cut off from the city.
>
> ZECHARIAH 14:1A, 2

When I read these words my spirit leaps for joy, for they reveal to me that the Day of the Lord is near! Indeed, today in our day, all nations, with the exception of the United States, are against Israel. And her leaders continue to divide up the land. GOD told Abraham that the land was his. They are not to give it away. But that's not what is happening. It seems nearly every month we see in the news another giveaway! In 1973 they gave back the Sinai to Egypt. Unfortunately no peace came from that deal. In 2002 they pulled out of Southern Lebanon. Immediately the Iranian backed terrorist group known as Hezbollah moved in. Again, no peace. Recently, the Gaza was handed back in the peace for land deal. This time the Syrian backed group called Hamas took over the leadership. Need I say that once again the hoped for result has eluded the leaders of Israel!

No, Israel will continue to be divided as the Day of the Lord approaches. Soon, I am sure one of her leaders will actually divide Jerusalem as Zechariah predicts here in these verses. When that happens, we are told that one half of the city will be taken (given) away and, as a result, houses will be rifled and women will be ravished. Therefore, dear believer, when you hear of the Israeli Prime Minister subdividing the City of the Great King, when he gives away half of Jerusalem in another pathetic attempt at brokering peace, know the Day of the Lord is so very near!

Continuing with Zechariah's prophecy concerning the birth of the baby, the next two verses read as follows,

> Then shall the LORD go forth, and fight against those nations, as when he fought in the day of battle. And his feet shall stand in that day upon the mount of Olives, which is before Jerusalem on the east...
>
> ZECHARIAH 14:3–4A

On that fateful day, when the armies of the world are poised in the Valley of Armageddon, surrounding Jerusalem and encompassing the breath of the Israel, then the Lord will go forth. The word from Zechariah states that Jesus will stand upon the Mount of Olives which is on the east of the city and overlooks the Temple Mount.

Of course, we remember that day two thousand years ago when our Lord also stood upon the Mount of Olives. From there he proceeded down the mount with his followers, crossed the Kidron Valley, and entered the city by the eastern gate. On this wonderful day, the same thing will happen! Only this time, Zechariah's words go on to say that there will be an earthquake announcing his arrival (Zechariah 14:4b). Also, instead of a sitting upon a donkey, Jesus will be riding on a majestic white horse as he once again enters the city via the eastern gate.

Now, some of you may be wondering, "the eastern gate, what are you talking about! That gate has been sealed shut for hundreds of years." That's the point. The gate has indeed been closed as it is waiting for the arrival of the One worthy to enter in. It is also of no coincidence that another name for the eastern gate of Jerusalem is the gate Beautiful. For indeed, the gate to the city that is reserved for Messiah is most beautiful!

Ezekiel has some words from the heavenly vision that he, like John, also witnessed, which we should consider at this point which speak of the eastern gate and its role in Second Coming prophecy.

> Afterward he brought me to the gate, even the gate that looketh toward the east: [the Eastern Gate] And, behold, the glory of the GOD of Israel came from the way of the east: And his voice was like a noise of many waters: And the earth shined with his glory...and the glory of the LORD came into the house [Temple] by the way of the gate whose prospect is toward the east [The Eastern Gate].
>
> EZEKIEL 43:1–2, 4

Obviously, these words are speaking of the same event that both Zechariah and John have also spoken about. These words tell of Messiah's arrival in glory. They speak of the second coming of Christ!

When I traveled to Israel in 1999 I learned that the enemies of Israel also have understood this prophecy. That's why they have shut up the eastern gate! It was clearly perceived by the Arabs, that if the gate were sealed, well, then Messiah could not come. For the prophecy clearly stated that he would enter the city by the Beautiful gate. Also if you've been to Jerusalem, as I have, you will note one other curious feature before the Eastern Gate. There is a cemetery there. The way before the gate is encompassed about with the tombs of dead men! The enemies of Messiah have surmised that no good Jew would walk over the bones of the dead upon his entrance to the city. Thus they have felt that by sealing the gate and placing dead men before it that they can keep the Jewish man of war from his arrival to save his people.

There is only one little problem to their plan. They didn't read the next chapter of Ezekiel! If they had they would have known that they were doing exactly what GOD predicted that they would do!

> Then he brought me back the way of the gate of the outward sanctuary which looketh toward the east [Once again, speaking of the Eastern Gate]; and it was shut. Then said the LORD unto me; This gate shall be shut, it shall not be opened, and no man shall enter in by it; because the LORD, the GOD of Israel, hath entered in by it, therefore it shall be shut. It is for the prince; the prince, he shall sit in it to eat bread before the LORD; he shall enter by way of the porch of that gate, and he shall go out by the way of the same.
>
> EZEKIEL 44:1–3

GOD told Ezekiel that the Eastern Gate would be shut because the Lord, the GOD of Israel, *had* entered in by it. When did that happen? When did the GOD of Israel enter in by it? On Palm Sunday, of course! On that day, when Jesus the Lord, the GOD of Israel, entered through the Eastern Gate, he fulfilled the first part of Ezekiel's prophecy. Now, on this day we are presently considering, the Prince will again enter via the closed eastern gate. How will he do it, considering it is closed and there are dead men in front of it?

I don't know for sure, but remember, there will be a massive earthquake which will split the city at the moment of Jesus' arrival upon the Mount of Olives. It may be that the Eastern Gate will miraculously open as well as the graves of those which are lying before the same. We'll just have to wait and see! But he *will* do it! He will enter by the gate Beautiful, for "it is written!"

His Eyes Were As a Flame of Fire

We saw in the last chapter that the Messiah will make war. But I skipped over the fact that he will also judge mankind upon that day. Yes, he will judge those who have actively fought against him as well as those who have passively sat by. Those who knew better, yet did nothing will also suffer the consequences of the Lord's vengeance on that day. For indeed, his eyes are a flame of fire. He can see into the hearts of men! First, let me show you the judgment of those who actively fought against him. In our next chapter we will consider the judgment of those who stood by with their hearts closed.

> And I saw the beast, and the kings of the earth, and their armies, gathered together to make war against him that sat on the horse, and against his army.
>
> REVELATION 19:19

As mentioned previously, the armies of the world will be gathered in the Valley of Megiddo, known as Armageddon. Again, they will be called together through the course of political events pitting Antichrist's European coalition in opposition to the king of the north (Russia), the kings of the south (the Arabs) and the kings of the east (China and her allies). We were told that GOD allowed frog-like devil spirits to accomplish his will in bringing these forces together to battle. Ironically, as they are all racing towards the conflict they will not even be aware that Jesus, the King from heaven will also on his way to this last battle.

But here in verse 19 we learn what will happen to these enemies when they see the Lord coming upon the clouds with great glory. Why, they will forget their differences realizing they have a "bigger fish to fry!" It will immediately become clear to the kings of the earth that they are on the wrong side against the One who is coming back with vengeance and great fury. Thus, in one last and ultimately pathetic act, they will turn their formidable weapons (by earthly standards) against our Hero who is sitting upon the white horse and against his army which is following.

The next two verses tell of their rapid and complete defeat.

> And the beast was taken, and with him the false prophet that wrought miracles before him, with which he deceived them that had received the mark of the beast, and them that worshipped his image. These both were cast alive into a lake of fire burning with brimstone.
>
> REVELATION 19:20

Here we see the end of the two leaders who deceive the many souls of men. They are burned out! We are also informed that it is their miracles which were their agents of deception. I must remind you *not* to fall for anybody speaking "great things" and having a seemingly powerful ministry if the fruit he is producing in his life is rotten! That is the mistake that the people who take the mark of the Beast will fall into. It is a tragic mistake indeed!

Next, we learn of the end of the other combatants who have massed in the Valley of Armageddon.

> And the remnant were slain with the sword of him that sat upon the horse, which sword proceeded out of his mouth: And all the fowls were filled with their flesh.
>
> REVELATION 19:21

Again, Jesus, the sustainer of all things, will speak the Word and those who have been committed to fight against that Word will die. The book of Hebrews gives me some spiritual insight of how this happens. It states emphatically in chapter 1:3c that the Son upholds *all* things by the word of his power! That means he sustains all things. He upholds his enemies as well as his friends. To a certain point, that is. In this final instance, this is where the Lord lets go of his enemies!

Next, after dealing with Antichrist, the False Prophet and their confederates, the Lord will turn his attention to the leader of the circus! The first of two judgments will fall upon the Dragon!

> And I saw an angel come down from heaven, having the key of the bottomless pit and a great chain in his hand. And he laid hold on the dragon, that old serpent, which is the Devil, and Satan, and bound him a thousand years, [Please note, dear reader, that only one angel is needed to bind Satan. Often, we can think of the Strongman as this incredibly powerful being who can only be subdued by legions of GOD's angelic forces! Not so! Only one angel is needed for the task of banishing the one who was previously known as Lucifer!] And cast him into the bottomless pit, and shut him up, and set a seal upon him, that he should deceive the nations no more, till the thousand years should be fulfilled:
>
> REVELATION 20:1–3A

There it is! That's the thousand year end of our adversary! With that the Lord will have subdued those who have actively opposed him. He will next ascend to his rightful place on the throne of David and there the separation of the sheep from the goats will occur.

And on His Head Were Many Crowns

And on his head were many crowns...

REVELATION 19:12B

"And I saw thrones, and they that sat upon them, and judgment was given unto them"...(Revelation 20:4a). The Bible tells us clearly that our Lord is to judge the world. It is on this day that that task will be completed. Just as Solomon ascended to the throne of Israel in the days of the Old Testament, the greater than Solomon will sit upon his throne in this day as Judge and Holy Ruler. The prophet Joel and the apostle Matthew give us much insight concerning how this will appear.

> Assemble yourselves, and come, all ye heathen, and gather yourselves together round about: Thither cause thy mighty ones to come down, O LORD. Let the heathen be wakened, and come up to the valley of Jehoshaphat: For there will I sit to judge all the heathen round about.
>
> JOEL 3:11–12

As we have so often noted, Joel was given an incredible vision of the last days. In these verses we are told that the Almighty will cause the mighty ones as well as all of the heathen to gather on that day in the valley of Jehoshaphat where they will be judged. Of course, the valley of Jehoshaphat is another name for the Kidron valley. You remember it is the Kidron which flows between the Mount of Olives and the Temple Mount immediately before the Eastern Gate. You see, the Lord will sit in judgment from the Temple Mount as all of the survivors of the seven year time of Jacob's Trouble will be gathered before him in the Kidron valley below.

There, we are told in Matthew's Gospel that Jesus will separate the sheep from the goats.

> When the Son of man shall come in glory, and all the holy angels with him, then shall he sit upon the throne of his glory: And before him shall be gathered all nations: And he shall separate them one from another, as a shepherd divideth his sheep from the goats:
>
> MATTHEW 25:31–32

We are about to consider one of the most famous, and oft quoted stories in the entire Bible. And, I hope at the conclusion of this discussion you will look at this story differently. For I hope you will see that many preachers have stood over their pulpits across the centuries and have misapplied this teaching which so clearly speaks of the judgment on the last day!

This story is found in Matthew 25 and is the final recorded words of our Lord as he sat upon the Mount of Olives and explained the things of the end-times to his apostles. In chapter 24 we were told of the birth pangs, of wars, and rumors of wars. We were told of the blossoming of the fig tree and of the Rapture where one would be taken and the other left behind. The discourse then continued with three parables found in chapters 24 and 25 which spoke of the importance of watching for his return (24:42–51), being ready for his return (25:1–13) and of being a good steward of the talents he has given while we wait for his return (25:14–30).

But then in Matthew 25:31 to the end of the discourse, the verses which apply to this discussion, the Lord shifts into another gear and instead of giving a last parable, he speaks plainly of what *will* occur at the last judgment. For you see, in verse 31, there is *no* mention of this story being another parable that we all should apply to our lives now. No, Jesus said that this is going to occur when he comes back in glory. He was not giving another parable as has so often been taught. He is about to reveal what the separation of the sheep from the goats entails and to whom it applies.

> And he shall set the sheep on his right hand, but the goats on the left. Then shall the King say unto them on his right hand, Come, ye blessed of my Father, inherit the kingdom prepared for you from the foundation of the world: For I was hungered, and ye gave me meat: I was thirsty, and ye gave me drink: I was a stranger, and ye took me in: Naked, and ye clothed me: I was sick, and ye visited me: I was in prison, and ye came unto me. Then shall the righteous answer him, saying, LORD, when saw we thee an hungered, and fed thee? Or thirsty, and gave thee drink? When saw we thee a stranger, and took thee in? Or naked, and clothed thee? Or when saw we thee sick, or in prison, and came unto thee? And the King shall answer and say unto them, Verily I say unto you, Insomuch as ye have done it unto one of the least of these *my brethren,* ye have done it unto me (emphasis mine).
>
> MATTHEW 25:33–40

Did you catch that? Jesus said that the criterion for being called a sheep or a goat is how one treats "his brethren." Well, who are Jesus' brethren? Why the Jews of course!

Jesus was and is a Jew. And his brethren are that clan who have been persecuted and butchered since their beginning. But also, those who call Jesus as their Lord have a brother in him. Thus, Jesus' brethren are both the Jews, and the Gentiles who call upon Jesus as their Savior. In this passage, Jesus was clearly stating that those end-time survivors who have treated their brothers with compassion and respect, instead of with disdain and indifference, will be judged as sheep and will inherit the kingdom prepared for them from the foundation of the world.

You see, in our age of grace, salvation is determined by faith in Jesus. But during the Tribulation, after the Rapture of the church, the rules will seem to change. In that day, it will *not* take faith to believe in Messiah. Signs will abound everywhere as we have discussed. No, in that day, salvation, being called a sheep instead of a goat, will be dependent upon how one views Jesus' brethren. It will be determined by how one treats the Jews and the Christians. Remember, in that day it will not be safe to be of either group. Thus, if a man or woman does not have compassion towards the Jews or Christians they will run the risk of losing their heads.

I think of the days of Nazi Germany to illustrate this idea. You may recall in the movie, *Shindler's List,* how Oskar Shindler, who was a Gentile, saved several hundred Jews who worked for him at the height of the Holocaust. He took great risk and today is celebrated in Israel for his stand. Well, this is what our Lord is saying to those who will be alive in this day. Those who treat his brethren with love and compassion by helping them in their time of need will be called into the Kingdom. If you read on you will see that those who did not feed, clothe, or visit his brethren in that day will meet an unpleasant end!

That's the meaning of this story. It's not a parable for us as we have been painfully taught so many, many times. If it were, we would all be sent to hell! For salvation today is determined by how I view Jesus, not by the works I do! But in that day, apparently good works will be imperative in regards to a man's salvation. It may be because in that day faith will no longer be needed during that time when the Lord is so clearly and power-fully revealing himself to every living soul.

Of course, I'm not saying that this story doesn't apply on some level to you and me, that's not my point. The Lord is pleased when I have compassion toward the needy. And he is especially happy as he views my behavior toward his brethren.

Paul tells us in the epistle to the Galatians, "As we have therefore opportunity, let us do good unto all men, *especially unto them who are of the household of faith*" (Galatians 6:10, emphasis mine). I have the second part of that verse highlighted in my Bible also!

So I want to be good unto all men, and especially to my brothers and sisters in Christ. But when I hear a preacher wrongly teach that the Lord will say to me "Well done, good a faithful servant" based upon how a treat the poor, I must remember that that is not really what these verses teach. I once again am thankful for the Cross. For it is in the redemptive blood of Jesus and my faith in him that I find salvation. No need for another "guilt trip" as Matthew is once again preached out of context!

•   •   •   •

Thus, on that day when the Judge of the entire universe, the sustainer of all things, sits upon the throne in Jerusalem, he will separate the sheep from the goats who have gathered in the Valley of Jehoshaphat. On that great day, the One who is wearing many crowns will separate the heathen based upon how they treated his brothers.

Next, it is time to consider his vesture which is dipped in blood. For it is the blood which covers sin but it is the blood which also pictures just how ugly sin is!

And He was Clo✝hed with a Vesture Dipped in Blood

In the first chapter of Revelation, John also saw the Lord in all of his glory. But in that scene there was no mention of any blood upon his clothes. Not so on this day we are now discussing. When the Lord returns in majesty on that day of vengeance and fury he will have blood upon his vesture.

In the book of Isaiah we find amplification of this picture. As you likely know, the prophet Isaiah was given much insight concerning both the first and second comings of our Lord. In fact, the last few chapters of his book is almost entirely prophecy of the coming Messiah, either his first or second visit to mankind. And as Peter has told us, Isaiah, like the other Old Testament prophets, did not quite understand the separation of their prophecies into two differing dispensations, yet they faithfully reported the words which the Spirit placed upon their hearts.

Let's remind ourselves of Peter's words concerning this dispensational separation of the first and second comings of Jesus,

> Of which salvation the prophets have enquired and searched diligently, who prophesied of the grace that should come unto you: Searching what, of what manner of time the Spirit of

> Christ which was in them did signify, when it testified before-
> hand the sufferings of Christ, and the glory that should fol-
> low.
>
> I Peter 1:10–11

The sufferings of Christ were the visions of the first coming of our Savior. Of course, the glory that should follow is speaking of our present topic. The prophets did not discern the difference between the first and second comings. They did not discern the valley between the two mountains of God's visitations to mankind just as if I were looking at a mountain range with one peak in front of another. From my perspective, looking at those two mountains I do not realize that there is a huge valley between those two mountains. That valley in prophetic time we call the Age of Grace. It has been the last two thousand years that the prophets of old did not discern. You may recall from our discussion of the Mystery of God found in Ephesians chapter 3, that the mystery of the Church Age was "hid in God" and was "unsearchable" so that the God of this world, Satan, would not comprehend God's plan of salvation. Remember Paul told us in First Corinthians 2:7–8 that if the princes of this world had understood the "hidden wisdom" of God, had they understood the mystery of the last two thousand years of God's grace, they would not have crucified the Lord of glory!

Thus, Isaiah's prophecies, like Jeremiah's, Micah's, and other Old Testament prophets, do not separate the first from the second coming as we read them. They didn't comprehend the difference, but we who are living in the valley between the mountain peaks can see them both. One peak is behind and the other stands before us.

So let's look at Isaiah's words which tell of his vesture dipped in blood,

> Who is this that cometh from Edom, with dyed garments from
> Bozrah? That this is glorious in his apparel, traveling in the great-
> ness of his strength? I that speak in righteousness, mighty to save.
> Wherefore art thou red in thine apparel, and thy garments like
> him that treadeth in the winefat?
>
> Isaiah 63:1–2

Isaiah asks who this One is that he sees traveling in glory and greatness out of Edom and specifically out of Bozrah. He asks who is this One with his garments as red as one would appear if he were treading out the juice from grapes? The answer is given in the next verses.

> I have trodden the winepress alone; and of the people there was none with me: For I will tread them in mine anger, and trample them in my fury; and their blood shall be sprinkled upon my garments, and will stain all my raiment. For the day of vengeance is in mine heart, and the year of my redeemed is come. And I looked, and there was none to help; and I wondered that there was none to uphold: Therefore mine own arm brought salvation unto me; and my fury, it upheld me. And I will tread down the people in mine anger, and make them drunk in my fury, and I will bring down their strength to the earth.
>
> ISAIAH 63:3–6

Truly our GOD is a consuming fire!

These verses clearly speak of the Messiah and his coming on that great day in vengeance and fury. Blood will stain his raiment as he treads down those who are fighting against him in the valley of Armageddon.

You may recall from our discussion of Revelation 14:20, that the winepress would be trodden without the city with blood coming out of it by the space of one hundred eighty miles. Remember, one hundred eighty miles is the length of the battlefield of Armageddon from north to south. Also remember that in the southern end of the battlefield is Petra, which is in the land of Edom and, specifically, is Bozrah (Bozrah in Hebrew means fortress of sheep). Recall that Petra, that rock fortress is where the Jews (the sheep) will be safely awaiting the Messiah during those last days of the Tribulation. Here we see Jesus, coming to Bozrah and spilling blood upon his vesture as he delivers his people from the clutches of Antichrist and his armies.

This day will also be the year of the redeemed! Blood will spill upon the vesture of the Conquering King as he redeems his brethren who are protected in the fortress of Bozrah, as he redeems the children of Jacob who are safely ensconced in the stronghold of Petra! On that awesome day, as the Lord descends over that great battlefield, he will destroy his enemies with the sword of his mouth over the entire one hundred eighty mile length of the Valley of Armageddon. And it will be bloody, for the judgment of sin is not a pretty picture. The blood, which Revelation 14:20 states will spill up the height of a horse's bridle will also be sprinkled upon the One coming in power and great glory.

And please remember as you are reflecting upon the horror of this scene, that this is not the first time our Lord has gotten his vesture bloody. No, not by a long shot. For before the Christ will climb Mount Megiddo in the future, he has, in the past, already climbed Mount Calvary. Before Jesus, the Lion, will bloody his vesture on that furious day in judgment of those who have rejected him, Jesus, the Lamb, went outside of the city and was brutally bloodied for the salvation of all those that would accept him! He bled on his vesture on that day with his own blood so that I could escape the righteous judgment that my sin requires. No, the blood of the lost which we see staining our Lord was proceeded by the blood of the redeemed upon his vesture and upon his body as he went to Mount Calvary and died for you and me.

Truly, as Revelation 5:6 tells us, on that day in heaven we will see him as a Lamb having just been slain!

Thus, on the day of the birth of the baby, we will indeed see blood and water. We will see judgment and grace. The world will feel the joy of a birth as well as hear the crying of the baby! As our text in Revelation 19:11–16 so powerfully states, we will see him that is called Faithful and True coming in righteousness to judge and make war. He will be the One with eyes as a flame of fire and upon his head will be many crowns. And his vesture will appear as scarlet, it will be dipped in blood!

Lastly, though, before we reach the end of this book as we consider the Millennium and the New Heaven and New Earth, we must consider his name. For in the name of the Lord we find all we need to know about the nature of GOD. For the *name* of GOD tells of the *nature* of GOD!

And His Name is Called ✝ he Word of God

The text we are studying gives us four insights into the nature of our God.

Let's remind ourselves of his words concerning his name.

> ... and he that sat upon him was called Faithful and True.... . and he had a name written, that no man knew, but he himself... . and his name is called The Word of God.... . And he hath on his vesture and on his thigh a name written, KING OF KINGS, AND Lord OF Lords.
>
> REVELATION 19:11B, 12B, 13B, 16

First, He is "Faithful and True" as we have previously discussed. Next, he has "a name which no man can know." This is *so* important to understand. He has a name which we cannot know! You see, we belong to and are married to a God who is so big that we will never be able to fully comprehend him! Even as he reveals himself to us in his name and even as we discover more and more about him in eternity to come, we will never come to the complete understanding of his entire essence. There are facets to God that will *never* be discovered. In considering his name I must first be reminded that he has a name which no man can know!

Thirdly, "And his name is called The Word of God" (Revelation 19:13b).

John opened his gospel with these words,

> In the beginning was the Word, and the Word was with God, and the Word was God.... And the Word was made flesh, and dwelt among us.
>
> JOHN 1:1, 14A

Jesus and the Word of God are one and the same!

The book of Hebrews opens with these confirmatory words, "God, who at sundry times and in divers manners spake in time past unto the fathers by the prophets, Hath in these last days spoken unto us by his Son" (Hebrews 1:1–2a). God's word first came by the prophets but now it is by, or better translated, "*in* his Son." For in the Son, in Jesus, we find the Word of God. Everything we need to know about God, everything that there is to know about God can be found in studying and looking at Jesus!

As John proclaimed, as he concluded his remarks about Jesus as the Word of God, "No man hath seen God at any time; the only begotten Son, which is in the bosom of the Father, he hath declared him" (John 1:18). Yes, Jesus, truly is the declared and entire Word of God.

David, in Psalm 138, made a statement which is hard to understand until I realize that Jesus is the Word.

> I will worship toward thy holy temple, and praise thy name for thy loving kindness and for thy truth: For thou hast magnified thy word above all thy name.
>
> PSALM 138:2

Even as a man is greater than his name, so too Jesus is greater than all of the names that tell of him! The Word has been magnified above the Name!

Lastly, these verses remind us that Jesus is, "KING OF KINGS, AND LORDS OF LORDS" (Revelation 19:16b). This title puts it all into perspective. For Jesus is *the* King! All who have come before, be they physical or spiritual kings, will bow before the One who will reign on that Day. Yes, Nebuchadnezzar and Alexander, Napoleon and Roosevelt will all say with one voice that Jesus is Lord. Likewise, Buddha and Mohammed, the Dali Lama, and Billy Graham will also proclaim on that wonderful Day that Jesus is the King!

We are now ready to consider the thousand year reign of Christ the King, the Era known as the Millennium. For it is the Millennium and the New Heaven and New Earth which are analogous to the joy that follows the birth of a baby!

✝he Millennial Kingdom

And I saw thrones, and they sat upon them, and judgment
was given unto them: And I saw the souls of them that were
beheaded for the witness of Jesus, and for the word of GOD, and
which had not worshipped the beast, neither his image, neither
had received his mark upon their foreheads, or in their hands;
and they lived and reigned with Christ a thousand years. But
the rest of the dead lived not again until the thousand years
were finished. This is the first resurrection. Blessed and holy is
he that hath part in the first resurrection: On such the second
death hath no power, but they shall be priests of GOD and of
Christ, and shall reign with him a thousand years.

REVELATION 20:4–6

Here we see that those millions who have died during the Tribulation time frame as martyrs for Jesus Christ will be resurrected
and will rule and reign with him for a thousand years. We also
learn that the rest of the dead, those who have never called Jesus
their Lord, will remain asleep until the thousand years have finished.

But to complete this thought, we must remember that those
other millions of believers over the ages who have also called
upon Jesus prior to the Tribulation time frame will have already

been resurrected seven years prior to this time in the event we know as the rapture. You will recall that Paul has taught us that the Lord himself will descend from heaven with a shout and with the trump of GOD and the dead in Christ will rise first. He then went on to say that we who are alive and remain will be caught up (raptured) to meet the Lord in the air (I Thessalonians 4:16–17). Therefore, we see that the first resurrection has two parts. That is, the resurrection of the believers on the day of the Rapture and the resurrection of new believers who come to the Lord and die during the Tribulation.

We will soon see that there will be a short-lived second resurrection at the end of the thousand year Kingdom for those who over the millennia have rejected the good news of Jesus Christ. At that time they will be judged according to their works and will experience the second death. It is that death which has been immortalized by Dante in his famous graphic depiction of hell!

• • • •

But before we consider the end of the thousand years, let's look at some of the many descriptions we have from other inspired Bible writers which give us more information of how this time frame will appear.

One of my favorites is found in Isaiah,

> And it shall come to pass in the last days, that the mountain of the LORD's house shall be established in the top of the mountains, and shall be exalted above the hills; and all the nations shall flow unto it. And many people shall go and say, Come ye, and let us go up to the house of the GOD of Jacob; and he will teach us of his ways, and we will walk in his paths: For out of Zion shall go forth the law, and the word of the LORD from Jerusalem.
>
> ISAIAH 2:2–3

Did you catch that! Jesus, the GOD of Jacob will teach us his ways! We will walk in his path. He will speak the word from Jerusalem!

Isaiah continues with his well-known prophecy concerning the end of war,

> ... and they shall beat their swords into plowshares, and their spears into pruning hooks: Nation shall not lift up sword against nation, neither shall they learn war any more.
>
> ISAIAH 2:4B

In chapter 11 of his book Isaiah adds this equally famous description of how the Millennial Kingdom will look.

> The wolf also shall dwell with the lamb, also the leopard shall lie down with the kid; and the calf and the young lion and the fatling together; and the little child shall lead them. And the cow and the bear shall feed; their young ones shall lie down together: And the lion shall eat straw like the ox. The suckling child shall play on the hole of the asp, and the weaned child shall put his hand on the cockatrice den. They shall not hurt or destroy in all my holy mountain: For the earth shall be full of the knowledge of the LORD, as the waters cover the sea.
>
> ISAIAH 11:6–9

What a time that will be. No wars! No strife. For all the earth will be full of the knowledge of the Lord! The prophet Micah gave a parallel account to Isaiah in his account found in 4:1–5. I would like to draw your attention to some additional information concerning GOD's provision for man during this wonderful day which is given by Micah.

> But they shall sit every man under his vine and under his fig tree; and none shall make them afraid.
>
> MICAH 4:4A

GOD is going to provide provision and shelter for all in that day. There will be no worries on that day when all things are made right. There will be enough for all! Zechariah has another important account which gives us more insight concerning our future time with Jesus.

And it shall be in that day, that living waters shall go out from Jerusalem...and the LORD shall be king over all the earth: In that day shall there be one LORD, and his name one...and it shall come to pass, that every one that is left of all the nations which came against Jerusalem shall even go up from year to year to worship the King, the LORD of hosts, and to keep the Feast of Tabernacles.

ZECHARIAH 14:8A, 9, 16

Every year, the people of the world who have survived the Tribulation will somehow travel to Jerusalem in September to see and worship the King in person. What a wonderful convocation that will be. Understand also, we who are ruling and reigning with Jesus, we members of the first resurrection, will be escorting those survivors and their children to the City of the Great King every autumn. We too, will travel with the "mortal sheep" that we are overseeing, to worship before the Lord each year during the Feast of Tabernacles!

Next, let's consider some of Ezekiel's words concerning the thousand year reign of the King of Kings and his special relationship to Israel during this Era.

Then I will sprinkle clean water [the Holy Spirit] upon you, and ye shall be clean: From all your filthiness and from all your idols, will I cleanse you. A new heart also will I give you, and a new spirit will I put within you: And I will take away the stony heart out of your flesh, and I will give you an heart of flesh. And I will put my spirit within you, and cause you to walk in my statutes, and you shall keep my judgments, and do them. And you shall dwell in the land that I gave to your fathers; and ye shall be my people, and I will be your GOD.

EZEKIEL 36:25–28

The Jews will be filled with the Spirit in that day. Thus, they will finally be able to follow GOD's Law as they are empowered by the Spirit within. And they will dwell close to the King. They will live in the land given to their fathers. They will dwell in Israel!

Ezekiel continues by speaking of Jesus, calling Him David.

And David my servant shall be king over them; and they shall all have one shepherd: They shall also walk in my judgments, and observe my statutes, and do them. And they shall dwell in the land that I have given unto Jacob my servant, wherein your fathers have dwelt; and they shall dwell therein, even they, and their children, and their children's children for ever: And my servant David shall be their prince forever. Moreover I will make a covenant of peace with them; it shall be an everlasting covenant with them: And I will place them and will set my sanctuary in the midst of them for evermore. My tabernacle shall also be with them: Yea, I will be their GOD, and they shall be my people. And the heathen [Gentiles] shall know that I the LORD do sanctify Israel, when my sanctuary shall be in the midst of them for evermore.

EZEKIEL 37:24–28

Wow! It would appear that during the Millennial Kingdom, that GOD, through his Son Jesus, will finally have the relationship which he sought to have with Israel when they first convocated below Mount Sinai on the day the Law was given to Moses. On that day they couldn't keep the covenant. During this new day, they will! Israel will at last get to realize that relationship which GOD had intended for them and also the world will get to witness that special calling that Israel was given. Indeed, the heathen (the Gentiles) will know that the Lord has sanctified the children of Israel.

Paul proclaimed this day with these words, "And so all Israel shall be saved: As it is written, There shall come out of Zion the Deliverer, and shall turn away unGODliness from Jacob" (Romans 11:26). But GOD has given us more to understand about the future.

Let's study Joel's prophecy concerning the restoration of this day.

And I will restore to you the years that the locust hath eaten, the cankerworm, and the caterpillar, and the palmerworm, my great army which I sent among you. And ye shall eat in plenty, and be satisfied, and praise the name of the LORD your GOD, that hath dealt wondrously with you: And my people shall never be ashamed. And ye shall know that I am in the midst of Israel, and that I am the LORD your GOD, and none else: And my people shall never be ashamed.

JOEL 2:25–27

The Millennium will be a time when all things are made right. All debts will be cancelled. All judgments rescinded. All wounds will be healed. For the Jews, they, as scattered sheep who have gone astray, will have come back to the Shepherd of their souls. As the prodigal son who has realized his folly, they have come back to the Father and have been given a robe and ring as they dine upon the fatted calf. Yes, the thousand year reign of Christ physically present upon Earth will be a time of incredible restoration. As our Lord said, "Behold, I make all things new" (Revelation 21:5b).

• • • •

When I'm bugged by worms and caterpillars, the little things that are destroying my peace and taking my abundance, I need to remember that GOD is the GOD of restoration. He has promised me in his Word that he will never leave me nor forsake me (Hebrews 13:5). He has said that nothing can separate me from his love (Romans 8:38–39). And he has stated that he knows my end and that it is an expected end (Jeremiah 29:11). It is an ending that will turn out well! Even though I may have lost everything today due to my folly and sin, GOD has promised to bring me in. He will bring me home!

Jesus said it better than I when he told his disciples, and tells me by extension, that he was leaving so as to go and prepare a home for you and me in heaven with him (John 14:2). He has a mansion, a honeymoon cottage, if you will, in store just for you, just for me!

What a day that will be!

• • • •

Next, I want to show you the love relationship that Israel,

including the spiritual children of Abraham (i.e. all believers in Jesus), will enjoy with the Lord on that day.

Look with me at some of the words of the prophet Hosea.

> And it shall be at that day, saith the LORD, that thou shalt call me Ishi; [My Husband] and shalt call me no more Baali *(My* LORD*)*.
>
> HOSEA 2:16

On that day, we will enjoy a spiritual intimacy with the Lord which he pictures for us by comparing it to the physical love that a husband and wife share. Incredibly, GOD will view us as a marriage partner and not as a servant!

Continuing,

> And I will betroth thee unto me for ever; yea, I will betroth thee unto me in righteousness, and in judgment, and in lovingkindness, and in mercies. I will even betroth thee unto me in faithfulness: And thou shalt know the LORD.
>
> HOSEA 2:19–20

Wow! What a deal. Righteousness, discernment, lovingkindness and faithfulness are the qualities I long for now but often fall woefully short of! All of these attributes will be given to me in the dowry of gifts I receive from my Husband.

Lastly, we come to my favorite prophecy concerning the Millennial Kingdom. It is found in the little Book of Zephaniah.

> In that day it shall be said to Jerusalem, Fear thou not: And to Zion, Let not thine hands be slack. For the LORD thy GOD in the midst of thee is mighty; he will save, he will rejoice over thee with joy; he will rest in his love, he will joy over thee with singing.
>
> ZEPHANIAH 3:16–17

Now did you catch that?

The GOD of the universe will *rejoice* over you with joy! He will *rest* in *his* love for you and me, and he will joy over us with *singing!* That verse is so far out there that I can hardly believe it! But GOD said it, so I choose to trust it nonetheless!

• • • •

Now, one little digression and we can move onto the end of the Millennium.

You, of course, understand that this time is called the Millennium because it is a thousand year period of unparalleled peace and prosperity for mankind. If you will, it's utopia!

But if we look at man's chronological history upon this planet from the biblical perspective, we see that Adam was on the scene just a little over six thousand years ago. (Genesis 5 and 11 give those chronological details.) That is, in our day now, we are starting the seventh Millennium. We also remember that in GOD's economy, a day is as a thousand years and a thousand years is as one day (II Peter 3:8). Thus, we are starting the seventh day.

The Millennium is the seventh day! Just as GOD rested on the seventh day in the creation account and just as the children of Israel were to rest on the seventh day in their weekly calendar, so, too, mankind will rest on the seventh day. The Millennium will complete the picture that GOD painted on the very week he created all things! For seven is that perfect number and on the seventh day mankind will rest from their labor.

Okay, back to our story!

Jesus is ruling and reigning from Jerusalem. We too are sharing in that responsibility. The lion and the lamb lay down together and we share in a love relationship with our Maker. This wonderful time lasts for a thousand years. But then something bad happens. Satan is loosed from his prison and trouble is on the way. The people have one more chance to reject their True King and side with the counterfeit. The result of that insurrection is our next stop.

The Great White ✝ hrone Judgment

And when the thousand years are expired, Satan shall be loosed
out of his prison,
And shall go out to deceive the nations which are in the four
quarters of the earth…to gather them together to battle: The
number of whom is as the sand of the sea.

REVELATION 20:7–8A, C

This blows me away until I consider what's going on in the background. Why would GOD let Satan out once again to mess things
up with mankind? This sounds a lot like the Garden of Eden
story, doesn't it?

That's the point!

You see, in that day we will have a world that is ruled in righteousness. There will be no internet porno or late night Letter-
man to waste time and energy on. There will be no need to steal
for bread or to lie to my boss. The mortals in that day will live a
life which we in our day have not known or even considered. It's
a world without Satan and the influence of the world's carnal system. Yes, humans will still have their sin nature that they inherited from Adam. But Satan and the world's influences will not be
weighty forces. Also, we overseeing priests and kings will pretty

much keep the desire of men to sin down to a minimum! Jesus does not tolerate sin, and we as his ambassadors will also rule with him with the rod of iron when it comes to the area of willful sin. Thus, the children of the world will have not known a choice. And that's the problem. For GOD is love and love demands an alternative.

If I married my wife because she was the only woman I could pick from, well, that wouldn't be all that great. But choosing my wife over many other women tells her that she is the one I love. So it is with GOD. The Creator wants a love relationship with his children. But at the end of the Millennium there will be generations of people who have not known a choice. It's not you and me and it's not the Tribulation saints who will be tripped up by Satan. We've already chosen the Lord. But the mortals born after the onset of the Day of the Lord will have not known that option. They will not have ever had the chance to desire GOD or to reject him. It's for that reason that Satan is again let on the loose. Love demands a choice and Satan once again is the agent that GOD will use to give mankind the opportunity to decide to love him or to choose to, in pride, love themselves.

So Satan will go out to the four quarters of the Earth and much reminiscent of the frog-like demons of the Tribulation, he will whisper into the ears of men that Jesus isn't really all that great! He will say that there is pleasure in sin and that Jesus is holding back. It will likely sound much like what he told Eve on that day in the Garden. He will appeal to the lust of man's eyes and to the lust of his heart. And he will appeal to man's awful pride and tell them that Jesus and the saints of heaven don't deserve to rule over them. He will say that it's time for a change of administration. Unfortunately, those who do not really love the Lord will choose badly.

I am reminded of the story of Absalom's rebellion against David's rule as I consider this section of scripture. Check it out as it is a good Old Testament picture of this very day. Absalom, as the handsome and gifted usurper, gathered an army of discontented subjects of David and tried to take over. And just as happened to Absalom, we will see a similar end to Satan and those who join in league with him on that day.

> And they went up on the breadth of the earth, and compassed the camp of the saints about, and the beloved city:
>
> REVELATION 20:9A

Once again, Jerusalem, the city of peace, will be surrounded by an attacking army! It's a recurring nightmare isn't it! From Sennacherib to Nebuchadnezzar, from Titus to Hadrian, from Saladin to Antichrist, Jerusalem has always been the site. It has always been the flashpoint.

Oh, and don't forget...the greatest battle of all time took place there around 33 a.d. Jesus the Christ took on Satan, and, as the Passover sacrifice, once and for all redeemed you and me out of the clutches of our adversary. That spiritual battle made these other physical ones pale in comparison!

> ... and fire came down from GOD out of heaven, and devoured them.
>
> REVELATION 20:9B-10

Many times GOD has sent fire down from heaven as his cleansing agent. I think of the fire that rained down upon Sodom and Gomorrah, as well as the hail mingled with fire that fell upon Pharaoh and Egypt. Later Elijah and Elisha called down fire upon GOD's enemies. During the Tribulation the two witnesses will use the fire proceeding forth from their mouths to defeat those who would try and stop them before they have finished their testimony. And lastly, we will soon consider the fire which will escort in the New Heaven and the New Earth. That fire is spoken of in Peter's 2nd Epistle and will usher in the eighth and last millennium of which the Bible speaks, found in chapters 21 and 22 of Revelation.

Yes, twelve words are all that are needed to tell of the end of this devilish rebellion. Indeed the judgment upon those who choose death over life at the end of the Millennium will be quick! Next, we see the end of Satan.

And the devil that deceived them was cast into the lake of fire and brimstone, where the beast and the false prophet are, and shall be tormented day and night for ever and ever.

REVELATION 20:10

No getting out after this judgment. Lucifer, the one who walked with GOD, as Ezekiel described, in the midst of the stones of fire and who was perfect in all his ways has now met his appointed end. Why? Because iniquity was found in him! His heart was lifted up because of his beauty! He corrupted his wisdom by reason of his brightness (Ezekiel 28:12–19). It was pride, little children! I must remember that I too am a little child or my pride can also burn me out!

The Bible does not say, "Before honor is pride." No, it says, "Before honor is humility." Let me show you; "The fear of the Lord is the instruction of wisdom; and before honor is humility" (Proverbs 15:33).

And I saw a great white throne, and him that sat on it, from whose face the earth and the heaven fled away; and there was found no place for them.

REVELATION 20:11

Eternal life is living in the presence of GOD. For those who have thus rejected GOD, they are about to receive their desire. That is, life apart from GOD. It is an existence that cannot stand in his presence. It is a life that must flee away from him. What does this mean? Why, life apart from GOD is eternal death. It is eternal destruction. It is the second death.

And I saw the dead, small and great, stand before GOD.

REVELATION 20:12A

On that day it will not matter if one is Andrew Carnegie or Elvis Presley. It won't make any difference as all, both small and great will stand before GOD. And all will say and do only one thing, "That at the name of Jesus every knee should bow...

and that every tongue should confess that Jesus Christ is Lord" (Philippians 2:10a, 11a).

> And the books were opened: And another book was opened, which is the book of life: And the dead were judged out of those things which were written in the books, according to their works.
>
> REVELATION 20:12B

This is a very important little verse. For in it we find the secret to our salvation. We must keep our name written in the Book of Life (Revelation 3:5). For the book of Life will be opened and as long as my name is in there then the words in the other books do not apply to me. Those other books are filled with words documenting man's works. Unfortunately for the unsaved, GOD has stated in Isaiah that all our works are filthy rags in comparison to his glory. But he has also told us who believe that he will remember our sins no more as we call upon him. Thus, I must call upon GOD's only provision for salvation, that is, Jesus, the Way, the Truth, and the Life to keep my name from being blotted out of the book of Life. Thereby, I will stay the other books, which hold the unrighteous works of those who have not had their sins erased, from being opened against me.

The result of judgment based upon works is seen in the last two verses of the Millennium.

> And death and hell were cast into the lake of fire. This is the second death.
> And whosoever was not found written in the book of life was cast into the lake of fire.
>
> REVELATION 20:14–15

These two verses really bother me. This is bad news for so many. I don't understand the ramifications of these verses at all! But they make me want to tell of the Good News of Jesus Christ. And they should! How Jesus went to the Cross and died for my sins so that I can live with him forever and ever. I feel it is appropriate to speak of what has been called the "Roman's Road" at this point.

Only three verses need to be memorized and you too, with the Spirit's help and prompting, can be a great evangelist!

1. "For all have sinned, and come short of the glory of GOD" (Romans 3:23).

2. "For the wages of sin is death; but the gift of GOD is eternal life through Jesus Christ our LORD" (Romans 6:23).

3. "That if thou shalt confess with thy mouth the LORD Jesus, and shalt believe in thine heart that GOD hath raised him from the dead, thou shalt be saved" (Romans 10:9).

There it is! All have sinned. The wages of sin is death (the second death we are now reading about). But GOD's gift to you is eternal life as you confess and believe in Jesus Christ. And as we have discussed before, this gift is free but it is not cheap! Jesus, the only innocent man, had to suffer and die for our sins in order for us to be able to stand before the One who otherwise causes all heaven and earth to flee away from the presence of his awesome glory!

•　•　•　•

Next, we are ready to consider the very last section of GOD's revealed plan. After Satan and those who have rebelled with him are judged from the books and cast away from GOD's presence, the heaven and earth that is now will also pass away. In its place will come a new heaven and a new earth. A place that even as it is described by GOD in his Word, is far too extraordinary for us to grasp this side of eternity! Nonetheless, let's consider these last of GOD's written words to us.

The Elements Shall Melt With Fervent Heat

Before we look at the beauty and wonder of the new heaven and new earth, I would like to speak of the end of our present heaven and earth. Peter, Isaiah, and Paul give some important insights.

> ... by the word of GOD the heavens were of old, and the earth standing out of the water and in the water: Whereby the world that then was, being overflowed with water, perished: But the heavens and the earth which are now, by the same word are kept in store, reserved unto fire against the day of judgment and perdition of unGODly men.
>
> II PETER 3:5B-7

Peter states that just a surely as the world before Noah was overflowed with water, so too the heaven and earth which are now will be reserved unto fire. As we have discussed, the book of Hebrews, in its introductory comments, reveals that Jesus upholds *all* things by the word of his power (Hebrews 1:3a). On this day we are discussing, he will let it go!

Listen and see how it will sound and look!

> ... the heavens shall pass away with a great noise, and the ele-

ments shall melt with fervent heat, the earth also and the works that are therein shall be burned up.

II Peter 3:10b

Heaven and earth will pass away to make room for the new heaven and new earth. But look what also will be burnt away... the earth and the *works* that are therein shall burn! That's why Peter continued by saying,

Seeing then that all these things shall be dissolved, what manner of persons ought ye to be in all holy conversation and God-liness, Looking for and hasting unto the coming of the day of God, wherein the heavens being on fire shall be dissolved, and the elements shall melt with fervent heat? Nevertheless we, according to his promise, look for the new heavens and a new earth, wherein dwelleth righteousness. Wherefore, beloved, seeing that ye look for such things, be diligent that ye may be found of him in peace, without spot, and blameless.

II Peter 3:11–14

Peter implored his flock to realize that works that don't matter will burn. But he suggested though, that some works, i.e. diligent, good works, will survive the cleansing fire of this day. Paul amplified this idea of good works remaining while trivial and evil works will burn.

For other foundation can no man lay than that is laid, which is Jesus Christ. Now if any man build upon this foundation gold, silver, precious stones, wood, hay, stubble. Every man's work shall be made manifest: For the day shall declare it, because it shall be revealed by fire; and the fire shall try every man's work of what sort it is. If any man's work abide which he hath built thereupon, he shall receive a reward. If any man's work shall be burned, he shall suffer loss: But he himself shall be saved; yet so as by fire.

I Corinthians 3:11–15

This is so important! Some of my works will abide. Others will not. Paul gives they key to knowing which of my works will abide the fire of that day in what is likely the most famous chapter of the entire Bible.

> Charity [love] never faileth...And now abideth faith, hope, charity, these three: But the greatest of these is charity.
>
> I CORINTHIANS 13:8A, 13

There it is! Love never fails. Love will not burn on that day. Nor will things done in faith and hope. I suspect every other work not done in faith, hope, or love will burn away! Isaiah speaks of this cleansing fire as a grand case of amnesia!

> For, behold, I create new heavens and a new earth: And the former shall not be remembered, nor come to mind.
>
> ISAIAH 65:17

In the new heaven and earth, I imagine that the things that do not survive the cleansing fire will not even be remembered. But again, as Paul has proclaimed, there will be works that will follow us to heaven. Those will be the things of gold, silver, and precious stones (faith, hope, and love). While the wood, hay, and stubble will be remembered no more nor come to mind.

At this point I need to remind you of the analogy we discussed in Book I of *A Woman's Silent Testimony* entitled "Parallels of Fetal and Earthly Life." You my recall, that the point was made that we don't remember our days in which we spent in-utero. All my memories of those nine months are lost! In like manner, those memories we have recorded as we wait in this present earthly womb for our delivery into the next that are without any faith, hope, and love will also fade away!

So you may say, "What's the point? If everything is going to burn, why should I even care?"

That's the point! Everything you or I do *is* going to burn... except those things done which build upon the foundation of the Lord Jesus Christ. Those works I do out of love, in faith, or with hope *will* last.

This changes everything. This makes it important that I redeem the things in my life that may be trivial but which give me pleasure. I love to fly planes, snowboard, play basketball, and golf. Are these things a waste? I'm not sure. Likely when they are enjoyed in the context of GOD's plan for my life, they will last. Those times when I should be somewhere else other than on the mountain or at the golf course will likely be lost.

What about my work? Is that going to last? Again, am I giving out in love or am I living for the weekend just wishing away my time? That's the question that matters.

What about my family? Will I remember our lives together? The answer should be obvious by now! Some memories I will keep and others will burn. That's why I want to live my life under Jesus' guidance and protection. Then my life now will count in eternity. Not only will I be saved as by fire, but some of my works will be also!

✝he Eighth Day

The dawning of this new day is one thousand years after the end of the Tribulation time frame and 2nd coming of Jesus. And the total time period of God's dealing with mankind from Adam unto this day is approximately seven thousand years. Thus, if you are tracking with me, we are about to consider the 8th Millennium. If you will, this day of the new heaven and earth is the eighth day according to Peter's analogy of one thousand years being equal to one day.

The reason this is so important is, of course, because God loves to give meaning to life by the way he uses numbers. Once again, this is the case. You may recall that "eight" is God's number of new beginnings and of super abundance. Thus, we should not be surprised that the new heaven and earth will begin on the eighth day!

Let me remind you of a few of the many other examples of the number "eight" being scripted by God to reveal newness and abundance. Leviticus 14 tells of the law of the leper in the day of his cleansing, i.e. a great picture of our final cleansing from our leprosy of sin! We learn that the cleansed leper will tarry abroad out of the tent for seven days and then on the eighth day will come before the door of the tabernacle. It is on the eighth day that the leper (us in the analogy) is allowed to come into the full presence of the Lord just like mankind for seven days (seven thousand years) lives outside of the new heaven and new earth waiting also for that eighth day!

God's weekly time frame is another obvious example. We were given seven days in the week and with the onset of the eighth day we start a new division of time. We noted in Book V of *A Woman's Silent Testimony*, entitled "Paul's Travail," that God has divided the book of Acts into eight divinely scripted sections. The eighth section tells of the new beginning to the book of Acts which has even continued into our present day. The super abundance of the eighth section of the book of Acts is revealed by the abundance of Scripture we were given which was penned during that time frame by Paul.

Another example of God's newness and abundance relating to the number eight is found in the line of David the king. We are told in Samuel's prophecy that David was the eighth son of his father Jesse. Jesse's youngest and most inexperienced shepherd boy was God's choice to bless Israel after the fleshly reign of King Saul.

Lastly, let me show you something about the greater than David, Jesus Christ, as it relates to the number "eight." The 2nd book of the Chronicles documents the kingly line of David until the fall of Judah at the hand of Nebuchadnezzar in 586 b.c. In that book are given the names of all of the kings from David to Zedekiah. Since we understand that Christ is the son of David, we can look at our Lord's kingly genealogy as found in Matthew chapter 1 to see something very wonderful. If you count the names of the men from David to Jesus who actually reined as a king in Israel you we see that there were seven. Their names are David, Solomon, Rehoboam (Roboam, Gk), Abijah (Abia), Asa, Jehoshaphat (Josaphat) and Jehoram (Joram). After Jehoram, Ahaziah became king while according to Matthew's account of our Lord's genealogy, a different son named Ozias continued in the chain of fathers leading to the birth of the Messiah and eternal King. You see, Jesus is the eighth son in his line who has and will reign! He is the new and everlasting King which God promised David. He is the super abundant eighth King!

Truly, GOD's ways are above our ways. But in reflecting upon the way GOD uses the number eight, I am not surprised to conclude that the new heaven and new earth will also be associated with that number!

✝he New Heaven and New Earth

Wonderfully, it is now time to look at GOD's overview of the new heaven and earth as given in the first seven verses of Revelation 21. To follow after, in our next chapter, will be the fine detail of which the rest of the Revelation will speak.

> And I saw a new heaven and a new earth: For the first heaven and the first earth were passed away; and there was no more sea. And I John saw the holy city, new Jerusalem, coming down from GOD out of heaven, prepared as a bride adorned for her husband. And I heard a great voice out of heaven saying, Behold, the tabernacle of GOD is with men, and he will dwell with them, and they shall be his people, and GOD himself shall be with them, and be their GOD. And GOD shall wipe away all tears from their eyes; and there shall be no more death, neither sorrow, nor crying, neither shall there be any more pain: For the former things are passed away. And he that sat upon the throne said, Behold, I make all things new. And he said unto me, Write: For these words are true and faithful. And he said unto me, It is done. I am Alpha and Omega, the beginning and the end. I will give unto him that is athirst of the fountain of the water of life freely. He that overcometh shall inherit all things; and I will be his GOD, and he shall be my son.
>
> REVELATION 21:1–7

Wow! These verses are loaded as I reflect upon them. In verses 1 and 2 we read of a *new dwelling for man.* That is, the new heaven and new earth as well as the new Jerusalem. In verse 3, we see a *new dwelling place for* God. The tabernacle of God is with men! In verse 4, we learn of a *new living experience for man.* No tears, no death, no sorrow and no pain! Verse 5 tells us that everything is new. And God punctuates this statement by saying that these words are true and faithful. You may remember from our study of the 2nd Coming, that Jesus is called Faithful and True. Once again, Jesus and God's Word really can't be separated, for Jesus *is* the revealed Word of God. He is faithful and true just as the Word is true and faithful!

Verse 6 is the guarantee that these things *will* come to pass. For the Alpha and Omega has said it! He is the beginning and the end! Also, verse 6 reminds me of the Spirit's presence in the new heaven and new earth. The Alpha and Omega will give to the thirsty the fountain of the water of life. This statement reminds me of Jesus' words concerning water, the Holy Spirit, and everlasting life.

> Jesus answered and said unto her, Whosoever drinketh of this water shall thirst again: But whosoever drinketh of the water that I shall give him shall never thirst; but the water that I shall give him shall be in him a well of water springing up into everlasting life.
>
> JOHN 4:13–14

And,

> In the last day, that great day of the feast [the day John is speaking of is the last day of the Feast of Tabernacles but these 10 words also are a picture of this time we are considering. They are a prophecy of the new heaven and new earth!], Jesus stood and cried, saying, If any man thirst, let him come unto me, and drink.
> He that believeth on me, as the scripture hath said, out of his belly shall flow rivers of living water. (But this spake he of the Spirit, which they that believe on him should receive: For the

Holy Ghost was not yet given; because that Jesus was not yet glorified.)

JOHN 7:37–39

Lastly, I want to consider the wonderful truth that verse 3 proclaims. For in reading it again we are reminded that the GOD of the universe will dwell with *us* and we will be *his* people. Imagine that, the infinite GOD dwelling in the presence of his finite creatures. What a trip that will be!

S✝reets of Gold

On this day, over a thousand years from now, we believers in Jesus Christ will actually experience what we are presently going to discuss. This is so great. I pray that our spiritual eyes and ears can take some of it in!

> And there came unto me one of the seven angels which had the seven vials full of the seven last plagues, and talked with me, saying, Come hither, I will show thee the bride, the Lamb's wife. And he carried me away in the spirit to a great and high mountain, and showed me that great city, the holy Jerusalem, descending out of heaven from God,
>
> REVELATION 21:9–10

Hold on! Wait a minute! I thought we are the Lamb's bride, you may be thinking. What is going on with this! This verse reveals that the Holy City, the New Jerusalem, is the Lamb's bride. How can this be?

Well the answer to this riddle is given in the book of Ephesians.

> Now therefore ye are no more strangers and foreigners, but fellow citizens with the saints, and of the household of God; And are built upon the foundation of the apostles and prophets,

> Jesus Christ himself being the chief cornerstone; In whom all the building fitly framed together groweth unto a holy temple in the LORD. In whom ye also are builded together for an habitation of GOD through the Spirit.
>
> EPHESIANS 2:19–22

You see, the bride of Christ and the new Jerusalem are one in the same in GOD's eyes. We, as the Lamb's bride, are being built together into a habitation for GOD! We are being fitly framed into a holy temple in the Lord. Later, we will see that in the new Jerusalem there is no temple. That's because verse 22 proclaims that the Lord GOD Almighty and the Lamb *are* the temple. And we understand that as part of the body of Christ, we go where he goes. I know this concept is abstract, but would you really expect anything else from GOD? Look to Book X of *A Woman's Silent Testimony,* entitled "The Marriage of the Lamb," for further amplification of these two incongruent concepts.

> Having the glory of GOD: And her light was like a jasper stone, clear as crystal.
>
> REVELATION 21:11

The Bible teaches that when we see him, we will be like him (I John 3:2). That's what is happening here. We, as the bride of Christ, the City of GOD, the Holy Jerusalem, will actually have the glory of GOD! This is a revelation that is simply mind-blowing!

You may remember from our study of Revelation chapter 4, when we first come up to heaven that we will stand before the One sitting upon the throne. We were told in Revelation 4:3 that he will appear as a jasper and a sardine stone. In today's English, a jasper is a diamond and a sardine is a ruby. He will have the blinding whiteness of light and the deep redness of love, for truly GOD is light and he is love! So, too, the holy city will appear as a diamond having the glory of GOD!

And had a wall great and high, and had twelve gates, and at the

gates twelve angels, and names written thereon, which are the twelve tribes of the children of Israel.
REVELATION 21:12

You will recall that twelve is the number of Israel. So it is not surprising that Holy Jerusalem should have twelve gates and their names would be the names of the twelve sons of Israel (Jacob). From a spiritual perspective, though, we can see something wonderful as we consider these gates named for the sons of Jacob. The gates to a city are the places of entry. In considering our access to the City of GOD, we believers have entered in via Israel. Yes, we Christians have gained our heritage from Israel. We were, as Paul has taught, grafted in unto the olive tree of Israel (Romans 11:13–26). We Gentiles have come into the City via the twelve gates of the Jews!

And the wall of the city had twelve foundations, and in them the names of the twelve apostles of the Lamb.
REVELATION 21:14

Here we see the foundation of the city walls as represented by the twelve apostles. This speaks of the New Testament. For the Gospel of Christ, found in the New Testament, speaking of how Jesus died for our sins, was buried, and on the third day rose again is the Good News which is the foundation to the City. Thus we have access to the city via the Old Testament, as it foretold of Jesus, and we have the foundation via the New, as it revealed him!

And he that talked with me had a golden reed to measure the city, and the gates thereof, and the wall thereof.
REVELATION 21:15

We are about to learn of the incredible dimensions of the city. Hang on!

And the city lieth foursquare, and the length is as large as the breath: And he measured the city with the reed, twelve thou-

sand furlongs. The length and the breadth and the height of it
are equal.

REVELATION 21:16

The length, breadth and height are equal. Thus, this city we
are considering is a perfect cube. It is unlike any city you have
ever seen. It is not two dimensional like our present day cities as
they sprawl across the valleys and coastlines of our planet. No,
this city is as high as it is long. It is as wide as it is tall!

The Bible tells us that the length of each side of the cube is
twelve (There is that number again!) thousand furlongs. How
long is that? Those of you who have ever watched a horse race
know that a furlong is a little over a tenth of a mile. Thus, twelve
thousand furlongs is equivalent to fifteen hundred miles. Each
side of Holy Jerusalem is same as the distance from New York to
Kansas City. And when considered in its cubic form, the city of
GoD is nearly the size of the Moon. Only it is hollow, with space
not merely on its surface but through and through!

And he measured the wall thereof, an hundred and forty and
four cubits...

REVELATION 21:17A

A cubit being eighteen inches means the walls are two hundred sixteen feet high! And we thought the Great Wall of China
was a wonder. As we read on we will see that this wall will be
magnificent! But first, did you notice the number, "one hundred
forty four?" Why that's twelve times twelve!

And the building of the wall of it was of jasper: And the city
was pure gold, like unto clear glass.

REVELATION 21:18

The walls and the city will appear as diamonds and gold.
What a sight that will be!

You know, the word "paradise" means "walled in garden."
And like the original paradise, the Garden of Eden, our final
home will also be a walled in garden. It will be Paradise!

> The foundations of the wall of the city were garnished with all manner of precious stones...And the twelve gates were twelve pearls; every several gate was of one pearl:
>
> REVELATION 21:19A, 21A

Interesting, that pearls came from an un-kosher sea creature. Yet in the new heaven and earth, that which was once considered unclean will be on display. I hope you can see the analogy!

> And the street of the city was pure gold, as it were transparent glass.
>
> REVELATION 21:21B

There it is! That famous mind-picture. Streets of gold!

> And I saw no temple therein: For the LORD GOD Almighty and the Lamb are the temple of it.
>
> REVELATION 21:22

In the Millennial reign of Jesus on Earth there will be a temple in Jerusalem. But now, in this City which is *so* different, there will be no temple. For GOD and his Son *are* the temple!

> And the city had no need of the sun, neither of the moon, to shine in it: For the glory of GOD did lighten it, and the Lamb is the light thereof.
>
> REVELATION 21:23

Again, dear reader, we must stop thinking of Jesus as the carpenter from Galilee. The whole Christ, the One who was transfigured on Mount Hermon and was seen by John in chapter 1 of the Revelation, has the countenance of the Sun!
The Lamb is really and truly, *all* the light we need!

> And the nations of them which are saved shall walk in the light of it: And the kings of the earth do bring their glory and honor into it.
>
> REVELATION 21:24

John told us that we shall be kings and priests with him (Revelation 1:6). You and I are the kings which will bring our glory and honor into the city! How do we do that? Because, as we have said, we are the city of GOD, we are the Lamb's bride. And, as discussed in verse 11, that city will incredibly be given the glory of GOD.

> And the gates of it shall not be shut at all by day: For there shall be no night there.
>
> REVELATION 21:25

Never will there be any darkness of the soul in the holy Jerusalem. That city, which is nearly as big as the Moon will sparkle like a diamond and shine like glassy gold. We, as a royal priesthood, will be immersed in his light and love. Oh, how fantastic will be that day!

> And he showed me a pure river of water of life, clear as crystal, proceeding out of the throne of GOD and of the Lamb.
>
> REVELATION 22:1

This pure, crystal-like water, may be a heavenly manifestation of the Holy Spirit. Ezekiel, in his heavenly vision found in chapter 47 of his book, also saw this river. In addition, that prophet got to take a swim in it! GOD had Ezekiel stand in the river up to his ankles, then knees. Next, he waded up to his loins and lastly, Ezekiel jumped totally in. Pastor Jon, in his commentary (*Jon Courson's Application Commentary*), teaches that this vision typifies for our lives now the levels that the Spirit will take you and me, if we allow. That is, first we get in to our ankles, we believe the Gospel, if you will. We get our feet wet! Next, the river comes up to our knees. We start to pray effectively as the Spirit leads. We get down on our knees. After that, the water can rise to our loins if we desire. That's the area of our reproduction organs. When we get into the water of the Spirit to that level we see addition to GOD's kingdom as we are led to witness to the lost; That is, we see reproduction. Lastly, we jump totally in the river. That typifies the baptism of the Spirit. We have become immersed and are able to just go with the flow of the Spirit. To be immersed in the Spirit is to go where he leads.

> In the midst of the street of it, and on either side of the river, was there the tree of life...
>
> REVELATION 22:2A

Just as the tree of life was in the Garden of Eden, so too it will be found in Paradise.

> And there shall be no more curse...
>
> REVELATION 22:3A

Do you remember the curse? It's found in Genesis 3. Adam and Eve cursed themselves in sinning against GOD's revealed Word to them. By extension they also cursed their progeny.

> Unto the woman he said, I will greatly multiply thy sorrow and thy conception; in sorrow thou shalt bring forth children... and unto Adam he said...cursed is the ground for thy sake; in sorrow thou shalt eat of it all the days of your life; Thorns and thistles shall it bring forth to thee; and thou shalt eat the herb of the field; In the sweat of thy face shalt thou eat bread, till thou return unto the ground; for out of it wast thou taken: For dust thou art, and unto dust shalt thou return.
>
> GENESIS 3:16A, 17A, C-19

Obviously women have been cursed in conception as well as labor and delivery. It's extremely hard. It is terribly difficult! Without the curse, this entire book about birth pangs makes no sense at all!

Obviously, the ground has been cursed. It rains too much here while in the next state they are having a drought. Weeds grow up in the fields and much sweat is used to bring forth the harvest.

And lastly, we have been cursed with aging and death. Yes, the curse of mankind...childbearing, the ground, and death. But on that wonderful day there will be no more curse! It will be the way GOD had intended all along.

Can you women imagine a world that didn't include the difficulty of childbearing? There would have been no wondering if the pregnancy test would have turned positive or worrying if a miscarriage would occur. Can you imagine a world that did not include the terrible agony of labor and delivery? Or a world that had no obstetricians and midwives!

How about you men? The ground would have brought forth abundantly while you sat under your vine worshiping and praising your GOD. And, of course, can you see a world that had no funeral parlors and cemeteries? No grief at the loss of a loved one. Oh, how different things would have been!

But on this day, the curse that fell at the beginning of the Book will be taken away at the end. What a happy ending to the story it will be!

> But the throne of GOD and of the Lamb shall be in it; and his servants shall serve him.
>
> REVELATION 22:3B

This won't be a bummer! No, not at all! You see that's really what I've always wanted to do. That's what I was created to do! If you love someone with all of your heart it's easy to put them ahead of you. It's easy to serve them. You lovers know what I mean. When you're in love, nothing gets in they way of your man or woman. You put them first! They are on a pedestal! And that's imperfect human love. Imagine how it will be when we are engrossed in perfect spiritual love. Why, to serve our Husband will be the only thing we want to do! And we will be *totally* fulfilled and blessed in doing so! No, it won't be a downer. In fact, it will be such an "upper" that I can talk about it now, but I know that I really don't get it at all! The way we are going to feel as we serve and love our Lord is completely unimaginable this side of heaven. But you wait, you watch, you'll see, it's going to happen!

> And they shall see his face;
>
> REVELATION 22:4A

Do I really even need to comment upon this verse? We will see the face of GOD for goodness sake! Moses, in the book of Exodus, only saw his backside. Before the curse was lifted, one would die to look upon the perfection and beauty of the face of GOD. As the Bible states, no man can see GOD and live.

But both Moses and David understood that someday they *would* see GOD's face. GOD gave Moses and Aaron this blessing to give to the children of Israel, "The Lord bless thee, and keep thee: The Lord make his face shine upon thee, and be gracious unto thee: The Lord lift up his countenance upon thee, and give thee peace" (Numbers 6:24–26).

And David sang this song, "As for me, I will behold thy face in righteousness"(Psalm 17:15a).

> ... and his name shall be in their foreheads.
>
> REVELATION 22:4B

Remember during the Tribulation era the mark of the beast included a chip in the hand or forehead identifying the fooled of the world's allegiance to the Antichrist. On this day we will have the mark (name) of the Lord on our foreheads! He is, and will be our wonderful allegiance. And because we have the name of the Lord on that place of prominence, we will be able to see the Lord in one another!

David also understood that he too would reflect the Lord's countenance in the very next verse of his song, "I will be satisfied, when I awake, with thy likeness" (Psalm 17:15b). And finally, on that day when we see his face and have his name on our foreheads we will finally fulfill the Great Shemah. We will at last be able to proclaim without any hint of reservation from our flesh that,

> Hear, O Israel: The LORD our GOD is one LORD: And thou shalt love the LORD thy GOD with all thine heart, and with all thy soul, and with all thy might.
>
> DEUTERONOMY 6:4–5

This wonderful proclamation which I read as a command,

that is, I *should* love the Lord with all my heart, soul and might... will turn into a promise. That is, I *will* love the Lord. It will be a complete love. Heart, soul, and might!

Epilogue

We have come to the end of this book. And we have come to the end of *the* Book! Jesus has some important last words for us as chapter 22 of Revelation concludes. They are important final reminders of the things he wants you and me to hold fast to as we wait for his blessed return.

> And he said unto me, These sayings are faithful and true... Behold, I come quickly: Blessed is he that keepeth the sayings of the prophecy of this book...
> And he saith unto me, Seal not the sayings of the prophecy of this book: For the time is at hand. He that is unjust, let him be unjust still: And he that is filthy, let him be filthy still: And he that is righteous, let him be righteous still: And he that is holy, let him be holy still. And, behold, I come quickly; and my reward is with me, to give every man according to his work shall be. I am Alpha and Omega, the beginning and the end, the first and the last...And the Spirit and the bride say, Come. And let him that heareth say, Come. And let him that is athirst come. And whosoever will, let him take the water of life freely. For I testify unto every man that heareth these words of the prophecy of this book. If any man shall add unto these things, GOD shall add unto him the plagues that are written in this book: And if any man shall take away from the words

of this prophecy, GOD shall take away his part out of the book of life, and out of the holy city, and from the things written in this book. He which testifieth these things saith, Surely I come quickly. Amen. Even so, come, LORD Jesus.

REVELATION 22:6A, 7, 10–13, 17–20

That's it! Jesus' final benediction to us as we read the last page of the Bible. Indeed, it's the final word about Jesus, from Jesus! He is the Alpha and Omega, the beginning and the end, the first and the last. Did you notice that he told the truth of his preeminence in three different ways?

The Lord says he wants us to know the end. Behold, I come quickly!

He says he does not want us to keep this a secret. Seal *not* the sayings of the prophecy of this book!

He warns that there is a point in time when a person's destiny is fixed. "He that is unjust, let him be unjust still…and he that is holy, let him be holy still" (Revelation 22:11a, d).

The Lord promises to come back with rewards according to our works. Thus, it is important to remember what it is…to do the work of the Lord!

Jesus answered and said unto them, this is the work of GOD, that ye believe on him whom he hath sent.

JOHN 6:29

My faith in Jesus, my love for Jesus, that's the work of GOD! Hence, the rewards he will return with will include all the blessing we have discussed. Such as our seven year honeymoon with him in Heaven, the wedding banquet, the Millennial Kingdom, and the new heaven and earth.

Unfortunately for the rejecter of the Gospel, the rewards will not be good. Judgment and destruction, outer darkness and eternal death will be their end. Consequently, I understand why Jesus wants to remind me of this bad news at the end of the book. It is so that I will remember the lost; so I will pray for the lost; so I will speak to the lost!

Next, the Lord gives a final invitation. "And the Spirit and the bride say, Come...And let him that is athirst come" (Revelation 22:17a, c). Isaiah echoed this sentiment beautifully, "Ho, every one that thirsteth, come ye to the waters, and he that hath no money; come ye, buy, and eat; yea, come, buy wine and milk without money and without price" (Isaiah 55:1).

Lastly, Jesus says not to add or detract from his words. If any man adds to his words, plagues will be added. If any man takes away from his words, well, his name and future home will be taken away!

So these are the Teacher's words to us today. We know the end of the story, don't keep it a secret, our destiny is safe, he has rewards for us, offer the invitation and respect his Word.

Pretty good advice from the One who gave his life for you and me!

God bless you as you walk in his incredible grace and mercy!

The grace of our Lord Jesus Christ be with you all. Amen.
REVELATION 22:21